——————————— *A Journal Briefing* ———————————

Whitewater
Volume II

A Journal Briefing

Whitewater
Volume II

From the Editorial Pages of
The Wall Street Journal.

Edited by Robert L. Bartley
with Micah Morrison and Melanie Kirkpatrick
and the Editorial Page staff

Library of Congress Catalog Card Number:
94-79762

ISBN 1-881944-04-2

Printed in the United States of America

The Wall Street Journal.
Dow Jones & Company, Inc.
200 Liberty Street
New York, N.Y. 10281

Introduction

"Whitewater" has been the expanding noun of the Clinton presidency. Originally a two-bit land deal in the Ozarks, it swelled to embrace an expanding list of scandals, flaps and misfortunes. On the eve of President Clinton's re-election campaign, the list was still growing, with migrating FBI files, further documents withheld from Congress and the resignation of the White House security chief after revelation of his bizarre résumé. The thread holding the meandering chain together is called "character," in several of the senses of that word, from essential nature to moral fortitude to personal reputation. By now, indeed, "Whitewater" and "the character issue" have become practically synonymous.

Broadly defined, this issue bids to be decisive in Bill Clinton's 1996 campaign, if not indeed his place in the annals of the Presidency. In the conventional view, the nation is at peace and the economy passably vigorous, so an incumbent President should be re-elected. A less conventional view is that Mr. Clinton is likely to be defeated because he is an accidental President, elected in a three-way race with 43% of the vote despite heading a party profoundly out of step with the voters and the times. Yet even if you take this view, as I tend to, the character issue looms large; as he bids to co-opt Republican issues, who will believe him?

The Wall Street Journal commentary on these issues has been praised by some as courageous and criticized by others as obsessive. Whatever else, it has compiled a record—one way of following a complex and moving story, a catalog of personalities and events as they emerge, submerge and re-emerge. In the fall of 1994, with the Congressional elections approaching and the appointment of a new investigator providing a natural stopping point, we collected our commentary to that point. As the Presidential campaign opens, we publish Volume II. Together they are an exhaustive exploration of the question asked by the title of the first editorial in the first volume, "Who Is Bill Clinton?"

Yet to us the story has always been more than that. We have stuck to the story while the rest of the press blew hot and cold because we think it speaks to something larger than one President and one state. We were led into Whitewater by a chain running from the still-unresolved scandal of the Bank of Credit & Commerce International, to Arkansas financial powerhouse Stephens Inc. (which thinks a statute of limitations ought to apply to its long-ago BCCI connections), to the Rose Law Firm, to Hillary Clinton, the late Vincent Foster, William Kennedy Jr. and Webster Hubbell—which is to say, to the "character" of the Administration.

Along the way, we discovered Mena, another still-unresolved mystery involving money, drug smugglers, arms and possibly intelligence agencies all swirling around an obscure airport in the wilds of western Arkansas. The spectacle of Clark Clifford's involvement in BCCI, and later the tribulations of the Harriman estate, suggested an end-of-dynasty collapse of the Democrats who dominated not only Arkansas but the District of Columbia. But against critics who claim our motives are partisan, we also raised questions about Republicans such as Oliver North. We continue to feel that "Whitewater" is an outcropping of a deeper vein relating to the character of not only the Clinton cronies but swaths of the American establishment, indeed, to the character of the nation itself at the dawn of a new century.

With this in mind, we've been content to march to our own drummer in covering and commenting on the story. We've persevered despite enmity from the White House, the criticism of some of our colleagues and repeated warnings that the scent was dead. Our Micah Morrison has made himself a familiar, and often controversial, figure in darkest Arkansas. We think we've resisted and even helped to dampen the eccentric conspiracy theories bound to swell—and in this day and age crowd the Internet—when full explanations are not available for mysterious events. But on serious charges and reasonable suspicions swirling around leaders, the voters must judge; we've given great weight to the public's right to know—a journalistic cliché sometimes honored in the breach.

Readers are of course under no obligation to share our own view of our efforts, but this introduction is an obvious place for a few comments on an editor's view of the spirit of an enterprise. We think readers will find these volumes stimulating, informative and a good read. As in Volume I, the articles are arranged chronologically, with connecting narrative at chapter headings. A chronology and index are added. Our fondest hope is that readers will find it helpful in thinking not only about the impending election but also about the nature of their society and their times.

Robert L. Bartley
Editor
The Wall Street Journal
August 7,1996

TABLE OF CONTENTS

Starr, GOP Take Over

The first volume of this collection opened with the 1992 campaign editorial "Who Is Bill Clinton?" It remarked, "Every four years the Democrats send us another Governor we have to get to know." Getting to know President Carter was a long experience, but Governor Dukakis's tank ride helped voters get a quick fix on him. With Governor Clinton, we observed in March 1992, "the Gennifer Flowers tank has already rumbled by. But where's the rest of them?" Somehow, Mr. Clinton's "new Democrat" rhetoric morphed into an attack on "the rich."

"The real question," the editorial continued, "is why the party that dominates Congress has to keep putting up unknowns to contest the world's most powerful political office. Why is Washington such dead ground for growing Democratic political timber? About this there is no mystery. It is because the political positions of the Democratic House Caucus are rigorously enforced on Congresspeople. Encumbered with this awful political baggage, none of them can win a presidential election. . . .

"So once again it comes down to this: Is there any real reason to trust an unknown Governor when he says he's different? We'll find out eventually, and with any luck at all, revelation will come before November."

The closing article in Volume I of *A Journal Briefing: Whitewater* was "Whitewater Status Report," concerning the impending 1994 Congressional election and a federal judicial panel's appointment of its own man to head the Whitewater investigation. It remarked, "The effort to bury Whitewater through the election was most obvious in the otherwise hilarious attacks on Kenneth Starr's appointment as special counsel. When the object of an investigation attacks the investigator, the ordinary citizen must figure the stars have moved into their proper places. But to hear Presidential mouthpiece Bob Bennett tell it, a special counsel probing White House conduct should be someone the President will like."

The editorial, and the volume, closed with the words, "The true importance of Whitewater does not lie in what happened in the Ozarks a dozen years ago. It lies in what happened to Justice and bank regulation during Bill Clinton's tenure as President. Were those processes subverted to cover up what happened in Arkansas, and conceptually to do future favors for future friends of the President? And has Congress discharged its role in policing such abuse? About this no prosecutor or judge can render a verdict; voters will have to make their own decisions."

Mr. Starr did take over, turning in a series of guilty pleas and ultimately a stunning guilty verdict against not only the first couple's Whitewater partners but also the sitting governor of Arkansas. And the voters did render a spectacular decision, cashiering the Democrats who had run Congress for 40 years. Yet as we close Volume II of the collection, we are somehow back in the same place. Another political campaign is starting, and the questions remain: Who indeed is Bill Clinton? And will he succeed in putting the resolution of Whitewater off beyond the impending election?

* * *

A brief review of Volume I may be helpful: As a public issue, Whitewater has waxed and waned since March 8, 1992, when the New York Times published a story by investigative reporter Jeff Gerth on the Clintons' links to Madison Guaranty Savings & Loan, and the Whitewater Development Co. partnership with Madison's owners, James and Susan McDougal. That article raised issues about the nature of the partnership and Mrs. Clinton's representation of Madison before regulators appointed by her husband. All this would turn out to be true, but in the heat of the Presidential primary campaign the Clintons' damage control team swung into action and deflated the story, killing Whitewater as a campaign issue.

Volume I traced the arrival of the Clintons in Washington,

expressed growing concerns about the inner circle of Rose Law Firm members, and recorded events such as the Travel Office firings, the death of Deputy White House Counsel Vincent Foster, the resignation of Webster Hubbell (another former Rose partner), Mrs. Clinton's commodity trades, and the Paula Jones sexual harassment suit. It provided in-depth critical commentary and reporting on the appointment of Robert Fiske as special Whitewater prosecutor and the first round of hearings in the Democratic-controlled Congress. It concluded with Mr. Starr's appointment.

*　*　*

At this point the present volume opens. The Starr appointment was quickly followed by another seminal event: a Republican sweep of the Congressional elections. In itself, the gathering Whitewater scandal was by no means decisive in the election. Few elections, and probably no midterm Congressional election, have turned more squarely on policy issues. The "GOP Contract" engineered by Rep. Newt Gingrich framed the issue of smaller versus bigger government. President Clinton, whose extravagant health care promises had dissolved, responded with a series of blistering attacks on "the 1980s." The 1980s won, resuming the Reagan revolution.

Yet Whitewater and character surely affected the climate of the election. Broadly, such issues as gays in the military, a vanishing middle class tax cut, and various appointments difficulties raised a problem of identity and credibility. More narrowly, the Travel Office firings, the death of Vincent Foster, and the legal troubles of the anonymous health care task force raised issues of propriety and legality. During the campaign, new questions arose from both Washington and Arkansas. We discovered Governor Jim Guy Tucker's problems at a place called Castle Grande. Another cabinet officer, Agriculture Secretary Mike Espy, got another independent counsel, Donald Smaltz, over dealings with another Arkansan, chicken king Don Tyson. An airport at Mena raised questions for both Democrats and Republicans.

Not least, the 1994 election put the investigative powers of Congress in Republican hands, as the judicial power was invested in Mr. Starr. From this flowed the revelations of the following two years.

REVIEW & OUTLOOK

All in the Family

When Lloyd Cutler moved in to dam up Whitewater as White House counsel, he went as a special 130-day government employee, avoiding many ethics rules. He also reserved the right to remain in contact with "one or two" clients, getting an ethics ruling to continue some work on estates and trusts. He told Legal Times, "I would continue to do that less as a lawyer, but more as a friend."

The client and friend, we now learn, just happens to be Pamela Harriman, whose trust and estate problems have blossomed into a lawsuit on behalf of Averell Harriman's heirs by a previous wife. She is accused of breach of fiduciary duty in handling trust money. Co-defendants Clark Clifford, Paul Warnke and William Rich III are accused of fraud and violations of RICO. Mr. Rich was head of a firm handling administration of the trusts. Messrs. Clifford and Warnke were of course law partners in Clifford & Warnke, and Mr. Clifford was also head of First American Bank when it was owned by the Bank of Credit and Commerce International.

Lloyd Cutler

What we have here, in short, are the grandees of the Democratic Party Establishment. As the brief filed for the plaintiffs by former U.S. Attorney Paul Curran notes, "Defendant Pamela Digby Churchill Harriman ('Pamela Harriman' or 'Harriman') is a citizen and resident of Virginia and presently also resides in the United States Embassy in France. Harriman is the United States Ambassador to France, and a highly sophisticated businesswoman and philanthropist, who was the founder and Chairwoman of Democrats for the 80s from 1980-90, and of Democrats for the 1990s in 1991. Her fund-raising for the Democratic Party was actively assisted by Clifford."

The suit alleges that through "negligence, gross negligence and willful malfeasance" the defendants stripped the Harriman trusts, at a cost to the beneficiaries of some $30 million, leaving some $3 million in cash and securities plus a bunch of mostly worthless investments. There was no income available for distribution, and insufficient capital to pay the beneficiaries the distributions on which they have relied. Mr. Harriman's daughters, Mary A. Fisk, 77, and Kathleen L. Mortimer, 76, have suffered a loss of income of $200,000 a year.

Clark Clifford

The trusts grew well under a conservative investment policy until late in 1989, the suit alleges, but then started to "diversify" into a New Jersey real estate speculation, with an investment in the Seasons Resort and Conference Center at Great Gorge. There followed a stream of transactions with the resort, various holding companies, their principals and others.

Despite the infusion of funds, the resort failed, as it had under Playboy Enterprises and other previous owners. Its principal asset, a 27-hole golf course, was also allegedly sold without benefit to the Harriman trusts, while the trusts' entire securities portfolio was pledged for an $18 million loan plowed into the resort. This and other actions violated the trust agreements, the suit charges, and some defendants profited from self-dealing transactions. In one series of transactions, the plaintiffs allege, they ended up guaranteeing trust disbursements to Mrs. Harriman.

The real estate investment took place, the complaint continues, without due diligence of the resort's sorry history, or of its current principals. "Even the most basic due diligence," it adds, would have discovered that Eugene W. Mulvihill, who proposed the investment, had pleaded guilty to six felony counts of fraud in unauthorized operation of an insurance company, and had been banned for life by the SEC. And that a second principal, Robert E. Brennan, had been investigated and sued by the SEC and NASD for his operation of First Jersey Securities Inc. (This summer the SEC charged Mr. Brennan with defrauding investors of $27 million in a penny stock scam.)

This cast of characters suggests that the Harriman suit is likely to prove far more than the family spat depicted in the society columns. The defense is yet to be heard from, of course. The Washington Post reported that Mr. Clifford said he was comfortable with his trusteeship, that Mrs. Harriman's lawyer denied she was a trustee of the relevant trusts, that Mr. Warnke says he did not know trust funds had been pledged for a loan. Mr. Cutler tells us that while serving as White House counsel he did have discussions of the dispute with Mr. Curran, but points out it did not concern the government. He also asks why the suit is of interest for an editorial in The Wall Street Journal.

Because we wonder what was going on here. The plaintiff's brief dryly notes that First American Bank "was the only lender to recoup its entire investment"; Mr. Clifford headed the bank, and Mr. Rich was a director of First American Bank of New York. While even our friends feel we see BCCI under every bed, we can't forget that in late 1989 the corrupt enterprise was under heavy cash pressure. In the fall of that year, the Bank of England and Monetary Institute of Luxembourg asked Price Waterhouse for a special audit of BCCI. Perhaps there is no connection, and perhaps we will never know, since the Clinton Justice Department struck a sweetheart settlement with BCCI's president and seems to be closing down any investigation.

The Harriman lawsuit may or may not tell us much about Mr. Clifford's other entanglements, but at the very least it will tell us something about the mores of a Washington establishment, mores that cannot be blamed on Arkansas.

Editorial Feature

Governor's Travels In Whitewater Country

By MICAH MORRISON

LITTLE ROCK, Ark. — As Election Day nears, the tentacles of the Whitewater affair are tightening around Arkansas's leading gubernatorial candidate, Democratic Governor Jim Guy Tucker.

Widely circulated news reports in Arkansas have linked Gov. Tucker, who stepped into the top post when Bill Clinton became president, to the alleged corrupt practices of James McDougal's Madison Guaranty Savings & Loan and David Hale's Capital Management Services, two companies at the center of the Whitewater investigation. Press accounts name him as a likely target for indictment by the Whitewater grand jury. The Resolution Trust Corp. is pursuing possible fraud claims against him, and he is fighting a broad RTC subpoena for documents.

In May and June, newspapers around the state ran a five-part Associated Press series on Governor Tucker's links to Whitewater; in August, the Arkansas Democrat-Gazette published a lengthy four-part investigative report. "Luckily for the governor," wrote Jeff Hankins, editor of the weekly Arkansas Business, "the saga went right over the heads of the average reader" and "won't be strong enough to deliver a victory" to Governor Tucker's GOP opponent, Sheffield Nelson. Governor Tucker has dismissed the reports as "nothing new," said a campaign spokeswoman, Dina Tyler.

But when the Byzantine pathways are cleared of debris, Governor Tucker's Whitewater problems have a familiar look to students of the affair. From 1983 to 1987, Mr. Tucker and firms he controlled reportedly received more than $2 million in loans from Messrs. Hale and McDougal through channels not available to ordinary folks. Some loans were not repaid; questions have been raised as to whether others were fraudulently obtained.

In 1983, following a loss to Bill Clinton in the 1982 Democratic gubernatorial primary, Mr. Tucker went into the cable business to try to make some extra money. A lawyer earning $170,000 a year, Mr. Tucker was burdened with a $250,000 campaign debt; he turned to his old friend David Hale, who had been Mr. Tucker's campaign co-chairman in an unsuccessful 1978 Senate bid.

Mr. Hale, a municipal judge, had formed Capital Management in 1978. Subsidized by the Small Business Administration, the company was licensed to provide funds to "socially or economically disadvantaged" individuals. When Mr. Tucker approached Mr. Hale with his venture, County Cable Inc., he was promptly lent $50,000. "Ultimately," the Democrat-Gazette reported, "companies that Tucker owned would borrow $725,000 from Hale's Capital Management for his cable television business through 1987." The cable business made Mr. Tucker a millionaire. Mr. Tucker has said he did not learn that Mr. Hale's company was supposed to lend only to the disadvantaged until reading Whitewater news reports in 1993.

Jim Guy Tucker

Mr. Hale is now cooperating with the independent counsel and seeking a lenient sentence after having pleaded guilty to fraud. He claims that Mr. Tucker, Mr. McDougal, and then-Governor Clinton pressured him into making illegal loans, including one for $300,000 to Mr. McDougal's wife, Susan. Some published reports say $100,000 of that loan ended up in an account controlled by Whitewater Development, the McDougal-Clinton land partnership.

The Democrat-Gazette series described Mr. Tucker's odyssey through "the land of Whitewater," where "political cronies doled out loans worth hundreds of thousands of dollars with a phone call; six-figure loans changed hands without applications or down payments, and debts were shed by walking away." In this land, Jim McDougal was king.

But Mr. McDougal's kingdom was one of financial chaos in which loans and land parcels were switched around with the speed of a hare, while the tortoise of regulatory scrutiny plodded along behind. Castle Grande, Mr. McDougal's plan for a neighborhood and shopping center south of Little Rock, is a good example.

In October 1985, a Madison Guaranty subsidiary, Madison Financial, paid $1.75 million for 1,000 acres of land, in partnership with Seth Ward, a prominent Arkansas businessman and father-in-law of Webster Hubbell, a Rose Law Firm partner and former Clinton administration associate attorney general. Mr. Tucker, meanwhile, was looking for a loan. Mr. McDougal agreed to lend Mr. Tucker $260,000 if Mr. Tucker purchased 34 acres of the Castle Grande land.

Mr. Tucker got his loan — without a down payment, the Democrat-Gazette reported, and without a written loan application. Mr. Tucker seldom bothered with loan applications. "I called Jim McDougal if I wanted to borrow money," he told the Democrat-Gazette.

The $260,000 loan is one of the transactions that has attracted federal investigators. The AP reported that Mr. Tucker may "have committed bank fraud" by misrepresenting to what uses he would put the money. Mr. Tucker has said he used $125,000 of the loan to pay for the Castle Grande land, with most of the rest going to pay off a loan he had guaranteed for a friend. Mr. McDougal claims Mr. Tucker was supposed to use the rest of the money for improvements to the land, but instead spent it on his cable business. Mr. Tucker told AP that he had not pledged to use the remaining funds for land improvement.

In the end, Mr. Tucker seems to have done all right with his 34 acres. The same month he bought the land for $125,000, it was appraised at $350,000. The appraiser, the Democrat-Gazette reported, turned out to have three loans outstanding at Madison Guaranty totaling more than $200,000. In 1987, a company partly owned by Mr. Tucker, Southloop Construction, bought the land from him for $353,000. That purchase was partly funded by a $100,000 loan from Mr. Hale's Capital Management to Southloop. Eventually, the RTC took over the property, reappraised at $120,000. Most of the original $260,000 note has been paid off. The $100,000 loan from Capital Management was never paid back.

Mr. Tucker ran into trouble with another Madison Guaranty transaction, the purchase of a sewer and water utility on the Castle

Grande property. In February 1986, an appraiser working for Madison valued the utility at $1.3 million, a figure later reduced to $640,000 by a 1992 RTC appraisal. (The original appraiser also was engaged in a profitable Madison transaction.) Two weeks after the first appraisal, a new Tucker partnership, Castle Sewer & Water Corp., bought the utility for $1.2 million. The $150,000 down payment came from Mr. Hale's Capital Management; the rest of the financing was provided by Madison. Among other issues, the independent counsel is investigating an elaborate scheme linking the Castle Sewer deals to an alleged $825,000 loan from Madison to Arkansas businessman Dean Paul.

By 1986, the regulatory tortoise was closing in on the Madison hare. In July, the Federal Home Loan Bank Board removed Mr. McDougal from Madison. According to the Democrat-Gazette, Mr. Tucker's Castle Sewer note "was one of the largest single delinquent loans on Madison Guaranty's books."

Castle Sewer, along with the entire development, was going down the drain. An anticipated new highway did not materialize. Many of the plots remained unsold. The sewer system was falling apart. Some of Mr. Tucker's land turned out to be on a flood plain.

With Madison now in the hands of federal regulators, the Tucker partnership renegotiated the Castle Sewer deal, arguing that Mr. McDougal had not fulfilled side agreements to bring in new sewer and water hookups. The loan was cut to $525,000. According to the Democrat-Gazette, the deal was contingent on new legislation allowing utilities to raise their rates. In June 1987, Gov. Clinton signed the bill. Four months later, Mr. Tucker's restructured loan was approved.

A year later, Castle Sewer was still missing payments on the renegotiated loan. The $150,000 down payment is still owed to Capital Management, according to the Democrat-Gazette. In June 1989, Mr. Tucker bailed out, selling his Castle stock to a partner for $10.

All this alleged fiscal chicanery so far seems to have had little impact on Arkansas voters. Private polls by both parties show Gov. Tucker with a comfortable 15-point lead over Mr. Nelson, the GOP candidate. Mr. Nelson has his own somewhat milder Whitewater problems. Not only was he once involved in a land deal with Mr. McDougal, but he has been criticized in Arkansas for bringing the Whitewater affair to national attention. The Nelson camp, fearing a backlash if it raises Whitewater again, has been reduced to praying for an indictment before the election. "We need a miracle," says a Nelson strategist. Over at Castle Grande, they'd settle for a decent sewer.

Mr. Morrison is a Journal editorial page writer.

Editorial Feature

Imagine '96: With a Heavy Heart, Sir...

With health reform dead, GATT held hostage by a single senator, Haiti occupied by Marines and Democrats fearing the Inquisition of Speaker Gingrich, it's not too soon to ask: Will President Clinton even be renominated by the Democrats in 1996?

While this thought may seem crazy, or at least wildly premature, it's the private buzz of much of Washington these days. Last January a Democratic senator, a well-known potentate, wisecracked in a visit to this newspaper that by 1995 Democrats in Congress might be trying to get rid of Mr. Clinton while Republicans worked to keep him on the ticket. Three months later TV interviewer Charlie Rose almost knocked over his coffee when my Journal colleagues, Dan Henninger and John Fund, predicted that Mr. Clinton wouldn't be renominated. They don't seem hyper-caffeinated now.

Potomac Watch

By Paul A. Gigot

Democratic losses this November are widely assumed to be either devastating, or merely awful. Giants of the party — great vote-getters all — are fighting for their lives: Mario Cuomo in New York, Ted Kennedy in Massachusetts, House Speaker Tom Foley in Washington and several committee chairmen. Party enthusiasm is so low that Mr. Clinton himself has had to travel to New York to coax blacks to turn out for Mr. Cuomo.

The private Democratic reaction is that things like this didn't happen until Bill Clinton became president. Unions grumble that he's delivered nothing to them in this historically liberal Congress.

One Democratic elder, a Beltway fixture for decades, says he doesn't believe Mr. Clinton can regain enough public consensus to govern. Liberal Garry Wills, who all but canonized Hillary Rodham Clinton in the New York Review of Books in 1992, now roughs up both Clintons in the same publication.

These are not signs of Hope. While it's possible the Comeback Kid could resurrect himself a la Harry Truman, and Republicans have been known to self-destruct, let's suspend disbelief and imagine how Democrats might try to avoid feeling Mr. Clinton's pain in 1995 and 1996:

The president starts out trying to repair his image by pursuing a new center-out strategy. But he's frustrated because his own credibility is low and the new Congress is even more polarized than the old.

Among House Democrats, liberals are more dominant than ever because so many moderates lost in 1994. Speaker Dick Gephardt moves left with his members, especially after the Black Caucus saves him from North Carolina Rep. Charlie Rose's leadership challenge. So he sides with Reps. Harold Ford and Maxine Waters when they stage a hunger strike against welfare reform.

Bill Clinton

The Gingrich Republicans, buoyed by 25 more House seats, pursue the strategy George Mitchell used against George Bush — back legislation that forces Mr. Clinton to oppose his own political base. Gridlock prevails but with few GOP fingerprints. Things are little better in the Senate, where Majority Leader Bob Dole and Phil Gramm are competing for anti-Clinton primary votes.

Meanwhile, the economy, the president's only safety net, begins to soften. Inflation heads toward 5%, and financial markets tank amid reports that Mr. Clinton plans to replace Alan Greenspan at the Federal Reserve with Alan Blinder.

Democrats, who always challenge their own president anyway (Truman, Johnson, Carter), begin to face 1996 with dread. Jesse Jackson's challenge is already under way on the left. On the right, Nebraska Sen. Bob Kerrey parlays his entitlement commission into a bid for disenchanted New Democrats. (A Jimmy Carter boomlet is hooted down.) Neither man thrills the party establishment, though, which prefers a more reliable liberal.

Sensing a debacle, that establishment concludes that Mr. Clinton cannot run again. A delegation of elders, led by West Virginia Sen. Robert Byrd (who rankles as ranking minority member on Appropriations), visits the president to deliver the bad news. You are unpopular because you have taken on the hard issues, they tell him, but it's best for the party and the nation if you pull an LBJ. The Clintons, furious and hurt, refuse to withdraw.

Which is when Democrats discover strange new respect for Senate Banking Chairman Al D'Amato. His Whitewater subpoenas begin to get bipartisan support. The Senate introduces America to such Arkansas icons as "Red" Bone. The New York Times editorializes that Paula Corbin Jones's accusations are part of a pattern that is more serious than it first thought.

This personal attack is a clean kill for liberals, because it implicates only the Clintons and Arkansas, not their ideas. Word leaks that George Mitchell is tired of feuding with George Steinbrenner and may make a presidential run. Mr. Clinton at last succumbs, declaring that the cause of "change" is too important to let his personal history, however distorted by right-wing critics, interfere. Vice President Gore, newly liberated and free of personal scandal, announces his bid.

Far-fetched? Maybe, but this is an era of political astonishment. Japan's LDP coalition is now led by a Socialist, Canada's conservatives lost 150 of 152 seats, and a governor from a small Southern state with a troubled if little-known past was elected, with 43% of the vote, to the most powerful job in the world. Imagine that.

REVIEW & OUTLOOK

Espy's World

Poor Mike Espy. This is a man who fell in with the wrong crowd. In descending order of bad influence, they are: the House of Representatives, Arkansas, the Clinton Administration and Tony Coelho.

Let's start with the Capitol Hill crowd the former Mississippi Congressman used to run with. Their influence must explain why

Donald Smaltz

shortly before the Agriculture Secretary resigned, he tried to argue that the 1907 Meat Inspection Act, barring Ag officials and inspectors from taking gratuities from meat and poultry interests, didn't apply to him. Mr. Espy must have thought he was still back in the House, exempt from the coverage of all the laws they impose on the rest of the country.

The Independent Counsel investigating the Espy case, Donald Smaltz, informed the Secretary that this defense was a non-starter. Mr. Smaltz also told Mr. Espy that his decision to pay back Arkansas chicken baron Don Tyson for the gratuities he'd received also didn't constitute a serious defense. Maybe all the House incumbents about to be voted out of their safe haven should pass through some sort of re-education camp to learn the rules in the real world.

Speaking of other worlds, we'll bet Mike Espy wishes he'd never heard of Arkansas. The place seems to function internally for the state's insiders as a kind of Twilight Zone, with no recognizable line between private interests and public office.

We imagine that the private sector there would argue that in a one-party state like Arkansas, you do what you have to do to survive the politicians' predations on your cash flow. Tyson's income derives from poultry processing, and it wasn't long after Mr. Espy settled in at Agriculture that he somehow ended up at sporting events, with tickets, transportation and lodging paid for by Tyson Foods and others. Even by the standards of Arkansas mores, this is fairly small change, but the Independent Counsel is checking out charges that the Agriculture Department held up fecal-contamination standards for poultry at the behest of Tyson Foods a few months after the Administration took office.

It's tempting to think about how the world of the Clinton Presidency must have looked early on from where Mike Espy was sitting. He's getting offers of freebies from Arkansas interests at the same time the new President is stocking his own office of general counsel, the Justice Department and White House Administration with unknowns from Arkansas (though of course we learn later the unknowns know a lot about something back home called Whitewater). An ambitious politician might be forgiven for thinking calls from the state needed his attention. Still, the political culture probably won't fly as a defense either.

Indeed, aficionados of the prevailing political culture should consult Brooks Jackson's account in "Honest Graft" of how then-House Whip Tony Coelho helped fund the original Espy House race in Mississippi with soft money. Mr. Coelho left office under his own cloud in 1989, but was recently recruited back to Washington by Mr. Clinton to informally run the Democratic National Committee.

The Espy case is big because it involves the resignation of a Cabinet Secretary. It's of a piece, though, with the larger story now of people in our politics who are unable to recognize any line at all between the realms of private and public life.

Editorial Feature

The Mena Coverup

By MICAH MORRISON

MENA, Ark. — What do Bill Clinton and Oliver North have in common, along with the Arkansas State Police and the Central Intelligence Agency? All probably wish they had never heard of Mena.

President Clinton was asked at his Oct. 7 press conference about Mena, a small town and airport in the wilds of Western Arkansas. Sarah McClendon, a longtime Washington curmudgeon renowned for her off-the-wall questions, wove a query around the charge that a base in Mena was "set up by Oliver North and the CIA" in the 1980s and used to "bring in planeload after planeload of cocaine" for sale in the U.S., with the profits then used to buy weapons for the Contras. Was he told as Arkansas governor? she asked.

"No," the president replied, "they didn't tell me anything about it." The alleged events "were primarily a matter for federal jurisdiction. The state really had next to nothing to do with it. The local prosecutor did conduct an investigation based on what was in the jurisdiction of state law. The rest of it was under the jurisdiction of the United States Attorneys who were appointed successively by previous administrations. We had nothing — zero — to do with it."

It was Mr. Clinton's lengthiest remark on the murky affair since it surfaced nearly a decade ago, in the middle of his long tenure as governor of Arkansas. And while the president may be correct to suggest that Mena is an even bigger problem for previous Republican administrations, he was wrong on just about every other count. The state of Arkansas had plenty to do with Mena, and Mr. Clinton left many unanswered questions behind when he moved to Washington.

Anyone who thinks that Mena is not serious should speak to William Duncan, a former Internal Revenue Service investigator who, together with Arkansas State Police Investigator Russell Welch, has fought a bitter 10-year battle to bring the matter to light. They pinned their hopes on nine separate state and federal probes. All failed.

"The Mena investigations were never supposed to see the light of day," says Mr. Duncan, now an investigator with the Medicaid Fraud Division of the office of Arkansas Attorney General Winston Bryant. "Investigations were interfered with and covered up, and the justice system was subverted."

The mysteries of Mena, detailed on this page on June 29, center on the activities of a drug-smuggler-turned-informant named Adler Berriman "Barry" Seal. Mr. Seal began operating at Mena Intermountain Regional Airport in 1981. At the height of his career, according to Mr. Welch, Mr. Seal was importing as much as 1,000 pounds of cocaine a month.

William Duncan

By 1984, Mr. Seal was an informant for the Drug Enforcement Agency and flew at least one sting operation to Nicaragua for the CIA, a mission known to have drawn the attention of Mr. North. By 1986, Mr. Seal was dead, gunned down by Colombian hitmen in Baton Rouge, La. Eight months after Mr. Seal's murder, his cargo plane, which had been based at Mena, was shot down over Nicaragua with Eugene Hasenfus and a load of Contra supplies aboard.

According to Mr. Duncan and others, Mr. Clinton's allies in state government worked to suppress Mena investigations. In 1990, for example, when Mr. Bryant made Mena an issue in the race for attorney general, Clinton aide Betsey Wright warned the candidate "to stay away" from the issue, according to a CBS Evening News investigative report. Ms. Wright denies the report. Yet once in office, and after a few feints in the direction of an investigation, Mr. Bryant stopped looking into Mena.

Documents obtained by the Journal show that as Gov. Clinton's quest for the presidency gathered steam in 1992, his Arkansas allies took increasing interest in Mena. Marie Miller, then director of the Medicaid Fraud Division, wrote in an April 1992 memo to her files that she told Mr. Duncan of the attorney general's "wish to sever any ties to the Mena matter because of the implication that the AG might be investigating the governor's connection." The memo says the instructions were pursuant to a conversation with Mr. Bryant's chief deputy, Royce Griffin. In an interview, Mr. Duncan said Mr. Griffin put him under "intense pressure" regarding Mena.

Another memo, from Mr. Duncan to several high-ranking members of the attorney general's staff in March 1992, notes that Mr. Duncan was instructed "to remove all files concerning the Mena investigation from the attorney general's office." At the time, several Arkansas newspapers were known to be preparing Freedom of Information Act requests aimed at Gov. Clinton's administration.

A spokesman for Mr. Bryant, Lawrence Graves, said yesterday that he was not aware of the missing files or of pressure exerted on Mr. Duncan. In Arkansas, Mr. Graves said, the attorney general "does not have authority" to pursue criminal cases.

From February to May 1992, Mr. Duncan was involved in a series of meetings aimed at deciding how to use a $25,000 federal grant obtained by then-Rep. Bill Alexander for the Mena investigation. In a November 1991 letter to Arkansas State Police Commander Tommy Goodwin, Mr. Alexander urged that, at the current "critical stage" in the Mena investigation, the money be used to briefly assign Mr. Duncan to the Arkansas State Police to pursue the case full time with State Police Investigator Welch and to prepare "a steady flow of information" for Iran-Contra prosecutor Lawrence Walsh, who had received some Mena files from Mr. Bryant.

According to Mr. Duncan's notes on the meetings, Mr. Clinton's aides closely tracked the negotiations over what to do with the money. Mr. Duncan says a May 7, 1992, meeting with Col. Goodwin was interrupted by a phone call from the governor, though he does not know what was discussed. The grant, however, was never used. Col. Goodwin told CBS that the money was returned "because we didn't have anything to spend it on."

In 1988, local authorities suffered a similar setback after Charles Black, a Mena-area prosecutor, approached Gov. Clinton with a request for funds for a Mena investigation. "He said he would get on it and would get a man back to me," Mr. Black told CBS. "I never heard back."

In 1990, Mr. Duncan informed Col. Goodwin about Clinton supporter Dan Lasater, who had been convicted of drug charges. "I told Tommy Goodwin that I'd received allegations of a Lasater connection to Mena," Mr. Duncan said.

The charge, that Barry Seal had used Mr. Lasater's bond business to launder drug money, was raised by a man named Terry Reed. Mr. Reed and journalist John Cummings recently published a book — "Compromised: Clinton, Bush and the CIA" — charging that Mr. Clinton, Mr. North and others engaged in a massive conspiracy to smuggle cocaine, export weapons and launder money. While much of the book rests on slim evidence and already published sources, the Lasater-Seal connection is new. (Thomas Mars, Mr. Lasater's attorney, said yesterday that his client "has never had a connection" with Mr. Seal.) But when Mr. Duncan tried to check out the allegations, his probe went nowhere, stalled from lack of funds and bureaucratic hostility.

Not all of the hostility came from the state level. When Messrs. Duncan and Welch built a money-laundering case in 1985 against Mr. Seal's associates, the U.S. Attorneys in the case "directly interfered with the process," Mr. Duncan said. "Subpoenas were not issued, witnesses were discredited, interviews with witnesses were interrupted, and the wrong charges were brought before the grand jury."

One grand jury member was so outraged by the prosecutors' actions that she broke the grand-jury secrecy covenant. Not only had the case been blatantly mishandled, she later told a congressional investigator, but many jurors felt "there was some type of government intervention," according to a transcript of the statement obtained by the Journal. "Something is being covered up."

In 1987, Mr. Duncan was asked to testify before a House subcommittee on crime. Two days before his testimony, he says, IRS attorneys working with the U.S. Attorney for Western Arkansas reinterpreted Rule 6(e), the grand-jury secrecy law, forcing the exclusion of much of Mr. Duncan's planned testimony and evidence. Mr. Duncan also charges that a senior IRS attorney tried to force him to commit perjury by directing him to say he had no knowledge of a claim by

Mr. Seal that a large bribe had been paid to Attorney General Edwin Meese. Mr. Duncan says he didn't make much of the drug dealer's claim, but did know about it; he refused to lie to Congress.

Mr. Duncan, distressed by the IRS's handling of Mena, resigned in 1989. Meanwhile, the affair was sputtering through four federal forums, including a General Accounting Office probe derailed by the National Security Council. At one particularly low point, Mr. Duncan, then briefly a Mena investigator for a House subcommittee, was arrested on Capitol Hill on a bogus weapons charge that was held over his head for nine months, then dismissed. His prized career in law enforcement in ruins, he found his way back to Arkansas and began to pick up the pieces.

Mr. Duncan does not consider President Clinton a political enemy. Indeed, he feels close to the president — a fellow Arkansan who shares the same birthday — and thinks Mena may turn out to be far more troublesome for GOP figures such as Mr. North than any Arkansas players.

These days, Mr. Duncan struggles to keep hope alive. "I'm just a simple Arkansan who takes patriotism very seriously," he says. "We are losing confidence in our system. But I still believe that somewhere, somehow, there is some committee or institution that can issue subpoenas, get on the money trail, find out what happened and restore a bit of faith in the system."

Mr. Morrison is a Journal editorial page writer.

REVIEW & OUTLOOK

Under BCCI's Rug

The headlines last week said Swaleh Naqvi got a stiff sentence for his role in the Bank of Credit and Commerce International – the maximum under his plea agreement, the longest of anyone associated with the rogue bank, etc., etc. Given our longstanding interest in the still-unresolved scandal, we've been poking around – and are scarcely surprised to come to a more skeptical and even suspicious assessment.

We should perhaps begin by restating our continuing interest in BCCI. The notion that it was another country and the wench is dead seems to be the conventional wisdom among law enforcement authorities, news organizations and no doubt many readers. But not only at $10 billion or so was BCCI the biggest bank heist in history; it is also a prototype for the future. Given the Latin American drug cartels and now what we see developing in Russia and China, the next century bids to become one of international criminal gangs operating in a shadowy world beyond the control of fragmented national authorities themselves subject to corruption.

Robert Altman

The banking system is particularly vulnerable, but also potentially an important choke-point against criminal cartels.

So the point about BCCI is that we still do not know what happened. The particular U.S. concern is discerning how a pack of Arab crooks got control of the biggest bank in Washington, D.C. We do know that in other nations BCCI prospered by corrupting politicians and regulators, and can reasonably suspect that it tried the same here. But nowhere have we had the kind of investigation that would determine who got what, or alternatively, that the penetration resulted merely from a string of mistakes and coincidences without actual corruption.

Mr. Naqvi's extradition from Abu Dhabi was to have been the big hope for that kind of housecleaning. But neither his testimony nor records released after long tenure in the emirate have led to any important public revelations. Federal investigators are ready to write him off as a dry hole. Robert Morgenthau, the Manhattan District Attorney, thinks that Naqvi has been stonewalling, and the threat of a truly serious sentence might produce some real information.

While ostensibly 11 years, the sentence levied by Judge Joyce Hens Green allows credit for nearly three years Mr. Naqvi served under house arrest in Abu Dhabi. It also includes a provision allowing the government to move for a reduction on the basis of cooperation. Gerald Stern, the Justice Department special counsel in charge of the case, tells us the original sentence did not take cooperation into account, and that Mr. Naqvi has indeed cooperated. So the ultimate sentence could be anything from eight more years to time served in Abu Dhabi.

In conjunction with the Naqvi case, also, a legal dispute has erupted between Mr. Stern and Harry Albright Jr., the court-appointed trustee for Washington's First American Bank. Mr. Albright succeeded in selling the banking assets for more money than anyone expected, and has also filed a civil suit against Clark Clifford and Robert Altman over their management of the bank. The government has now filed a forfeiture order for BCCI's interest in the proceeds of the sale; the order is opposed by Mr. Albright on the grounds that it is a big step toward collapsing his trusteeship and not so incidentally his suit against Mr. Clifford and Mr. Altman. If successful, the suit would provide more funds for eventual distribution to victims of the scam, and also a lot more information about BCCI's ownership of First American.

Mr. Stern has filed a court response saying not to worry; the government would never do such a thing. The legal argument devolves into intricacies of state vs. federal law, whether shareholders own only their shares or the underlying assets, and the implications of the RICO law. Our sympathies lie with the guy trying to keep the investigation as active as possible, not with the guy who's moving to close things down.

All the more so given the net of influence surrounding this case and the checkered history of the Clinton Justice Department. No doubt innocent people will be swept up in the following, and some will no doubt accuse us of innuendo. But we remember charges that the Meese Justice Department was impeached by the "sleaze" of the Wedtech case, a two-bit affair at most. In unraveling BCCI's $10 billion web, you have to start somewhere:

Mr. Clifford was of course dean of the Washington establishment. Deputy Attorney General Jamie Gorelick represented him in trying to get First American to pay his legal bills to his lead lawyers. These were Robert Fiske, onetime Whitewater special counsel, and Robert Bennett, President Clinton's lawyer in the Paula Jones case.

Clark Clifford

Webster Hubbell, the resigned attorney general and former law partner of Hillary Clinton, is now ensconced at an office at G. William Miller & Co., a Washington investment boutique run by the Carter Administration Fed chairman and Treasury Secretary. Miller principal Michael Cardozo, also head of the President's legal defense fund, says that while Mr. Hubbell has an office, he has "no formal affiliation" with the firm.

We previously wrote that at least Mr. Stern had no BCCI connection, only to be upbraided in the American Spectator by former colleague James Ring Adams, from whom we have learned much about the case. Mr. Adams points out that Mr. Stern was formerly general counsel of Occidental Petroleum, headed by Armand Hammer, who was involved in the original financial maneuvering over First American and sold some of his company's shares to BCCI front man Ghaith Pharaon. Mr. Stern says this was all before his time at Occidental, let alone Justice.

Oh, Mr. Naqvi's lawyer is Joseph E. diGenova of Manatt, Phelps & Phillips, a firm Mr. Stern used at Occidental and where Trade

Representative Mickey Kantor was a partner. Mr. diGenova has said he is working without pay, in the hope that Abu Dhabi will eventually pick up the tab. Mr. Naqvi is reported as destitute and unable to pay the $255 million judgment Judge Green levied against him.

This string of associations, if not conclusive of anything, starts to show why an unresolved scandal of BCCI's scope raises so many questions. It is going to continue to attract suspicions, and spread them, until someone picks up the case and shakes it until we're sure no more dirt has been swept under the rug.

Review & Outlook

The GOP and Whitewater

Since we've been assiduous about Whitewater and the BCCI scandal, both of which primarily focus on Democrats, we ought to pause in this election season to remark that Republicans also have some questions to answer. And that, perhaps understandably, Democrats don't seem very good at asking them.

Drug smuggling, the Contras and Oliver North, for example, have been flitting through the hot Virginia Senatorial contest. The Washington Post reported that Drug Enforcement Agency officials had complained that Mr. North did not pass along reports that aircraft and crew used in a humanitarian assistance program for the Nicaraguan Contras may have been involved in drug smuggling. This provoked a retort from former Assistant Secretary of State Elliott Abrams, saying, "All of us who ran that program, including Oliver North, were absolutely dedicated to keeping it completely clean and free of any involvement by drug traffickers."

Oliver North

We believe Mr. Abrams says what he believes to be true. But in connection with Whitewater we've been investigating the happenings at Mena airport in Arkansas, where the names of the Contras and Mr. North keep popping up. As we said Friday in detailing the BCCI connections in the Clinton Justice Department, we wish we had a good explanation of Mena if only to clear the innocent.

This much we know: Barry Seal was smuggling drugs and kept his planes at Mena. He also acted as an agent for the DEA. In one of these missions, he flew the plane that produced photographs of Sandinistas loading drugs in Nicaragua. He was killed by a Colombian drug gang in Baton Rouge. The cargo plane he flew was the same one later flown by Eugene Hasenfus when he was shot down over Nicaragua with a load of Contra supplies. These bare facts are, so far as we know, undisputed.

As we've detailed in articles on Mena on this page June 29 and Oct. 18, it's clear that a great many strange things were going on at the airport, even if you discount the extreme speculations in Terry Reed's book "Compromised." In particular, there is abundant evidence that drug investigations of Mena were blocked at both the state and federal levels. We also know, of course, that Mr. North was point man in the Contra operation. So lacking any clear explanation of what was taking place, it's almost inevitable that a lot of informed and competent people in Arkansas suspect that Mr. North was involved.

These suspicions are fed by a lot of backbiting within the law enforcement community. Some DEA officials blame Mr. North for the leak of the Seal photo, blackening the Sandinistas but also exposing one of the DEA's agents. A 1988 Foreign Relations Committee report on some of these issues said that DEA agents testified that Mr. North suggested that the proceeds generated by the Sandinista sting operation be funneled to the Contras.

Ollie North is of course one of the most thoroughly investigated individuals in U.S. history, and Iran-Contra special prosecutor Lawrence Walsh showed little interest in extensive materials he was given on Mena. Still, given the facts on their face, Mr. North and others really do owe the Republic a complete explanation. His opponent, Senator Chuck Robb, is somewhat restricted in flogging the drug issue because of rumors circulating around the Virginia Beach parties he attended. Nor, as things stand, is the matter likely to be aired by a Congressional probe; which party would launch it?

*　*　*

In Texas, similarly, GOP gubernatorial candidate George W. Bush is being targeted for his involvement in Harken Energy Corp. Incumbent Ann Richards has been charging that he may have been guilty of insider trading when he sold nearly two-thirds of his stock in the company for some $840,000. The stock rose on news of an off-shore oil concession in Bahrain, and fell when bankers complained that loan covenants were violated.

Now, insider trading is the least of our problems with the Harken investment, as we made clear back during the Bush Presidency ("Bush and BCCI," October 29, 1991). The real question is how Harken, with next to no relevant experience, was ever selected for the Bahrain concession. Did it have anything to do with the fact that the son of the President sat on its board and was a prominent investor?

George W. Bush

Indeed, Harken is one of the intriguing links between BCCI and Whitewater broadly defined. The deal was outlined in "False Profits," the BCCI book by Peter Truell and Larry Gurwin. Harken's investment bank was Arkansas giant Stephens Inc. One of its principal investors was Sheik Abdulla Taha Bakhsh, sometime business associate of BCCI figures Ghaith Pharaon and Khalid Bin Mahfouz. The Bahrain deal, the book reports, was put together by "former Stephens executives." This was in fact David Edwards (with his brother), longtime Little Rock buddy of Bill Clinton. Mr. Edwards's connection to Mr. Clinton might go some way toward mitigating Mr. Bush's fear that, as he told us Friday, "Ann Richards will turn BCCI into a commercial." Mr. Bush added that he had been "against the Bahrain deal. I thought it was wrong for the company. And I had no idea that BCCI figured into it."

*   *   *

While we're at it, we might take note that in England, Margaret Thatcher's son Mark is fighting charges by a dissident Saudi diplomat that he made £12 million in commissions on an arms deal Mrs. Thatcher helped to secure with Saudi Arabia when she was prime minister. Perhaps President Clinton's discussions in Saudi Arabia last week included his own efforts to obtain a civilian aircraft order for Boeing, now on the rocks over financing difficulties.

All of which is to say that a great deal of quite understandable suspicion revolves around the once-storied Arab petrodollars, the banking system, the Western intelligence agencies, the drug cartels and electoral politics. And further that all political factions have their problems, so that it's not clear that much will be forthcoming in Congress. Yet with the Cold War over and the Arabs living under Western military protection, it's time for a thorough laundering of dirty linen. Perhaps candidates like Mr. North and Mr. Bush, and also the Clinton Administration figures we mentioned in "Under BCCI's Rug" last Friday, could see some advantage in a Blue Ribbon Commission. At this stage in our national life it would not be easy to find an appropriate chairman; while he may be shocked at the suggestion, we nominate retired Supreme Court Justice Byron White.

REVIEW & OUTLOOK

The Rest of Him

"Where's the rest of me?" was one of Ronald Reagan's most famous screen lines, from his depiction of an amputee in the 1942 picture "King's Row." Tuesday, the American electorate answered the question, producing the rest of the revolution President Reagan initiated back in 1980.

Ronald Reagan

As President for eight years, Mr. Reagan accomplished no few things, cutting taxes to reinvigorate economic growth, arming the military to win the Cold War and renewing the spirit of America and the world. But throughout his presidency he was hampered by opposition control of the Congress, which holds such real levers of power as the power of the purse and the prerogative to investigate. Now these powers have been turned over to a new generation of Republicans reared under President Reagan. You can bet there is going to be "change" in American politics.

The momentousness of Tuesday's results can hardly be overstated, as the accompanying table depicts. These numbers mean a new, more conservative spirit has infused the U.S. system. Philosophically, the domestic politics and legislative enactments of the United States will move power away from large and bureaucratic entities and toward individuals and the country's many local governing institutions. This, broadly, is American conservatism.

With the unmistakable decisiveness of Tuesday's vote, the American electorate has joined hands with voters elsewhere in the world who have been forcing this new political spirit into their systems. Electorates as diverse as Japan's, Italy's and the Czech Republic's all have signaled their wish to live more by their own lights and less by bureaucratic edict.

It is no accident that the United States should be among the last major nations to fully seize this reorganizing global spirit, since America's Founders saw virtue in a deliberate political process. But they also designed a national system able to reflect fundamental shifts as we have just witnessed; now the world should prepare to see this country swiftly lead the new direction.

Seismic Shift

The extent of the shift in American political power starts with a few figures:

- Republicans will take control of the Senate for only the fourth time since World War II.
- Republicans will take over the House of Representatives for the first time in 40 years, with a gain of at least 52 seats, the largest GOP victory since 1946.
- House Speaker Tom Foley has conceded defeat in his home district. Three Democratic committee chairmen also lost – Dan Rostenkowski of Ways and Means, Jack Brooks of Judiciary, and Dan Glickman of Intelligence.
- No incumbent Republican Senator or House member lost. Two incumbent Democratic Senators and 35 House incumbents were defeated.
- Republican House gains were distributed as follows: Eastern states, 4 seats; Southern states, 19 seats; Midwest states, 15 seats; Western states, 13 seats.
- Oklahoma's J.C. Watts will join Gary Franks of Connecticut as the second black Republican in the House.

Under that system the presidency commands enormous powers of authority, especially in foreign affairs. But if the presidency constitutes the engine of authority, it is Congress that runs the system's switchyard controlling the levers of power. The content and direction of this new political generation's policies will emerge soon enough. For one technical but enormously powerful example, we can almost certainly expect to see the elimination of the perpetual-spending device called the "current services budget," whereby current programs rather than current spending becomes the test of a budget "increase" or "cut." Similarly, many of the most grandiose and costly laws passed over the past 20 years — affecting water, pollution, air, endangered species, disabilities and the like — will undergo rigorous tests of economic rationality when their reauthorizations arrive. A school prayer amendment is no longer a non-subject.

But with partisan control changing hands in both chambers of Congress, it is important to note the election's negative effect, that is, what the voters have put a stop to. Congressional power resides mainly in its standing committees and their chairmen. This means that as of January 1, for example, John Dingell, longtime chairman of a committee that deploys an army of staff investigators, will no longer be able to smear and ruin the careers of such Americans as Nobel laureate David Baltimore. It is now less likely that committee chairmen and their staff will use the enormous police powers and litigation budgets of the federal agencies to bully private citizens and local governments. These intrusions, so commonplace that they got scant publicity (if not approval), will decline, a gain in both personal and economic liberty that can hardly be overstated.

At the same time, the defeats of Ollie North in Virginia and, apparently, Michael Huffington in California suggest that the American electorate did not engage Tuesday in some unconsidered partisan sweep. A word also must be said about this election's moral dimension. Amid all the charged argument about the "religious right," abortion, crime, school prayer and the like, what emerges from this election's results is an unmistakable sense that the American people are searching thoughtfully for ways to refresh the moral quality of their society. The change of party control ensures that this subject will not be intimidated or ridiculed off the public agenda.

The tables are now turned, with a Republican Congress confronting a Democratic President. Bill Clinton and his Administration will have to choose how to deal with this reality, whether by cooperation or confrontation, neither an attractive alternative. No doubt there remains plenty of room for Democratic maneuver and Republican mistakes, but this election is likely to prove a defining moment. The electorate has found that "kinder and gentler" Republicans don't work, and that there are not yet any "new Democrats." So they are returning to the 1980s, providing another chance for the never-quite-completed agenda of Ronald Reagan.

REVIEW & OUTLOOK

Gridlock Upended

In his news conference yesterday, President Clinton accepted "responsibility" for Tuesday's Democratic debacle, and then asserted that his own agenda was largely in sync with the country's wants and desires. Something's wrong with this picture.

We have been given to believe for some months now by various Beltway choruses that the nation's number one problem was "gridlock" in Congress, in particular the opposition stance of Republican members of Congress. We now have an election result in which voters have sent unprecedentedly larger numbers of these same Republicans to serve in Congress. This suggests to us that much intellectual work needs to be done inside the Beltway on accurately identifying the temper of the times.

Clinton aides say they've gotten the voters' message, but many of those aides have acted in recent years as if they were disconnected from national politics. Instead of at all engaging the GOP ideas born in the 1980s, those initiatives were rejected as wholly "failed," as Mr. Clinton reiterated yesterday. The better course, they thought, was to remake the U.S. health care system. How is it surprising that this gulf produced "gridlock"? Someone needs a reality check.

We suggest a look at some intriguing post-election polls. The Fabrizio/McLaughlin polling firm has often asked Americans if they preferred a bigger government that provided more services or a smaller government that provided fewer. In 1988, Americans divided about equally on that. Then early this year, 59% favored smaller government. Now, in a Tuesday poll of 1,000 voters, 68% wanted a smaller government and only 21% wanted a bigger one.

Only 16% of voters on Tuesday described themselves as liberal, but 52% described Mr. Clinton as a liberal. This week, Democrats paid a high price for that yawning philosophical gap between the President and the people.

Again, for two years the White House has railed against "gridlock," and that view has been popular in Washington. But surely it's now clear that gridlock occurred because President Clinton and the Democrats chose to govern against the temper of the country and the times. Republicans may now plausibly argue that the President's veto power could become the chief source of gridlock over the next two years.

It strikes us that the way to really break gridlock is for the White House to recognize, in the words of Bob Dylan, that "the times they are a changing." Yesterday, as so often has been the case, Mr. Clinton got the words exactly right: He expressed a desire to work for "smaller, more effective government." With the big-government Congress now turned out of office, he indeed has the opportunity to find partners at the other end of Pennsylvania Avenue willing to end the gridlock.

Skirmishes & Stalling

In the early months of 1995, national attention was focused on the new Congressional majority. But skirmishes continued over Whitewater. The Senate Banking Committee issued final reports on the summer's Whitewater hearings, focusing on the swirl of high-level Executive Branch meetings in late 1993 over the Resolution Trust Corp.'s confidential criminal referrals on Madison Guaranty. The Journal wrote that the reports demonstrated that "the hearings, though limited to the narrowest slice of the sprawling Whitewater controversy, clearly showed a massive breach of the confidentiality of the criminal process, and strongly suggested a White House in full coverup mode."

Investigations in Arkansas also were meeting with stiff resistance. Independent Counsel Donald Smaltz, appointed to investigate Agriculture Secretary Mike Espy's ties to agribusiness, found his probe curtailed by the Justice Department shortly after he ventured into Arkansas to look into poultry giant Tyson Foods. The Arkansas state trooper who led the investigation of Mena airfield, Russell Welch, was suddenly stripped of his post and threatened with the loss of his pension.

Independent Counsel Starr's probe appeared to be making headway in February when he indicted an Arkansas banker for bank fraud, and in June a Little Rock grand jury handed up indictments against Arkansas Governor Jim Guy Tucker and two associates in a complex scheme to fraudulently buy and sell cable television systems. But Mr. Starr's fortunes seemed to dim when the Tucker case was assigned to Federal District Judge Henry Woods, a longtime Clinton crony.

REVIEW & OUTLOOK

One Big Arkansas?

With the Republican tide swooshing through Capitol Hill, it's not surprising that last week's Whitewater reports from the Senate Banking Committee made no big splash. Still, the reports make clear the scandal isn't going away. With two independent counsels already in the field, indeed, it's likely to prove more illuminating than the ethical flaps that have been in the news these past two weeks.

The main Banking Committee report, written by the Democratic staff, provides an exhaustive account of conflicting testimony during the committee's six-day public inquiry into contacts between the White House, Treasury and Resolution Trust Corp. regarding RTC probes into Madison Guaranty Savings & Loan. While providing a 227-page factual base, the former majority's report studiously avoids drawing any significant conclusions, leaving that to the new majority's separate document. To wit, "The Committee and the American people witnessed a parade of high-level government officials experiencing various degrees of memory loss and delivering conflicting, contradictory and inconsistent testimony designed to obfuscate the truth about their actions."

The reports focus on the whirlwind of high-level meetings and phone calls between two bookend dates: late September 1993, when the RTC's Kansas City field office prepared to forward a new set of confidential criminal referrals containing allegations against current

Arkansas Governor Jim Guy Tucker and mentioning Bill and Hillary Clinton as possible witnesses to or beneficiaries of illegal actions. And February 28, 1994, when the statute of limitations on civil claims for fraud and misconduct concerning Madison was scheduled to expire; in the event, Congress extended the statute.

The reports make clear that in this period Roger Altman, Deputy Treasury Secretary and interim RTC head, was talking about the Madison case to the White House Counsel's office; Republicans point out that he "told the White House the single most important fact about the investigation, that it probably would not be concluded until after the statute of limitations had expired."

The Counsel's office in turn was talking to political operatives such as Bruce Lindsey and Harold Ickes. They in turn were talking to outside parties, in particular James Lyons, the Denver lawyer who crafted the Clinton campaign's Whitewater response.

The "gist" of Mr. Altman's key report was also reported to the President and Mrs. Clinton by Mr. Ickes. The President, in turn, held a private meeting with Governor Tucker, one of the suspects. The President also directly approached one regulator, Comptroller of the Currency Eugene Ludwig, to discuss the case. In short, the hearings, though limited to the narrowest slice of the sprawling Whitewater controversy, clearly showed a massive breach of the confidentiality of the criminal process, and strongly suggested a White House in full coverup mode.

*   *   *

The Republicans have written Independent Counsel Kenneth Starr asking that he start a formal review of possible criminal violations in testimony by Mr. Altman, Jean Hanson and Joshua Steiner of Treasury, and White House aides George Stephanopolous and Mr. Ickes. The Republicans point out that the President and First Lady gave Special Counsel Robert Fiske sworn depositions on what took place at these meetings, and promise "strenuous efforts to obtain these depositions or to obtain the information in some other manner."

They want to know, for example, "Did President Clinton inform Jim Guy Tucker that he was mentioned in the RTC's criminal referrals. . .?" They also say the committee "must question Webster Hubbell," the former Associate Attorney General who has confessed to overbilling at the Rose Law Firm; they want to know about his knowledge of the referrals and about the initial decision not to pursue them made by Paula Casey, the Clinton friend who is U.S. Attorney in Little Rock. They also want hearings on the disposition of the papers taken from Vincent Foster's office following his death.

Though Chairman Al D'Amato once promised early hearings, Republicans now say they will defer to Mr. Starr "until we believe such hearings will not impede" his investigation. The key to the postponement, it seems, is that the Republicans have acquired a confidence in Mr. Starr they did not have in Mr. Fiske.

And indeed, the Starr investigation is showing signs of vigor. He got a guilty plea from Mr. Hubbell. And another plea, portentous to those who understand loan-kiting, from the real estate appraiser for many Madison transactions. Our Ellen Joan Pollock reported from Little Rock on December 30 that he will soon decide whether to indict Governor Tucker, Madison owner James McDougal, his former wife Susan, her brothers and others involved in Madison.

While arguably Mr. Fiske's investigation laid the basis for much of this progress, in recent days Mr. Starr has taken grand jury testimony from the rescue workers and Park Policemen who discovered Mr. Foster's body in Fort Marcy Park. Both sides of the Banking Committee accept that Mr. Foster's death was a suicide. Yet it would appear that Mr. Starr has some reason, whether simple thoroughness or new information, to start from the ground up.

Meanwhile, loud cries are coming from Arkansas about independent counsel Donald Smaltz, appointed to study the actions of former Agriculture Secretary Mike Espy but broadening his investigations to include other activities of poultry giant Tyson Foods, a big node in the loose network that has long dominated the political landscape of Arkansas.

* * *

This is all to the good, but we continue to have doubts about a simply legalistic approach. We have little desire to criminalize the efforts of executive officials to put the best face on their actions before hostile Congressional questioning. While the Clinton Administration should be held responsible for its lapses, embarrassing the President and his aides is not the point. What we really want to know is whether Whitewater and its ilk represent something systemic.

Consider for a moment the Whitewater and Arkansas casualties so far. Mr. Foster is a suicide. Mr. Hubbell is a confessed felon. William Kennedy III, the third Rose Law Firm partner in the Administration, slipped out the White House door November 18. Secretary Espy has resigned over Tyson contacts. David Watkins left his post as White House director of administration over a helicopter ride. Mr. Altman, Mr. Nussbaum, Ms. Hanson and Mr. Steiner have resigned.

The White House payroll still includes, however, two aides who visited Mr. Foster's office the night of his death: Patsy Thomasson, former top associate of Little Rock drug convict Dan Lasater, and Maggie Williams, Mrs. Clinton's chief of staff, who also delivered the Foster papers to the White House family quarters. Meanwhile, the President is appealing a ruling that he has to give a deposition in the Paula Corbin Jones lawsuit. A federal judge has asked U.S. Attorney Eric Holder to study whether health czar Ira Magaziner committed perjury in the lawsuit against the secrecy of the First Lady's health-care task force. HUD Secretary Henry Cisneros is beleaguered over questionable testimony regarding arrangements with a former mistress, and Surgeon General Joycelyn Elders has been forced from office.

The sweep of this list suggests something deeply wrong. At the very least, it seems to raise the question of whether Washington is becoming one big Arkansas. But in a larger sense, we quickly admit, that's unfair to Arkansas. We've recently seen some of the most powerful figures in Congress embarrassed by ethical lapses, chased from Congress and even indicted. Not least, we've learned that Clark Clifford, the epitome of the Washington establishment, was involved in the world's biggest scam — a front-man, to put it charitably, for the Bank of Credit & Commerce International, which not so incidentally had Arkansas connections.

Nor, though Democrats have been in Congressional power too long for their own good, is this limited to one party. During the campaign we remarked on suspicions about Whitewater and BCCI touching George Bush Jr. and Oliver North. While we don't think Chairman D'Amato is in any way unfit for his duties, he'll inevitably take knocks for hot-issue trading, which the financial world understands as inherently suspect. One thing the voters wanted in handing power to the Republicans, we think, was some kind of an ethical accounting.

This mandate will not be redeemed by such Beltway establishment nostrums as new rules on lobbyists. It will be redeemed by sunshine. On BCCI, we still need to know how a band of Arab crooks came to own the biggest bank in the nation's capital. And on Whitewater, we need to know not merely whether some laws were broken, but whether the whole Administration was designed and staffed to preclude investigation of the Whitewater-Madison transactions in Arkansas, and to provide a framework for similar wheeler-dealing in Washington.

Letters to the Editor

White House Coverup? It's News to Me

Your Jan. 13 editorial "One Big Arkansas?" which purports to describe the Senate Banking Committee's recent Whitewater reports, seriously mischaracterizes the facts, which do not support your "strong" suggestion of "a White House in full coverup mode."

The contacts between White House and Treasury officials concerning the RTC's Whitewater activities have been the subject of no fewer than five exhaustive inquiries. In each of those inquiries the White House cooperated fully and completely. No documents, whether or not subject to a proper claim of executive privilege, were withheld from the independent counsel. No relevant documents were withheld from the Senate and House committees. White House officials appeared before a grand jury and were interviewed by FBI agents working under the direction of the independent counsel. They agreed to interviews in the course of my own internal review of the contacts, to depositions by the Treasury and RTC Inspectors General, to interviews by the House Banking Committee, to depositions by the Senate Banking Committee and to testimony taken in public hearings before both committees. This degree of cooperation is without precedent. And it is hardly the stuff of which a "coverup" is made.

Furthermore, none of these inquiries − including the one conducted by the Senate Banking Committee − reached the conclusion that the Treasury-White House contacts had any effect whatsoever on what the RTC actually did. Indeed, the RTC civil investigation of

Madison Guaranty Savings and Loan is proceeding under Jay Stephens — the private counsel selected by the RTC, who is a vocal political opponent of President Clinton — while the criminal investigation into Madison's affairs is in the hands of an independent counsel with teams in Washington and Little Rock.

Your editorial claims that the Senate report (which, incidentally, was signed by both then-Chairman Riegle and then-Ranking Republican Senator D'Amato) "studiously avoids drawing any significant conclusions." But how can that claim be reconciled with the chairman's statement on releasing the report — significant by any standard — that the committee found that the contacts were not prohibited by any law or ethics standard? Furthermore, the committee announced that its findings were consistent with the conclusions of the Office of Government Ethics that there was no violation of ethics standards by any Treasury official, and with my own conclusion that there had been no violation of ethics standards by any White House official.

A further indication of your editorial's eagerness to leap to adverse conclusions is its uncritical acceptance of the assertion by some committee Republicans that Roger Altman [then-deputy treasury secretary and interim RTC head] told White House officials that the RTC investigation of potential civil claims would not be concluded until after the expiration of the statute of limitations. Yet the report discredits this conclusion and states that everyone who remembered the details of Mr. Altman's briefing at which he is supposed to have made such a statement testified that he did not (See report 103-433, vol. II at 77).

As I testified to the Senate and House committees, my own investigation led me to conclude that it would have been better if some of the contacts between White House and Treasury officials had not occurred, and if all such contacts had been confined to Treasury and White House Counsel. As we promised in the hearings, and as the Senate Committee report recommended, new procedures are now in place to more carefully limit and control such contacts in the future. Plainly, it is time for all of us to move on to other more important affairs.

LLOYD N. CUTLER
Former White House Counsel
Washington

Editorial Feature

How Shocking!
Press Exhumes Troopergate

By R. EMMETT TYRRELL

Why last Friday did the Washington Post on its front page report hoary tales of President Clinton's extramarital affairs? When, as editor of the American Spectator, I published the original stories just over a year ago, I was disparaged for practicing tabloid journalism.

Andrew Sullivan, editor of the New Republic, cried the crocodile's tears that the conservative Spectator had been reduced to pubic hair and women in hotel rooms. And the author of the disappointing piece, David Brock, was abominated by many of the greatest eminences of mainstream media. Among the herd journalists it became a matter of received wisdom that the American Spectator was a magazine of reproachable taste and judgment.

What is happening at the Washington Post? Why its sudden recklessness? And the Post's piece relied solely on the testimony of one person, Betsey Wright. Mr. Brock relied on four sources, two on the record. Did the Post's writer ever stop to think that Miss Wright might be lying about our president? The Post's writer, Ann Devroy, was reporting on a forthcoming Clinton biography written by a Post reporter, David Maraniss. Is this not a conflict of interest?

After the grief I have endured for publishing Troopergate, a series of stories on Whitewater, and an account a couple of months back about Clinton operatives handing out "walking around" money that now seems to have aroused the interest of the independent counsel, I can tell you that our journalists are very fussy about what they call "journalistic standards."

According to the front-page story in the New Washington Post — soon to be in tabloid format? — "The belief among Clinton's aides that his extramarital affairs were a problem appears throughout the [Maraniss] book, but it is most telling in a few short paragraphs describing a session Clinton had with Wright, his chief of staff when he was Arkansas governor and a longtime political confidant."

Mr. Maraniss writes that Miss Wright confronted Bill Clinton about his affairs when he was considering a run for the presidency in 1988 because, "she was convinced that some state troopers were soliciting women for him and he for them, she said."

Well, Miss Wright's belief could only have been strengthened when she read David Brock's piece. A second Troopergate piece by the American Spectator's Danny Wattenberg introduced state trooper L.D. Brown, and Mr. Brown not only added evidence that Mr. Clinton misused state credit cards but stated that the governor had provided the troopers with women.

Miss Wright should have let out a yell of gratitude — "Hooray, the truth is out!" But, no, she characterized the troopers' statements as "lies" and "falsehoods"; and along with

Betsey Wright

practically every voice in the major media, she completely ignored the Wattenberg story, though it revealed misdeeds transcending mere sex.

In Miss Wright's inhospitable response to our investigative journalism, she introduced the term "gold-digger," implying that many of those who claimed knowledge of Mr. Clinton's satyriasis were out to make a buck.

But Miss Wright's disparagement of the American Spectator and of David Brock in particular actually had a suave charm compared with the shrieks of others. Michael Kinsley accused Brock and his editors of "dishonesty" and "fundamental bad faith." "Who would believe anything this fellow wrote? Not me," quipped Mr. Kinsley in the course of a characteristically specious denunciation of us that appeared in the New Republic and the Washington Post.

In Newsweek, Joe Klein accused Mr. Brock of being the "purveyor of uncorroborated and hyperbolic accusations by a handful of gold-digging Arkansas state troopers." Gold-digging? Has Joe, too, fallen under Betsey's spell? The Washington Post's E.J. Dionne Jr. again charged Mr. Brock with writing up unsubstantiated gossip because Mr. Clinton "is trying to alter the country's political landscape and its assumptions about government. And he's actually doing it."

TV commentator Paul Duke, in his solemnizing wrap-up of 1993 for "Washington Week in Review," adjudged Mr. Brock the year's "loser" who "wrote that slimy magazine article that revived all those old charges about Bill Clinton's personal behavior." Now the Post is out front in the running for Mr. Duke's 1995 award. Oh, woe!

The slandering of Mr. Brock has actually gained momentum over the year. On "Reliable Sources," Ellen Hume, a retired Journal journalist now embalmed at something called the "Washington Annenberg Program," intoned soap-opera like, "You're not a journalist, David."

The herd journalists are a menace to language. David Brock is clearly a journalist as well as an author. The herd journalists of America have taken the Cartesian formulation, "I think, therefore I am" and replaced it with a credo of their own, "I conform, therefore I am." Mr. Brock has not conformed, so he is not a journalist.

The Washington Post's vindication of the American Spectator will, I fear, not redound to our credit. There is an infantile quality about the American journalist's mind; our journalists do not revise their thoughts when confronted by earlier errors. The Post's revelations will most likely only occasion more reference to how untrustworthy Brock and the Spectator are.

As always I commit the old-fashioned foolishness of having evidence for what I say. In a newsletter read by many of the giants of this city, the White House Bulletin, of Feb. 3, an anonymous White House TV correspondent testifies as to why David Maraniss's account of Clinton's infidelities is serious stuff. "This is not the American Spectator, this is a very credible Washington Post correspondent." Maybe the troopers were lying.

Mr. Tyrrell is editor-in-chief of the American Spectator.

Editorial Feature

Who Is David Edwards?

By Micah Morrison

As the lens of "Whitewater" pans from tight focus to the full panorama of Bill Clinton's Arkansas, no more intriguing Friend of Bill appears than Edwin David Edwards.

Not that there is any suggestion that Mr. Edwards played a role in the Whitewater land development or Madison Savings & Loan, or any evidence of anything illicit where the Little Rock investment adviser has been involved. But Mr. Edwards keeps popping up, both as one of the president's oldest friends and as a symbol of the Saudi Arabian links that loom surprisingly large on Razorback terrain.

David Edwards

Mr. Edwards has been a Friend of Bill since at least 1969, when he briefly shared an apartment in England with Mr. Clinton and Strobe Talbott, the current deputy secretary of state. He vacationed with the Clintons on the Riviera, according to "Off the Books," by Robert Hutchison (William Morrow, 1986). Mr. Edwards was instrumental in the Saudi contribution for a Middle East studies center at the University of Arkansas announced just after the presidential election. He was on hand for the president's emotional departure from Little Rock for Washington (see the rendering of an Associated Press photo). On a visit to Little Rock the weekend before the suicide of

Deputy White House Counsel Vincent Foster, the president spent a four-hour dinner alone with Mr. Edwards.

Mr. Edwards and his brother Mark now run their own Little Rock investment placement firm, Edwards Brothers. While Mr. Edwards refused repeated requests for interviews for this article, his principal client appears to be a mysterious Jidda investor, Abdullah Taha Bakhsh, who at one time owned nearly 10% of Little Rock's Worthen Bank. Before leaving to form their own firm in 1990, both brothers worked for Stephens Inc., the powerhouse Arkansas investment firm that handled the brokerage when Middle Eastern front men for the Bank of Credit & Commerce International made an early attempt to buy First American Bank in Washington, D.C. While at Stephens, Mr. Edwards also played an important role in securing an offshore drilling contract in Bahrain for Harken Energy Corp., on whose board sat George W. Bush, presidential son and current governor of Texas.

If only as a matter of curiosity, David Edwards is a Friend of Bill worth a few moments of attention. The tales of the university donations and the Harken deal are particularly interesting.

Much of Mr. Edwards's tenure at Stephens was devoted to the investment firm's European and Middle East operations, though his precise role is murky.

In 1989, officials of the University of Arkansas at Fayetteville approached Jackson Stephens, the billionaire head of Stephens Inc. and a university board member, for help in raising funds for international studies. Mr. Stephens referred them to his employee, Mr. Edwards, say university officials. Mr. Edwards quickly turned to his Saudi contacts, including Mr. Bakhsh. Two executives associated with the investment firm say Mr. Edwards brought the low-profile Saudi to Stephens in 1987.

Reports in this newspaper and the BCCI book "False Profits," by Peter Truell and Larry Gurwin, say Mr. Bakhsh was a co-investor in Saudi Arabia with alleged BCCI front man Ghaith Pharaon. Khalid bin Mahfouz, another BCCI figure and head of the largest bank in Saudi Arabia, was Mr. Bakhsh's banker. University of Arkansas officials say Mr. Edwards sought to involve Mr. Bakhsh in a project to create a Middle East studies center at the school. In a letter to a university official, Mr. Edwards said he would bring the reclusive Saudi to Fayetteville to talk "about designing a simple mosque somewhere on campus."

In a written statement, Mr. Bakhsh's attorney, Paul Meyer of Rogers & Wells, noted that the Saudi financier "was not involved in any way in any of the matters or transactions that constituted the BCCI scandal." Mr. Meyer added that Mr. Bakhsh "was not a participant" in Mr. Edwards's funding effort for the University of Arkansas.

When the Edwards brothers departed for their own firm, they took the university project with them. But friction was increasing between David Edwards and the university. The globe-trotting investment adviser claimed several hundred thousand dollars in Saudi travel expenses, says a university official. Others at the school found Mr. Edwards's abrasive manner and pro-Arab bias inappropriate for an academic setting. In a letter to university officials written less than a month before the Iraqi invasion of Kuwait, Mr. Edwards commented on rising tensions in the region and complained that "we are giving our money to the Israelis to do what we tell them not to do."

Gov. Clinton, university officials say, was an enthusiastic supporter of the project, and Mr. Edwards worked closely with him — on at least one occasion conducting business from the Governor's Mansion, according to a document obtained by the Journal. But Gov. Clinton may have had some Saudi resources of his own. Mr. Clinton was a Georgetown University classmate of Turki bin Feisal, the current head of Saudi intelligence.

Sources in Arkansas say Mr. Clinton's famous networking skills also put him in contact with Prince Bandar bin Sultan, the Saudi ambassador to the U.S. University of Arkansas officials participated in a Clinton-Bandar meeting in the spring of 1991, when they and Mr. Edwards joined the governor in delivering a request for a major gift to the ambassador. According to a 1991 gubernatorial disclosure statement, Mr. Clinton and Prince Bandar also were together on June 23, when they traveled from Aspen to Little Rock on a jet leased by the Saudis.

Despite such contacts, no progress in raising money was made until Gov. Clinton received the Democratic presidential nomination. One month later, Mr. Edwards handled an anonymous lead gift to the university of $3.5 million for a Middle East studies program. Individuals familiar with the gift say it came from the Riyadh

Chamber of Commerce. According to the Cyprus-based Arab Press Service, the gift was approved by Saudi Arabia's King Fahd at the recommendation of Prince Turki.

Under Mr. Edwards's direction, and despite some objections from University of Arkansas officials, the unusual gift was transferred to a

President-elect Clinton bids farewell to David Edwards.

university account in the form of Treasury bonds. The resulting confusion was the last straw for university officials. They insisted that Mr. Edwards withdraw from the project. Curiously, documents obtained by the Journal indicate that extra bonds were delivered to the university, with a face value of $3.5 million promised and $3.9 million delivered. A financial administrator at the university says that "excess bonds were put in the account by a mistake in the electronic transfer" and were "returned."

One month after President Clinton's inauguration, Arkansas Gov. Jim Guy Tucker announced that Prince Bandar had delivered a $20 million gift to the University of Arkansas.

A few years earlier, Mr. Edwards provided important help to a company linked by family ties to then Vice President George Bush. In 1987, Mr. Edwards and Mr. Bakhsh rode to the rescue of Harken Energy, a struggling Texas oil company that included George W. Bush on its board. Harken's web of Middle East connections was detailed in a 1991 Wall Street Journal report. Stephens officials, including Mr. Edwards, came up with an unusual arrangement to help cash-poor Harken: Union Bank of Switzerland would give the oil company a $25 million cash infusion in exchange for stock. UBS, the Journal noted, was not known as an investor in small U.S. companies and was a joint-venture partner with BCCI in a Geneva-based bank.

When UBS began to hit regulatory snags, it decided to unload its Harken stock. Stephens brought in a new buyer: Mr. Bakhsh. The Saudi tycoon ended up with a 17% stake in Harken, and his American representative, Chicago businessman Talat Othman, wound up with a seat on Harken's board. By August 1990, Mr. Othman was attending White House meetings with President Bush to discuss Middle East policy. Mr. Meyer, who serves as attorney for Mr. Othman as well as Mr. Bakhsh, says the Chicago businessman was invited to the meetings only because of his "longstanding involvement in Arab-American affairs."

In April 1989, the government of Bahrain was looking for an oil company to explore its offshore holdings. According to a 1990 article in Forbes, the Bahrainis turned to Houston oil consultant Michael Ameen, a former head of governmental relations for Aramco. Mr. Ameen, the Journal noted in its 1991 report, is another "BCCI notation in the Harken story." As a top Aramco official, Mr. Ameen "had close-up dealings for years with the Saudi royal family and its advisers," including Kamal Adham, a BCCI principal and former head of Saudi intelligence. Mr. Ameen also reportedly is close to Mr. Bakhsh.

Mr. Ameen and Harken officials did not respond to interview requests. But according to Forbes the Bahrainis called Mr. Ameen, looking for a small company that would give them full attention. Mr. Ameen said he didn't know of any. By coincidence, Mr. Ameen's friend David Edwards called 10 minutes later on an unrelated matter. Mr. Ameen mentioned his problem. Mr. Edwards mentioned Harken.

Mr. Ameen negotiated the Bahrain deal, earning a $100,000 consulting fee. George W. Bush says he opposed it. "I thought it was a bad idea," Gov. Bush said recently, because of Harken's lack of expertise in overseas and offshore drilling. Gov. Bush added that he "had no idea that BCCI figured into" Harken's financial dealings.

In June 1990, Mr. Bush sold some 60% of his Harken stake for about $850,000, earning a handsome profit. In November 1993, he resigned from Harken's board. Four months later, his successor was named: Michael Ameen. Harken has yet to discover any oil off Bahrain.

Mr. Bakhsh appears to have been pleased with Stephens's investment strategies. From February 1989 through October 1990, he purchased more than one million shares in the Stephens-controlled Worthen Bank, paying more than $10 million for 9.6% of stock, according to Securities and Exchange Commission disclosure statements. Mr. Bakhsh's attorney says he no longer is a Worthen shareholder.

Mr. Bakhsh has a wide range of U.S. investments, concentrated mainly in apparel, energy, real estate and financial services. In November, the Chicago Tribune reported that Mr. Bakhsh's First Commercial Financial Group, a commodities brokerage firm, was forced to shed its customer accounts after regulators raised concerns about capital shortfalls and customer complaints. Mr. Bakhsh owns First Commercial through Dearborn Financial Inc., an investment company run by Mr. Othman. Their attorney, Mr. Meyer, says that First Commercial was completing "the final phase of its long-term strategic restructuring plan" by transferring its customer accounts to other firms. Mr. Meyer says that Mr. Edwards was not involved in Dearborn and First Commercial.

Mr. Edwards, though, has long been familiar with complicated financial transactions. In "Off the Books," financial journalist Robert Hutchison details Mr. Edwards's central role in a Byzantine tale of international banking and currency trading. In 1975, Mr. Edwards, then a Citibank junior executive in Paris, accused a senior currency trader of taking kickbacks and raised questions about the offshore parking of foreign-currency transactions. In order to avoid European taxes, Mr. Edwards charged, Citibank was booking fake transactions through its Bahamas branch, concealing them through a series of coded telex messages and other methods.

The "Edwards Affair," as it became known, lasted until 1983, entangling the SEC, Congress, and regulatory officials of six European countries. It concluded with the senior Paris trader cleared of the kickback charges and Citibank paying minor fines and back taxes in several countries. Following a long investigation, in 1982 the SEC declined to take steps against Citibank.

By that time, Mr. Edwards was long gone. In one of his first acts as head of Citibank's International Banking Group, Thomas Theobold fired Mr. Edwards in 1978, saying that Mr. Edwards was unable "to provide any substantive, factual corroboration of the allegations." Mr. Edwards responded by going to the SEC and filing an ultimately unsuccessful $14 million wrongful dismissal suit.

Citibank officials are bitter about their eight-year wrestling match with Mr. Edwards and worry that he may now be serving as an unofficial adviser to the president. "We fired him for being a lousy trader and he got back at us," says a former top Citibank official. "The next thing we hear, he's down in Arkansas. Wherever there's a smell rising from the river, Edwards seems to turn up."

Mr. Morrison is a Journal editorial page writer.

REVIEW & OUTLOOK

Razorbacks Hold Firm

The pregnant words in the indictment of Arkansas banker Neal T. Ainley read "and others known and unknown to the Grand Jury." Independent Counsel Kenneth Starr charges that the defendant was part of a conspiracy to violate banking regulations by not reporting large cash withdrawals in connection with Bill Clinton's 1990 gubernatorial campaign.

The five-count indictment says that in 1990 Mr. Ainley failed to report more than $52,000 in cash withdrawals, in violation of federal laws requiring the filing of Currency Transaction Reports with the Internal Revenue Service for cash transactions of $10,000. Mr. Ainley is also charged with making false entries in banking records and submitting a false statement to the Federal Deposit Insurance Corp. In one case, the indictment charges, he went into the bank's mail room and filched a CTR envelope addressed to the IRS, but kept a copy of the report in the bank's records. If convicted, he faces as many as 20 years in jail and $1 million in fines.

The question, of course, is who are the other parties to this conspiracy, "known and unknown to the Grand Jury." It is the world's most open secret that they start with Bruce Lindsey, long-time Clinton confidant now ensconced as a high White House aide. Mr. Lindsey was treasurer of the 1990 campaign. He signed four $7,500 checks that were bunched together for a cash withdrawal of $30,000. The indictment says another unreported $22,500 cash withdrawal was "delivered to a representative of the 1990 Clinton Campaign."

Presumably this representative also was Mr. Lindsey, as indeed the New York Times reported yesterday.

Of course, the money already belonged to the Clinton campaign; the only thing to be concealed was that it was being moved around in hunks of cash, rather than paid by check for TV spots and the like. The indictment does not speculate on why anyone would like to conceal this, but you could always ask Ed Rollins. After the Christie Whitman victory in New Jersey, he stirred a national furor by claiming that the campaign paid black ministers to suppress the turnout for her opponent. In denying that it did anything wrong, the Clinton camp says the money was used in a get-out-the-vote effort.

"Walking around money" has long been a pretty standard feature of political campaigns in Arkansas and some other states. In

Bruce Lindsey

1990, Governor Clinton had a difficult primary challenge, and in the general election was worried about a television onslaught by opponent Sheffield Nelson. With his eyes already on a presidential race, winning again as Governor was absolutely essential. Apparently the Perry County deposits were in addition to the usual efforts of the party machine, and it is no great leap to suspect that the ultimate cash disbursements would not sustain much scrutiny.

Now, "walking around money" may be only a petty legal or moral violation, but conspiring to violate the banking laws is quite another matter. The purpose of Currency Transaction Reports is to help trace the movement of drug money and other illicit funds. A willingness to tamper with this reporting mechanism suggests a casual contempt for the law, which seems to be a recurrent theme in the series of scandals under the Whitewater rubric.

With the excitement over the Simpson trial and the GOP contract, Whitewater has not been much in the news since the close of Senate hearings. It is worth pausing to call the roll: Webster Hubbell has resigned as associate attorney general and confessed to a felony. William Kennedy III, like Mr. Hubbell a former law partner of Hillary Clinton, has resigned from the White House counsel's office. Counsel Bernard Nussbaum and Deputy Treasury Secretary Roger Altman have been forced into resignation. Agriculture Secretary Mike Espy has also resigned, and a separate independent counsel has been appointed to investigate his relations with Arkansas's Tyson Foods. Various ethical clouds also bedevil Commerce Secretary Ron Brown, Transportation Secretary Federico Pena and HUD Secretary Henry Cisneros. Not all of these problems concern the Whitewater land development, of course, but something here seems to be contagious.

The White House has recently been congratulating itself that no big names will be indicted; Mr. Starr will be able to land only little fish like Neal Ainley. The line "others known and unknown to the Grand Jury" adds some perspective. What transparently is going on here is a battle over Mr. Ainley's testimony. Prosecutors no doubt think that if he were willing to relate the relevant conversations about the Currency Transaction Reports for the campaign withdrawals, they could probably land Mr. Lindsey. But Mr. Ainley won't cop a plea, so he'll have to face a 20-year sentence.

An indictment is not a conviction, and Mr. Ainley's lawyer says he'll mount a vigorous defense. Perhaps he wasn't in the mail room at all. Or maybe he's willing to take the fall to protect the White House, in the interests of the President of the United States, or perhaps Razorback loyalty. The Ainley indictment is further evidence of Bill Clinton's ability to inspire loyalty among his backers, even in the face of their own personal misfortunes. With the exception of a few stray state troopers, the Arkansas contingent has held firm. Clearly it is a tight-knit state.

REVIEW & OUTLOOK

Mena Again

The strange story of what was going on at an airport in Mena, Arkansas, 10 years ago is an embarrassment to both the Democratic governor who ran Arkansas in the 1980s and to the Republicans who ran the White House. But two dogged Arkansans, former Internal Revenue Service Investigator William Duncan and Arkansas State Police Investigator Russell Welch, have kept the story alive. For more than a decade, Messrs. Duncan and Welch have been stitching together evidence of Mena-related schemes to smuggle drugs, launder money and ship weapons, possibly involving both Arkansas law enforcement and the U.S. intelligence community.

On Tuesday, Mr. Welch was summoned to Little Rock to appear before the State Police Commission. A review panel had demanded his immediate transfer to Little Rock. The reason? Inadequate attention to paperwork and the "need for closer supervision," says Wayne Jordan, a police spokesman. "It has nothing to do with" the Mena probe.

Repeated attempts to bring the Mena affair before state and federal authorities have failed. Mr. Duncan's stubborn insistence on investigating Mena, detailed on this page October 18, resulted in the destruction of his career in federal law enforcement. So naturally, when his colleague Russell Welch finds himself in a disciplinary hearing before the State Police Commission, we think it at least worthy of public note regardless of the official explanation. One year short of qualifying for his pension, Mr. Welch's transfer clearly would be tantamount to demotion and prelude to dismissal.

Mr. Welch tells us that his troubles started a little over a year ago, when he responded to inquiries from The Wall Street Journal and "CBS Evening News." Until then, he says he had always received above-average ratings on his performance reviews and high marks from his peers. Suddenly, questions were being raised about his paperwork. On one occasion, Mr. Welch says his commander, Major Charles Bolls, the chief of the Criminal Investigation Division, complained that Mr. Welch was "becoming like the two troopers" who provided the press with details on Governor Clinton's alleged sexual misadventures. In February, a police panel persistently questioned him about whether he was writing a book about Mena.

Russell Welch

Two weeks ago, Mr. Welch was notified of the administrative hearing and ordered not to work on his appeal during office hours. Among those rising to his defense was Charles Black, a former Mena-area public prosecutor who once had attempted to investigate the drug charges surrounding the airfield. Today Mr. Black is a deputy county prosecutor in Texarkana. Concerned about what was happening to Mr. Welch, who had no lawyer to represent him, Mr. Black went to Tuesday's hearing in Little Rock.

There, Mr. Black got the opportunity to question Major Bolls. According to observers of the proceeding, Major Bolls grew agitated when questioned about the Mena investigation and denied that it had anything to do with the transfer. Mr. Welch, Major Bolls said, was "consumed" with Mena and needed to be brought to Little Rock "so we would know where he was and what he was doing." By day's end, Mr. Black had won a 30-day continuance and Mr. Welch was placed on paid administrative leave.

A conflict of interest most likely prevents Mr. Black from further involvement in the case. He told us, however, "I'm convinced that Russell's activities in investigating Mena and talking to the media are playing a role in this whole mess." Mr. Jordan, the state police spokesman, hints that Mr. Welch's personnel file contains more damaging information and urges Mr. Welch to OK its release. At the least, Russell Welch clearly needs a lawyer, and a very tough one at that.

Mr. Welch's new lawyer might want to talk to Linda Ives, who drove up to Little Rock for the hearing. In 1987, Mrs. Ives's teenage son Kevin and his friend Don Henry were murdered near the railroad tracks south of Little Rock. She has waged a long campaign to prove their deaths are linked to drugs and Mena and a coverup. This troubling incident was reported by the Los Angeles Times in May 1992.

"That hearing was not about a trooper who didn't do his job," Mrs. Ives told us. "It was about a trooper who did his job only too well. Anybody who tries to tell the story is discredited and ruined."

REVIEW & OUTLOOK

Tyson's Corner

In a little noted development late last month, Attorney General Janet Reno set the bit in Independent Counsel Donald Smaltz's teeth and gave the reins a good yank. According to a report in the March 27 Legal Times, the probe by Counsel Smaltz has been "significantly curtailed by the Justice Department." What's going on here?

Mr. Smaltz was appointed in September to investigate charges that then-Agriculture Secretary Mike Espy had accepted gratuities from agribusiness. He recently sought permission from Ms. Reno to broaden his investigation. In what may be the opening shot in a battle over Mr. Smaltz's future, she turned him down. Neither side will comment on the precise area where Mr. Smaltz sought to broaden his authority, but it's clear that once again the larger subject is Arkansas.

Donald Smaltz

Like Heraclitus, Mr. Smaltz appears to have learned that he cannot step twice into the same river; having waded into Mr. Espy's business, Mr. Smaltz was borne quickly downstream to chicken king Don Tyson's corner of the sprawling Whitewater affair. There, he got into rough water. "Reno's ruling — which cannot be appealed to the court that oversees independent counsel — is apparently good news for President Clinton since Smaltz was reportedly edging closer to Clinton's own relationship with Tyson Foods, a major force in Arkansas business and politics," Legal Times reported.

Mr. Smaltz began the Tyson part of his probe by investigating reports that Mr. Espy improperly accepted such gratuities as football tickets and rides on the Tyson corporate jet. In return, it was suggested, Mr. Espy might have held off on stricter regulations for the poultry industry and intervened on Tyson's behalf in a permit dispute with Puerto Rico. In October it emerged that a Tyson foundation had provided a $1,200 scholarship to Mr. Espy's girlfriend. Mr. Espy walked the plank, announcing he would resign in December. By then Mr. Smaltz's investigation had expanded to include Mr. Tyson's business practices and ties to Arkansas politicians, including Bill Clinton.

Whitewater aficionados will recall the name of Jim Blair — Mr. Tyson's lawyer, longtime Friend of Bill and the man who guided Mrs. Clinton's dazzling commodities trades. Other Tyson executives helped fund Mr. Clinton's many campaigns. Mr. Smaltz set up shop down the road from Tyson headquarters in Springdale, issued subpoenas and began talking to Tyson employees.

Don Tyson

In late December, Time magazine's Richard Behar reported that a former Tyson pilot named Joseph Henrickson claimed that in the 1980s he had delivered six cash-filled envelopes from Tyson headquarters to Little Rock. Mr. Henrickson told Time that he believes the envelopes were intended for delivery to Mr. Clinton. Tyson Foods and Mr. Clinton's personal lawyer both denied the claim.

Tyson officials and others in Arkansas have reacted with outrage to Mr. Smaltz's aggressive investigation. Tyson spokesman Archie Schaffer called it "a politically motivated witch hunt." Mr. Schaffer added, "Neither Tyson Foods nor Don Tyson has ever been involved in the trafficking of illegal drugs." That reference is to decade-old allegations about Mr. Tyson and cocaine, which have resurfaced recently, mostly in police documents circulated by President Clinton's political enemies. Tyson employees report that Mr. Smaltz's investigators questioned them about these matters. Tyson has denounced the drug reports, asserting "they are totally false."

The Tyson camp has struck back. In January, Rep. Jay Dickey, the Republican congressman from Mr. Tyson's home district, placed calls to the Justice Department to explore ways to limit Mr. Smaltz's jurisdiction. A Tyson vice president launched a defamation suit against the wife of pilot Joe Henrickson for remarks she made about the alleged cash payments. In February, lawyers for Mr. Tyson and Mr. Espy filed sealed motions seeking to quash some of Mr. Smaltz's subpoenas to former Tyson employees. Mr. Schaffer and the company's chief lobbyist went to Capitol Hill to complain about Mr. Smaltz. So now we have reports of the Attorney General's actions on the Smaltz investigation.

It is a matter of record that we have not been fans of the independent counsel, at least not those, like Lawrence Walsh, who act accountable to no one. We generally have preferred open congressional hearings about which the public can make a political judgment.

As to the current lines of responsibility and authority, the independent counsel is appointed by an autonomous three-judge federal panel. Thereafter, the independent counsels are answerable to the attorney general. The attorney general can fire a counsel and must approve any expansion of an investigation.

At the same time, Mr. Smaltz's charter from the federal panel gives him the authority to investigate not only Mr. Espy, but also "other allegations or evidence of violation of federal criminal law . . . by any organization or individual developed during the Independent Counsel's investigation."

If within this structure, Attorney General Reno has cause to believe that Mr. Smaltz has abused his charge or that his investigation lacks any basis, then she should fire him. If that is not the case, then we suggest that Mr. Smaltz has all the authority he needs to do his job and should get on with it.

Review & Outlook

Deleting BCCI

In this world of instant communication, torrents of money moving down wires with the speed of light, shadowy banks springing up in Phnom Penh and Moscow, and drug lords taking over countries, you might think a $10 billion international bank heist would be of some continuing interest. But one of our duties in the world, it seems, is to remind everyone that we still haven't learned the complete story of the Bank of Credit & Commerce International.

This comes to mind because last week London solicitor David Sandy surrendered at JFK Airport to representatives of Manhattan District Attorney Robert Morgenthau. Mr. Sandy is a partner in the British firm Simmons & Simmons, which represents the London interests of the majority shareholders of the Bank of Credit & Commerce International – mainly the potentates of Abu Dhabi. Mr. Sandy was indicted on charges of suppressing evidence related to Mr. Morgenthau's long probe of BCCI.

Mr. Sandy does not deny he erased computer disks belonging to a high BCCI executive. John Wing, his New York lawyer, tells us that "the disk deletion was for legitimate purposes wholly unrelated" to the Morgenthau investigation. Those purposes, Mr. Wing says, "will come out at trial." He says his client "did not suppress evidence," and "is not guilty of these charges and intends to vigorously assert and establish his innocence." The erased documents were copied and eventually turned over to investigators. "This prosecution is a novel, untested and unprecedented application of

New York law," Mr. Wing says.

Still, disks were erased containing, according to the indictment, portions of a business diary that BCCI chief executive officer Zafar Iqbal kept in his laptop computer. The diary allegedly contains summaries of many conversations and transactions Mr. Iqbal had with BCCI officials and bank auditors from April 1990 to July 1991, when BCCI finally was shut down due to massive fraud. In a December 1991 plea agreement with U.S. authorities, BCCI had agreed to open all its documents to inspection. In January 1992, Mr. Sandy learned that liquidators from Touche Ross were examining BCCI records at the secured Shareholders Coordination Office in Abu Dhabi, the indictment charges, and he went to the office with Simmons & Simmons attorney Shaun Elrick. "While an agent of the liquidator was occupied examining other files nearby, David Sandy and Shaun Elrick secretly placed three computer disks containing the diary of Zafar Iqbal in a briefcase of Shaun Elrick" and spirited them away, not bothering to sign a receipt, it charges.

Robert Morgenthau

Mr. Sandy later copied the data from the disks, directed that information on the originals be destroyed and attempted to return the doctored disks, the indictment alleges. Investigators first learned of the diary in early 1994 from Mr. Iqbal. When demands for the information mounted and their game started to become undone, Mr. Sandy allegedly lied about the disks on several occasions. Finally, a printout of the disks was placed in the bottom of one of 1,580 trunks containing 80 tons of BCCI documents to be shipped to England. The suspicion, of course, is that the printout is merely a sanitized version of the original diary.

In London, Mr. Sandy's indictment has been greeted with dismay. "London's legal community is perplexed and uneasy," the Financial Times reports. The legal establishment "has been shaken by the spectacle of one of its own facing serious criminal charges." Mr. Morgenthau's aggressive investigation has long been at odds with Britain's slack pursuit of the BCCI affair. Suspicious minds might detect a degree of official complicity in the scandal — or at least in Britain, as well as the U.S., a strong desire that the whole mess would go away.

BCCI has reshaped our understanding of complex criminal enterprises and their often very respectable front men. It laundered drug money and spread a pool of political corruption across several continents. But it managed to acquire the services of such luminaries as Clark Clifford in Washington and Lord Callaghan in London. Among the beneficiaries of largesse from its executives were the Carter Center in Atlanta and the British Conservative Party. Among its clients were Manuel Noriega, Saddam Hussein and the Central Intelligence Agency.

Mr. Sandy is of course entitled to the standard presumption of innocence, and we look forward to the explanation of his legal basis for erasing documents. We would be particularly interested to know whether he did it for his client and his money, or whether he intended to help others in the London establishment. Similarly, when Robert Altman, Mr. Clifford's associate, was acquitted of criminal charges, it left hanging the whole question of how BCCI succeeded in buying into the U.S. banking system. Indeed, with Mr. Altman's acquittal, the testimony in his case was sealed under New York State law.

With the collapse of the Soviet empire and the growing economic clout of drug lords in Latin America and the Far East, sophisticated international criminal enterprises are on the rise. Unless we learn everything we can about the first BCCI, it's unlikely to be the last.

Yet with solicitors erasing tapes and testimony being sealed, the full story will not be easy to learn. It's about time that someone in authority — the House of Commons or the Senate Banking Committee — gets started on broad-ranging hearings on BCCI and, before a second one explodes, preventing future BCCIs.

Letters to the Editor

BCCI Shareholders Unfairly Maligned

Your April 19 editorial "Deleting BCCI" pays lip service to the presumption of innocence while questioning whether a British solicitor who formerly acted for the majority shareholders of BCCI erased a computer disk on behalf of "his client." Your accusation, as usual, is wide of the mark.

The majority shareholders were not aware of, nor did they authorize, the actions of David Sandy, the British solicitor. Shortly after learning of the incident last year, the majority shareholders authorized this firm to inform Manhattan District Attorney Robert Morgenthau. Indeed, the district attorney stated in a recent news release that "[t]he evidence shows that the majority shareholders were unaware of Sandy's . . . activities." Finally, contrary to the statement in your editorial, Simmons & Simmons (Mr. Sandy's firm) no longer represents the majority shareholders.

All this information was, of course, available to you before you wrote the editorial. As usual in your reporting on BCCI, however, the opportunity to make a scurrilous accusation against a Middle Eastern sovereign seems to have overcome a fair review of the evidence.

W. CAFFEY NORMAN III
U.S. Counsel to the
Majority Shareholders
Patton Boggs

Washington

REVIEW & OUTLOOK

Arkansas Bank Shot

One of the last of the Arkansas inner circle, deputy White House counsel Bruce Lindsey was the treasurer of Bill Clinton's 1990 gubernatorial campaign. On Tuesday, Arkansas banker Neal Ainley pleaded guilty to two misdemeanors related to the illegal concealment of funds from that campaign. Two months ago, Mr. Ainley faced much stiffer charges: five felony counts brought by Independent Counsel Kenneth Starr. Mr. Ainley is now "actively cooperating" with the Whitewater investigation, the Office of the Independent Counsel

Bruce Lindsey

announced. Mr. Ainley has told the prosecutors that Mr. Lindsey "directed him to illegally conceal cash payments to Mr. Clinton's 1990 campaign," Stephen Labaton of the New York Times reported yesterday.

The gist of the charges against Mr. Ainley involve failure to file IRS Currency Transaction Reports for more than $52,000 in campaign funds. Now, we're frank to admit that on the basis of what's publicly known, this is not the world's biggest crime, or that many campaigns likely couldn't stand such scrutiny. What we have here, however, is another strong impression in the pattern of what we've come to recognize as Arkansas mores. That is, a casual contempt for obeying the law, which seems to be at the bottom of Whitewater.

Associate Attorney General Webster Hubbell resigned and confessed to a felony. William Kennedy III, the Travelgate operative who like Mr. Hubbell and Vincent Foster was a former partner in the Rose Law Firm with Hillary Rodham Clinton, quietly slipped out of the White House counsel's office and returned to Little Rock. White House director of administration David Watkins left his post after an expensive, unauthorized golf trip using a presidential helicopter.

Washington casualties have included White House Counsel Bernard Nussbaum, plus Roger Altman, Jean Hanson and yuppie diarist Joshua Steiner — all senior officials gone from the Treasury Department due to contacts between the Resolution Trust Corp., Treasury and the White House over criminal referrals concerning Madison Guaranty of Arkansas.

As to the Whitewater investigation itself, Mr. Starr has issued a string of indictments and seems to be patiently building a case from the ground up. The other independent counsel, Donald Smaltz, has elicited furious protests for probing poultry giant Tyson Foods, a major player in the Arkansas political landscape. The investigations in Arkansas appear to be gathering momentum. Also yesterday, Susan Schmidt of the Washington Post reported that Mr. Starr is "looking into more than $800,000 in campaign-related loans...an amount much larger than previously known," according to sources close to the investigation. These sources "dismiss as premature recent press reports that the probe ultimately will amount to only minor cases" like that of Mr. Ainley.

Working the minor cases is standard procedure in this business. As in eight-ball, you see a lot of bank shots being made to get to the money balls. When a Neal Ainley goes from facing five felony counts to pleading two misdemeanors, you get the feeling something's up.

REVIEW & OUTLOOK

Echoes of Oxford

Reading President Clinton's pointed attack on citizen militias at Michigan State University last Friday, we were struck by one potent line in particular:

"I say to you, all of you, the members of the Class of 1995," said Mr. Clinton, "there is nothing patriotic about hating your country or pretending that you can love your country but despise your government."

Where had we heard that last part about despising government before? Sure enough, from Mr. Clinton himself, in his now famous letter from Oxford to Colonel Eugene Holmes, his Arkansas ROTC director, on December 3, 1969. Here are some excerpts from that letter's very strong anti-government sentiment:

"As you know, I worked for two years in a very minor position on the Senate Foreign Relations Committee. I did it for the experience and the salary but also for the opportunity, however small, of working every day against a war I opposed and despised. . . .

"I have written and spoken and marched against the war. One of the national organizers of the Vietnam Moratorium is a close friend of mine. After I left Arkansas last summer, I went to Washington to work in the national headquarters of the Moratorium, then to England to organize the Americans here for demonstrations Oct. 15 and Nov. 16. . . .

"From my work I came to believe that the draft system itself is illegitimate. No government really rooted in limited, parliamentary democracy should have the power to make its citizens fight and kill and die in a war they may oppose. . . .

"One of my roommates is a draft resister who is possibly under indictment and may never be able to go home again. He is one of the bravest, best men I know. His country needs men like him more than they know. That he is considered a criminal is an obscenity. . . .

"I am writing too in the hope that my telling this one story will help you to understand more clearly how so many fine people have come to find themselves still loving their country but loathing the military. . . ."

While we recognize those were the passionate thoughts of a young man, Mr. Clinton has always stood by them. Regarding Vietnam, he has recently said Robert McNamara's book makes him feel "vindicated." Mr. Clinton praises his draft resisting friends as patriots though they "despised" their government and even "loathed" their military. So is despising a government at war better than despising a government for its gun laws? If breaking gun or tax laws is "wrong" now, as he rightly insists, then why was breaking the draft laws brave and noble then?

In his Michigan State speech, Mr. Clinton referred once to the 1960s, saying that while "many good things happened," the "Weathermen of the radical left who resorted to violence" were "wrong." The President is eager to distinguish between his own anti-government positions during the 1960s and those who used such anti-government themes to justify violence. Yet regarding militias and others who are anti-government today, he paints with a broad moral sweep that ties their sentiment to the evil bombers of Oklahoma City.

We agree with President Clinton that America could use a discussion over the obligations of citizenship. But we suspect he'd speak with greater moral authority to more Americans if he made a few more critical distinctions, starting with the contradictions in his own past.

Letters to the Editor

Clinton Didn't Express Hatred of Government

Your May 9 editorial "Echoes of Oxford" wouldn't persuade an alert grade-school child. To attack President Clinton, you first quote from his recent speech: ". . . there is nothing patriotic about . . . despis[ing] your government." Then you ask, "Where have we heard that last part about despising government before?" You answer your own question in the next paragraph by quoting from Mr. Clinton's letter of 26 years ago: ". . . a war I opposed and despised. . . ."

You falsely equate despising our government with despising one specific act of our government: the Vietnam War. Despising our government means despising it in its entirety. Despising a particular war is merely to despise one specific act of our government. I despise individual acts of our government, including many where I find myself in agreement with you. But I don't despise the government itself. (I might add that I was a World War II officer, supported the Vietnam War and have misgivings about President Clinton's performance.)

How can you expect your readers to be persuaded by your positions when your arguments are so confused?

ALBERT SANDERS

New York

Editorial Feature

Mena Coverup? Razorback Columbo to Retire

By MICAH MORRISON

LITTLE ROCK, Ark. – To the many people he has helped over the years, Russell Welch is a kind of country Columbo. Working as a state police investigator in the western reaches of Arkansas, Mr. Welch has investigated murders, all sorts of backwoods mayhem – and Mena. For more than a decade, Mr. Welch has been one of a small number of Arkansas-based law-enforcement officials who've probed reports of guns, drugs, spies and money-laundering at tiny Mena Intermountain Regional Airport. Most of the alleged activities occurred on the watch of a Democratic governor and Republican presidents. It's the story that both political parties wish would go away. Last week, it looked for a time as if some folks in Arkansas were going to make sure that Russell Welch went away.

Friday, in a case closely followed by Arkansas law enforcement, Mr. Welch fought off a transfer that would have brought a distinguished career to a ruinous halt. The offense? According to the state police: sloppy paperwork, tardiness, and not producing enough new cases. After more than 19 years on the job and with only 11 months to go until retirement, Mr. Welch had been ordered to transfer immediately from remote Mena to Little Rock for "closer supervision."

Texarkana deputy county prosecutor Charles Black, who stepped in as Mr. Welch's attorney when it appeared he would not get adequate counsel, says the real reason for the transfer attempt was the Mena probe. "There is a coverup of Mena under way," Mr. Black says.

Police officials scoff at this. "Mena is a diversion," says spokesman Wayne Jordan. "There is no coverup in the Arkansas State Police. This is a simple case of a man not doing his job. The media is devouring this stuff because of Clinton."

The known facts of this persistent issue center around drug smuggler Barry Seal, whose operation was run out of Mena airport. At the height of his career, Mr. Seal was importing as much as 1,000 pounds of cocaine per month and claimed to have made more than $50 million from his illicit activities. Mr. Seal became a DEA informant and

Russell Welch

on at least one occasion worked for the CIA in a Nicaraguan drug sting. He was gunned down in Baton Rouge, La., in 1986. A year later, his plane, with an Arkansas pilot at the wheel and Eugene Hasenfus in the cargo bay, was blasted out of the sky by the Sandinistas.

Pursuing the Seal money trail that ran out of Mena, Mr. Welch and his partner, former Internal Revenue Service investigator William Duncan, put together a money-laundering case in 1985 and brought it to a federal grand jury in the Western District of Arkansas, where it fell apart. There has never been an adequate public explanation for the failure to pursue such an obviously major case. Mr. Duncan, whose bitter 10-year battle to bring Mena to light was detailed on this page Oct. 18, says that "investigations were interfered with and covered up" and charges that U.S. Attorneys "directly interfered with the process." Eight other state and federal probes were aborted. It doesn't take Columbo to figure out something is going on here.

As an investigator who also happened to be a member of the state police, Mr. Welch occupies a difficult position in the Mena story. A memo recently obtained by this newspaper indicates that state police officers were keeping close tabs on Mena, and even let a suspect in the probe pore over state police records to trace Mr. Welch's phone calls. The memo summarizes a conversation between Mr. Welch's suspect and an official with the State Police Criminal Investigation Division:

"Furr [the Welch suspect] was sent by his boss to the State Capitol in Little Rock where he checked the State Police telephone records and determined that Russell Welch and what I understood to be the FBI had been corresponding by telephone. . . . [Furr] stated that he took most of the day at the capitol building checking these records and that the gentleman that was helping him there told him he could not copy these records; however, he could sit down with the records and make hand notes from them and that Colonel Goodwin [commander of the Arkansas State Police] had been advised of his being there and periodically checked back to see if he was still there and each time the colonel checked back, the man would walk in and say Mr. Goodwin just called back to see if you were still here and how you were doing."

The author of this 1987 memo is now a member of the state police team involved in Mr. Welch's current review. Col. Goodwin, now retired, did not respond to a request for comment.

As well as acting as Mr. Welch's attorney, Mr. Black also could be counted as a member of the poignant assembly − the mothers of murdered sons, brothers grieving for brothers lost − that turned out on Friday to support Mr. Welch. Mr. Black's mother was murdered in 1986; Mr. Welch brought the killer to justice.

Mr. Black had planned to mount an aggressive Mena defense at the hearing, but at the last minute he negotiated a settlement. Mr. Welch will be allowed to serve out his time in Mena and retire, provided that he "clean up" his remaining cases and make a 160-mile daily round trip to Hot Springs to report to a superior. Mr. Welch for his part conceded that he had been remiss in keeping up with paperwork and late for some police functions.

It's unlikely, however, that among the cases Mr. Welch will "clean up" is the one connected to cocaine and the CIA. The wonder is that the Arkansas law-enforcement establishment isn't helping this effort, rather than hindering it.

Mr. Morrison is a Journal editorial page writer.

Editorial Feature

Independent Counsels: Accountable to Whom?

Kenneth W. Starr, the independent counsel investigating Whitewater, delivered the commencement address Saturday to the graduating class of Duke University School of Law. His theme was the accountability of independent counsels. Excerpts follow:

Concerns about an independent counsel's lack of accountability to the president and the attorney general have prompted Congress to impose some constraints on independent counsels.

For example, in reenacting the Independent Counsel Act in 1994, Congress was quite concerned that one previous independent counsel in particular had spent too much money — an amount far in excess of what the Department of Justice would have spent in conducting a similar investigation. For that reason, Congress imposed restrictions on the compensation and expenses of an independent counsel and his staff and required periodic reports and audits of expenses.

Congress also became concerned that independent counsels spend too much time on their investigations, thereby subjecting the persons under investigation to years of uncertainty and stress as they wait to learn the results of the investigation. Congress has therefore empowered the Special Division of the D.C. Circuit to determine after two years of an investigation whether termination of the office of the independent counsel is appropriate.

These constraints on the cost and duration of an independent counsel investigation, while important, ultimately are skeletal. They do not directly affect the day-to-day substance of an investigation —

the decisions whether to subpoena certain documents, to investigate certain issues, to grant immunity, to indict, or to agree to a plea bargain. Those decisions are the life of a federal prosecutor's office, and an independent counsel's office is no different. With one crucial distinction: Unlike other federal prosecutors, an independent counsel does not report to the attorney general or the president.

It is true that Congress has encouraged independent counsels, in making substantive decisions, to follow Department of Justice policy and practice to the degree practicable. But an independent counsel is still left with a huge amount of unchecked discretion. For that reason, our office has taken steps to guard against arbitrary and capricious decisionmaking.

Let me describe some of the steps:

To ensure accountability, we have endeavored to mirror the existing practices and mechanisms of accountability at the Department of Justice.

First, personnel. I have recruited experienced Department of Justice prosecutors, familiar with the policies and practices of federal criminal law enforcement both at the department and within a diverse assembly of U.S. attorney's offices throughout the country.

We have prosecutors from the Public Integrity Section of the Justice Department. Also with us are current and former career federal prosecutors from the U.S. attorney's offices in such places as Illinois, Tennessee, Iowa, Virginia, the District of Columbia and Texas. Included within that superb cadre of prosecutors is Hickman Ewing, a career federal prosecutor who served as a first assistant U.S. attorney during the Carter Administration and then as the U.S. attorney in Tennessee for 10 years. Steve Learned, an assistant U.S. attorney from Virginia, who served as senior litigation counsel for the Dallas Bank Fraud Task Force, which was at the epicenter of the S&L earthquake in the 1980s, heads up our Madison investigation. And leading the Capital Management Services investigation is Brad Lerman, deputy chief for special prosecutions in the Illinois U.S. attorney's office.

We also have attorneys experienced in dealing with the very difficult and sensitive issues regarding the separation and balance of powers that the Office of Legal Counsel, ably headed by Prof. Walter Dellinger, is ordinarily called upon to handle in high-profile investigations of senior government officials.

In addition, Prof. Sam Dash, the legendary chief counsel for the Senate Select Committee on Watergate . . . serves not only as our office's ethics counselor, but also as a senior adviser on all matters. The criminal defense bar is represented within our ranks with senior lawyers such as my Little Rock deputy, Bill Duffey, who practiced with Judge Griffin Bell at a leading Atlanta law firm, and my Washington deputy, Mark Tuohey, who in the 1970s served as assistant U.S. attorney in Washington and as a special counsel to Attorney General Benjamin Civiletti.

Second, we have established safeguards to ensure that our major actions and decisions are subject to the most searching and rigorous internal scrutiny. Witnesses are called before the grand jury only in consultation with senior attorneys and deputies in Little Rock and

Kenneth Starr

Washington. In addition, we have set up an indictment review process mirroring that of the Justice Department. Detailed prosecution memos are prepared before any indictment is presented to the grand jury. Those memos are circulated to the senior prosecutors both in Washington and Little Rock — and to Prof. Dash. There follows an extensive series of meetings and discussions before any final decision is made. By that time, literally all attorneys on the staff will have had the opportunity to participate in the decision-making process, and we seek to operate on a consensus basis on all major decisions.

Third, one of the most fundamental obligations of a prosecutor's office is to maintain the confidentiality of its work. All attorneys and staff in our office have agreed to conduct themselves in accordance with the strictest ethical and legal standards for guarding the confidentiality of grand jury secrets, investigative materials and national security information. In this respect, serious concerns were raised a few years ago when a young attorney on the staff of Judge Lawrence Walsh, hired fresh out of law school, authored a book about his work on the Oliver North case based on his own memory and thousands of pages of notes and documents that he had taken with him when he left the office. These sensitive documents reflected internal deliberations, discussed possible criminal charges and revealed investigative plans and results. Judge Walsh sued his own lawyer in what proved to be a vain attempt to prevent him from publishing this book. Obviously, a prosecutor — whether an independent counsel or not — should take steps to prevent such a flagrant disregard for the fundamental obligations of a federal prosecutor.

The mechanisms I have described are designed to ensure effective and fair decisionmaking. However, the most important mechanism that guides what we do is the accountability that we have to each other. Not a day goes by that we do not seek to discuss and judge what we are doing, why we are doing it, and the impact of what we are doing on others. In this regard, we are not different from other lawyers, in other practices, serving other clients.

Review & Outlook

Clinton, Espy, Cisneros, Brown . . .

Bill Clinton has Kenneth Starr, the Agriculture Secretary got Donald Smaltz, the Housing Secretary's independent counsel is yet to be named and yesterday Attorney General Janet Reno announced she wants an independent counsel to deconstruct Commerce Secretary Ron Brown's business world.

We've been longtime critics of the institution known as independent counsel, but the Clinton Administration is certainly putting our position to the ultimate test. Aside from constitutionality or politics, how do you handle the simple volume? Our view has been that Congress is the appropriate venue for airing these matters, but even in the former days of fat staffs Congress wouldn't have the personnel to simultaneously check out so many Cabinet Secretaries. Bowing in this direction yesterday, the Senate voted 96 to 3 to create a special Whitewater committee. The enabling resolution was jointly offered by Banking Committee Chairman Al D'Amato and ranking minority member Paul Sarbanes.

We're not quite ready to call for the establishment of a fourth branch of government to handle the caseload being tossed up by a generalized decline in political morality, but the Clinton phenomenon invites comment on precisely what the system, in the persons of these independent counsels, is trying to achieve here.

The Clinton White House's contribution of late has been either to question the counsel's usefulness (as suggested by Abner Mikva, who supported the law as an appellate judge before he became Counsel to the Clinton White House), or minimize the appointment of such counsel. The President yesterday, while calling Ron Brown's performance "unparalleled," added that "the legal standard for such an appointment is low."

Yesterday on this page, we carried excerpts from a recent address by Kenneth Starr, the independent counsel investigating Whitewater. Mr. Starr's theme was ensuring that these prosecutors, who operate independent of virtually any political control, somehow remain accountable, if only to the highest standards of the profession. Mr. Starr's argument was eloquent and persuasive, and it must be admitted that the team he has assembled is impressive both in expertise and bipartisanship.

Our own bias on the subject is simple: Get the facts out.

That, more than anything, has been the cause of our misgivings about special prosecutors. Their charges are confined solely to what is indictable. But we aren't much interested in whether a Roger Altman should be indicted and sent to jail for lying to Congress; we want a full public record of who did what at the Clinton White House in the critical period after Vincent Foster's death. Similarly with Whitewater and the political culture of Arkansas in the Clinton years and now the political culture of a Ron Brown. There is sufficient cause to wonder whether something is rotten in Denmark, but reason to worry that an independent counsel, even one as capable and fastidious as Ken Starr, may never disclose to the public the nature of the rottenness.

Ron Brown

As readers of these columns are aware, whether the issue is Whitewater or BCCI or Ron Brown's business deals, our concern has been the increasing entanglements of high public office with illicit private interests. Not just here in the U.S., but Japan, France, England, Mexico and Russia have had to wrestle with the destructive phenomenon of political corruptions. Human nature being what it is, some of this is unavoidable. But democratic systems entrust public officials with enormous authority over the levers of financial power. If this arrangement is to be seen as credible rather than rigged in the eyes of citizens, it will be crucial that the system find a way to present the public with a full set of facts about these troubling cases. For ultimately it is the voters who must balance the political value of any particular government or official against their failings.

We hope the special Senate Whitewater panel will serve that purpose. Certainly congressional committees can run out of control, as the Bork and Thomas hearings attest. But the D'Amato and Leach hearings were well run and informative, and even the Iran-Contra hearings, despite the circus atmosphere, offered the public a basis for judging the Republicans in power then.

For now, the Clinton Administration's troubles will pass through the sieves of grand juries and congressional committees. One school of observers will mainly want to know only if laws were broken. Our view is that the stakes are fundamentally and appropriately political. That is, they are the voters' business.

REVIEW & OUTLOOK

Gathering Steam

With the indictment of Jim Guy Tucker, present Governor of Arkansas and sometime political ally of Bill Clinton, Kenneth Starr's Whitewater investigation is building a head of steam. Two Tucker associates were also indicted Wednesday, and yesterday a third, Stephen Smith, pleaded guilty to a misdemeanor and agreed to cooperate with the independent counsel.

At the heart of the Tucker indictment is a complex scheme to fraudulently buy and sell cable television systems. The first step, the indictment alleges, was to obtain a federally backed loan from Capital Management Services, a Small Business Administration-chartered company run by David Hale. The indictment says that in June 1987, Mr. Tucker and a business associate, William Marks Sr., made false statements to obtain a $300,000 loan from Mr. Hale. The funds were then used as collateral for an $8.5 million bank loan for Messrs. Tucker and Marks to buy into a cable television venture. Later, the indictment charges, a bogus bank-

Jim Guy Tucker

ruptcy claim was cooked up with Mr. Tucker's lawyer, John Haley, in order to sell off part of the cable system at a hefty profit and defraud the IRS.

Mr. Tucker made millions from the cable business in the 1980s. In a statement issued Wednesday night he said he had "fully repaid all of the loans involved" and looked "forward to an aggressive presentation of the facts of my business transactions in a public forum." So do we. Fully repaying an illegal loan does not make it legal, a fact that seems to have escaped attention in Arkansas.

Naturally, Governor Tucker is complaining that the prosecution is political, though Mr. Starr was recently applauded for his discretion in not indicting White House aide Bruce Lindsey over the financing of Mr. Clinton's 1990 gubernatorial campaign; the reported irregularities could have been painted as felonies and used to try to force Mr. Lindsey to implicate the President. This is the sort of

David Hale

thing Lawrence Walsh did with, for example, Elliott Abrams. But Mr. Starr desisted, in line with regular Justice Department guidelines. In the Tucker case, the guidelines instead suggested prosecution.

The White House responded to the news of Mr. Tucker's ill fortune with a terse statement noting that it was "not aware of anything in the indictment that relates to the President." While this is certainly true in the narrow sense, it's equally certain that the indictment paints an unflattering picture of the political and business atmosphere that nurtured the President. Mr. Hale's Capital Management, licensed by the SBA to make loans to socially or economically disadvantaged parties, seems to have been a piggy bank for the Arkansas political elite.

That includes Bill Clinton, according to Mr. Hale's plea-bargain testimony. The heart of Whitewater is Mr. Hale's claim that in 1986 then-Governor Clinton and James McDougal, president of Madison Guaranty Savings & Loan and a partner with the Clintons in the Whitewater Development Co., pressured him into making a $300,000 loan to Mr. McDougal's wife, Susan; $100,000 of that loan allegedly ended up in a Whitewater account. Mr. Starr's Thursday plea bargain with Stephen Smith also relates to a false loan from Capital Management run through Madison. Since Mr. Hale has confessed to crimes, his accusations against the President are of course suspect, but these indictments seem likely to bolster his credibility.

Especially so given the events since Mr. Clinton's inauguration. Mr. Hale was refused a plea bargain, remember, by Paula Casey, inserted as U.S. Attorney in Little Rock after the Administration took the unprecedented step of firing all incumbent U.S. Attorneys. Also recall the flurry of White House activity connected with the confidential Resolution Trust Corp. criminal referrals on Madison Guaranty in late 1993. In early October of that year, White House aide Bruce Lindsey informed President Clinton about the referrals. Mr. Lindsey later told Congress that he did not mention any specific targets, but according to published reports, Mr. Tucker was named as a target of the investigation.

Within 48 hours of Mr. Lindsey's briefing of the President, however, Governor Tucker was at the White House. On November 18, Mr. Clinton again saw Mr. Tucker, this time for a private meeting in Seattle. The subject of these conversations, we're asked to believe, was to discuss pressing matters involving the Arkansas National Guard.

REVIEW & OUTLOOK

Who Is Henry Woods?

Last year, the President was reminiscing with Connie Bruck of The New Yorker about his 1990 gubernatorial race. At one point, he said, he was undecided about running and an influential Arkansan came up with a substitute: Hillary Clinton. The powerful member of the Arkansas political family "desperately wanted her to run for governor," the President told Ms. Bruck, "and it got out and around the state."

Henry Woods

That gentleman was Judge Henry Woods of the U.S. District Court for the Eastern District of Arkansas. "Henry," a friend of the judge told Ms. Bruck, "just hangs the moon on Hillary." Judge Woods has contributed 15 years of distinguished service to the judiciary, particularly in the long-running Little Rock school desegregation cases. At a critical point in 1987, Judge Woods named Mrs. Clinton counsel to a citizens' committee working for racial balance in the schools. "I called on Hillary a lot," he told Ms. Bruck. "She was not just functioning as adviser to the committee."

Judge Woods will soon be back in the news, starting with tomorrow's arraignment of Arkansas Governor Jim Guy Tucker and two associates. They're charged with defrauding the government in a scheme linked to David Hale's Capital Management Services. While the arraignment will take place before other magistrates in Little

Rock, the trial is scheduled to unfold in the courtroom of Mrs. Clinton's biggest fan.

Governor Tucker has angrily declared his innocence and says he may challenge Independent Counsel Kenneth Starr's jurisdiction. "None of the allegations," Governor Tucker said, "involve President Clinton, Mrs. Clinton or any other person in the executive branch that the regular U.S. Attorneys would have had a conflict in prosecuting." As we have noted in regard to the Clintons, this is correct in a narrow sense; but it is also true that the indictments and guilty pleas so far obtained by Mr. Starr paint a disturbing picture of the political and business landscape from which the President and First Lady emerged.

Understandably, for example, Governor Tucker would have preferred that "the regular U.S. Attorney" handle his case. That would be Paula Casey, the longtime Friend of Bill who first received criminal referrals from the Resolution Trust Corp. allegedly naming the Clintons and Mr. Tucker. After making some crucial decisions, Ms. Casey belatedly recused herself from the Madison Guaranty case, in November 1993, in the midst of a six-week period which saw Treasury contacts with the White House, Bruce Lindsey informing the President about the referrals, two Clinton-Tucker meetings, and Associate Attorney General Webster Hubbell's own recusal from Whitewater matters.

The problem, of course, is that everyone from the Arkansas political culture comes from the Arkansas political culture. When it came time for Mr. Hubbell to plead guilty to a scheme to defraud the government and his former partners at the Rose Law Firm, he stood before U.S. District Court Judge William Wilson in Little Rock. Two days after the plea, Judge Wilson stepped down from the case, saying his contacts with the Clintons over the years might be misconstrued. "Not only must you do justice," Judge Wilson said, "you must have an appearance of doing justice."

Naturally Judge Woods has the same sort of associations. Now 77, he was for some 40 years a close associate of Arkansas financier and legislator Witt Stephens — head of the Stephens Inc. investment giant until his death in 1991. "Mr. Witt" first earned a reputation as a political kingmaker with the 1948 election of Governor Sid McMath; Henry Woods was Governor McMath's top aide. Mr. Woods later fought segregationist Governor Orval Faubus and was a supporter of current Senator Dale Bumpers and Rep. Ray Thornton, among others. Messrs. Clinton, Tucker, Hale, and James McDougal of Madison Guaranty fame all got their early political education from one of the towering figures in Arkansas politics, former Senator William Fulbright. It's a tight, if sometimes feuding, family.

Mr. Woods actively supported Mr. Bumpers' 1970 gubernatorial run. In 1974, Governor Bumpers knocked Senator Fulbright out of the Democratic primary and went on to the Senate; Mr. Fulbright went to work for the Saudis and Stephens Inc. In 1978, Mr. Woods supported Mr. Stephens' nephew, Mr. Thornton, in a three-way primary race against then-U.S. Rep. Tucker and David Pryor for the Democratic nomination to the Senate. President Carter nominated Mr. Woods to the federal bench in 1979; when he was sworn in, Governor Clinton saluted him, saying he was a man who would "feel the pain" of the people.

The defendant to the contrary, the Tucker case is not just another case, but one pregnant with implications for the President, the First Lady and the whole circle of the judge's friends and associates. Judge Woods can best honor his distinguished record on the bench by following Judge Wilson's example and stepping aside.

REVIEW & OUTLOOK

Investigate Mena

For more than a year we have been reporting on the mysteries of tiny Mena airfield in western Arkansas. The clouded tale of drug smugglers and spy operations in the 1980s is a potential embarrassment to the Democratic governor who ran the state and the Republicans who ran the White House. But the big story here is not primarily about who did what 10 years ago. It's about a very 1990s concern: drugs. How has our system broken down so that illegal drugs can be moved into this country on such a large scale?

This week, the American Spectator magazine adds another piece to the Mena puzzle with a story about Arkansas State Trooper L.D. Brown written by Spectator editor R. Emmett Tyrrell. Now, the account's weakness and strength are one and the same − L.D. Brown himself. Its weakness is that it is a single-source account; its strength is that L.D. Brown is an important source. A potentially key player in the Whitewater saga, Mr. Brown corroborates part of David Hale's claim that Mr. Clinton put pressure on him for financial help.

Mr. Brown now says that while working on then-Governor Clinton's security detail, he applied to the Central Intelligence Agency, with the governor's support. Following CIA testing and an exchange of letters − supplied to Mr. Tyrrell by Mr. Brown − the state trooper claims he was contacted by Mena drug smuggler Barry Seal. Soon after, he was on two Central American flights from Mena airport aboard Mr. Seal's C-123K, running guns to the Contras. Mr. Brown, a former narcotics officer, says that when Mr. Seal showed him cash and cocaine shipments, he quit. When he confronted Governor Clinton about the drugs and money, Mr. Brown allegedly was told not to worry about it. "That's Lasater's deal," Mr. Brown claims Governor Clinton told him.

To be sure, Dan Lasater is a colorful figure. He ran a free-wheeling bond house in Little Rock, and was friend and campaign supporter to Bill Clinton. In 1986, in a case that also involved Mr. Clinton's brother, Roger, Mr. Lasater pleaded guilty to a cocaine distribution charge and went off to prison for a brief stay. The federal prosecutor who handled the case was George Proctor, a Carter-era appointee who now heads the Justice Department's Office of International Affairs; Mr. Proctor's office has authority over aspects of another of our longstanding concerns, BCCI. One of Mr. Proctor's predecessors at OIA, Michael Abbell, was in the news recently when he was indicted on racketeering charges in connection with the Cali drug cartel.

Our own reporting about Mena points more toward Washington than Arkansas. We want to know what the federal government knew about drugs and money flowing through the area. Our Micah Morrison has painstakingly separated fact from fiction regarding Mena and Barry Seal's involvement with the CIA, the Contras and cocaine traffic. Mr. Seal, a sometime informant for the Drug Enforcement Agency, smuggled several billion dollars' worth of drugs into the country. In our October 18 story "The Mena Coverup," we detailed the short-circuiting of nine separate state and federal probes into Mena. Reliable sources in the intelligence community now tell us that in the years after Mr. Seal's death, some activities continued around Mena: an AWACs-Patriot system was tested, CIA contract planes were repainted, and the area was included in a counterterror exercise run out of nearby Fort Chaffee.

But the heart of Mena, we suspect, is narcotics, and on this aspect answers are lacking. Drugs? Arkansas officials wave off the question, saying Mena was a federal responsibility. The CIA blames a "rogue DEA operation"; the DEA isn't talking; the FBI says "no comment."

The betting around here is that L.D. Brown and others in the Arkansas State Police know a lot more about the matter — including what the feds were up to — than they are letting on. State police officers are starting to show up all over the Mena story. While we discount the extreme speculation in self-proclaimed CIA operative Terry Reed's book about Mena, "Compromised," it's interesting to note that Mr. Reed is making headway in Little Rock with his lawsuit against former State Troopers Tommy Baker and Buddy Young; Mr. Young also served for a time as Governor Clinton's security chief. Mr. Reed's lawyers have deposed several state troopers in connection with the case, Mr. Tyrrell says. Last year "CBS Evening News" reported that a top Arkansas State Police official played a role in derailing an early effort to advance the Mena probe.

Some reports to the contrary, we see no indication that Independent Counsel Kenneth Starr is investigating Mena or Mr. Lasater. Mr. Starr appears to be sticking close to his mandate to examine matters arising from Madison, the Whitewater Development Co., or Mr. Hale's Capital Management Services.

Yet Mena cries out for investigation. A congressional committee with resources, subpoena power, and the perseverance displayed by some past chairmen should look into this. If some chips fall on the Republican side, so be it. Important questions need to be answered.

Was Mena simply a remote outpost of the Cold War? Or was it a major trans-shipment point for drugs and money laundering? To what degree were government officials involved? Where did all the cocaine and cash involved in the Barry Seal operation go? Were Arkansas financial institutions involved in laundering drug money?

Again, how Mena worked is of some present moment as the U.S. continues to wrestle with illegal drugs — their use apparently on the increase again among teenagers — and the attendant corruption. Mena may provide a window into one of the big sources of this problem.

Hearings

In July 1995, new Whitewater hearings opened on Capitol Hill. New York Senator Alfonse D'Amato convened a special Whitewater Committee to investigate the Byzantine affair. In the House, Jim Leach, the new chairman of the Banking Committee, continued his probe of Madison. But the new Republican majority met a solid phalanx of Democrats tossing up roadblocks and complaining that Whitewater was nothing but a partisan witchhunt. Yet amid the heated committee battles and furious spin control from the White House, the Journal noted, "evidence continues to mount that the Clintons used Madison as their personal piggy bank."

The Senate probe first returned to the events surrounding the death of Vincent Foster. New evidence came to light about Mr. Foster's concerns over the Whitewater investment, a matter he was handling while serving simultaneously as the Clintons' personal lawyer and White House deputy counsel. When questioned about their activities in the hours and days after Mr. Foster's death, top White House aides suffered extensive memory loss.

In the House, RTC investigator Jean Lewis testified about her probe of Madison. Ms. Lewis said she found evidence of "inside abuse, self-dealing, money laundering, embezzlement, diversion of loan proceeds, payments of excessive commissions, misappropriation of funds, land flips, inflated appraisals, falsification of loan records...and illegal campaign contributions." Among the "suspects" were Madison owners James and Susan McDougal, Jim Guy Tucker, and the Bill Clinton Political Committee Fund.

Democrats on the House committee devoted themselves largely to efforts to discredit Ms. Lewis, the Journal complained. But Kenneth Starr appeared to have found her credible. On August 17, following the road maps provided by Ms. Lewis and Arkansas insider David Hale, Mr. Starr indicted Governor Tucker and the McDougals on multiple counts of bank fraud and conspiracy.

REVIEW & OUTLOOK

Why Webster Hubbell

The Senate's special Whitewater committee begins hearings today with former Clinton confidant Webster Hubbell as the lead-off witness. As the hearings progress, the tea-leaf readers (a reality of our time is that we live in an age of tea-leaf politics) will want to know whether Senator D'Amato's investigators have come up with "anything new" that could "damage" the Clintons. If nothing new, then the Republicans "run the risk" of being accused of only trying to "get" the President. Like Dungeons and Dragons, this is fascinating stuff.

Non-professional observers might reasonably wonder, though, if something is more important here than a political game. There is, and no better carrier of that import could be found than Webster Hubbell. Beyond the immediate issue of what happened to Vincent Foster's papers, the larger issue goes to the structure and staffing of the Clinton Administration. Was the whole rig designed from the first with the overriding priority of suppressing unpleasant baggage from Arkansas, leaving public purposes in the lurch?

Bill and Hillary Clinton came to Washington by way of Georgetown, Wellesley, Oxford, Yale Law and leadership of the National Governors Association. The Clintons were long on a first-name basis with the best and brightest Democrats around the country. So we drew attention very early on that the Clintons had brought with them and assigned to remarkably high Administration positions three partners from the Little Rock, Ark.,

Rose Law Firm — Webster Hubbell, Vincent Foster and William Kennedy. Mrs. Clinton was herself a partner at Rose, now clearly seen as a deeply troubled law firm.

Mr. Foster was named No. 2 in the White House general counsel's office and was joined there by Mr. Kennedy (who quickly became embroiled in charges of misusing the FBI in the Travelgate affair). Meanwhile, the Clintons sent Webster Hubbell over to Justice, eventually as Associate Attorney General, occupying an office close by Janet Reno's. One of Ms. Reno's first large acts was to have to publicly reclaim the authority of her office after it was reported that President Clinton had been dealing with Mr. Hubbell on the Waco affair, leaving Ms. Reno out of the loop.

We've long supported letting Presidents have trusted advisers in key positions, including at Justice, but the Hubbell regency was discomfiting. The respected deputy attorney general, Philip Heymann, resigned and returned to Harvard Law, a "pushee" in the words of a Washington Post editorial.

Webster Hubbell

More worrisome was the decision by both Ms. Reno and Mr. Hubbell to fire all 32 sitting U.S. attorneys in 1992. The single replacement that cries out for a closer look was the naming of Paula Casey, Friend of Bill, as the federal prosecutor in Little Rock. One of Ms. Casey's first acts in September 1993 was to turn down a plea bargain offer from the attorney for Judge David Hale, the Little Rock figure who wanted to talk about "the borrowing practices" of Arkansas' political elite. A month later, Ms. Casey wrote RTC investigator Jean Lewis that her criminal referral regarding Madison Guaranty was insufficient "to warrant the initiation of criminal investigation." After these key decisions, Ms. Casey recused herself from the Madison probe.

The hearings beginning today will now listen to who was running where with Vincent Foster's files in the days after his death. So tangled are the accounts offered by such luminaries as White House Counsel Bernard Nussbaum, Patsy Thomasson and Hillary Clinton aide Margaret Williams that the committee will take testimony from the White House cleaning staff. And there is the matter of Webster Hubbell physically preventing a Park Police investigator from talking to Mr. Foster's sister then.

We fear amid this jumble of broken-down memories and rambling senatorial musings, the morning-after reports will conclude "nothing new." This comes very close to saying that only the gotcha of a smoking gun can drive Washington's political juices anymore. We expect that those who take the time to understand will indeed find more evidence of rot, but that aside, the controlling theme here is accountability. A presidential administration brings with it the highest positions of public office in this country, and those persons in turn are invested with degrees of authority and power far beyond that of anyone in private life. Public accountability helps ensure that these persons don't abuse their outsized, temporary authority. That above all is what is going on in this week's hearings not only on Whitewater but the Waco tragedy.

The broader public wants reassurance that their interests lie at the center of these appointees' official acts and behavior. The committee should try to discern whether Webster Hubbell's tour of duty in Washington was about something else.

REVIEW & OUTLOOK

Call Fiske

From the report of the Independent Counsel in Re Vincent W. Foster, Jr., Robert B. Fiske Jr., Independent Counsel:

During his time as White House Deputy Counsel, Foster continued to handle some personal legal matters for the President and Mrs. Clinton, as he had while a member of the Rose Law Firm. Among those matters was Foster's role in arranging for the Clintons' accounting firm to prepare Whitewater tax returns for the years

1990-1992. We have reviewed all of the Whitewater-related documents from Mr. Foster's files that were delivered to the Clintons' personal attorney after his death. However, Rule 6(e) of the Federal Rules of Criminal Procedure precludes us from disclosing the content of these documents since they were obtained by grand jury subpoena.

Those who worked in the White House during the first half of 1993 all stated that Whitewater was not an issue of any significance within the

Robert Fiske

White House during that period. The issue had received virtually no attention in the press since the spring of 1992, during the Presidential campaign. As one person put it, Whitewater issues were "not on the screen" at the time. It was not until October 1993, three months after Foster's death, when it was disclosed that the Resolution Trust Corporation had issued criminal referrals involving Madison Guaranty and Whitewater, that the matter again received public attention.

Each of Foster's co-workers, friends and family whom we questioned was explicitly asked whether Foster had ever mentioned Whitewater or Madison Guaranty related matters as a cause of concern or distress. According to each of these people, Foster had never expressed any concern about these matters. . . .

Obviously, the fact that Foster never expressed a concern about Whitewater or Madison to anyone does not mean that he did not, in fact, have such a concern. Thus, we cannot conclusively rule out such a concern as a possible contributing factor to his depression. What we can conclude is that there is no evidence that he did have such a concern against a background in which Whitewater/Madison issues were neither a matter of expressed concern in the White House, nor the subject of media attention.

No evidence, we learn from the documents released at the hearings this week, except in working on the tax returns, Mr. Foster wrote things such as:

"More importantly, would result in an audit of proof of basis

"can of worms you shouldn't open."

Or:

"Sometimes relied on Clinton's return as evidence

"Don't want to go back into that box.

"Was M=D trying to circumvent bank loss — why HRC getting loan from other"

Or:

"Discussion points

"1. An argument that they were protected against loss

"A) Wash [?] is consistent w/this theory."

* * *

Anyone whose mother tongue is English, we should think, would conclude that Whitewater was very much a concern to Mr. Foster in the weeks before his death. Indeed, it has since been revealed that in preparing the Clinton tax returns he was already very deep into much that has been subsequently disclosed. Presumably these handwritten notes, pried out of the White House by Congressional probers, were among the papers Mr. Fiske's report says his investigators examined but could not release because of grand jury secrecy. Yet in inviting the public and Congress to believe the demurrers of the White House staff, Mr. Fiske wrote that there was "no evidence" that Mr. Foster harbored any such concern.

The public and the Congress deserve an explanation. Asked about this apparent discrepancy yesterday, Mr. Fiske said of the tax matter that his investigation "saw no evidence that that issue, discussed back in April, was a factor" in the July suicide. And he reiterated that under the limitations of Rule 6(e), he couldn't reveal which documents they looked at. Yet when an Independent Counsel writes "no evidence," even those of us congenitally suspicious of the whole institution would assume this applies to everything the Counsel has examined, not merely what he feels free to release.

The now-released notes make clear that, with his responsibility for the Clinton finances, Mr. Foster understood that the Whitewater transactions would not sustain much scrutiny. Even with the tax issue momentarily resolved, this must have played a role in his depression, even if he preferred to vent his frustration at our Rose Law Firm editorials, which did make clear that scrutiny was coming. Since our editorials are still being cited, not only in Mr. Fiske's report but as recently as this week in Webster Hubbell's testimony to the D'Amato committee, some might like to make an independent judgment about whether they were harsh or hysterical by the standards applied to Bob Packwood or Newt Gingrich.

We accept the conclusion that Mr. Foster suffered from depression, which is a clinical disease and not a moral failure, and that he committed suicide. But we can't be 100% sure, and conspiracy theories are understandable, because of the incredibly sloppy way in which the death was investigated. The D'Amato committee could help by proposing to amend the laws to give the FBI automatic jurisdiction over any death of a high official, whether assassination (already covered), suicide or apparently natural causes.

It could also help by taking a close look not only at the first investigation by the Park Police, but also the second investigation by Mr. Fiske. At the very least, it could call him and provide a forum to elaborate his explanation of why the Foster notes are no evidence of concern over Whitewater.

REVIEW & OUTLOOK

More 'Small Fry'

If any sentient being still doubts that Whitewater and the Clinton's personal finances were preoccupying the late Vincent Foster before his death, yesterday's testimony by two secretaries in his office should settle the matter. In testimony and previous depositions to Senate investigators, Linda Tripp and Deborah Gorham added their names to the list of "small fry" contradicting testimony by White House bigwigs.

"Whitewater was not on his mind," former White House counsel Bernard Nussbaum said in his exculpation to the New York Times last week, "It was an innocuous issue then." This of course has been the White House line from immediately after the death, when President Clinton declared, "We'll just have to live with something else we can't understand." The no-Whitewater worry was also the official conclusion of Robert Fiske, the first independent counsel.

This was contradicted by Foster's handwritten notes saying that Whitewater was a "can of worms you shouldn't open." He was intent on not subjecting Whitewater to an IRS audit by claiming the capital loss the Clintons said they had suffered.

Now it turns out that in addition, Ms. Tripp, a secretary to Mr. Nussbaum, had bearded him about Mr. Foster spending "an inordinate amount of time" on the Clintons' personal finances. She told Mr. Nussbaum that in her experience it was not the role the counsel's office had played, and he explained that Mr. Foster had been the Clintons' attorney in Arkansas and had continued in that capacity in

Washington. Ms. Tripp also said that Ms. Gorham, Mr. Foster's secretary, told her that her long hours were spent partly working on "a real estate matter for Mr. Foster."

Ms. Gorham's own testimony yesterday was even more explosive. She said that on July 22, two days after the death, an index detailing the Clintons' personal files that Foster had worked on was missing from a file drawer. The White House has asserted that no files were removed from the office until later that day, and Maggie Williams, Hillary Clinton's chief of staff, has denied she took files during her visit to the office the night of the death. She has brandished lie detector tests to bolster her account, but depositions show that the tests were administered by an expert located by her attorney and who gave her several practice tests before the one she passed. Another "small fry," security guard Henry O'Neill, says he saw Ms. Williams take out an armful of files. Since the index would obviously be the key document, Ms. Gorham's report of its absence powerfully corroborates his testimony.

Vincent Foster

More amazing yet, Ms. Gorham says Mr. Foster asked her to put two large manila envelopes in his safe. One was marked "For Eyes Only," and was addressed to William Kennedy III, then associate White House counsel and former law partner of Mr. Foster, Mrs. Clinton and Webster Hubbell. The second was addressed to Attorney General Janet Reno. To date, the White House has never acknowledged the existence of any of these envelopes, let alone their final disposition. Ms. Gorham reports that shortly after the death Mr. Nussbaum asked her for the combination to the safe.

Ms. Gorham also testified yesterday that following the death she told Mr. Nussbaum she'd seen "something yellow" in the bottom of Mr. Foster's briefcase, and that he had questioned her intensively about what she'd seen. Yesterday, Park Police Sergeant Peter Markland testified that Mr. Nussbaum had refused him a chance to examine the briefcase at a July 22 meeting, but looked into the briefcase and indicated it was empty. Last week, Foster family lawyer Michael Spafford testified that on the same day he heard White House lawyer Cliff Sloan comment that he saw scraps of paper inside Foster's briefcase, and Mr. Nussbaum set the case aside, commenting that he would get to that later. The White House contends the Foster note wasn't discovered until the 24th, and not released to investigators until the 26th.

Little wonder that the White House has been extraordinarily sensitive about this note, releasing its version of the text but making the original available only in the Justice Department press room. We have sued for its release under the Freedom of Information Act, and won in Federal District Court. But appeal is still pending, after attorneys representing Mrs. Foster intervened with assertions of privacy rights. By now copies of the note have been widely circulated on Capitol Hill, and even displayed on television screens in the hearing room. This has become ridiculous, and a copy of the note is reprinted alongside. Of course, the events described above show that the chain of custody is much in doubt, so we do not know whether it is the same yellow pieces of paper Ms. Gorham saw but Mr. Nussbaum did not.

Yesterday's hearings were not widely televised despite their revelations; at least until today, the consensus of the Beltway press corps is that nothing much has happened. The Williams-O'Neill conflict got some play, but the Spafford testimony on yellow scraps very little. Questioning of Patsy Thomasson about her association with drug convict Dan Lasater got none except on this page, though the background of people visiting the office the first night is clearly relevant. The lack of press coverage should mostly be laid at the feet of Chairman Alfonse D'Amato, who has conducted the hearings in a way calculated to win empty plaudits for "judiciousness" in deferring to Democrats, not to make the truth clear. Yesterday he joined Democrats in complaints about "leaks" through which the public might actually learn something.

Senator D'Amato can of course redress much of the damage by getting Ms. Williams back for further questioning following yesterday's revelations. And in his defense, the hearings have clearly revealed a great deal — it's only that it takes some effort to pry it from the record. Most obviously, there is by now a mountain of evidence that Mr. Foster was working on and concerned about the First Family's finances. Even more to the point, on this issue we haven't been told the truth. So we have to wonder about the truth of everything else this White House has been saying about Whitewater and related affairs.

August 2, 1995

Editorial Feature

The Note That Won't Go Away

The following note was said by the White House to have been found in Vincent Foster's briefcase following his death.

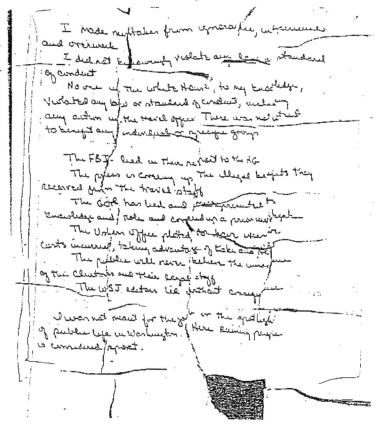

I made mistakes from ignorance, inexperience and overwork

I did not knowingly violate any law or standard of conduct

No one in the White House, to my knowledge, violated any law or standard of conduct, including any action in the travel office. There was no intent to benefit any individual or specific group

The FBI lied in their report to the AG

The press is covering up the illegal benefits they received from the travel staff

The GOP has lied and misrepresented its knowledge and role and covered up a prior investigation

The Ushers Office plotted to have excessive costs incurred, taking advantage of Kaki and HRC

The public will never believe the innocence of the Clintons and their loyal staff

The WSJ editors lie without consequence

I was not meant for the job or the spotlight of public life in Washington. Here ruining people is considered sport.

Editorial Feature

D'Amato Plays Judge Ito— For Real

Republicans in the 1980s had an ironic little prize they called Strange New Respect. The honor went to Republicans such as David Stockman, whose change of mind or style suddenly made them Beltway favorites.

Who would have thought that the first winner of the 1990s would be Alfonse D'Amato?

Potomac Watch

By Paul A. Gigot

When the in-your-face New Yorker was in the Senate minority, liberals loathed him. He was "Senator Pothole," an ethical briar patch, proof that Republicans were barbarians.

In Whitewater hearings last year, Mr. D'Amato met those lofty expectations. His opening statement declared: "The White House has concealed, disguised and distorted the truth," and the evidence backed him up.

Zeroing in on Clinton officials, Mr. D'Amato's favorite word was "incredulous!" White House aide and New York rival Harold Ickes was always "Ickkkkk-eeeeez," as if he were uttering a curse. His tenacity kept the hearings in the news and the Clinton White House on defense.

But this year Mr. D'Amato is chairman of the Whitewater probe and an altered statesman. Suddenly he's a model of judicial cool. His opening summary was so bland it barely offered a road map for what the hearings would show. His most ferocious line to date has been, "This is troubling" — delivered in soft tones that suggest it grieves him to have to say it.

Liberals have responded with the best press of his career. Washington Post columnist Mary McGrory wrote he was trying to "impersonate a senator." Another described his "admirable delicacy," two words never before seen in the same sentence with Al D'Amato. The New York media have admired his rise in social rank with his celebrity girlfriend. The Times even ran a front-pager praising his "soft-spoken gravity" and heralding "a politician at the top of his game." Strange New Respect.

There's no doubt Mr. D'Amato has gone out of his way to accommodate Democrats. Whenever North Carolina Republican Lauch Faircloth tries to expand a line of questioning, the smooth, confident Democrat Paul Sarbanes of Maryland objects that it's beyond "the scope of inquiry." Mr. D'Amato usually agrees.

The erstwhile terror has also tread softly around Maggie Williams, Hillary Rodham Clinton's chief of staff, though her testimony has now been contradicted by at least three people. Mr. D'Amato first promised Republicans

Al D'Amato

he'd recall Ms. Williams as a witness but reneged after Democrats objected.

When Mr. Faircloth suggested the committee call Mrs. Clinton to testify, Mr. D'Amato was quick to knock it down. It's as if having apologized earlier for mocking Lance Ito's ethnicity, Mr. D'Amato has decided to adopt his forgiving judicial style.

All of which has some Republicans wondering, at least in private, if Mr. D'Amato has lost his zeal for the chase. They note that while last year's hearings made headlines, this year reporters seem bored. The media standard seems to be that unless the First Couple are indicted, who cares?

This is partly Mr. D'Amato's fault for not explaining that political accountability involves more than criminal offenses. His skilled chief counsel, Michael Chertoff, leads witnesses through questions that reveal contradictions but provide no context. They expose facts but not meaning. Reporters and the public are left with a pudding but no theme.

Mr. D'Amato's defenders say just relax and wait. Kit Bond, the Missouri Republican and one of the better questioners, says, "We're having to build a case from circumstantial evidence, and that's a lot tougher than having John Dean or someone come out and say, 'The butler did it.'"

Others say that given his reputation for rascality, Mr. D'Amato had to take a less partisan road. The hearings are a marathon, not a sprint, and Whitewater's story line will become clear to all. Credibility built up now will pay off later, as the hearings get closer to the Oval Office.

They also promise fireworks next week, when former White House counsel — and now designated White House fall guy — Bernie Nussbaum testifies. On the other hand, Mr. Nussbaum's testimony will have to compete with Jim Leach's House hearings, which start next week.

Mr. D'Amato is a shrewd enough pol to know liberals won't love him forever. His ties to presidential candidate Bob Dole also give him incentive to pursue Whitewater wherever it leads — especially now that elite Arkansans (chicken king Don Tyson) are advertising their frustration with Bill Clinton and their donations to the Dole campaign.

Yet, so far, it's hard to disagree with Democrats who think they're winning the battle of the summer hearings. Democrat Chuck Schumer, the Brooklyn motor-mouth, dominated the House Waco hearings against less experienced GOP chairmen. His debates with New Hampshire Rep. Bill Zeliff should have been stopped on grounds of cruel and unusual punishment.

And despite the drip of facts, the White House spin of guileless blunders still dominates press coverage on Whitewater. The new, statesmanlike D'Amato has his virtues, but more of the old tenacity might help get to the truth.

Editorial Feature

Who Is Dan Lasater?

By MICAH MORRISON

CHICAGO – Last week, the Federal Deposit Insurance Corp. issued a report criticizing Little Rock's Rose Law Firm for conflicts of interest in representing the government. It was harsh on convicted felon Webster Hubbell in one case, and in another laid much responsibility on the late Vincent Foster. But it minimized the role of a third partner, Hillary Rodham Clinton, on questions about her relationship with drug convict Dan Lasater and Rose's role in suing him on behalf of the government and First American Savings & Loan of Oak Brook, a Chicago suburb.

The FDIC didn't exactly say Mrs. Clinton had no conflict of interest, but it did say that in the First American case she billed for only two hours, reviewing some work in the absence of Mr. Foster, the lead attorney. It said Mrs. Clinton met Mr. Lasater only twice, though he had contributed $16,000 to her husband's gubernatorial campaigns and had a close friendship with Virginia Kelley, Mr. Clinton's mother, and Roger Clinton, Mr. Clinton's half brother. It said that in the end Mr. Foster got a settlement of $200,000 from Mr. Lasater, against a loss to the thrift of $361,000 – not at all bad by the standards of bankrupt thrifts. There seems little reason to doubt that these facts are accurate, as far as they go.

Yet some time probing the affairs of First American here in Chicago suggests that the FDIC's bland recitation conceals a much more interesting story. First American of Oak Brook – not to be confused with the First American Bank in Washington illicitly owned by the Bank of Credit & Commerce International — happened to be owned by former Illinois Governor Dan Walker, like Mr. Lasater now an ex-con. The $361,000 figure was established in a lawsuit by Mr. Walker against Mr. Lasater for unauthorized trading of Treasury bonds. Mr. Lasater's defense was that the trades were authorized and there was no breach of fiduciary relationship. But in a broader

Dan Lasater

sense, given Mr. Lasater's financial relations with First American and Gov. Walker, he may have had reason to believe he owned the bank. Court records relating to Mr. Lasater's curious trades with First American also suggest that he may have taken more than the disputed $361,000 out of the thrift. And, to connect the Illinois affair with the probe of Little Rock's Madison Guaranty, the savings and loan at the heart of the Whitewater scandal being aired in congressional hearings this week, there's reason to wonder whether Mr. Lasater was doing the same thing with Madison, where he also held a trading account.

In short, who is Dan Lasater?

The FDIC is quite correct that he was not Hillary's friend; he was Bill's friend, and according to many Little Rock sources, partying companion. The FDIC's $16,000 in campaign contributions does not appear to include donations Mr. Lasater encouraged from associates, nor such favors as the use of the Lasater plane for campaign-related events. The FDIC says that "a full report of the investigation" will be made available to the public, but so far it has not elaborated on Mr. Lasater's other favors for the Clinton family.

In a 1986 interview with the FBI, for example, Mr. Lasater said that he gave Roger Clinton a job as a stablehand at the governor's request; later, Roger Clinton approached Mr. Lasater for help in paying off a $20,000 cocaine debt. Mr. Lasater told the FBI that he arranged an $8,000 "loan" to help the governor's brother. Copies of FBI interviews with Mr. Lasater and his associates were obtained by The Wall Street Journal. Mr. Lasater did not responded to interview requests.

Roger Clinton went to jail for connections to the same cocaine ring that ultimately put Mr. Lasater himself behind bars. Mr. Lasater was convicted of social distribution of cocaine and served six months; Gov. Clinton later pardoned him — effecting his "relief from civil liabilities," as Senate Banking Committee Chairman Alfonse D'Amato (R., N.Y.) so delicately put it in hearings last week.

Also, Mr. Lasater for almost 10 years employed Patsy Thomasson, now a top White House aide and one of the three people to visit Mr. Foster's office the night of his death. When Sen. Lauch Faircloth (R., N.C.) sought to question Ms. Thomasson about her relations with Mr. Lasater and Madison Guaranty during her Banking Committee appearance, Sens. Paul Sarbanes and Christopher Dodd objected it was beyond the "scope" of the hearings; after several exchanges, Chairman D'Amato ultimately ruled, "I'd ask the senator to withhold at this time."

Mr. Lasater also did favors for a number of other former governors, including Dan Walker. Mr. Walker was the Democratic governor of Illinois from 1972 to 1976 and had been planning a late entry into the 1976 presidential race when a gubernatorial primary loss brought his political career to an abrupt end. Following a string of failed business ventures, Mr. Walker bought First American in 1983. The same year, Mr. Lasater sold Mr. Walker a 48-foot yacht. Mr. Lasater's partner David Collins handled the $350,000 sale, "and money was lost in the deal," Mr. Lasater told the FBI. Mr. Lasater also told the FBI that he had loaned Mr. Walker $200,000 and received stock in First American as collateral. (In the same FBI interview, Mr. Lasater said he delivered a $300,000 cash loan to a former Kentucky governor in a paper bag, and through an intermediary offered a former New Mexico governor a consulting job. At the time, Mr. Lasater owned Angel Fire, a New Mexico resort and airstrip.)

Initially, First American enjoyed spectacular growth, with assets zooming from $13 million in 1983 to more than $80 million by late 1985. News reports have attributed the growth mainly to an inflow of brokered jumbo certificates of deposit. But in 1985, Mr. Walker sued Mr. Lasater for unauthorized T-bond trading through First American. In 1986, Mr. Walker's thrift was declared insolvent and placed in conservatorship. A year later, Mr. Walker pleaded guilty to looting the thrift of nearly $1.4 million. A federal judge sentenced him to seven years in prison, castigating him for using the S&L as "a personal piggy bank."

Mr. Walker had accused Mr. Lasater of "front-running" trades —

essentially, trading Lasater accounts "in front of" First American accounts. According to an analysis prepared by commodity trading expert Leslie Jordan for First American when it was represented by Mr. Foster, trading tickets linked to Lasater & Co. likely were doctored; "someone stuck the loser in First American's account," Ms. Jordan said in a deposition related to the case. She added that there were other "questionable trades" not listed in the First American suit and that "there may have been illegal practices that just weren't caught at the time."

First American and another failed Illinois thrift, Home Federal Savings & Loan of Centralia, also appear to figure into the mysterious case of Dennis Patrick, a Kentucky resident who discovered millions of dollars worth of unauthorized trades being run through his Lasater & Co. account. In an interview with Mr. Patrick's lawyer, two former Lasater traders claimed that repurchase agreements related to the Patrick account had been dumped in First American and Home Federal. In 1988 the Centralia thrift also sued Lasater & Co. for unauthorized trades. Ms. Jordan, the commodity trading expert, analyzed some of the Lasater trades done for Home Federal, noting "a lot of suspect activity." In 1989, Vincent Foster advised Home Federal's management to accept a $250,000 out-of-court settlement with Mr. Lasater.

At both thrifts, the suspect trades occurred between March and May of 1985, intersecting the spectacular fall of Bevill, Bresler & Schulman Asset Management Corp. in April. The New Jersey firm went under with $200 million in losses in an uncollateralized repurchase-agreement scandal that sent shock waves through the securities industry. The fall of Bevill is also mentioned in the interview with Lasater traders. According to bankruptcy notices filed in Chicago, both First American and Home Federal were listed as creditors of a Chicago securities firm that went under with Bevill. Another firm that did not survive was Collins Inc. of Little Rock, run by Mr. Lasater's former partner David Collins, who sold Mr. Walker the Lasater yacht at a loss.

The biggest apparent loser in the Bevill collapse, though, was Little Rock's Worthen Bank, which held $52 million in repos with Bevill on which it had failed to secure the collateral. The Worthen repos actually represented Arkansas state funds. Little Rock's investment giant Stephens Inc. recapitalized Worthen to cover the loss, assuming a much larger stock interest and placing a Stephens executive as CEO. Initially, this positioned Stephens as a hero, but after the Clinton presidential election it became controversial in light of the law against mixing investment banking and commercial banking. After Stephens sold its interest in Worthen last March, the Federal Reserve dropped a two-year investigation, declaring the issue "moot."

As for Mr. Lasater's relations with Madison, the thrift opened a trading account with him in 1984, but it's not known whether it was extensively used. Before Sen. Faircloth's questioning was cut off, Ms. Thomasson said her employment by Lasater involved only a short time at the bond house, and she did not know about the trading account. She did confirm, however, that Mr. Lasater was involved in Emerald Isle Resort, a Madison-financed real estate deal.

While no evidence has emerged linking drug money to Mr. Lasater's bond business, his cocaine conviction and links to troubled thrifts have raised questions about possible money laundering activities. Last month, Greg Hitt of Dow Jones News Service reported that Resolution Trust Corp. investigators had passed documents concerning Mr. Lasater and Madison Guaranty to then-Special Counsel Robert Fiske. Mr. Hitt quoted minutes from a high-level RTC meeting in June 1994: "Dan Lasater may have been establishing depository accounts at Madison and other financial institutions and laundering drug money through them via brokered deposits and bond issues."

Also last month, the American Spectator magazine reported the claim of an Arkansas state trooper, L.D. Brown, that when he told Gov. Clinton he'd seen drugs on flights from remote Mena airfield in western Arkansas, the governor replied, "that's Lasater's deal." While there is no way to substantiate Mr. Brown's account of the conversation, the time frame, at least, seems to fit. Barry Seal, the admitted drug smuggler with whom Mr. Brown said he flew, was active in the early to mid-1980s, and Mr. Lasater admittedly was involved with cocaine during the same time. So was Roger Clinton. In 1985, Roger Clinton was offered a deal at the end of a long drug probe centering around Mr. Lasater and his associates, including former partners George Locke, a former state senator, and David Collins. Roger Clinton pleaded guilty to reduced charges, testified against the Lasater circle — most of whom were indicted — and went to jail for 15 months.

The man who cut the deal was George Proctor, a former state legislator who had been named U.S. attorney for the Eastern District of Arkansas by President Jimmy Carter in 1979. Shortly after Roger Clinton's testimony, Mr. Lasater pleaded guilty to the minor social distribution charge and went briefly to prison. Mr. Proctor now heads the Justice Department's Office of International Affairs, which deals with, among other things, aspects of the BCCI case. Oddly enough, BCCI first attempted to enter the U.S. through Arkansas in the late 1970s, in a deal initially handled by Stephens Inc., which says it has had no contact with BCCI investors since 1978.

Early 1986 must have been a tough time for Bill Clinton. His brother was in jail. Mr. Lasater was on his way to jail. Federal regulators had removed James McDougal from the board of Madison Guaranty. Mr. Clinton was planning his fifth run for governor and thinking about a bid for the presidency. His GOP rival Frank White was making his association with Mr. Lasater an issue. Into this atmosphere drifted the threat of the Walker lawsuit, which had been taken over by the Federal Savings and Loan Insurance Corp.

FSLIC handed the Lasater suit to Hopkins & Sutter, a Chicago firm where former Gov. Walker had worked for 13 years prior to his political career. Hopkins & Sutter dismissed the previous Little Rock counsel, Hardin & Grace, and hired the Rose Law Firm; Vincent Foster took the case. Mr. Lasater hired Wright, Lindsey & Jennings — Gov. Clinton's old firm. In less than a year, the case was settled under a seal of confidentiality, vanishing from public view. Even the fact that a settlement had been reached was put under seal, until revealed in a Chicago Tribune story last year. While the FDIC took a different view, the Tribune suggested Mrs. Clinton's participation in the suit may have constituted a "glaring conflict of interest."

Mr. Lasater, it seems, was of great interest to the overlapping circles of law enforcement, finance and legal representation in Little Rock and beyond. If who Dan Lasater is and what he was up to remain beyond the "scope" of congressional hearings, the hearings probably won't reveal very much.

Mr. Morrison is a Journal editorial page writer.

REVIEW & OUTLOOK

What Is Whitewater?

With Whitewater hearings under way on both sides of Capitol Hill and White House and Congressional Democrats in full spin mode, it's a good time to review what the sprawling affair is all about. It is not about some two-bit land deal a decade ago, as the defense team is fond of saying. It is about the conduct of the Clinton Presidency in the here and now.

The question is at heart whether this President and his associates have abused the authority of the nation's highest public office. Specifically, did they use the power of the Presidency to cover up the embarrassment of decade-old transgressions? And more generally, is the Clinton team now repeating in the White House the patterns and style of conduct evident in the matters dating back to Little Rock — the cut corners, the convenient losses of memory, the use of surrogates and associates to maneuver in the gray areas of what is legal and what is not?

Yesterday, over the huffing and puffing of Henry Gonzalez and Barney Frank, the government's investigators made clear they felt obstructed in their investigation of Whitewater, Madison Guaranty Savings & Loan and the Clintons' participation in and benefit from illicit money. And Chairman Leach produced documents to support his charges that at every step of the way the White House has claimed one thing while "the facts are otherwise."

It's true that in this the dollar amounts are small, even in comparison with Hillary Clinton's $100,000 profits in the futures markets.

But at the same time, there was no little to cover up. Among other things, it seems the future President and his wife had been cheating on their taxes. "Mrs. Clinton knew," Jeff Gerth of the New York Times reported on Sunday, that Whitewater Development Co. "had made payments for which she and her husband later claimed the deductions, on their 1984 and 1985 tax returns."

More broadly, evidence continues to mount that the Clintons used Madison Guaranty as their personal piggy bank. Funds from Madison and David Hale's Capital Management Services, said House Banking Committee Chairman Jim Leach on Monday, "were used to reduce the Governor's personal debt and campaign liabilities" and "to purchase a tract of land from a company to which the state had given a significant tax break."

The message we draw from the Clintons' Arkansas years is this: Theirs was a world in which there was no normal demarcation line between public and private life. Like aristocracy in some medieval barony, the Clintons felt entitled to support, and it was the responsibility of subordinates and minions to make sure that money and excuses were always available to keep the Clintons' permanent political campaigns and careers above water.

This is the world the Clintons brought into the Oval Office, as quickly became apparent in the Travelgate affair, in Webster Hubbell's intervention in a political corruption case, in the firing of both U.S. Attorneys and White House ushers. And in the handling of the late Vincent Foster's papers by Maggie Williams, the First Lady's chief of staff, and Patsy Thomasson, one of the most suspect members of the Arkansas political mafia.

We will hear more about this as Bernard Nussbaum defends his peremptory disposition of the papers. There are of course valid concerns about executive privileges, precedents on the powers of the presidency and so on. But it is precisely the whole checkered history of this White House that calls his motives into question. Yes, he was entitled to be concerned about the prerogatives of the Presidency, as Richard Nixon was entitled to fire Archibald Cox. But now as then, the public is entitled to draw the conclusions and extract the political price the context suggests.

As we listen to Mr. Nussbaum, the question to keep in mind is, who was his client? He was not Bill Clinton's personal lawyer; he was an employee of the United States government. Yes, difficult questions arise when the President's personal papers turn up on government property; the papers never should have been there in the first place. A normal presidency would have arrived in Washington and immediately transferred the President's tangled private matters to a lawyer's office at someplace like Williams & Connolly. Not this one. The local lawyer handled it down the hall, serving at taxpayer expense as deputy White House counsel.

Now, there is a law, 18 U.S.C. 641, that prohibits government officials from using subordinates for personal services. We might be more willing than others to look the other way in the case of a President. But when the personal lawyer/government official dramatically kills himself, the American people are entitled to inquire about the implications of this strange setup.

Bernard Nussbasum

If Mr. Clinton's defenders wish to argue that the Republicans' own pedigree was besmirched by Watergate and Iran-Contra, they are entitled, though their objections drip with hypocrisy given their aggressive investigations then and their stonewalling on Whitewater when they held the majority. In any event, the Clinton Presidency is the one that now occupies the White House. Its political character is a fair subject for the hearings now being conducted by Senator D'Amato and Congressman Leach, as well as a relatively small number of determined journalists amid a huge and largely indifferent Washington press corps.

The evidence mounts that in reaction to Whitewater the White House grabbed every lever of power it could reach to distort and dissemble, not because the stakes were so high, but simply because that's the way they'd learned to behave back in Arkansas.

REVIEW & OUTLOOK

Ira Beats the Rap

Ira Magaziner, the czar of the ill-fated Clinton health care task force, is off the hook. After a six-month investigation, U.S. Attorney Eric Holder announced last week that Mr. Magaziner wouldn't be prosecuted on perjury charges related to his claims about the eyes-only task force. We agree with Mr. Holder that perjury requires a

Ira Magaziner

high degree of proof, but we question his belief that because White House and Justice Department lawyers were so incompetent no one can be held accountable for the decision to have the task force work in secret in violation of open-meeting laws.

In an 18-page letter to Attorney General Janet Reno, Mr. Holder said a "confusing" March 1993 statement drafted for Mr. Magaziner by the late Vincent Foster, then deputy White House counsel, left Mr. Magaziner "open to charges that portions were inaccurate." The statement claimed federal open-meeting laws didn't apply because all task force members were government employees. This at a time when a horde of volunteers and representatives of special interest groups were part of the task force.

Mr. Holder also criticizes White House and Justice lawyers for going "back after the fact" and trying to reclassify outside consultants as government employees. Indeed, in an attempt to comply with the law, Mr. Foster even signed Federal Register notices for meetings that had already taken place. Stunts like that are what prompted federal judge Royce Lamberth to accuse the Administration of "evasive" behavior. Last December, he indicated he intended to fine the White House for its "misconduct," but asked Mr. Holder to first look at Mr. Magaziner's statement, which Judge Lamberth termed "misleading, at best," to see if he had committed perjury. Mr. Holder found that Mr. Magaziner's claims were "strained," and anyway had been made for him by Mr. Foster and other Administration lawyers.

Rep. Bob Barr of Georgia, a former U.S. Attorney who now sits on the Judiciary Committee, isn't buying it. Yesterday, he wrote Attorney General Reno demanding that she investigate the role that government lawyers played in misleading Judge Lamberth. He says Mr. Holder's letter effectively means that clever legal wordsmiths can nullify the federal open-meeting law. "Mr. Holder shouldn't be allowed to redirect blame for the undermining of our sunshine laws away to government lawyers without a follow-up investigation," he told us.

Rep. Barr has been part of the Whitewater hearings this week, and he is struck by similarities between the two cases. The same players — former White House counsel Bernie Nussbaum, the late Vincent Foster and the now-imprisoned Webb Hubbell — were involved in both, and the modus operandi was the same: a pattern of evasion and stonewalling and the mishandling of documents. In Whitewater, the designated fall guy appears to be Bernie Nussbaum, who will take the heat before a Senate committee today. When it comes to Mr. Magaziner's whoppers on health care, it looks as if the blame is being passed to Vincent Foster, who can't defend himself.

The President and First Lady claim to be clueless about how the health care task force that designed the crown jewel of their policy initiatives was being misused. Given a choice between being portrayed as ethically adrift or incompetent, members of this administration consistently choose the latter defense. We prefer to acknowledge their intelligence.

REVIEW & OUTLOOK

The Lewis Testimony

Former Resolution Trust Corp. investigator Jean Lewis is the latest small fry in the federal government to come forward with testimony regarding the political mores of the Clinton Administration.

Ms. Lewis's experience amid the mighty oaks of official Washington has been similar to other small fry who've talked about Whitewater or the wandering Foster files. They discover that they have to win at a special Beltway board game called "No Big Deal" in which the squares are marked Nothing New, Not Proved, Just Numbers, Political Bias and so on till the player staggers into oblivion.

Jean Lewis

Ms. Lewis, from Kansas City, spent a day delivering testimony to the House Banking Committee about the 10 criminal referrals she filed to the Justice Department, mostly about the money running through and around people involved with Madison Guaranty S&L and the Whitewater real estate development. Ms. Lewis encountered her biggest hurdle when she landed on the Not Proved square. It was pointed out that the Bush-appointed federal attorney in Little Rock didn't think that her case was prosecutable and that a career lawyer at the Justice Department thought the referrals' factual support was weak.

As a popular sportscaster used to say, let's go to the videotape. Let's look at Jean Lewis's work product. Obviously some in the

Justice Department professed to believe the material extracted alongside didn't add up to anything worth pursuing. But as it happens, Independent Counsel Kenneth Starr has had the referrals for months, and has been pursuing them. The indictments and guilty pleas to date show that Ms. Lewis's referrals are sticking.

Testifying Tuesday about her work, Ms. Lewis stated, "Between May 1993 and August 1993, the Madison criminal investigative team researched several transactions involving insider abuse, self-dealing, money laundering, embezzlement, diversion of loan proceeds, payments of excessive commissions, misappropriation of funds, land flips, inflated appraisals, falsification of loan records . . . and illegal campaign contributions." She added that these "referrals identified multiple suspects, including the Bill Clinton Political Committee Fund, James and Susan McDougal, Jim Guy Tucker, Chris Wade and several former Madison officers and borrowers." Elsewhere, Ms. Lewis identified Clinton aide Stephen Smith and Larry Kuca, a business partner of Jim McDougal.

In March Chris Wade, an Arkansas real estate agent, pleaded guilty on a charge unrelated to Whitewater but committed to cooperating with Mr. Starr's office in that investigation. In June, Mr. Starr's office issued an indictment of Arkansas Governor Jim Guy Tucker, involving allegations of false statements to obtain a federally backed $300,000 loan from David Hale's Capital Management Services and a bogus bankruptcy. Stephen Smith pleaded guilty to misusing a federal small-business loan. Last month, Larry Kuca also pleaded guilty to conspiring to fraudulently obtain such a loan.

While the conventional wisdom insists that nobody following this affair can ever get past the Just Numbers square, it looks to us as if this lady from the Kansas City RTC office knew very well how to follow the tangled money trail of a financial fraud. Somehow the committee's Democrats didn't want to debate Ms. Lewis about the innards of the Little Rock fraud establishment. So instead we got Rep. John LaFalce trying to discredit her by noting her lawyers are from the conservative Landmark Legal Foundation (apparently the Nan Aron Alliance for Justice combine didn't offer to help her find an attorney).

There was a time when Democrats welcomed whistleblowers into their midst. Now they try to banish them. Democrats during the hearing routinely charged that the Independent Counsel's office had "no trust" in Ms. Lewis and two RTC colleagues who appeared with her. Mr. Starr's office thereupon got out a statement that the assertions were "categorically untrue" and that in fact Mr. Starr's office was investigating their obstruction charges.

This suggests that the Starr investigation isn't over yet. Indeed it looks to us as if the Independent Counsel is still working his way through Jean Lewis's list.

Editorial Feature

Hard Evidence
From a Federal Investigator

Evidence presented on Tuesday to the House committee investigating Whitewater by Resolution Trust Corp. (RTC) investigator Jean Lewis:

The first Madison criminal referral [or report], which was assigned the number C0004, was supported by substantial detail and extensive exhibits. It was completed on Aug. 31, 1992, and submitted to the FBI and U.S. Attorney by Kansas City RTC senior management in the investigation unit on Sept. 2, 1992, in full compliance with RTC procedures and guidelines.

Among other things, the referral provided specific check numbers, dates, account names, account balances, particular uses of funds, and the names of individuals and entities involved in various check kiting schemes. The referral also stated that among those who stood to benefit from this activity were Stephen Smith, Jim Guy Tucker, then-Gov. Bill Clinton and Mrs. Clinton inasmuch as "[t]he overdrafts and 'loan' transactions, or alleged check 'swapping' and kiting, between the combined companies' accounts ensured that loan payments and other corporate obligations were met, thus clearly benefiting the principals of each entity." . . .

Very specific information was provided in this first referral. For instance, it states, in part, the following:

". . . Each instance in which Whitewater's actions resulted in an overdraft, no service charge or fees were assessed, with the exception of two in 1985, both of which were refunded. The two largest checks written by Whitewater during this time frame, check #137 for $25,000, payable to Ozarks Realty Co., and check #138 for $30,000, payable to James McDougal (alleged 'loan repayment' — although the records show no indication of any loan from McDougal to Whitewater) were both force paid as there were insufficient funds in the account to cover either check. When the $25,000 check paid, placing the [negative] balance at $24,470.90, the overdraft was covered by a check from Flowerwood Farms for $24,455.90 (the amount of the overdraft, less the $15 service charge which was later refunded). The Flowerwood funds came from the proceeds of a $135,000 cashiers check drawn on Stephens Security Bank, Stephens, Ark. The $30,000 check written from Whitewater to James McDougal was written when Whitewater had a balance of $270.13. When the check was force paid, the balance went to [a negative] $29,744.87, where it remained for two weeks until a $30,000 check from Madison Financial Corp. (subsidiary of MGS&L) was deposited into Whitewater's account. There was no explanation given as to why Madison Financial would have given (or even 'loaned') Whitewater Development $30,000."

. . . I would also point out to the Committee that the $135,000 Stephens Security Bank Loan was paid off with funds from the $300,000 Capital Management loan to the McDougals' Master Marketing Co. in 1986. . . .

Between May 1993 and August 1993, the Madison criminal investigative team reviewed and researched several transactions involving insider abuse, self-dealing, money laundering, embezzlement, diversion of loan proceeds, payments of excessive commissions, misappropriation of funds, land flips, inflated appraisals, falsification of loan records and board minutes, chronic overdraft status of various subsidiaries, joint ventures and real estate investments, regulatory violations of investments in subsidiaries, wire fraud, and illegal campaign contributions. . . .

Again, these referrals provided significant detail. For instance, Criminal Referral No. 730CR0196 states, in part, the following:

"Prior to funding $38,940 of the $50,000 loan proceeds to Quapaw Title Co. on April 5, 1985, Peacock allegedly diverted $6,000 from the proceeds to purchase two cashier's checks on April 4, 1985; check numbers Q2497 and Q2498, drawn on MGS&L account #7001312. Each check was in the amount of $3,000, each was purchased in the name of either a Peacock relative or business associate, and each was payable to Bill Clinton, individually rather than the Bill Clinton Political Committee. These two checks were subsequently deposited to the Bill Clinton Political Committee account (#81-313) at the Bank of Cherry Valley, Cherry Valley, Ark.

"On the same day, Flowerwood Farms Inc., an entity owned and operated by James B. and Susan H. McDougal, issued check #000192 to Madison Guaranty for $3,000; this referral re-incorporates the allegation contained in previously submitted RTC criminal referral #C0004, that these funds were used to procure MGS&L cashier's check #Q2496 for $3,000, purchased in the name of former Sen. J.W. Fulbright and payable to the Bill Clinton Campaign Fund. According to information obtained from an interview with James. B. McDougal, conducted by former Special Investigative Counsel Jeff Gerrish of the Memphis law firm Borod & Huggins, hired by the MGS&L board of directors in late 1986 to investigate the McDougals' activities at the thrift, McDougal admitted that he had been 'signing documents' for Sen. Fulbright 'for 20 years,' lending a strong degree of probability that the cashier's check in question was in fact purchased by McDougal and obtained in conjunction with the two checks from Peacock, as evidenced by the sequential order of the checks (#Q2496, 2497, 2498 and 2499). It should be noted that the signature on the Flowerwood Farms check is allegedly that of Susan McDougal. However, it bears no resemblance to Ms. McDougal's signature as it appears on numerous other MGS&L documents.

"In addition, check #688 for $3,000 payable to the Bill Clinton Campaign Fund was issued from James B. McDougal's personal account on April 4, 1985, signed by Susan McDougal, which appears to be her actual signature. As previously referenced in RTC criminal referral #C0004, this check was written on the McDougals' account when the balance was at a negative $7,897.73; the check was force paid, allegedly on McDougal's authority, subsequently overdrawing the account to [a negative] $10,897.73. Both the check from McDougal's personal account and cashier's check #Q2496 were deposited into the same Bill Clinton Political Committee account at the Bank of Cherry Valley. . . ."

Thus far, of those identified as suspects and witnesses in these

RTC referrals, the independent counsel's investigation has resulted in guilty pleas from Chris Wade, Stephen Smith, Larry Kuca, and the indictment of Governor Jim Guy Tucker.

The Committee should note that these nine referrals, submitted to U.S. Attorney Paula Casey on Oct. 8, 1993, were in her possession and available for her review when she rejected Referral #C0004 on Oct. 27, 1993.

REVIEW & OUTLOOK

Whitewater Contradictions

Today four weeks of Whitewater hearings on Capitol Hill are scheduled to come to an end. Any careful observer of these proceedings could not help but notice a striking motif that played over and over through the witnesses' appearances. And that was the conflicting testimony, memory lapses, and lower-echelon figures contradicting the Big Fish at the White House.

Start with the matter of Vincent Foster's files.

On the key issue of what happened to the files in Mr. Foster's office, Secret Service Officer Henry O'Neill testified before the Senate Banking Committee that he saw Maggie Williams, Mrs. Clinton's chief of staff, exit the counsel's suite on the night of Mr. Foster's death — July 20, 1993 — "carrying what I would describe, in her arms and hands, as folders." Ms. Williams: "I took nothing from Vince's office." She offered in her defense lie-detector test results, though later it emerged that Ms. Williams had first taken several "practice" tests, which may have skewed the results.

Park Police officials in charge of the investigation testified that earlier in the evening a request was made to presidential aide David Watkins to secure Mr. Foster's office. Sgt. Cheryl Braun testified that Mr. Watkins "said yes, he acknowledged my request." The office, however, was not sealed. Sgt. Braun added that Mr. Watkins did not mention that a few minutes earlier he had dispatched his deputy, Patsy Thomasson, to search Mr. Foster's office. Mr. Watkins told the Senate panel he "did not hear" a request from Sgt. Braun to secure the office.

* * *

Mr. Foster's secretary, Deborah Gorham, testified that when she was called to Mr. Foster's office on July 22, two days after his death, to search the files with White House Counsel Bernard Nussbaum, an index detailing the Clintons' personal files was missing. Ms. Gorham's claim that a document was missing from Mr. Foster's office supports Officer O'Neill's statement that papers were removed the night of the death.

The White House has said that no files were removed from Mr. Foster's office until later that day.

Later on the day of the search by Mr. Nussbaum and Ms. Gorham,

Maggie Williams

Ms. Williams moved the files to the Clintons' personal residence. Ms. Williams says this was her idea, not Mrs. Clinton's. Thomas Castleton, a young White House aide, told the Senate committee that he moved the Foster files "either from Maggie Williams's office or the First Lady's office" to the residence. Ms. Williams's told him "they needed to be reviewed by the First Lady," he testified. "My understanding, from the conversation I had with Ms. Williams, was that the First Lady would be reviewing them," Mr. Castleton said. Ms. Williams does not recall the conversation.

Another White House aide, Carolyn Huber, testified that on July 22 Miss Williams called her "and said that Mrs. Clinton had asked" that the files be moved to the residence. A former Nussbaum aide, Clifford Sloan, said at the hearings that his notes from the day after Mr. Foster's death include the lines: "Get Maggie [Williams] – go thru office – get HRC [Mrs. Clinton] and WJC [President Clinton] stuff."

Mr. Nussbaum testified that he told Ms. Williams to check with the Clintons about where to store Whitewater and other files. But Ms. Williams testified that it was Mr. Nussbaum who had instructed her to give the files to the Clintons' personal attorney, and that she had only stored the files in the residence because she was tired.

Another Nussbaum aide, Associate White House Counsel Stephen

Neuwirth, told the Senate panel that Mr. Nussbaum told him that Mrs. Clinton had expressed concern about investigators having "unfettered access" to Mr. Foster's office, which brings us to Susan Thomases.

Notice of Mrs. Clinton's concern had been delivered in an oblique phone call by Susan Thomases. Mr. Nussbaum told the Senate that during the call from Ms. Thomases — one of more than a dozen she placed to the White House in the aftermath of Mr. Foster's death — the longtime adviser to Mrs. Clinton had said "people" were concerned about the search of Mr. Foster's office that was about to take place.

Ms. Thomases this week told the Senate that Mr. Nussbaum brought up the search, not her. She added that she "never received from anyone or gave to anyone any instructions about how the review of Vince Foster's office was to be conducted or how the files in Vince Foster's office were to be handled."

Philip Heymann, the former Deputy Attorney General, testified that Mr. Nussbaum imposed plenty of fetters when he sent two career Justice Department prosecutors to the White House to examine Mr. Foster's office. Mr. Heymann recalled that after Mr. Nussbaum blocked the prosecutors from looking at Mr. Foster's papers,

Susan Thomases

he angrily phoned the counsel, asking, "Bernie, are you hiding something?" Mr. Nussbaum said he did not recall Mr. Heymann's remark.

Contradictions and omissions also surround the torn-up note found in Mr. Foster's briefcase. Michael Spafford, a Washington lawyer representing the Foster family, told the committee that two days after Mr. Foster's death, Nussbaum aide Clifford Sloan saw scraps of paper at the bottom of Mr. Foster's briefcase and told Mr. Nussbaum, who replied that they would get to it later. Mr. Sloan told the committee that the incident "did not happen."

Ms. Gorham, Mr. Foster's secretary, testified that she too saw something in the bottom of Mr. Foster's briefcase days before Nussbaum aide Stephen Neuwirth says he discovered the note. During his testimony, Mr. Neuwirth acknowledged that when the FBI questioned him about the events he did not mention that Mrs. Clinton had inspected the note.

While the Senate has been probing the handling of the Foster files, the House Banking Committee this week has been hearing the career federal investigators who examined the tangled affairs of Madison Guaranty Savings & Loan. Jean Lewis, a Resolution Trust Corp. investigator, testified that there was "a concerted effort to obstruct, hamper and manipulate the results" of the Madison probe, which had turned up evidence of "rampant bank fraud." Ms. Lewis said that she had suffered "personally and professionally" in the time since she forwarded the Madison criminal referrals to Washington and to U.S. Attorney Paula Casey in Little Rock. The referrals were, now famously, rejected.

In February 1994, Ms. Lewis said, she received RTC Washington official April Breslaw as a visitor to her Kansas City office. Ms. Breslaw told her that top RTC officials "would like to be able to say Whitewater did not cause a loss to Madison." Ms. Breslaw has asserted that her conversation with Ms. Lewis has been mischaracterized.

* * *

Yesterday, the Banking Committee released records of previously undisclosed phone calls between Ms. Breslaw and then-Associate Attorney General Webster Hubbell. Ms. Breslaw's lawyer says the contacts were innocuous. Possibly, but more phone records might help clear up some of the many "can't recalls" floating through the air these days. We have our own list.

We wonder, for starters, if in addition to Ms. Breslaw, whether Mr. Hubbell also spoke during this period with Paula Casey, the former Little Rock attorney Mr. Clinton appointed federal prosecutor there. Likewise, a look at phone records might lay to rest the troubling allegation of a call from the Clintons' babysitter to Little Rock on the night of Mr. Foster's death — a call that allegedly took place before the White House says it learned of the death.

There is also the mystery of when Mrs. Clinton knew of Mr. Foster's death. Mrs. Clinton was on an official plane heading east from Los Angeles around the time Mr. Foster died, and made a stop in Little Rock. We are told that Andrews Air Force Base keeps a log and taped records of all communications with the presidential fleet. Subpoenas for these phone records might go a long way toward laying to rest or getting to the bottom of some of these mysteries.

As we have been noting throughout these hearings, Beltway wisdom appears to have created a standard of proof guaranteed to ensure that stonewalling is now a legitimate defense. Unless the opposition produces irrefutable evidence — a tape recording, explicit memoranda, aerial reconnaissance photos through the windows of the official residence — nothing is proven so nobody did anything.

This may be the rule by which life is lived in the Colosseum called Washington, where the players measure results solely in terms of either survival or personal destruction, but it is not the basis on which the American people make their contribution to the nation's politics. They do that in the voting booth, and those decisions about sitting presidents or their challengers are based on complex individual judgments about performance and character. The Whitewater hearings these past weeks, we think, have offered valuable insights into the political ethos that has animated the Clinton White House since January 1993.

Editorial Feature

Nussbaum Shows What He Learned From Watergate

It took a while, but this week one large difference between Whitewater and its Watergate cousin of two decades ago became clear: Richard Nixon never had Bernie Nussbaum on his side.

The Trickster's lawyer was John Dean, who helped in the coverup but then cracked like bone china when the going got tough. President and Mrs. Clinton were smart enough to hire Mr. Nussbaum, who isn't a cut-and-run guy.

During Watergate Mr. Nussbaum was working against Nixon. The New York litigator was the "senior associate special counsel" to the House Judiciary Committee that impeached Nixon. In that role he met Hillary Rodham Clinton, introducing her to smash-mouth politics.

Potomac Watch

By Paul A. Gigot

In that role, too, Mr. Nussbaum helped rebut Nixon's infamous defense of "executive privilege." So it was with astonishment, if not amusement, that senators this week heard Mr. Nussbaum roll out the Nixon defense to justify his own Whitewater behavior. After Vincent Foster's death, he had stonewalled Park Police, cordoned off Justice Department lawyers and otherwise mucked around, Mr. Nussbaum explained, because "it was my ethical duty as a lawyer."

"It was my duty to preserve the right of the White House — of this president and future presidents — to assert executive privilege, attorney-client privilege and work-product privilege," he said.

Never mind that this may be the first time in history that executive privilege has been invoked not against Congress but against another department of the same executive branch! You have to admire that kind of brass.

Especially since this super-Nixon defense seems to be working for Mr. Nussbaum, and by extension for the Clintons. Bernie's a standout as a stand-up fellow. He interrupts senators, rebuts their skepticism, concedes nothing. Remorse is not in his vocabulary.

Of course, Mr. Nussbaum's tale requires that we believe some improbable events or contradictions: That he somehow wouldn't remember, despite his Watergate experience, when the deputy attorney general asked him if he were "hiding something." That no fewer than three Justice attorneys were wrong in concluding they had an agreement with him on how to search Foster's office.

Also that White House aides were stricken by grief the night of Foster's death, but not too stricken to scour his office for a suicide note.

Bernard Nussbaum

That despite this preoccupation with a note, Mr. Nussbaum overlooked the one that wasn't found in Foster's briefcase until days later.

And that everything in Foster's office was properly accounted for, even though Foster's secretary says she saw an index file that has never turned up, and even though she saw Mr. Nussbaum and the first lady's chief of staff searching through Foster's files.

Above all else, we are supposed to believe that Mr. Nussbaum made every decision on his own, without any word from the Clintons. For if the buck stops with Bernie, the Foster mystery hits a dead end. Any political fault lies with Mr. Nussbaum, who is tough enough to take it and no longer works in the White House.

The only crack in his stalwart front is a difference he has with Susan Thomases, the first lady's best friend and renowned armbreaker. Mr. Nussbaum says Ms. Thomases called him two days after Foster's death and said "people were concerned" about how much access police would have to Foster's office. Another attorney has testified that Mr. Nussbaum told him something similar.

But Ms. Thomases says Mr. Nussbaum was the one who brought up the plan for a search. All she said was, "sounds good to me." This is the same Susan Thomases who underwent a personality transplant for the hearings. The heavy of campaign legend emerged as Miss Manners. In 17 phone calls to White House officials during two critical days after Foster's death, Ms. Thomases says she was merely a consoler.

She never asked about, and barely heard about, how to handle any Foster probe. This line tested even the credulity of Massachusetts Democrat John Kerry, the Clintons' most reflexive defender, who managed a skeptical question or two.

In essence, we are left with two Whitewater story lines. One comes from the most senior White House officials. It holds that the post-Foster blundering was caused merely by grief and bumptious Bernie. The messiness was innocent, typical of this White House's confusion. As for the Clintons' Arkansas past, there was nothing to hide. If you choose to believe ...

The other story is the one told by lesser officials who observed all of this around the edges. They tell of contradictory testimony, spirited papers and multiple phone calls close to the time outside probers were stymied. This story includes evidence that Vince Foster indeed had Clinton taxes and finances on his mind. And as House hearings showed this week, those Arkansas finances were sleazy and the taxes underpaid.

By Watergate standards, this is no "smoking gun." But it does show a White House that was worried about more than it let on, that used its power to block and dissemble, and that surely acted as if it had something to cover up. It's enough to leave a skeptic wondering if the most important lesson Bernie Nussbaum learned from Watergate was that Nixon should have burned the tapes.

Letters to the Editor

A Fearsome Judge Broke Open Watergate

Even Mr. Gigot (Potomac Watch, Aug. 11) seems to have forgotten the critical difference between Watergate and Whitewater. It is not Bernie Nussbaum; it is not even Bob Woodward. The battering ram that broke open the Watergate was Judge Sirica. But for the 20-year sentences passed out by Maximum John (for breaking and entering without theft!), Watergate might have terminated at the stonewall, just as Whitewater appears destined to do. The only holdout was Gordon Liddy, who was remanded to the most violent prison in the D.C. area. John Dean did not need to be made of bone china to break at the prospect of facing this jurist or his like.

In my view, it is to the credit of Republicans that, unlike the Democrats vis a vis Nixon, they show no passion to "get" the president — at whatever cost to the nation — but appear to seek only a modest gain of a few talking points for '96.

RALPH M. REYNOLDS

Venice, Calif.

REVIEW & OUTLOOK

Asides

Paula's Pass

So RTC investigator Jean Lewis did reveal something pertinent during the Leach Whitewater hearings after all. Ms. Lewis testified that her referrals on Madison Guaranty S&L named "multiple suspects," among them Jim and Susan McDougal and Arkansas Governor Jim Guy Tucker. Yesterday, Independent Counsel Kenneth Starr indicted Jim McDougal on 19 felony counts, his wife on eight counts and Governor Tucker on 11 — most for fraud of various kinds. So Jean Lewis was onto something. What now needs to be explained is why Friend-of-Bill federal attorney Paula Casey in Little Rock refused to investigate Lewis's case and why she earlier refused the plea and cooperation of Judge David Hale, whose Capital Management Services is also named in the indictments. A 15-year-old mystery? No, Paula Casey passed on all this less than two years ago.

More Skirmishing

The fall of 1995 was marked by courtroom skirmishes and clashes over documents. In the BCCI case, U.S. District Judge Joyce Hens Green dismissed procedural motions against the trustee of First American Bank, allowing a civil suit against Clark Clifford and Robert Altman to move to discovery and trial. "Because nearly everyone else has forgotten," the Journal wrote, "we always have to apologize for our continued interest in the Bank of Credit & Commerce International—instead of more contemporary scandals such as Bob Packwood's boorishness or Newt Gingrich's book deal. All that BCCI represents, after all, is the prototypical 21st century criminal enterprise." The "numerous intriguing conjunctions between the BCCI history and the Whitewater scandal," the Journal added, was also a matter worthy of note.

In Little Rock, U.S. District Judge Henry Woods dismissed tax fraud charges against Arkansas Governor Jim Guy Tucker and two associates, ruling that the independent counsel lacked jurisdiction to bring the case. Mr. Starr appealed to the Eighth U.S. Circuit Court in St. Louis.

In Washington, the third White House counsel in three years, Abner Mikva, abruptly announced his resignation. The job was turned over to Jack Quinn, a former Al Gore operative, who continued the White House stonewall on document requests by Congress. In late October, following rebuffs from the White House over long-sought documents, Rep. William Clinger's Government Reform and

Oversight Committee launched hearings into the Travel Office affair. The summary firings of Travel Office head Billy Dale and six others would turn out to be a ticking time bomb for the Administration.

LEISURE & ARTS

Brother Act: The Man From Hopeless

By Maria-Caroline Perignon

At the time of his arrest in 1984 on drug charges, Roger Clinton says he was ingesting five to seven grams of cocaine a day and had been for some years. Mr. Clinton has now ordered his recollections, such as they are, in a selective saga of his life, "Growing Up Clinton: The Lives, Times and Tragedies of America's Presidential Family" (Summit, 195 pages, $19.95).

Roger begins his autobiography with the confrontation that has become part of official Clinton mythology: When Bill Saved The Family. Defending Roger and his beleaguered mother, the 16-year-old future president stood up to his alcoholic stepfather and warded off a scissors-wielding, "Psycho"-style attack. It's clear that Roger, 10 years younger, idolized his half-brother from a very early age – and perhaps for good reason.

Bookshelf

"Growing Up Clinton: The Lives, Times and Tragedies of America's Presidential Family"
By Roger Clinton

Roger's tale is touching at times, particularly when he describes his early years. He conveys some of the flavor of his odd Arkansas childhood when he notes that his mother, Virginia Cassidy Blythe Clinton Dwire Kelley, a devoted follower of the horses, taught him to read at Oaklawn racetrack "using the racing form." Later, she would sneak Roger and Bill out of the house to the nearby Capri Motel to escape his father's drunken rages. At one point Roger states simply — and poignantly — that "for all children of alcoholics, there are no second chances at childhood."

At 15, Roger smoked marijuana for the first time and, unlike his brother, seems to have inhaled deeply. By the time Bill became governor in 1978, Roger was a major-league doper. Zonked on drugs, Roger glided in and out of the guest house at the governor's mansion until confronted by an assertive Hillary, who demanded that he call first.

During the years of his drug addiction, a charmed Roger also moved across state lines with "ounces and ounces" of cocaine stashed on his body. Roger says that the reason he was driven to drugs was that he was screwed up inside. Perhaps so. But his self-presentation in "Growing Up Clinton" — a mixture of feel-good homilies and hillbilly tales — doesn't always seem credible. For example, while Roger notes that he once borrowed $8,000 to pay off a cocaine debt, he neglects to mention that the lender was his good buddy, Whitewater figure Dan Lasater. Roger also neglects to mention that when he went to Lasater, he overstated his debt by $4,000 and pocketed the difference — a fact that has been well-documented by other chroniclers of Clintonian follies.

Lasater is a not unimportant figure in the history of the Clinton family. A controversial Little Rock investment banker and racehorse owner, he was introduced to the Clinton brothers in the late 1970s through his racetrack friendship with Virginia Kelley. By the early 1980s, Lasater was providing significant support to Mr. Clinton's gubernatorial campaigns and employed Roger as a stable hand. Roger, charged with conspiracy to distribute cocaine in 1985, cut a deal and testified against Lasater. They both served relatively brief jail terms. The reader of this book, however, learns virtually nothing about this. One gets the impression that Roger wanted to purge his conscience without really spilling the beans.

Where Roger could have given us some insight — about his time behind bars — he regales us instead with diary entries of bone-crunching dullness. His prison journal mostly sounds like a 12-year-old writing home from camp. Roger opens his mail. Roger washes his clothes. Roger makes friends with a convicted murderer. Compulsory daily readings of Roger's "Prison Proverbs" could prove more effective as sheer punishment than serving time in an Arkansas jail. "Never brag on what you can do," reads one, "unless you can brag on what you do!"

The second half of the book, which might be called Roger Goes to Hollywood, is not much better. In 1991 Roger began work on the set of "Designing Women," produced by Clinton cronies Harry Thomason and Linda Bloodworth-Thomason. Of the latter, Roger notes that — with her "take-no-prisoners attitude" — she "is the kind of person you want working with you and not against you. In that respect, she's a lot like Hillary." Later he spars with Rush Limbaugh on the set of "Hearts Afire."

Of course the big event in the book's second half is Inauguration Day. Roger watches with "pride and awe" as Bubba undergoes a startling transformation into President Bill Clinton. Preceded by 10,000 Maniacs, Roger performs at the MTV inaugural gala, then hangs out with Barbra Streisand.

"Growing Up Clinton" has its amusing moments, but generally it is unsatisfying. Characters are not portrayed in depth, and even references to Roger's own anguished journey are cloyingly saccharine. Apparently Roger didn't want to write a kiss-and-tell expose of the presidential tribe. Even so, he might have given us a more interesting glimpse into their world.

Ms. Perignon is a free-lance writer and radio commentator based in New York.

REVIEW & OUTLOOK

BCCI Opening

Because nearly everyone else has forgotten, we always have to apologize for our continued interest in the Bank of Credit & Commerce International – instead of more contemporary scandals such as Bob Packwood's boorishness or Newt Gingrich's book deal. All that BCCI represents, after all, is the prototypical 21st century criminal enterprise. A stateless entity, it ripped off depositors worldwide of $10 billion, laundered money, corrupted governments, and consorted with terrorists and drug dealers. In the U.S., BCCI crooks somehow managed to acquire the biggest bank in the nation's capital, as well as banks in at least six other states.

The global struggle with corruption, further, is one of the most dramatic stories of our time. Money scandals have contributed to the collapse of governments in Italy, Japan and France. Drug pushers with Pharaonic pretensions influence councils of state in Colombia, Mexico, Nigeria and Thailand. Powerful criminal gangs are on the rise in Russia and China. The life blood of all these enterprises, of course, is money; the international banking system is at once particularly vulnerable to, and a potentially important checkpoint against, criminal cartels.

So we'd like to know precisely what happened with BCCI, in particular how it managed to penetrate American banking. And we do not know, at least to our satisfaction. At the head of their U.S. effort, the Arabs and Pakistanis running BCCI placed Washington icon Clark Clifford and his partner, Robert Altman, to run companies controlling First American Bank in Washington. Movers and shakers in both parties became the beneficiaries of BCCI's largesse. Naturally, this created a strong incentive to downplay the entire affair when the bank came to a screeching halt in 1991.

This effort has been a great success. When criminal charges were brought by Manhattan District Attorney Robert Morgenthau, Mr. Clifford was dropped from the case due to age and infirmity. Mr. Altman was acquitted at a criminal trial in New York; precisely why is difficult to ascertain because under curious and probably unconstitutional New York law the testimony is sealed. While various legal proceedings limped on, the journalistic community soon lost interest in murky and complex charges. Case closed, it would seem.

Clark Clifford

In the depths of August, though, came proof of the adage that it ain't over until it's over. In a civil case against Mr. Clifford and Mr. Altman and others in U.S. District Court for the District of Columbia, Judge Joyce Hens Green dismissed procedural motions to throw out charges for common law fraud, misconduct, conspiracy and racketeering. She threw out objections that the trustee bringing the action was exceeding his authority; that First American lacked standing; that the statute of limitations had run; that the plaintiffs failed to adequately state the charges against them. Judge Green turned thumbs down on all the arguments and ordered the BCCI case to move swiftly to discovery and trial.

Robert Altman

That's big news for anyone who professes to be concerned about big-time corruption. A civil trial opens up an avenue for finally getting to the truth about BCCI. We would like to know a lot more, for example, about how Mr. Clifford and Mr. Altman got the Federal Reserve to approve the acquisition of First American by BCCI front men. There have been suggestions, for example, that the New York jury acquitted Mr. Altman because it concluded the Fed was not deceived, but knew who the true owners were.

The civil suit now headed to trial is the result of the diligence of the First American trustee, Harry Albright, with the help of Mr. Morgenthau and the Justice Department. The suit has already netted some $350 million in settlements, including $239 million from Sheik Zayed bin Sultan and other parts of the royal household of Abu Dhabi, $27 million from Kamal Adham, formerly intelligence adviser to the king of Saudi Arabia, and $10 million from Khalid bin Mahfouz, one of Saudi Arabia's leading bankers. Including the sale of First American Bank, Mr. Albright and his associates have recovered some $1.4 billion for the trust funds to repay defrauded parties world-wide.

As we keep noting, there are also numerous intriguing conjunctions between the BCCI history and the Whitewater scandal that besets President Clinton. BCCI's first attempt to acquire First American, for example, was put together in Arkansas by investment giant Stephens Inc. Jack Ryan, one of the Fed officials most involved in approving the First American acquisition, was (and still is) head of the Resolution Trust Corp. when RTC investigator Jean Lewis pressed her case against Madison Guaranty, the Whitewater S&L. And while there's no evidence that BCCI was connected to activities at Arkansas's Mena airport, both seem to have involved the same netherworld of money laundering, drugs and intelligence agencies.

Congressional committees, even under Republican control, have been leery of opening the broader aspects of Whitewater. Perhaps this is because Senator D'Amato has turned statesman, or perhaps it's because a wider investigation would tar not only Democrats but Republicans. The GOP needs to recognize that voters disgusted with Washington want someone to clean house and let chips fall where they may, and will find somewhere else to turn if Republicans don't deliver.

Beyond Washington and outside of partisan politics, though, people like Harry Albright doggedly pursue their own duties. If we ever do learn the full story of BCCI and the rest, it will be because the diversity of our governing system gives it a profound strength.

REVIEW & OUTLOOK

Henry Comes Through

Federal District Judge Henry Woods, the Clinton crony who once wanted Hillary to run for governor when Bill was undecided, lit up the week by throwing out one of the indictments of Arkansas Governor Jim Guy Tucker. The tax fraud allegations weren't connected to Whitewater, he ruled, and therefore Independent Counsel Kenneth Starr didn't have the authority to prosecute.

Though the Supreme Court upheld the constitutionality of the independent counsel law, Judge Woods adopted the logic of the lone dissenter. "While Justice Scalia's dissent did not carry the day in Morrison v. Olson, he made some highly pertinent observations about the officials having supervision over the independent counsel. He or she is responsible to no elected officials, but only to a panel of three appointed members of the Federal judiciary."

Henry Woods

Those of us who agreed with Justice Scalia at the time can only find this hilarious. As it happens, though, the law went the other way. Indeed, Mr. Starr's grant of authority says that he is to investigate Whitewater, Madison Guaranty, Capital Management Services and the rest, and that in addition, he has authority to investigate "violation of any federal criminal law, other than a Class B or C misdemeanor or infraction, by any person or entity developed during the Independent Counsel's investigation referred to above and connected with or arising out of that investigation."

Mr. Starr investigated, and out of that investigation came the tax fraud indictment of Governor Tucker and two others. For that matter, the dismissed indictment does involve Capital Management, since it alleges that Mr. Tucker submitted a bogus loan application there, then used the funds to buy and later sell a cable television company, allegedly conspiring to evade paying taxes on the sale.

Judge Woods, though, managed to read the above sentences concerning authority as saying that Mr. Starr is limited to prosecuting only crimes directly connected to Whitewater Development and other

Paula Casey

named entities. He says that for things such as tax fraud, "jurisdiction was vested in the Attorney General or the United States Attorney for the Eastern District of Arkansas."

Now, Judge Woods should never have been sitting on this case, as we argued back on June 21. He's been active in Democratic Party politics in Arkansas for more than 40 years, and developed particularly close relations with Mrs. Clinton when he appointed her to a citizens' committee in his long-running school desegregation case. The Tucker case, we noted, was "pregnant with implications for the President, the First Lady and the whole circle of the judge's friends and associates."

Judge Woods now suggests that the Tucker prosecution be referred to the U.S. Attorney. Namely, Paula Casey, the former Clinton campaign worker appointed to the Little Rock post after the incoming Administration took the unprecedented step of removing all sitting U.S. Attorneys at a swoop. Ms. Casey did receive the criminal referrals from the Resolution Trust Corp. naming the Clintons and Mr. Tucker as possible beneficiaries of criminal acts. She refused them, though Mr. Starr's Whitewater indictments follow them closely. She also rejected plea bargain attempts from David Hale of Capital Management. After this, and in the midst of a flurry of Executive Branch contacts concerning the referrals, Ms. Casey recused herself from the Madison case.

Instead of relying on Ms. Casey to prosecute the governor, Mr. Starr is appealing Judge Woods's decision to the Eighth U.S. Circuit

Court in St. Louis. The chief judge of the Eighth Circuit is Richard Arnold, another Arkansan with strong political ties to the President. Judge Arnold has been widely regarded as one of Bill Clinton's short-list candidates for a Supreme Court seat. At Senate hearings, David Watkins testified that Judge Arnold recommended Patsy Thomasson's appointment to the White House staff.

Down in Arkansas, there's nothing here but business as usual. Commenting on our earlier editorial, Democrat-Gazette columnist John Brummett conceded there were powerful reasons for Judge Woods to recuse himself, but that if he did, a Republican judge might get the case, and there is no reason Democrats should "unilaterally disarm." The notion of judicial independence, it seems, is entirely foreign to the state. Mr. Starr really ought to seek a change of venue, moving the Whitewater prosecutions to, say, Minnesota.

Judge Woods's ruling, by the way, came in the face of a brief supporting Mr. Starr from Janet Reno's Justice Department. In the wake of the ruling, the Attorney General has the authority simply to co-appoint Mr. Starr as her special counsel, as she originally appointed Robert Fiske. Or more simply, she has authority to ask the independent counsel court to expand Mr. Starr's jurisdiction to include the Tucker matters. One way or another, Attorney General Reno could solve the Henry Woods problem by the end of the week.

Review & Outlook

A Grueling Job

"I'm running out of gas," White House counsel Abner Mikva told the Associated Press after his resignation was announced yesterday, "I feel good, but this is a grueling job."

Evidently so, since Judge Mikva is the third prominent counsel burned out by the Clinton White House. Bernard Nussbaum went down in flames to protect Maggie Williams, Patsy Thomasson and the rest of the White House staff. Lloyd Cutler sagely signed up as a temp, departing as soon as another reassuring name could be landed. Mr. Mikva said he told President Clinton of resignation plans in mid-July, but promised to stay until a replacement was found. He said the new counsel, Jack Quinn, currently chief of staff for Vice President Al Gore, was a surprise choice in recent days.

Mr. Mikva's job has been especially grueling, however, just this week. On Monday, Mr. Nussbaum drew the line at playing fall guy, issuing a statement saying it was "preposterous" to suggest he was responsible for withholding Vincent Foster's handwritten notebook on the Travelgate scandal. This suggestion arose in a letter from Mr. Mikva to Chairman William Clinger of the House Committee on Government Reform and Oversight. Yesterday, the day of the resignation, was also the deadline Chairman Clinger had set for the White House either to produce a disputed set of documents or offer a formal claim of executive privilege.

Mr. Clinger has identified 907 pages of withheld documents; 507 remained outstanding after Mr. Mikva delivered a first installment.

So merely for illustrative purposes, let's trace the Foster notebook:

Mr. Nussbaum took the Travelgate notebook from Mr. Foster's briefcase two days after his death, during the famous search in which investigators were not allowed to examine papers. This was the same briefcase in which Mr. Foster's torn-up note was discovered, and the one Ms. Thomasson testified she peeked into during her visit to Mr. Foster's office the night of his death.

The notebook was in the White House counsel's office from July 22, 1993, to April 5, 1995, when it was delivered to Independent Counsel Kenneth Starr. Mr. Mikva said it and related documents were made available for review by "interested members of the press" after July 6, 1995. Shortly thereafter it was mentioned in Newsweek.

Abner Mikva

"We were stunned to learn of the existence of this document," reads a Justice Department memo by Michael E. Shaheen Jr., head of the Office of Professional Responsibility. He'd learned that it included a line-by-line response to the FBI report on the Travel Office; before resigning as Deputy Attorney General, Philip Heymann had directed OPR to review the performance of the FBI and try to learn what Mr. Foster meant in writing that "the FBI lied in their report to the AG." But the Newsweek story was the first hint of a handwritten critique of the report.

"We believe that our repeated requests to White House personnel and counsel for any information that could shed light on Mr. Foster's statement regarding the FBI clearly covered the notebook, and that even a minimum level of cooperation by the White House should have resulted in its disclosure to us at the outset of our investigation," Mr. Shaheen wrote. He cited previous complaints of lack of cooperation, describing the notebook as "yet another example," and added a footnote that "ours may not have been the only investigation" to draw this response.

For nearly a year, in short, the White House stonewalled official investigators over a clearly relevant document. Grueling work indeed. And assuming Republican probers ever get their act together, there will be more ahead. The White House's dwindling credibility raises the questions of what further documents are still undisclosed, and the record of Senator Alfonse D'Amato's Whitewater hearings is littered with intriguing leads.

To wit: Two folders from the National Security Agency Mr. Foster kept in a safe in the Counsel's suite. Also two manila envelopes addressed to Attorney General Janet Reno and "eyes only" to since-departed Associate White House Counsel William Kennedy, a partner with Mr. Foster, Mrs. Clinton and Webster Hubbell at the Rose Law Firm. What were in these documents, and whatever became of them?

The redoubtable Senator Lauch Faircloth has also noticed that on the day of Mr. Foster's death Mrs. Clinton arrived unannounced in Little Rock; the White House has refused his request for her flight plan and phone records. The White House has also refused phone records in the matter of Helen Dickey, the Clinton babysitter who phoned a report of the Foster death to the governor's mansion in Little Rock, possibly prior to the time the body was discovered in Fort Marcy Park. Perhaps all of these matters can be cleared up easily, but if so, why not release the documents?

The innocent explanation is that this White House stonewalls as a matter of routine. The records of Hillary Clinton's health care task force, for example, were pried out in extended litigation that sent Judge Royce Lamberth ballistic. And, of course, there is the grand-daddy of missing Whitewater documents, the records Susan MacDougal said were delivered to the Clinton governor's mansion. Perhaps stonewalling has a genetic explanation.

On the other hand, perhaps Judge Mikva got a peek at what was in some of the remaining documents, and saw ahead a still more grueling job.

REVIEW & OUTLOOK

Who Is Jack Quinn?

We explained yesterday that the resignation of White House Counsel Abner Mikva came as controversy again swelled over documents the White House withheld from investigators. Now let us introduce his replacement, John M. "Jack" Quinn, a man who believes the trouble in the White House is that former Counsel Bernard Nussbaum was too forthcoming with investigators.

The newly appointed counsel, it turns out, has already been deposed by Congressional investigators looking into the Whitewater mess and the handling of the papers in Vincent Foster's office. Mr. Quinn describes a conversation in which he was dispatched by then Chief of Staff Thomas "Mack" McLarty to find out how Mr. Nussbaum intended to handle the search of the Foster office. Mr. Quinn reports that he objected to Mr. Nussbaum's plans to accommodate the investigators. He said Park Police investigators should not be allowed in the Foster office until the White House Counsel's office had vetted everything there.

Jack Quinn

In the event, Mr. Nussbaum compromised between Mr. Quinn's absolutist viewpoint and the needs of investigators by having the Park Police stand in the corner while he reviewed the documents. It worked fine, Mr. Quinn reported Mr. Nussbaum telling him afterward. Evidently so, since the long-distance scrutiny of the Park

Police did not prevent the White House from concealing from investigators Mr. Foster's handwritten notebook on the Travel Office scandal, taken from his briefcase during the search.

The most recent controversy concerned 907 pages of withheld documents identified by Rep. William Clinger's Committee on Government Reform and Oversight. Yesterday Chairman Clinger reached agreement with Mr. Mikva on a schedule for delivering most of the remaining documents. After Mr. Quinn takes over Nov. 1, he will carry his absolutist views into such discussions; indeed, we have no doubt that's why he's been named to the post. We hope the celebrated Confederate general wouldn't mind if we appropriate his nickname for Stonewall Quinn.

The first three Clinton White House counsels — Mr. Nussbaum, Mr. Mikva and Lloyd Cutler — had each built distinguished careers in the law. Mr. Quinn is a longtime partner in Arnold & Porter, and also obviously a political animal to his core. He's been adviser to numerous Democratic political candidates, and a participant in many of the political meetings at the current White House. He is precisely the kind of man you might want on a sensitive mission such as talking to Mr. Nussbaum the morning of the office search, or tending the White House Counsel's office as an election year approaches.

"It was not unusual for McLarty to have asked me to take on special assignments. This had happened on other matters," he explained to questioners who asked why he was sent to Mr. Nussbaum. Indeed. As he prepares to become the top White House lawyer, Whitewater investigators might want to ask what special assignments he may have undertaken in the fall of 1993, when the Whitewater story was starting to break in earnest.

Below, for example, we have an extract of the incoming message log of Webster Hubbell, then Associate Attorney General and now a convicted felon. Jim Lyons, the Denver lawyer who managed to bury the Whitewater issue during the Presidential campaign, called the number-three official of the Justice Department, instructing him to bring documents to a lunch with vice-presidential aide Jack Quinn. Mr. Lyons further left word that he was meeting with Presidential confidant Bruce Lindsey.

We of course have no idea what documents were being passed from the Justice Department to the White House to the Whitewater defense expert, or Hubbell-to-Quinn-to-Lyons. We do know that the date of Mr. Lyons's call, October 27, 1993, was the same date that Paula Casey, the Clintons' handpicked U.S. Attorney in Little Rock, rejected the first criminal referral concerning the Arkansas political elite's involvement in Madison Guaranty Savings & Loan.

We inquired about this yesterday, and White House spokesman Mark Fabiani reported that Mr. Quinn did recall the lunch, that it was social, and that he neither saw nor discussed any documents that Mr. Hubbell might have had with him. Mr. Fabiani added that Mr. Hubbell did pass documents to Mr. Lyons, and noted that in the past Mr. Hubbell had said they were related to Whitewater.

Perhaps Mr. Quinn could also be asked about a series of phone calls to Webster Hubbell on December 20, 1993, at the same time Mr. Hubbell was taking calls from the Fosters' personal attorney, Mr. Foster's widow, and others. Simultaneously, the Clintons' personal lawyer, David Kendall, was requesting that Justice issue a subpoena for Foster documents that had been turned over to him, meeting the letter of the law while effectively walling them off from public view.

We look forward to getting to know Mr. Quinn better, and we hope our feeling is shared by the relevant committees on Capitol Hill.

Editorial Feature

The Whitewater Story?
What Whitewater Story?

By L. Brent Bozell III

One has to wonder why the national news media — particularly the television networks — that so relished investigating and reporting any and all allegations against the Reagan administration, no matter how unfounded, have so pathetically rolled over with this Democratic administration.

Hillary Clinton

I refer, of course, to the alphabet soup of political scandals surrounding Bill and Hillary Clinton, the mere mention of which will cause liberals reading this piece to roll their eyes in disbelief: There go the conservatives again with their wild conspiracy theories. Anyone demanding media coverage is excoriated for having a political "agenda" by a press corps that has no stomach for the story. It is not only that the media refuse to investigate the past (everything before Mr. Clinton's election is somehow deemed irrelevant) — they are refusing to cover what is unfolding before their very eyes.

Last week Abner Mikva, President Clinton's third White House counsel in three years, abruptly resigned after less than a year on the job. A former member of Congress and former chief judge of the U.S. Court of Appeals in Washington, Mr. Mikva had told the Washington Times earlier that he would remain at least through the end of the president's first term. Eleven months later he announces, "I'm running out of gas," and is gone.

The national news media accepted that explanation without reservation. Brief stories announcing Mr. Mikva's resignation appeared in all the major dailies (The Wall Street Journal ran a 163-word report) as well as on CNN and in U.S. News & World Report. ABC, CBS, NBC, Time and Newsweek didn't bother reporting anything at all. But something is wrong with taking that explanation at face value. One week before Mr. Mikva's announcement, the White House had been rocked by yet another scandal. It was revealed that Mr. Mikva's predecessor, Bernard Nussbaum, had taken key documents pertaining to the Travelgate scandal out of Vince Foster's briefcase after his death and that the White House had hidden them from investigators for two years, something that Mr. Mikva would want no part in.

Is this a reach? Are they two completely different stories connected only in the twisted minds of conspiracy buffs? Perhaps, and if that's true it would be correct for the news media to deal with them separately. But a search of the records shows that none of the networks devoted a single story on their evening newscasts to the new Travelgate bombshell; nor did most major newspapers, the Journal included, cover it as a news story.

What explains this silence? Let's dig deeper into the excuse file. How about: This is a very serious accusation and the media would be irresponsible to run allegations without a formal accusation, no matter how tangible the evidence may appear. Well, that's certainly a convenient post-Reagan rewrite of the journalistic rules of engagement, but for argument's sake let's legitimize that rationale.

Remember Jean Lewis? She was the lead Resolution Trust Corp. investigator whose riveting testimony this summer before the congressional committee investigating Whitewater included a formal charge that the administration was obstructing justice. Mr. Clinton's Democratic allies tried to question her credentials, but they are impeccable; they tried to impugn her motives but found them unimpeachable. And this wasn't closed testimony. It was covered live by C-SPAN and PBS. What did our hallowed news media think about that? The networks did only one story each, none of them leading the newscasts; and no network chose to explore this charge with an investigation of its own. Among the news magazines, there was nothing in U.S. News, a paragraph in Time and 500 words in Newsweek under the headline "An End In Sight (Maybe)." Contrast this with the feverish 13-year investigation of the "October Surprise" nonevent by many of these same organizations.

Let's try another line of defense, the one we hear constantly from Clinton apologists like Eleanor Clift: The public just doesn't care about this Whitewater stuff. That may be true, but then again, the surveys show the public had the same indifference to the Iran-Contra affair before the infamous hearings. While we're at it, Richard Nixon was re-elected in the largest electoral landslide in history in the midst of the Watergate investigation. Does it follow, then, that these liberal pundits would maintain these stories should not have been investigated for lack of public interest?

Or maybe it's because this Whitewater business just isn't "newsworthy" – during the hearings this past summer there were more important news items that simply bumped the scandal off the news media's radar screen. What earth-shattering events bumped Whitewater while the hearings were in progress? On Aug. 2, CNN World News reported nothing on Whitewater but did deem it important to cover a story on the benefits of soy-based tofu food products; on Aug. 10, the same network opted not to cover the hearings in favor of stories like Joe Namath's donation of pantyhose to a Planet Hollywood restaurant. The network morning news shows were even worse. These programs regularly declined to report on the hearings in favor of more important items like rollerblading technique in New York City; the art of catching butterflies; women who smoke cigars; and an Elvis convention in Mississippi.

No, the principal reason the news media have spiked the Clinton scandals is their utter disdain for the emerging conservative press, those Rep. Henry Hyde (R., Ill.) once labeled as "the great unwashed" in the eyes of the liberal elite in Washington. If Rush Limbaugh & Co. think it's important, they won't touch it.

But this story just won't go away and is getting out in spite of the network news blackout. It is being covered meticulously by the Washington Times, The American Spectator and on the Journal's editorial page. A couple of other newspapers deserve an honorable mention for occasional stories: the Washington Post and the Los Angeles Times.

The most prominent venue for coverage of the continuing Clinton scandals is, of course, talk radio. Talk show hosts nationwide refuse to buckle under the intimidation from the liberal national news media, and continue to report the story the networks do not want the public to hear. This helps explain why the talk format is now the most popular programming option on AM radio, and why seven of the nine most popular talk show hosts in the country are conservatives — at a time when the mainstream media (print and network news) are losing audiences. It also explains why they, along with the afore-mentioned print outlets, are Public Enemy No. 1 in the eyes of the ever-more-embattled Clinton administration.

Mr. Bozell is chairman of the Media Research Center.

Editorial Feature

Arkansas Judge Runs the Clock On Whitewater

By MICAH MORRISON

"Dear Vince," U.S. District Judge Henry Woods wrote the late Deputy White House Counsel Vincent Foster in July 1993. The judge had been approached by a reporter; she wanted to interview him about Hillary Clinton. "I have not responded to her phone calls, as I mentioned to you on the phone. Today I received the enclosed letter. Would you take this up with Hillary or her press secretary and give me instructions as to whether this interview should be granted?"

The judge seeking "instructions" about press coverage of the first lady is the same judge whose rulings in the Whitewater trial of Arkansas Gov. Jim Guy Tucker are now under appeal by Independent Counsel Kenneth Starr. Last month, Judge Woods threw out Mr. Starr's indictments of Gov. Tucker and two associates for defrauding the government in a scheme linked to David Hale's Capital Management Services. The judge held that Mr. Starr exceeded his jurisdiction, even though his mandate includes a clause authorizing him to pursue any crimes "arising out of" his probe of Madison Guaranty S&L, the Whitewater Development Co., or Capital Management. Mr. Starr has appealed to the Eighth Circuit Court in St. Louis.

In Arkansas, the political family looks out for one another. And as already reported, Judge Woods has a longstanding relationship with Bill and Hillary Clinton. The judge also was a longtime associate of the late Arkansas political kingmaker Witt Stephens, founder of investment giant Stephens Inc., and Sen. Dale Bumpers, among others. His financial disclosure statements include a trading account at Stephens Inc. and shareholdings in Worthen Bank. In 1987, Judge Woods appointed Mrs. Clinton as counsel to a special panel on desegregation cases, and wanted her to run for governor herself when Bill was doubtful. More recently, according to reports in the Arkansas press, he was an overnight guest at the White House the night of the 1994 midterm elections.

Judge Woods's ruling on Mr. Starr's jurisdiction is merely one of the legal fronts being contested in Arkansas courts. A second round of fraud and conspiracy charges against Gov. Tucker and former Madison owners James and Susan McDougal are being heard by another judge, George Howard Jr. Last week lawyers for Gov. Tucker lobbed a dozen procedural smoke bombs into Judge Howard's chambers, including motions to dismiss the second round of charges on grounds that the independent counsel law is unconstitutional and that Mr. Starr has again exceeded his jurisdiction, though the Supreme Court upheld the basic provisions of the independent counsel law in a 7-1 decision.

Henry Woods

The appeal of Judge Woods's decision is being heard by the Eighth Circuit Court in St. Louis, whose chief judge is another Arkansan, presidential golfing buddy Richard Arnold. The Eighth Circuit also is considering appeals in the Paula Jones sexual harassment case; in December, a Little Rock judge decided the case could be delayed until after the president leaves office. In an interview yesterday, Judge Arnold said he had recused himself from both cases. "I don't plan to sit on any cases in which the independent counsel appears," he added.

Judge Arnold, Judge Woods and Judge Howard were appointed to their present positions back in 1979, in what was then known as "the three-way deal." Sen. Bumpers brokered the deal on behalf of his good pal Henry when a new judgeship was created for the Eastern District of Arkansas. The senator persuaded President Jimmy Carter to elevate Judge Arnold from the Eastern District to the Eighth Circuit, allowing Mr. Carter to honor a campaign pledge of more black judges by naming Mr. Howard to the new judgeship and giving Mr. Woods the second vacancy.

Judge Woods could, of course, recuse himself from the Tucker lawsuit, which after all was brought by an independent counsel appointed to investigate his friends the Clintons. Judge Arnold has taken that course. Earlier, William Wilson, another U.S. District Judge in Little Rock, recused himself from the sentencing of former Associate Attorney General Webster Hubbell, citing the need to preserve not only justice but "the appearance of doing justice." Mr. Starr has the option of seeking a writ of mandamus forcing the judge to recuse himself, though this would be another time-consuming set of proceedings.

Paula Casey, named U.S. Attorney for the Eastern District after the Clinton administration abruptly fired all sitting U.S. Attorneys, did finally recuse herself from the Whitewater cases. But only after rejecting the Madison criminal referrals naming the Clintons as possible beneficiaries and witnesses, and rebuffing the plea-bargain offers of Mr. Hale. And Mr. Hubbell was delivering Whitewater documents to Clinton damage-control operatives even after he had recused himself from Whitewater. In his guilty plea for felonious billing at the Rose Law Firm, Mr. Hubbell agreed to cooperate with prosecutors, but Mr. Starr took no action to reduce his sentence as a reward for cooperation.

Judge Woods is likely to be overruled eventually, and indeed faces a series of rulings that would blacken his judicial reputation. But he is already on senior status and near the end of his career, and as close Arkansas observers understand, the game is to run out the clock. The procedural maneuvers push any denouement closer and closer to two deadlines: In April 1996, the statue of limitations expires on bank fraud offenses connected to Madison. And in November 1996, voters are scheduled to vote on giving President Clinton a second term.

Mr. Morrison is a Journal editorial page writer.

REVIEW & OUTLOOK

Whither Whitewater?

Whitewater hasn't been rushing, but it continues to bubble. Independent Counsel Kenneth Starr's Arkansas prosecutions are in procedural holding patterns, and the Senate Banking Committee is planning new hearings, replowing the contacts between the White House and Treasury. The statute of limitations expires in April, and Bill Clinton will run for a second term in November. We may well go into the campaign with important questions still unanswered, or for that matter unasked.

The most important question does not concern what happened in the Ozarks 10 years ago, but what happened in Washington during Mr. Clinton's Presidency. The pressing concern is not the Whitewater Development Co. land scam or the looting of Madison Guaranty Savings & Loan, though those are alleged crimes worthy of Mr. Starr's investigation. But the Senate has its own calling different from a court of law. It should be turning its attention not to legal technicalities, but to a grander political theme. To wit: Did the President and his associates abuse the highest office in the land to cover up transgressions in Arkansas? Indeed, was suppressing Whitewater and the like the theme unifying the basic architecture of the Clinton Administration?

Former Associate Attorney General Webster Hubbell, now a confessed felon, was after all the Administration's legal cornerstone. His Rose Law Firm partners, the late Vincent Foster and the departed William Kennedy, ran interference at the White House Counsel's office. White House Counsel Bernard Nussbaum is also departed, as present White House Counsel Abner Mikva soon will be. Roger Altman, the Deputy Treasury Secretary who was also regulating thrifts as head of the Resolution Trust Corp. has also departed, along with Treasury General Counsel Jean Hanson and for that matter Treasury Secretary Lloyd Bentsen. The question is, whatever was going on here?

Now, recall that concerns were growing about Whitewater as early as March 1993, only two months after the inauguration. An RTC probe of Madison was perking, and on March 24 Mr. Altman faxed press clips about Madison and Whitewater to Mr. Nussbaum. At the same time, Attorney General Janet Reno, acting on White House

orders, took the unprecedented step of firing every sitting U.S. Attorney in the land. The White House says it moved so abruptly because of pressure from Senators wanting to nominate their own candidates.

The Justice Department firings facilitated the appointment of Paula Casey, a longtime Clinton associate, as U.S. Attorney for the Eastern District of Arkansas. In this capacity she proceeded to reject the first RTC criminal referral on Madison. She also turned down plea bargain overtures from David Hale, a Clinton crony who was facing indictments for fraud involving his SBA-backed Capital Management Services, and who claimed to have information on the banking practices of the Arkansas political elite. After making these key decisions, she recused herself.

Al D'Amato

Much here demands explanation. Again, the Congress's job is oversight, not enforcing the criminal law. That oversight properly includes asking whether the powerful apparatus attached to the White House was bent to thwart justice. Senate hearings would let the officials concerned explain themselves, and allow the public to judge for itself. So far, however, Committee Chairman Alfonse D'Amato seems to have spent an inordinate amount of time adjudicating internal disputes and threatening to sic the FBI on staffers who talk to the press to inform the public. The public would profit if he regained some of the old fire he showed in the minority.

In the next round of hearings, we suggest, he should skip the small fry and call Attorney General Reno as the first witness. The country deserves an explanation as to how the decision was made to fire the U.S. Attorneys, and whether Webster Hubbell or any one else in the Clinton inner circle was involved.

The second witness should be Paula Casey, who should be asked if there were communications of any sort between her office and the Clinton White House and its operatives, particularly regarding the Madison referrals and the case of Mr. Hale. A prosecutor's decision not to prosecute is not normally reviewable in court, leaving it to the Senate to make such officials justify their decisions.

In addition, there is the general line of inquiry: What was Webb Hubbell up to at the Justice Department? Some of his phone records and appointments are now available. On August 31, 1993, for example, he met with Whitewater damage-control specialist Jim Lyons. On the same day, he was called twice by U.S. District Judge Henry Woods, a force to be reckoned with in Arkansas politics and a close friend of the Clintons.

Henry Woods, as it happens, presides over one of the cases brought by Mr. Starr against Arkansas Governor Jim Guy Tucker. Last month, he threw out Mr. Starr's indictment,

Kenneth Starr

arguing that the independent counsel had exceeded his jurisdiction. Judge Woods's move could delay proceedings past the statute of limitation for further indictments, an outcome that doubtless would mightily please the White House. Mr. Starr is appealing, and asking that Judge Woods be removed from the case given his ties to the Clintons. Certainly Judge Woods's action does not dispel the thought that officials have been abusing their powers to protect the Clintons.

Mr. Starr also asked that Sen. D'Amato delay the Whitewater hearings, saying he was worried they might disrupt "important investigative steps and crucial judgments in the upcoming weeks." Sen. D'Amato turned down the request, but offered to coordinate matters as much as possible. No doubt some of the committee Democrats, having first used the Independent Counsel to delay and limit hearings, would now love to use hearings to derail Mr. Starr, for example by compromising key witnesses. In the end, though, the Senate owes the public the responsibility of oversight.

From the first we've argued that the overriding priority is letting the public know how its government is being conducted. That remains the priority, but it won't be served by hearings narrowly conceived around issues of criminal responsibility. What the country needs are hearings conceived around commonly recognized notions of political accountability. There are plenty of reasons for the Senate to demand an account.

REVIEW & OUTLOOK

Travel Mysteries

Less than a month after he took office, President Clinton sat down with his old Hollywood pal Harry Thomason to discuss a $500,000 sole-source contract for an air charter company that Mr. Thomason partly owned. After this face-to-face lobbying, the President passed on the written proposal to senior White House staffers, checking a box labeled "ACTION" and adding a handwritten note: "These guys are sharp. Should discuss with Panetta and Lader" — that is, the director and deputy director of the OMB. The Thomason proposal for a celebrity set-aside rattled around the White House before being shelved in the wake of the Travel Office scandal involving the same Arkansas players.

We get this glimpse into the inner workings of the Clinton Administration because the House Oversight Committee under Rep. Bill Clinger finally held hearings this week on the mysterious May 1993 firings at the White House Travel Office. The hearings end two years of what Chairman Clinger calls "hide-and-seek" with relevant documents. Even today, Mr. Thomason is refusing to comply with document requests or to be interviewed by committee investigators.

In the Travel Office putsch, of course, the White House summarily fired seven longtime employees, indicating they were under criminal investigation. Catherine Cornelius, a 25-year-old Clinton cousin, was appointed to head the office. It seems the Thomason air charter firm, TRM Inc., had been rebuffed on overtures to run press charter flights. Soon afterward, Mr. Thomason told White House officials that Travel Office employees were accepting "kickbacks" and were "on the take." He had dinner with Hillary Clinton the night before auditors were called in to examine the Travel Office.

As criticism over the firings mounted, documents released to the Oversight Committee last month indicate, White House aides David Watkins and Patsy Thomasson asked Ms. Cornelius to lie if she was asked whether Mr. Watkins had read her memos suggesting that she take over the office. As for the firings, a 1993 White House review found they had been unfair and five of the workers were reinstated in other federal jobs. Billy Dale, former head of the office, goes on trial today on charges that he embezzled $55,000; he says the money went for purposes such as tips in moving press baggage. UltrAir, the firm that had been the subject of Mr. Thomason's "kickback" allegations, was cleared of wrongdoing in a two-year IRS audit that started a week after the firings.

William Clinger

In the early days of the Clinton Administration, both Mr. Thomason and his TRM partner Darrell Martens were given coveted White House passes. Mr. Martens came up with the idea of having TRM solicit a consulting project from the White House to audit the government's 1,874-aircraft civilian fleet and find ways to "revitalize" it. April memos to White House aide Bruce Lindsey asked that the President "issue an executive order" and "enter into a consulting agreement with TRM." The firestorm over the Travel Office firings came the next month, and the consulting project was formally shelved by White House Counsel Bernard Nussbaum shortly after Vincent Foster's death in July. Mr. Foster had been following the Travel Office affair and was deeply concerned about the White House's mishandling of it.

Given such petty machinations in executive corridors, it's understandable that Chairman Clinger is especially concerned with what he describes as "White House resistance to appropriate oversight." The Administration has stonewalled Rep. Clinger for months on turning over documents, and he has only now been told he can examine another 300 pages of relevant materials, perhaps including draft executive orders promoting Mr. Thomason's contract. One reason for the delays may be that the new deputy White House counsel is none other than Bruce Lindsey, the aide who was deeply involved in discussions over Mr. Thomason's contract.

The Chairman says the pattern was established when Mr. Nussbaum kept from investigators the Travel Office file compiled by Mr. Foster. This was finally turned over this summer. Michael Shaheen, head of the Justice Department's Office of Professional Responsibility, told the Oversight Committee this week that the White House's lack of "cooperation and candor" was "unprecedented."

Chairman Clinger says the stonewalling means that when both the executive and legislative branches are controlled by the same party the minority members of Congressional committees must be given their own subpoena powers. We hope he can sell this statesmanlike conclusion to the Republican majority. But it's also clear that this particular Administration has a lot to hide, that it entered the White House with habits of cronyism and corner-cutting carried from the governor's mansion in Arkansas.

REVIEW & OUTLOOK

Why the Mystery?

It is more than two years since Vincent Foster's body was discovered in Fort Marcy Park, and Senate hearings relating to his death will still be going on this week. A cloak of mystery still surrounds events before and after the death of President Clinton's former Deputy White House Counsel.

Tomorrow the Senate Banking Committee will recall Maggie Williams, Hillary Clinton's chief of staff, and Susan Thomases, the New York lawyer and adviser to the Clintons. The Committee was dissatisfied with their previous testimony concerning events after Mr. Foster's death. In its wider probe of the Whitewater land deal and related matters, it has also issued 49 subpoenas to parties at the White House and in Arkansas.

Vincent Foster

Senators want to explore the implications of newly released phone records, showing the following sequence of telephone calls on the morning of the official search of Mr. Foster's office, July 22, 1993: 7:44 to 7:51 EDT — from Ms. Williams to the Little Rock home where Mrs. Clinton was staying; 7:57 to 8:00 — from Mrs. Clinton to Ms. Thomases' hotel room in Washington; 8:01 — from Ms. Thomases to Bernard Nussbaum's pager at the White House. The records also show three calls by Ms. Thomases to Ms. Williams's office later that morning, three more from her to White House Chief of Staff Thomas "Mack" McLarty, and a call from Ms. Williams to Mrs. Clinton 20 minutes before the search began. This, of course, is when Mr. Nussbaum reneged on the previously reached agreement on ground rules for the search.

Ms. Thomases and Mr. Nussbaum have testified they did discuss the impending search that morning, with each insisting the other raised the issue. Mr. Nussbaum said Ms. Thomases told him that otherwise unidentified "people," were concerned about giving investigators "unfettered access." Ms. Thomases said her conversation with Mrs. Clinton that morning was an explanation of her decision not to attend the Foster funeral. Senators are naturally curious about why this conversation took place before 7 a.m. Little Rock time, and why she paged Mr. Nussbaum a minute later.

The suspicion that Mrs. Clinton ordered restrictions on the search of the Foster papers is further stoked by revelations in the Travel Office probe. A handwritten note, the White House listing David Watkins as the source, describes a May 14, 1993, phone conversation between Mr. Watkins and Mrs. Clinton: "Harry says his people can run things better; save money, etc., And besides, we need those people out — We need our people in — We need the slots."

Susan Thomases

All of these documents have had to be pried out of the White House. Michael E. Shaheen Jr. and Nancy Kingsbury, who reviewed the Travel Office affair for the Justice Department's Office of Professional Responsibility and the Office of Management and Budget, respectively, both complained about a lack of cooperation. Usually, Congressional document requests are enough to get White House material; the last two instances in which Congress felt full-fledged subpoenas necessary were a 1992 dispute over servicemen missing in action, and the Watergate scandal in 1973.

* * *

The day after Mr. Foster's death we wrote — to some ridicule — that in the confusion of multiple investigators, "A direct appointment such as special counsel within Justice would make clear who is in charge and directly responsible." If that advice had been heeded we would not now be left with an investigation with no crime scene photos, no X-rays of the wounds, and the FBI yet again visiting the park to seek the never-located bullet.

The lack of a vigorous initial investigation naturally leads to festering conspiracy theories. Given the unanswered questions and the by-now manifest inadequacy of the Fiske report, we're frankly happy to have Christopher Ruddy and James Dale Davidson and others pushing the envelope. But just as frankly, our checks with law enforcement sources we trust find that the handwriting analysts who argue the Foster note was a forgery are not widely known. Similar checks lead us to doubt reports that Mr. Foster made secretive trips to Geneva. We hope that Independent Counsel Kenneth Starr can provide some comfort about these items, as well as reports that witnesses have not been adequately interviewed, that a phone call about the death to the Arkansas governor's mansion came before the discovery of the body, and so on.

In the absence of any compelling evidence to the contrary, we continue to accept the simplest explanation, which is that Mr. Foster committed suicide in Fort Marcy Park, and that the missing links are the result of bungling in the midst of confusion. Clinical depression is distressingly real. We were initially put off when friends and relatives denied that Mr. Foster suffered from depression, but psychiatrists say such denial is common among bereaved. Subsequent recollections seem more compelling; we were especially impressed with Lisa Foster's account of her husband's depression in her interviews with Peter Boyer in the September 11 issue of The New Yorker.

* * *

Events following the death strike us as much more suspicious, however, and may shed some light on the question of what burdens weighed so heavily on Mr. Foster. Within hours, we know, his office was being searched by Mr. Nussbaum, Ms. Williams and longtime Arkansas operative Patsy Thomasson. A Secret Service guard has testified he saw Ms. Williams leaving the office with a stack of files and Ms. Williams has denied it. Ms. Thomasson testified that she peeked into Mr. Foster's briefcase the night of his death but did not see the famous torn-up note.

Park Police Sergeant Peter Markland has said that during the July 22 search, Mr. Nussbaum did not let him examine the briefcase, but looked into it and indicated it was empty. This was the day, we now know, that Mr. Nussbaum spirited from the briefcase the Foster

Travelgate diary, only now disclosed after two years. A Foster family lawyer, Michael Spafford, testified that on the same day he heard White House lawyer Clifford Sloan comment that he saw scraps of paper inside the briefcase; Mr. Nussbaum said he would get to it later. Deborah Gorham, Mr. Foster's secretary, testified that she told Mr. Nussbaum after the death that she had seen "something yellow" at the bottom of the briefcase and that Mr. Nussbaum had questioned her intensively about what exactly she had seen. The White House says the note was not discovered until July 24.

Ms. Gorham has also testified that a safe Mr. Foster used in the Counsel's suite contained two manila envelopes — one addressed "eyes only" to associate counsel and former Rose Law Firm partner William Kennedy III and the other to Attorney General Janet Reno — as well as two National Security Agency binders. These too seem to have vanished. There are also reports of another Foster "diary" said to be in the hands of the Foster family lawyer. Mr. Foster's office was never properly sealed, and a proper chain of custody was never established over the documents, which at one point Ms. Williams delivered to the White House family quarters.

*   *   *

Clearly, Mr. Foster's office, his papers and the possibility of a note were matters of anxiety. In her New Yorker interview, Mrs. Foster discusses one possible source of particular concern, rumors of an affair between her husband and Hillary Clinton. During the 1992 campaign, she reports, Mr. Foster gathered the family together to deny it. Mrs. Foster says, "I just have faith in Vince and faith in Hillary that they did not have an affair. If they did, who cares now? You know? Who cares? I sincerely believe that they didn't." Though every reporter covering Arkansas has heard these rumors, they are unsubstantiated and thus not widely reported; but they should at least be on record as something possibly on the minds of the trio visiting the Foster office.

More broadly and importantly, look at Mr. Foster's job. It was to clean up the Clintons' tangled finances so they could sustain some public scrutiny, and to defend such governmental practices as the Travel Office firings and the secrecy of the health care task force. The inner circle of the White House knew then and knows today that this was a series of hot buttons. And Mr. Foster and the Arkansas crowd probably had some sense that the road ahead was littered with land mines such as $100,000 commodity deals.

Indeed, we now have testimony that Linda Tripp, Mr. Nussbaum's secretary, complained to her boss about Mr. Foster spending "an inordinate amount of time" on the Clintons' personal finances. Ms. Tripp added that Ms. Gorham said she spent long hours working on, among other things, "a real estate matter for Mr. Foster." As the New Yorker's Mr. Boyer puts it, "it is reasonable to suppose that Foster was well aware the Clintons could face future political embarrassments over their Little Rock land deal." But the White House line, blandly echoed in the Fiske report, is that this was not on his mind at the time of his death.

There is one big reason, in short, that Mr. Foster's death remains cloaked in mystery after two years. To wit, from that night's visit to this week's hearings, the White House's inhabitants have acted like people with a lot to hide.

Editorial Feature

What's Ken Starr Looking For?

Have the president and first lady committed any crimes in connection with the Whitewater affair? This is the question Independent Counsel Kenneth Starr is charged with answering. What are the specific crimes Mr. Starr has under investigation and what would he need to find to charge either of the Clintons?

Let's begin with conspiracy, a crime often mentioned but rarely discussed with any precision. Federal law provides that "if two or more persons conspire . . . to commit any offense against the United States, and one or more of such persons do any act to effect the object of the conspiracy," each person is guilty of a felony.

Rule of Law

By Paul G. Cassell

Mr. Starr's indictment of James and Susan McDougal, along with Arkansas Gov. Jim Guy Tucker, illustrates the way in which prosecutors charge conspiracy.

The indictment alleges that, among other things, Mr. and Mrs. McDougal fraudulently obtained a $300,000 loan from Capital Management Services Inc., an investment company supported through Small Business Administration funding. Capital Management was run by David Hale and was authorized to make loans to socially or economically disadvantaged small businesses. In April 1986, it loaned $300,000 to "Susan McDougal d/b/a Master Marketing," a company the indictment alleges "was not in operation and had no ongoing business." Proceeds from the loan were deposited into the McDougals' joint account at Madison Guaranty Savings & Loan Association and diverted to personal purposes unrelated to Master Marketing and contrary to the loan documentation.

The press release from Mr. Starr's office takes pains to note that "the Indictment does not charge criminal wrongdoing by President William Jefferson Clinton or First Lady Hillary Rodham Clinton." The question that is worth examining here is what would Mr. Starr need to prove to broaden the conspiracy to include the Clintons?

On this score, the most serious allegation against Mr. Clinton (and indirectly against Mrs. Clinton) comes from Mr. Hale, who has pleaded guilty to fraud. He claims he was "pressured" by Mr. Clinton into making the illegal $300,000 loan. According to newspaper interviews of Mr. Hale, Mr. McDougal asked for help in clearing up some obligations involving "the political family." Later, Mr. Hale says Mr. Clinton asked him if he was going to be able to "help Jim and me out."

James McDougal

In February 1986, Mr. Hale met with Mr. McDougal and Mr. Clinton on how to structure a loan using Capital Management funds. "Bill said they could use some raw land in the Ozarks as collateral, but that his name couldn't appear on any of the documents," Mr. Hale recounted, although the land-for-collateral offer was not permitted under Small Business Administration regulations. As a result, again according to Mr. Hale, they all agreed to make a loan in the name of Susan McDougal, an agreement that culminated two months later in the $300,000 loan that forms the basis for the indictment. Mr. Hale is now cooperating with the Independent Counsel's office.

The White House says that Mr. Clinton has no recollection of any meeting with Mr. Hale about a loan. Mr. McDougal claims the meeting never occurred. But it is clear that, after the alleged February meeting, Mr. Hale loaned $300,000 to Mrs. McDougal in April. Ultimately $25,000 of the loan was used to fund part of a real estate purchase by Whitewater Development Company Inc., owned by the McDougals and the Clintons.

If Mr. Starr confirms Mr. Hale's story — plainly a big if — would a criminal conspiracy involving Mr. Clinton be proven? Not automatically. The critical question would be whether Mr. Clinton agreed to an unlawful loan. Mr. Hale's allegations provide some strong indications that a fraudulent loan was contemplated, notably Mr. Clinton's suggestions that his name not appear on the documents and that the loan be made in the name of Susan McDougal when the intended beneficiaries were others. But another possible interpretation is that Mr. Clinton understood the loan would be legitimate, thereby placing him outside the sweep of the conspiracy.

The conspiracy statute is probably the one Mr. Starr is spending the most time analyzing in connection with the Clintons' Whitewater activities in the 1980s. But what about allegations of more recent misconduct? The statute most commonly mentioned is obstruction of justice.

David Hale

Here, the most relevant statute provides that "whoever corruptly . . . influences, obstructs, or impedes . . . the due and proper administration of the law under which any pending proceeding is being had before any department or agency of the United States, or the due and proper exercise of the power of inquiry under which any inquiry or investigation is being had by" any congressional committee, shall be guilty of a felony.

How does this language apply to more recent Whitewater allegations? Among the most serious charges come from congressional testimony this summer by Resolution Trust Corp. investigator Jean Lewis. Supported by two supervisors, Ms. Lewis testified that she believed high-ranking government officials made "a concerted effort to obstruct, hamper and manipulate" her investigation of Madison. If Mr. Starr's office finds corroborating evidence — again, a big if — then obstruction charges against the responsible officials would be possible.

A complicated legal issue arises out of the possible obstruction of the investigation of Vincent Foster's suicide. Some have suggested that actions by Maggie Williams, Mrs. Clinton's chief of staff, impeded the investigation. Even assuming such allegations are true, would the investigation constitute a "proceeding" that could be obstructed within the terms of the statute? As to the Park Police investigation of the suicide, maybe not. Some courts have held that a mere police investigation is not a formal "proceeding" protected under the statute.

A related question is presented by the actions of former White House Counsel Bernard Nussbaum, who blocked Justice officials' investigation of Mr. Foster's office. Again assuming that Mr. Starr finds a corrupt motive, would the somewhat informal Justice investigation constitute a "proceeding" under the statute?

Mr. Starr will have to answer all these questions before considering criminal charges. Criminal law does not allow generalized accusations. If the president and Mrs. Clinton were to be charged, it would be on the basis of specific, provable criminal conduct, not speculation about conspiracy or obstruction. Sorting out the facts to determine who is responsible for what may turn out to be Mr. Starr's biggest challenge. It is also why he was appointed.

Mr. Cassell, a former federal prosecutor, is a professor at the University of Utah College of Law.

More Hearings

The Senate Whitewater Committee hearings ground on, despite opposition by committee Democrats and a White House spin effort to dismiss them as irrelevant and boring. By attempting to explore in detail the actions of White House operatives in handling information from confidential criminal referrals and in searching Vincent Foster's office, the Journal wrote, the Committee had "in fact focused on the critical Whitewater issue: the misuse of power by top Clinton Administration officials."

In November, a Washington jury indirectly offered its opinion on another apparent misuse of power, acquitting Billy Dale in less than two hours on charges that he embezzled $68,000 in White House Travel Office funds. In the House of Representatives, Rep. William Clinger's Government Reform and Oversight Committee pressed on with its effort to obtain Travel Office documents from the White House.

By December, Constitutional clashes over executive privilege loomed as Rep. Clinger and the Senate Whitewater Committee moved on separate tracks toward subpoenas in the face of continued White House stonewalling. The White House backed down from its fight with the Senate committee later in the month and produced former Associate White House Counsel and Rose Law Firm member William Kennedy's notes from a November 1993 Whitewater damage-control meeting. Mr. Kennedy's notes included the pregnant lines: "Vacuum Rose Law files WWDC [Whitewater Development Co.] Docs—subpoena+documents—never know go out—Quietly."

REVIEW & OUTLOOK

Irrelevant and Boring?

We have been watching the Senate's Whitewater hearings these past two weeks. So has White House lawyer Mark Fabiani. Mr. Fabiani's view is that the hearings have "reached new lows of boredom and irrelevance." That is, when career lawyers from the inspector general's office of the Treasury Department appear before a congressional hearing and testify that the department's high political appointees turned over confidential Treasury depositions to the White House in the middle of the review, this is "irrelevant and boring." If so, it is only by the standards common in Washington since January 1993.

Senator Alfonse D'Amato and his special Whitewater Committee have in fact focused on the critical Whitewater issue: the misuse of power by top Clinton Administration officials. And what we have learned from these important D'Amato hearings is that during this "irrelevant and boring" time frame, significant parts of the Clinton White House operation had put aside the nation's business to plug up holes popping in the Clinton dam and mop up what was relevant information spurting out of cracks in the bureaucracy.

The hearings have raised the following issues:

• Within 48 hours of Vincent Foster's death, top White House operatives leaned on the White House Counsel to block a Justice Department search of his office.

• Those same aides then developed memory loss and offered conflicting stories when questioned about their actions in the aftermath of the suicide.

- The Secretary of the Treasury conveyed to the White House Counsel transcripts containing confidential information about a criminal probe touching on the President and First Lady.

- Treasury officials passed confidential information about an internal department investigation to targets of the probe.

- Other Treasury officials could not remember discussions about providing the White House with confidential transcripts of witness depositions in advance of Congressional hearings.

Boring and irrelevant? Try this: Read back through that compendium and substitute names like Ed Meese and Don Regan and Nancy Reagan. These hearings would be running daily off the front pages, and the networks, now totally silent, would be pre-empting soap operas and Oprah to run live coverage.

This week, we heard testimony about then-Treasury Secretary Lloyd Bentsen turning over to then-White House Counsel Lloyd Cutler confidential transcripts from an internal Treasury probe of witnesses to the famous flurry of contacts between the White House, Treasury and the Resolution Trust Corp. in late 1993 over the Madison Guaranty criminal referrals.

Both Mr. Bentsen and Mr. Cutler testified this week that they saw nothing wrong with this, since they had agreed not to share the information with the witnesses and thus give them the opportunity to get their stories straight. But did they share the information with their boss, the President? We suppose some ethicist might untangle this casuistry.

The hearings also revealed this week that Francine Kerner, a Treasury lawyer, passed on information about the inspector general's Treasury probe to targets of the investigation, and we witnessed other Treasury officials fall victim to the dreaded Whitewater loss-of-memory affliction when questioned about contacts with the White House.

RTC officials testified this week that they were dumbfounded by Treasury's conduct. "I was astonished, and I was angry," said Patricia Black, general counsel to the RTC inspector general. "This was an investigation into Treasury's improper leaks to the White House and there they were doing it again."

Finally, let us convey your attention to events noted below, under the headline "(202) 628-7087." Susan Thomases and Maggie Williams, respectively external and internal White House operatives for Hillary Clinton, proved unable to explain a series of early-morning phone calls involving White House Counsel Bernard Nussbaum on July 22, 1993, two days after the death of Mr. Foster. Shortly after these calls, Mr. Nussbaum reneged on a pledge to allow Justice Department investigators to examine files in Mr. Foster's office. Ms. Thomases offers that she was merely calling to console people, but Senators last week produced letters from the White House showing that no staffers remembered talking to her.

We have previously said that we are prepared to accept, as the simplest explanation, the independent counsel's conclusion that Vincent Foster committed suicide. On the same basis, we have to conclude that Susan Thomases and Maggie Williams are lying.

We'd still like to know what it is these people are hiding. We now have testimony that they were in fact hiding something from career officials at the White House, Treasury, Justice and Resolution Trust Corp. We persist in thinking that if the answer can ever be pried out from the evasions and lies, it is not likely to be irrelevant, or boring.

---

(202) 628-7087

Does anyone know anything about this mysterious phone number? Bell Atlantic says it hasn't been in service since 1978. If you dial it today, you'll get a recording saying it's not in service. But someone seemed to be there on July 20, 1993.

At least it shows up in the list of phone records turned up by the Senate Whitewater Committee's investigation of the aftermath of the suicide of Vincent Foster. From the Tuesday discovery of the body through the Friday funeral, First Lady Hillary Clinton was staying at the Rodham household in Little Rock. The flurry of telephone calls from the Rodham home included a call to the mysterious (202) 628-7087 — ten minutes at 10:41 p.m. Little Rock time on July 20.

The list includes calls to Maggie Williams and Susan Thomases, as widely reported. Also to the Department of Justice Command Center (Webster Hubbell, perhaps) and Carpinteria, Calif., which is Harry

Thomason. There is also a 15-minute call on the 21st to someone staying at the Sunnyside Lodge in Tahoe City, Calif. But committee investigators are especially stumped by the unidentified Washington number.

The indefatigable Senator Lauch Faircloth displayed the number at the hearings and suggested that since Ms. Thomases and Ms. Williams couldn't explain it, perhaps Mrs. Clinton could. The first lady has not been forthcoming, so anyone with information about the mystery number should contact the Senator. Or fax us at (212) 416-2658, attention Editor.

Letters to the Editor

That Mysterious Number

In response to your Nov. 10 editorial "(202) 628-7087," the mysterious, out-of-service phone number that is on "a list of phone records turned up by the Senate Whitewater Committee's investigation of the aftermath of the suicide of Vincent Foster." A call was made to the mysterious (202) 628-7087 from the Rodham household in Little Rock for 10 minutes starting at 10:41 p.m. Little Rock time on July 20.

While I was in the military, I was engaged in special operations. From time to time we needed "anonymous phone numbers," ones that could not be traced back to any locale or identity. They were "dead" for all intents and purposes. It's quite easy for the government to establish such a number, even though the phone company may have no record of it. It is selected from a database of unassigned numbers. The number has no origin and no real terminus; it exists only in the cloud of the telecommunications infrastructure, and has the ability to ring anywhere in the world. Such numbers are routinely used by any number of federal agencies for purposes of "national security." The ability to track them down will prove futile because they do not exist.

What does this particular mysterious number indicate? Plain and simple: It was established by someone inside the White House administration for the purposes of "secure communications." Given that the top secret Health Care Task Force was in operation at the time, a search of the phone records of the task force possibly could yield the destination of the number or the identity of the person to whom it was assigned.

ROBERT K. MORGAN

Fairfield, Conn.

* * *

Perhaps, after dialing that number, a special code can be dialed to access "something more," such as occurred with the special software in the recent movie "The Net." If you know a computer hack with spare time and a spare phone line he may be able to write a program to try keypad combinations to break the code, if one exists.

FREDRIC M. STEINBERG, M.D.

Decatur, Ga.

* * *

The "mystery number" Hillary Clinton called on the day of Vince Foster's death was clearly identified during the Senate Whitewater hearings on Nov. 2. Calling this number allows you to then place a call that can't be traced by the phone company. If the folks at NYNEX offered such a service they might name it "call laundering." While I don't expect the mainstream press to investigate this inconvenient bit of intrigue, I'm disturbed that yours is the only news source in which I've seen even mention of it. Keep up the good work. Despite the media's nonreporting of yet another Whitewater bombshell, we "conspiracy nuts" keep growing in numbers.

RODNEY S. SCHECK

New York

* * *

There is nothing mysterious about this phone number. It is the phone number of the earth docking station for the planet Xenos. Now that you know, you can tell your fellow Republican nut cases on the Whitewater committee and they can issue subpoenas accordingly. I am looking forward to seeing you on the next night of the full moon, when your braying can do some good.

WILLIAM E. SCHRAMBLING

Martinez, Calif.

* * *

Applying your "simplest explanation" approach, I'll bet Socks, the Clintons' cat, knocked the phone off the hook and stepped on it, randomly pressing a bunch of numbers. Then I'll bet there was a power surge in Bell Atlantic's computer system, scrambling the numbers Socks dialed, inadvertently coming up with the mystery phone number. In the meantime, the party who really received Socks's call slipped on a banana peel in her kitchen, knocking herself out for those key 10 minutes. See? There's no mystery at all. When you look at it rationally, the only thing you have is a Republican witchhunt, trying to get the president by going after his wife.

DAVID I. THOMPSON

Cincinnati

* * *

It's very possible that you have finally uncovered Elvis Presley's number. Seems a little coincidental. Let's look at the facts:

1. Per official sources, neither number has been in service for a while.

2. Seems Brother Bill has been getting a little bigger lately. Somewhat like the King.

3. They are both from the same part of the country.

4. They are both into music. (Elvis was much better.)

Maybe we are onto something here. I'll let you guys take over from here, as I'm just an average taxpayer, not a Woodward or Bernstein. Let me know if this turns into something big.

JACK BITTNER

Coral Springs, Fla.

REVIEW & OUTLOOK

BCCI: The Memory Hole

Today in Federal District Court in Washington, Judge Joyce Hens Green will hear oral arguments on whether to take another step consigning the BCCI scandal to the memory hole. A state judge in Manhattan is considering yet another. Obviously, there are powerful

forces trying to rewrite history on the Bank of Credit & Commerce International so that the $10 billion heist never happened.

Meanwhile, Toshihide Iguchi managed to conceal a missing $1 billion from regulators in both Japan and the U.S., jeopardizing the existence of Daiwa Bank and unsettling relations between the two nations. And Great Britain, Germany and Singapore are still trying to figure out what to do about another stray $1 billion that went through the hands of Nicholas Leeson and did in

Robert Altman

Barings Bank of storied history. The bold suggestion here is that none of this might have happened if we'd ever got to the bottom of BCCI. More important still, the next few Iguchis and Leesons might not happen if we do so even now.

Accordingly, this newspaper has filed suit in New York state court to unseal the transcript of the trial that resulted in the acquittal of Robert Altman, who teamed with Clark Clifford to run First American Bank in Washington while it was secretly and illegally owned by BCCI. Against the common-law tradition that courts are public places, New York has a law sealing the records of criminal cases not proven beyond a reasonable doubt. But in sealing the Altman transcript, Judge John Bradley specified the seal would be lifted if the defendant sought further relief, which has now happened with Mr. Altman and Mr. Clifford seeking reimbursement of their legal fees from the trustee of the bank that was traduced while they headed it.

Our suggestion that the seal order needs clarification has produced results both outrageous and amusing. William Shields, a lawyer for Mr. Altman and Mr. Clifford, seemed able to keep a straight face while filing a motion requesting that his clients be referred to only as "Robert A." and "Clark C." – presumably to protect fragile egos. Oral argument produced several angry exchanges between lawyers for Mr. Altman and Manhattan District Attorney Robert Morgenthau, but then Judge Bradley proceeded to seal the transcript of our case, at least until he decides on the merits. He promises a ruling shortly.

Clark Clifford

Judge Green's case, by contrast, is anything but amusing. The U.S. Department of Justice has moved to reduce the sentence of Swaleh Naqvi, number-two man in BCCI now in U.S. prison. Mr. Naqvi struck a plea bargain on fraud and conspiracy charges upon his 1994 extradition from Abu Dhabi, where the ruling family under Sheik Zayed al-Nahyan was a long-time shareholder in BCCI and wound up with controlling interest as it collapsed. He was sentenced to a nominal 11-year term, but with a three-year reduction for time served under "house arrest" in Abu Dhabi. We wrote at the time that, with the possibility of parole and so on, this was not a sentence likely to produce true cooperation, nor one fitting for a 20-year career of truly grand larceny.

Now the Justice Department has moved to further reduce the sentence on the basis of "cooperation," raising the question "what cooperation?" In its memorandum to the court, the Justice Department says Mr. Naqvi has rendered "substantial assistance," but concedes that his "cooperation has not led directly to any additional federal charges within the past year." Mr. Morgenthau, who has filed separate New York charges against Mr. Naqvi, is opposing the reduction.

He relates one case in which Mr. Naqvi refused, unless promised absolutely no additional time on New York charges, to cooperate in  prosecution of a top BCCI figure, Syed Ziauddin Ali Akbar, on charges of extorting $15 million from Mr. Naqvi's BCCI, by threatening to reveal its true financial position. Similarly, he's refused cooperation with Great Britain's Serious Fraud Office in the case of Abbas Gokal, a key BCCI player.

It smells to us like a deal: Sheik Zayed would extradite the suspect, allowing U.S. authorities to look tough, and U.S. authorities would make sure nothing came of it. The facts would embarrass everyone, so down the memory hole — no matter the risk of encouraging the Iguchis and Leesons.

Swaleh Naqvi

REVIEW & OUTLOOK

BCCI Updates

It looks like Swaleh Naqvi, the number two man working for one of history's greatest criminal financial enterprises, the Bank of Commerce & Credit International, could be back on the street in about four years. On Monday, Federal Judge Joyce Hens Green knocked 30 months off Mr. Naqvi's nominal 11-year sentence. As we've reported, the U.S. Justice Department moved for a sentence reduction in the case of Mr. Naqvi, extradited from Abu Dhabi last year. With the sentence already reduced by three years for time spent under "house arrest" in Abu Dhabi, and expected time off for good behavior, Mr. Naqvi is facing a very short stretch.

Mr. Naqvi's lawyers argued that he had rendered substantial assistance to U.S. authorities, and Justice agreed. But New York District Attorney Robert Morgenthau and Britain's Serious Fraud Office both opposed a reduction in Mr. Naqvi's sentence, saying that he had not cooperated in their ongoing probes. Indeed, in Justice's own filing before Judge Green, it conceded that Mr. Naqvi's "cooperation had not led directly to any additional federal charges." So why the get-out-of-jail-early pass? We continue to wonder if the ruling family of Abu Dhabi under Sheik Zayed al-Nahyan, BCCI's central financier, would have extradited its chief banker without some assurance that nothing embarrassing would emerge. Nothing has.

At least not in Washington. By coincidence, legal authorities elsewhere were delving into a branch of BCCI that served as a global laundromat for narco-dollars. In a Hong Kong courtroom recently, authorities accused four former Bank of Credit & Commerce officials of helping drug kingpin Law Kin-man launder $33 million in U.S. heroin profits in the late 1980s. The drug money flowed from a Liberian-registered shelf company via Bankers Trust to BCC Hong Kong, the South China Morning Post reported. The BCC bankers apparently will escape prosecution under Hong Kong's relatively liberal currency transaction regulations.

Meanwhile, in a New York State Supreme Court this week, Judge John Bradley ruled against a motion by this newspaper to unseal the transcript of the trial that resulted in the acquittal of Robert Altman. Mr. Altman and Clark Clifford ran First American Bank when it was secretly owned by BCCI. Judge Bradley had specified that the seal would be waived if the defendant sought relief, which seemed to be the case to us when lawyers for Messrs. Altman and Clifford moved for reimbursement of legal fees from First American's trustee. Judge Bradley ruled that we lacked standing to assert a waiver of the seal on that basis. So the seal remains.

Letters to the Editor

Forget the Insults— There's No Coverup

Two editorials published the week of Nov. 13, "BCCI: The Memory Hole" and "BCCI Updates," pursue your obsession that powerful forces around the globe continue to cover up the BCCI scandal more than four years after the bank was shut down. Your scurrilous accusations about Sheikh Zayed bin Sultan Al Nahyan, president of the United Arab Emirates and ruler of Abu Dhabi, require a response.

You allege a secret deal between Sheikh Zayed and the U.S. to extradite Swaleh Naqvi, former BCCI chief executive, in return for an "assurance that nothing embarrassing would emerge." This is as insulting to the Justice Department and the Manhattan District Attorney as it is to Abu Dhabi, where Naqvi was convicted of criminal charges in 1994.

In May 1994, pursuant to an agreement signed by the Justice Department, the Manhattan District Attorney and the Federal Reserve Board, Naqvi was sent from Abu Dhabi to the U.S. to assist in U.S. investigations and to stand trial. No restrictions were placed on what he could say to the authorities, how he would be treated, or where he would be tried. His cooperation, plea agreement and sentencing have been solely in the hands of American prosecutors and U.S. courts, who have neither requested nor received any input from the United Arab Emirates.

We don't expect an editorial from you praising Sheikh Zayed's government for sending Naqvi to the U.S. to face the charges against him here. That would not feed your conspiracy theory, or appeal to whatever audience you think is still interested in BCCI. We ask, however, that you print this letter for the benefit of any unwary readers who, unfamiliar with your longstanding bias against legitimate Arab institutions, might get the mistaken impression that Sheikh Zayed is involved in a coverup.

W. Caffey Norman III
U.S. Counsel
for Sheikh Zayed bin Sultan Al Nahyan

Washington

NOVEMBER 17, 1995

REVIEW & OUTLOOK

Asides

White House Travels

A jury took less than two hours yesterday to acquit Billy Dale, the former director of the White House Travel Office, on charges that he embezzled $68,000. Jurors were apparently influenced by testimony that records that would have cleared Mr. Dale may have been removed in May 1993 after seven veteran Travel Office employees were fired so that Catherine Cornelius, a Clinton cousin, could take over the office. For example, Lee Johnson, deputy director of the White House Office of Records Management, warned his superiors after the firings that Ms. Cornelius had taken "boxes" of papers and "we have heard nothing from her since." Rep. Bill Clinger, chairman of the House Government Oversight Committee, says the Dale trial was "a transparently political prosecution"; he will now demand that the Justice Department that wanted Mr. Dale jailed for 20 years explain its actions. It's possible that crimes were indeed committed in the Travel Office, but with Mr. Dale's acquittal the focus of proper attention now moves back to the White House. At the news conference he called yesterday to imprecate the "congressional Republican budget," Mr. Clinton was asked about the Dale acquittal. The President replied, "I'm very sorry that Mr. Dale had to go through this." The former Travel Office director surely appreciates the sentiment.

REVIEW & OUTLOOK

On Abuse of Power

In the hearings that resume today, Senator Alfonse D'Amato's special Whitewater Committee gets to the central issue of the controversy, the conduct of government while Bill Clinton was President of the United States. It is not whether crimes were committed in a two-bit land deal in the Ozarks, but whether executive power was abused to short-circuit investigations that might embarrass a sitting President and his wife.

To this end, the D'Amato committee offers an intriguing witness list through Friday. The public will get its first look, for example, at Paula Casey, who was installed as U.S. Attorney in Little Rock after the Administration took the unprecedented step of sacking U.S. attorneys nationwide. Also appearing will be Randy Coleman, the lawyer who attempted to plea bargain with Ms. Casey on behalf of David Hale, the self-confessed bagman for the Arkansas political elite who has accused Mr. Clinton of being a party to bank fraud.

There will be RTC officials Jean Lewis, April Breslaw and Richard Iorio to discuss whether Ms. Lewis was thwarted in her attempts to investigate Madison Guaranty Savings & Loan. Also, former Associate Attorney General Webster Hubbell, former White House associate counsel William Kennedy and senior White House aide Bruce Lindsey. Senator D'Amato has invited a number of "small fry" from the White House, Justice, FBI, RTC and SBA to testify; as aficionados of political scandals know, sometimes those "small fry" say the darndest things.

Whether this cast will make headlines we do not pretend to know. Perhaps they will accomplish no more than the previous D'Amato hearings on efforts to thwart a Justice Department search of Vincent Foster's office, which left it obvious to any sentient being that White House operatives Susan Thomases and Maggie Williams were lying about the maneuvers. Clearly, too, the Democrats intend to put Ms. Lewis on trial, with tactics proven on Gennifer Flowers, Lani Guinier, Paula Jones and Kimba Wood.

And if there are to be headlines, someone has to write them. The press corps once asked what President Nixon knew when, and for that matter hounded Gary Hart out of the presidential race. But now White House spokesman Mark Fabiani pronounces Whitewater "boring" and "irrelevant" at every opportunity, and the Beltway press corps gets back to the important business of the ethical implications of Newt Gingrich writing a bestseller and blowing off steam over a presidential snub.

Publishers and TV executives worried about declining newspaper readership and network news ratings might stop to take notice of the news coverage on burgeoning talk radio and the information-age Internet. A kind of media counterculture will be tuning in to the hearings this

Al D'Amato

week, hoping that C-SPAN will cover them live or that the Senate will send the transcripts out on the World Wide Web.

Meanwhile, amazing nuggets are being found by the few determined journalists wading through the swamp of information, allegations and conspiracy theories. On November 14, Jerry Seper of the Washington Times, for example, reported that during last year's Office of Government Ethics probe, Treasury Counsel Jean Hanson said that RTC Senior Vice President William Roelle told her that the language of the criminal referral concerning Madison Guaranty "could lead to the conclusion that if additional work were done, that is, further investigative work, the President and Mrs. Clinton might possibly be more than just witnesses." Two days later Ms. Hanson informed the White House of the supposedly confidential referrals. Moreover, in a version of the deposition given to the Senate panel by the Treasury last year, the "more than just witnesses" remark was redacted. Senators may want to know why the phrase was deleted, and by whom.

A document, reprinted nearby, has also surfaced in which a second RTC investigator reports an experience similar to Ms. Lewis's, to wit that Ms. Breslaw said that senior RTC personnel discouraged an investigation of Madison. Also, today Senators will question officials of the Small Business Administration and the White House about a "heads up" on yet another investigation, the SBA's probe of Mr. Hale's company. The White House had confidential files for five or six days, until retrieved after the Justice Department threatened a probe of how they were used. "A classic case of no harm, no foul play," says Mr. Fabiani.

And with these intriguing witnesses on hand, perhaps someone may ask William Kennedy about that "eyes only" letter Vince Foster left for him in the safe in the White House Counsel's suite. And some brave soul may even ask RTC investigator Richard Iorio what prompted him to tell his superiors, according to minutes of an RTC meeting obtained by Dow Jones News Service in June, that Clinton crony Dan Lasater "may have been establishing depository accounts at Madison and other financial institutions and laundering drug money through them via brokered deposits and bond issues."

The picture that steadily emerges is of a widespread and pretty concerted effort to cover up transgressions back in Arkansas, conducted by the same Administration that asks us to trust it on the likes of Bosnia and Medicare. Perhaps the transgressions were indeed petty, but the abuse of the powers of the White House is anything but.

Editorial Feature

A 'Sensitive' Investigation

Kansas City Office
INTEROFFICE MEMO

DATE: February 18, 1994

TO: L. Richard Iorio
Field Investigations Officer

From: Gary Davidson
Investigator/Civil Fraud

Subject: #7236 - Madison Guaranty Savings and Loan
Little Rock, Arkansas
Discussion with April Breslaw/PLS

On January 11, 1994, you requested that I conduct a preliminary investigation into Madison Guaranty, for possible Civil Fraud claims. Procedures for conducting a Civil Fraud investigation require a systematic approach of gathering information by reviewing available documentation and interviewing RTC personnel. On January 13th or 14th, I called the assigned PLS attorney, April Breslaw, for the purpose of asking whether she knew of any fraudulent activity that was not addressed in the Criminal Referrals.

Before I could ask my intended question, April asked if I was conducting an investigation into Madison Guaranty. After acknowledging that I was, she indicated that what she was about to tell me was being stated as politely as she could. April felt I should know there are some RTC people in management positions that would take a "dim view" of me investigating Madison Guaranty. She also advised that I should be very careful of who I talk to and what I say, because of the people associated with Madison Guaranty.

After hearing April's comment, I stated that I had read the Criminal Referrals and was aware of the names associated with Madison Guaranty. I also stated that I was informed of the sensitivity of the investigation into the institution. I then asked the question of whether she knew of any fraudulent activity other than what is addressed in the Criminal Referrals. April indicated that there was no fraudulent activity to her knowledge, and we ended the conversation.

REVIEW & OUTLOOK

Whitewater Memories

We hope the Clinton people making our policy in Bosnia aren't drinking the same White House water as the ones who appeared Tuesday before Senator D'Amato's Whitewater Committee. These people can't remember anything. Meetings? What meetings? Personal notes? Beats me.

Despite the dead White House memories on display, Senator D'Amato's special Whitewater Committee in fact broke new ground Tuesday by focusing on Administration actions concerning David Hale, the former Arkansas municipal judge and confessed felon who ran Capital Management Services, a Small Business Administration-financed venture capital firm in Little Rock.

In May 1993, Mr. Hale was the target of a fraud probe by the Small Business Administration. Somehow, of all the penny-ante frauds the SBA chases, this one attracted the explicit interest of the Clinton White House.

By September, Mr. Hale's lawyer was looking for a deal, offering Clinton-appointed U.S. Attorney Paula Casey in Little Rock information on the "banking practices" of the political elite in exchange for a plea bargain. Ms. Casey turned him down. Mr. Hale went on to charge that then-Governor Clinton and Madison Guaranty S&L owner James McDougal pressured him to make an illegal $300,000 loan. This, in the narrowest sense, is Whitewater.

On Tuesday, former SBA official Wayne Foren testified that in May 1993 he told his boss, SBA Administrator Erskine Bowles, a

Clinton political appointee, about the confidential criminal probe of Mr. Hale. According to Mr. Foren, Mr. Bowles informed then-White House Chief of Staff Mack McLarty. Mr. Foren's account is supported by deputy associate SBA administrator Charles Shepperson. Mr. Bowles is now deputy White House chief of staff. Both he and Mr. McLarty deny discussing the Hale matter.

But someone appears to have had an abiding interest in the Hale case. According to Mr. Foren, in August 1993 an assistant U.S. attorney in Little Rock, Fletcher Jackson, took the unusual step of sending to the SBA a draft of the planned indictment of Mr. Hale. Mr. Foren says he gave it to Mr. Bowles. Mr. Bowles says, "I don't recall receiving this memorandum."

That September, New York Times reporter Jeff Gerth interviewed senior White House aide Bruce Lindsey about Mr. Hale. After the interview, Mr. Lindsey called another Clinton friend, James Blair of Hillary commodities fame. Mr. Lindsey's notes of that conversation were displayed at the Tuesday hearing. First Mr. Lindsey is asked if he called Jim Blair. He replies: "There's a note that reflects at some point I spoke to Jim Blair about this." Shortly, when the committee asks Mr. Lindsey about details of his conversation with Mr. Blair about the Gerth interview, he replies: "All I remember is what's reflected in these notes. I have no independent recollection of the conversation with Jim Blair."

In November 1993, Neil Eggleston, a lawyer in the White House Counsel's office, asked SBA General Counsel John Spotilla for the file on Mr. Hale. Mr. Spotilla, a political appointee, turned it over. Learning of the file transfer, the Justice Department raised strong objections, and Mr. Spotilla returned it.

The committee also revealed a previously undisclosed November 5, 1993, meeting concerning Whitewater at the office of the Clintons' personal attorney, David Kendall. Under questioning, Mr. Lindsey acknowledged he was at the meeting, but claimed attorney-client privilege. Senator D'Amato noted that the White House had prepared a memo about the meeting, but refused to turn it over.

Denials, memory failures, improper transmission of SBA information and documents, withheld memos, undisclosed meetings. Senator D'Amato has given us another chapter in the extraordinary saga of a crowd acting like it has something to hide. It remains the task of these valuable hearings to get to the bottom of it.

Editorial Feature

Senate Dems Play 'Gennifer' Card; Really

Whoever said politics makes strange bedfellows might have had the Senate Whitewater hearings in mind.

Who would have believed that Senate Democrats, in trying to defend President Clinton, would invoke the example of his most notorious woman accuser, Gennifer Flowers, to smear the motives of his most upright woman accuser? Whatever else one thinks about it, this would seem to be a high-risk gambit.

This thought occurs after watching Senate Democrats run Jean Lewis through their political Cuisinart this week. Ms. Lewis is the former Resolution Trust Corp. sleuth who made the mistake of following her boss's order to probe Whitewater.

Potomac Watch

By Paul A. Gigot

Her criminal referrals, which named the Clintons as witnesses, have been the basis for several indictments by independent Whitewater counsel Kenneth Starr. But they've also caused her no end of personal grief.

Her latest misery was appearing before the Senate Whitewater tribunal on Wednesday. Democrats on that panel are led by Paul Sarbanes, an urbane, white-shoe Maryland lawyer, who made his reputation during Watergate. His chief counsel, Richard Ben-Veniste, is a bulldog attorney who also made his bones against Richard Nixon.

In Whitewater, however, the pair long ago lost interest in what the president knew and when. They're in full defense array. And their defense strategy is to play offense against any witnesses who say anything inconvenient about the First Couple or their friends. In short, play by Arkansas Rules: Accuse the accuser.

By now this is a well-worn administration pattern. Secret Service agent Henry O'Neill, who saw documents being taken from Vincent

Jean Lewis

Foster's suite on the night of his suicide, is a loser who wants to climb in the ranks. Paula Jones is a trailer park bimbo. Arkansas troopers are liars looking for a book contract. Billy Dale gets indicted (and later acquitted) after disputing the official Travelgate line. And everyone else must be a political enemy with irrational hatred as motive.

This last is the elevated line Mr. Ben-Veniste took against Ms. Lewis. What she found matters less than why she was even looking. Had she ever called Mr. Clinton a "lying bastard?" he asked her, laying his trap. She didn't recall.

"I'll help you recall," the smooth lawyer said, citing a 22-page, February 1992 personal letter Democrats had pulled from one of her computer disks.

Ms. Lewis: "I confess, I'm curious where you got this letter."

Mr. Ben-Veniste: "We got it from you."

Ms. Lewis: "I don't think this was on a disk I gave you, counsel."

Mr. Ben-Veniste, in high sarcasm: "Apparently you didn't think it was on the disk but it was. That's the funny thing about these disks. I don't understand how they do it, but they can find the stuff on the disk that nobody thinks is there. I hate it when that happens, but here it is, Ms. Lewis."

She acknowledged writing the letter, and then the fun began. Mr. Ben-Veniste tried to move on. But it turns out Republicans hadn't even seen the letter. When they did get a copy, they found the context of Ms. Lewis's curse had been an off-hand comparison of her stepson's honesty to Mr. Clinton's denial of a 12-year affair with the tell-all cabaret singer. It read:

Her stepson's "ability to lie surpasses that of our most astute politicians (Gennifer who?? I never slept with that woman . . . quoth the illustrious Governor Bill Clinton! Everybody in Arkansas knows he did, the lying bastard, and then put her on the state payroll!)"

Having been handed a howitzer, Republicans fired. "Is the statement not true?" asked North Carolina's Lauch Faircloth. Dick Shelby of Alabama averred that "millions of other Americans" agree with Ms. Lewis that Mr. Clinton hadn't been honest when he called Ms. Flowers, back in January 1992, nothing more than a "friendly acquaintance." (Democrats did not rush to defend their president on this point.)

Rarely in politics has a sleazy hit been met with a more deserving boomerang. Especially because it may be an invasion of privacy that Democrats even dug up Ms. Lewis's personal letter. Ms. Lewis's lawyer says she'd deleted the letter from her computer disk long before it was subpoenaed by the Senate. So Democrats would have had to go to unusual technical means to "undelete" that file, an assertion backed up by Senate sources.

"We're going to examine what if any remedies we have," says her co-counsel, Mark Levin of Landmark Legal Foundation.

Mr. Ben-Veniste says his Senate staff did nothing more than "put the disk in the computer, push a button and stuff comes out." Then why didn't he bring up the "lying bastard" letter at Ms. Lewis's deposition, or even inform her lawyers or Chairman Al D'Amato about this line of questioning?

"They had the disk," Mr. Ben-Veniste replies, adding that a witness's motives are fair game. His old nemesis, Mr. Nixon, would have admired that retort.

As for Ms. Lewis, she suffers from high blood pressure, which soared under the nasty questioning. She left the hearing prematurely, in obvious distress, and was still in the hospital yesterday morning.

REVIEW & OUTLOOK

Absolutely Unbelievable

Any more weeks like the last, and someone's going to have to start a news show called "Whitewater Week in Review." Maybe someone already has on an alternative information source like the Internet. Senator D'Amato's Whitewater hearings last week surfaced a nice share of new leads and moments of high viewing drama.

For starters, readers may recall our November 10 editorial "202-628-7087." Well, it now looks as if we may finally get an answer to the mysterious Washington number that Hillary Clinton called from her mother's Little Rock home on the night of Vincent Foster's death. Last week, the White House agreed to a request by the Senate's special Whitewater Committee to have Mrs. Clinton provide written answers about the call.

The second unexplained call we wondered about in that editorial was on July 21 to Sunnyside Lodge in Tahoe. This call turns out to have been made to Diane Blair, a longtime friend of Hillary's and wife of Clinton commodities adjunct Jim Blair. Thanks to Senator D'Amato's now-vigorous investigation, we also learned last week that Mrs. Blair was among those present at the White House family residence a week after Mr. Foster's death, when the Clintons' then-personal attorney, Robert Barnett, retrieved Mr. Foster's files. Also at the residence were Mrs. Clinton's chief of staff, Maggie Williams, and Whitewater damage-control operative Susan Thomases.

"The exit and entry logs show Thomases, Barnett and Williams all going up to the White House residence within moments of each other on the afternoon of July 27," reported Susan Schmidt of the Washington Post, "and all exiting the residence within moments of each other about an hour and a half later. Blair was also in the residence during some of that period."

In a potentially damaging letter released last week by a White House under the pressure of the Senate investigation, it was revealed that Mr. Barnett had reviewed the files at the personal residence in the presence of Ms. Williams. This is news to us. In earlier depositions and testimony, and amid numerous lapses of memory, Ms. Williams minimized the Barnett encounter, stating merely that she had bumped into him and unlocked the closet containing the files.

The letter indicates that Mr. Barnett was at the White House for almost 90 minutes and was in Ms. Williams's presence while reviewing the Foster files. Senator D'Amato announced that the committee will again recall Ms. Williams and Ms. Thomases, and expects to hear from Mr. Barnett. The Foster-review letter, plus visitors' logs from the White House residence obtained by the committee, bolster the belief that the full story is yet to be known.

Testimony before the committee also made it clear that we are far from the full story on the Little Rock political elite's relationship with Madison Guaranty Saving & Loan. Senators raised the issue of the involvement of Rose Law Firm members Hillary Clinton and Webster Hubbell in legal work on behalf of Madison in its 1985 Castle Grande development project. Bank examiners later found that parts of the deal, some involving Mr. Hubbell's father-in-law, revolved around a series of fictitious transactions designed to inflate profits. Subsequently, FDIC lawyer April Breslaw, who testified on Thursday, hired Rose to act against Madison; no one at Rose bothered to mention the conflict of interest to her. We'd still like to know how Ms. Breslaw found her way to Rose in the first place.

Eventually, of course, Ms. Breslaw traveled to the Resolution Trust Corp. and there had her now-famous 1994 tape-recorded conversation with RTC investigator Jean Lewis suggesting that the "head people" would like to be able to say that "Whitewater did not cause a loss to Madison." The televised colloquy about that incident topped even the week's earlier spectacles of White House lawyer Bruce Lindsey testifying that he didn't know what his own notes meant of a phone conversation with Jim Blair and Democratic counsel Richard Ben-Veniste's invocation of Gennifer Flowers's memory to discredit Jean Lewis.

The committee — and TV audiences — had listened at length to the formidable Ms. Breslaw testify confidently and in clipped speech about her actions at the time. Then after the audio of her taped conversation was played into the committee room, she preposterously replied, "I don't know what my voice sounds like on tape."

Senator D'Amato replied that Ms. Breslaw's remark was "absolutely unbelievable." It was a fitting conclusion and one, we suspect, that will now persist.

Editorial Feature

Castle Grande: Hillary's Bills, Starr's Appraiser

By MICAH MORRISON

While Sen. Alfonse D'Amato is conducting Senate hearings on Whitewater, Independent Counsel Kenneth Starr is conducting an investigation that may produce further indictments. The two interact, and have to be considered together.

Last week, for example, former associate attorney general and current jailbird Webster Hubbell defended Hillary Clinton, saying she did "very little work for Madison," the savings and loan at the heart of the Whitewater scandal. In particular, he said she had only "minor" billings on a Madison development called Castle Grande. The Banquo's ghost at this hearing was an obscure Little Rock businessman and real estate appraiser named Robert Palmer. A year ago, Mr. Starr announced that Mr. Palmer had entered a guilty plea to backdating property appraisals for Madison and agreed to cooperate with the independent counsel.

Just what was the Castle Grande project? Students of Whitewater understand it as one of the great black holes of Arkansas corruption: Everyone disappears inside it. Federal examiners have criticized the deal as a series of fictitious transactions designed to inflate profits and evade state regulations.

In 1985, Madison Financial — the real-estate arm of Jim McDougal's S&L — bought 1,000 acres south of Little Rock for $1.75 million. Since Madison had an investment limitation of $600,000, it extended an insider, non-recourse loan to one of its employees, Seth

Ward, the father-in-law of Mr. Hubbell, then a partner in the Rose Law Firm. Mr. McDougal immediately sold a 34-acre Castle Grande plot to Arkansas businessman Jim Guy Tucker, the current governor, to build a shopping center — never mind that half the land was on a flood plain.

An appraiser valued the property at $350,000 — roughly triple its true worth, federal regulators would later discover. On the basis of the appraisal, Mr. McDougal loaned Mr. Tucker $260,000, charging him $125,000 for the land. Mr. Tucker later flipped the land to a company he partly owned, borrowing $100,000 from David Hale's Capital Management Services for that particular transaction. Meanwhile, Mr. Tucker also was buying a 39-acre sewer and water plant at Castle Grande. For the purchase, he received a $150,000 loan from Mr. Hale and a whopping $1,050,000 loan from Madison. The appraiser of the property was Mr. Palmer, who valued it a $1.3 million; the Resolution Trust Corp. later put its true value at $640,000. The inflated appraisals, of course, were used to support the inflated loans.

In his plea bargain with the independent counsel, Mr. Palmer admitted to falsifying 25 appraisals for Madison. At least one other of the appraisals involved property owned by Mr. Hale, who is also now cooperating with Mr. Starr. Mr. Palmer's appraisal provided a basis for Madison to loan $825,000 to a straw man for Mr. Hale, who took $500,000 of the proceeds to leverage $1.5 million out of the Small Business Administration. Of this, he loaned $300,000 to Mr. McDougal's wife, Susan, and part of this money showed up in the Whitewater account. This is the same loan Mr. Hale asserts Bill Clinton pressured him into making in order to take care of "the political family." Then there are the 23 other appraisals.

How does Mrs. Clinton figure in all this? She either was or was not the attorney on the deals in which Mr. Palmer was the appraiser. In the wake of the S&L crisis, federal regulators brought more than 150 cases against lawyers who represented wayward thrifts. In the Lincoln Savings & Loan case, the blue-blood firm of Kaye, Scholer, Fierman, Hays & Handler had to cough up a settlement of $41 million after regulators peremptorily froze its assets.

Mrs. Clinton has always maintained that she did very little work for Madison in return for her $2,000 monthly stipend in 1985 and 1986. Last week, however, the Senate Whitewater Committee produced accounting records from an RTC probe of the Rose Law Firm showing that Mrs. Clinton billed more than $6,000 on the Madison account in 1986. According to Rose accounting records, Mrs. Clinton did more work on Madison than anyone at her firm except one junior associate — another small fry who might cause trouble for the First Couple. Of particular interest to the committee was $2,730 in Mrs. Clinton's billings for services in connection with the Castle Grande land deal.

"Looking at the bills," said Sen. Robert Bennett (R., Utah), "Mrs. Clinton was not just the billing partner but heavily involved in Madison." And records uncovered so far could be just the tip of the iceberg. After spending last Friday exploring the Rose billings, Sen. D'Amato said Mrs. Clinton's previous accounts of her work on behalf of Madison had been "grossly misleading." Getting answers won't be easy. Mrs. Clinton declines invitations to appear before the committee, and the Rose Firm has said it has no records of Madison activity from 1983 to 1986.

Hillary Clinton

David Kendall, the Clintons' personal attorney, says Mrs. Clinton's Madison billings reflect her work on state law issues, not Castle Grande. But Mrs. Clinton's involvement in state issues might prove even more nettlesome. Among the services Rose billed to Madison was "research on what approvals, permits, etc., are necessary to operate sewer and water facilities." Later in 1986, when Madison passed into the hands of federal regulators, Mr. Tucker's million-dollar sewer loan was the largest single delinquent loan on Madison's books. Mr. Tucker and his partners negotiated it down to $525,000, contingent on new legislation allowing utilities to raise rates. A few months later, Gov. Clinton signed the legislation into law.

Mr. Starr has already indicted Gov. Tucker on fraud charges relating to Madison and Castle Grande. He has indicated the investigation is ongoing, and last week's testimony gives a glimpse of the evidence he's pondering. The issue may be how broad a net to cast.

Mr. Morrison is a Journal editorial page writer.

Review & Outlook

Subpoena Time

The issue of White House stonewalling is now headed for the courts. Both Senator Alfonse D'Amato of the Senate Banking Committee and Rep. William Clinger of the House Government Oversight Committee are threatening subpoenas in the face of White House stonewalling of their investigations.

Senator D'Amato wants to know more about a meeting on November 5, 1993, to discuss Whitewater. The two-hour meeting was hosted by Donald Kendall, the Clintons' private attorney at Williams & Connolly, the Beltway's topflight criminal defense firm. James Lyons, the Denver lawyer who handled Whitewater during the Presidential campaign, also attended, as did another Clinton personal attorney, Steve Engstrom. Also present were a number of lawyers on the government payroll: Bernard Nussbaum, then White House Counsel. William Kennedy III, then associate counsel. Bruce Lindsey, now deputy counsel. And Neil Eggleston, then associate counsel.

This legal firepower assembled shortly after White House officials had obtained confidential information about Resolution Trust Corp. criminal referrals that mentioned the Clintons in connection with the failed Madison Guaranty, the savings and loan owned by Clinton Whitewater partner James McDougal. Senator D'Amato and his committee are curious about whether confidential governmental information was passed along to the private defense team. (Aren't you?)

Asked about this, Mr. Lindsey and Mr. Kennedy refuse to answer.

Mr. Kennedy said he had to be careful to follow White House "instructions." The White House has been careful not to claim "executive privilege"; not only would that smack of Nixonian stonewalling, but the White House would also have to implausibly claim that Whitewater concerned weighty affairs of state. So the witnesses are instead contending that they cannot tell Congress what took place at the meeting because of attorney-client privilege.

This is even more preposterous than an executive privilege claim. To begin with, the attorney-client privilege has to be claimed by the client, not his lawyers. At the very least, President Clinton should himself assert the privilege and not hide behind White House lawyers. But the privilege only protects communication between an attorney and a client, and Mr. Clinton wasn't present at the November 1993 meeting. In any event, neither Mr. Lindsey nor Mr. Kennedy were attorneys for Mr. Clinton; they were government officials.

William Clinger

So we have the spectacle of a President ordering officials paid by taxpayers not to answer questions from the rest of the government about what they discussed with the private attorney defending his private interests in the midst of an independent counsel's investigation of potential criminal violations. Senator D'Amato's committee plans to vote this morning on subpoenas for notes and other documents relating to the meeting.

Meanwhile, Rep. Clinger is threatening to issue subpoenas to Harry Thomason, the President's Hollywood pal who orchestrated the White House Travel Office firings. He's been refusing to turn over records on the scandal, hiring superlawyer Bob Bennett to say he won't cooperate with "a political fishing expedition" that is designed to "embarrass the White House." Mr. Bennett also happens to represent President Clinton, having won a ruling burying the Paula Jones sexual harassment case until after the next election. The legal nightmare Mr. Thomason's Travel Office putsch caused for Billy Dale, the office's former director, is described nearby by John H. Fund.

In the face of the subpoena threat, Mr. Thomason finally did turn over 200 pages of material this week. But they are woefully incomplete. For example, Mr. Thomason turned over his meeting records for only an 11-day period in May 1993, when the Travel Office firings occurred. But Rep. Clinger needs more to establish if Mr. Thomason's role in the White House made him a special government employee subject to ethics laws. More negotiations with Mr. Bennett are under way.

Two White House aides are also refusing to meet with investigators for Mr. Clinger's committee unless Democratic staffers are present. Rep. Clinger, citing several recent leaks of sensitive information from the committee, says that's inappropriate. So the Travel Office investigation has proceeded without the testimony of Patsy Thomasson and Catherine Cornelius, who may have removed key documents from the Travel Office.

On yet a third front, federal Judge Royce Lamberth is weighing sanctions against the White House and Justice Department in ongoing litigation about the secrecy of Mrs. Clinton's health care task force. Calling government arguments for exemption from open-meeting laws "preposterous," the judge ruled for the plaintiffs, the Association of American Physicians and Surgeons. The association has asked that the Clinton Administration pay its $350,000 in legal bills. It's also asked the judge to prescribe ethics classes for the government's lawyers, including Mrs. Clinton, "an experienced lawyer with governmental experience who supervised directly the task force." The government's response brief has just been delivered.

Both the New York Times and the Washington Post have editorialized this week that the stonewalling should cease, and even Democrats in Congress are advising that stonewalling Congressional committees is a political loser. Yet the Clinton White House goes from one cockamamie excuse to the next, with a constant drain on what little credibility it retains.

Editorial Feature

A Kafkaesque Prosecution

By John H. Fund

Billy Dale began working in the White House Travel Office the year that John F. Kennedy became president. In 1982, he became its director and served without a blemish on his record until May 19, 1993. On that day, he and the other six Travel Office employees were ushered into a room where White House aide David Watkins told them they were fired and had to be out of the building within two hours.

During their meeting with Mr. Watkins — who a few months later was fired for using a presidential helicopter to visit a golf course — a 25-year-old cousin of President Clinton took over the Travel Office and began removing and throwing away key documents. White House aides told reporters that the Federal Bureau of Investigation was investigating allegations of criminal conduct by the Travel Office employees. Mr. Dale was soon subjected to a 30-month legal ordeal that ended only last month with his swift acquittal on what appear to be politically inspired embezzlement charges.

The White House was eventually forced to offer Mr. Dale's six colleagues jobs elsewhere in the government. But Mr. Dale was pursued with a vengeance by a White House eager to find some justification for its clumsy putsch. Mr. Dale was accused of embezzling $68,000 in money collected from news organizations that paid reporters to go on presidential trips. Mr. Dale admitted that he kept sloppy records and had made the egregious mistake of routing some of the money through his own bank account. But the petty cash notebook he maintained would clear him couldn't be found.

Rather than inquire after the missing records, the Internal Revenue Service pursued Mr. Dale with the relish of the police inspector in "Les Miserables." Mr. Dale was never interviewed so he could defend himself, but his daughter was interrogated as she returned from her honeymoon and asked where she had gotten the money for her wedding. Agents called Mr. Dale's sister to ask her about a check he had written her in 1988, apparently thinking she might be his mistress.

After an 18-month investigation, Mr. Dale was indicted for embezzlement. At his trial, the Clinton-appointed judge refused to allow into evidence testimony about the missing Travel Office records or the political motivations behind the firings. We now know they were inspired by Hillary Clinton's demand to "get our people" into the Travel Office. The FBI investigation of the office was based on what Mr. Watkins called "rumors of criminal activity" by its employees. The groundless allegations were raised by Catherine Cornelius (a presidential cousin who wanted to run the Travel Office), Harry Thomason (the president's Hollywood pal), and Darnell Martens (Mr. Thomason's partner in an air charter firm that had been rebuffed by the Travel Office in a bid to run press charter flights). All three had a financial interest in seeing the Travel Office taken over by Clinton cronies.

Even though Mr. Dale was allowed to make only a narrow defense, the jury still heard intriguing testimony. Dennis Sculimbrene, a 23-year FBI veteran, testified that he saw White House aides who lacked security clearances rummaging through Travel Office files after the firings. A longtime Travel Office employee testified that he saw White House administrator Patsy Thomasson in the Travel Office early one morning after its locks had been changed.

What jurors didn't hear was that Ms. Thomasson had ordered the removal of the office's computer hard drives two days before an audit of the office was initiated. Jurors were also not told that the late Vincent Foster had noted in his personal diary that his fellow White House lawyer William Kennedy "says someone told him that . . . documents are being thrown away." Mr. Kennedy's own diary contained an entry in which he discussed having "found a petty cash notebook" in Mr. Dale's office.

Even though they only heard hints of the machinations surrounding the Travel Office firings, jurors took only two hours to acquit Mr. Dale of all charges. The 58-year-old Mr. Dale has had to spend his life savings on legal bills and has no right to government reimbursement. He's convinced that "the investigation of me was political scapegoating." He hopes that the hearings planned by Rep. William Clinger (R., Pa.), chairman of the House Government Oversight Committee, will uncover the real story behind the firings.

There remain many questions. Mr. Thomason has declined to talk to Rep. Clinger's office, or supply it with all the relevant documents in the case. A memo outlining the allegations against the Travel Office is apparently missing. Mrs. Clinton refused to grant the General Accounting Office an interview about her role in the affair.

Mr. Dale thinks his ordeal had its origins at an even higher level. On the weekend that his office was suddenly audited he says an aide to President Clinton told him that "there was one person only that was responsible for what happened in your office this weekend, and that person occupies the Oval Office." After Mr. Dale's acquittal, Mr. Clinton declined to apologize and would only say he was "very sorry" about what had happened, and that he hoped Mr. Dale "can get on with his life."

Mr. Dale, who still faces a possible IRS audit of his finances, says he finds it difficult to believe the president's sincerity. Apparently, there are limits to this president's ability to "feel the pain" of others, and that especially means anyone who gets in the way of the sharp-elbowed Arkansas mores this administration has brought to Washington.

Mr. Fund is a member of the Journal's editorial board.

Review & Outlook

Will Sarbanes Filibuster?

Today marks a key milestone in the White House defense strategy on Whitewater. Up in New Hampshire, it's the filing deadline for the February primaries. The defense team has managed to obstruct and delay long enough that President Clinton will face no

substantial challenge from within his own party. The next objective is to deal with Republicans by stalling everything past next November's elections.

Let's call it the Paula Jones ploy. The President won a delay of her sexual harassment case until after he leaves office, and is appealing the judge's ruling that depositions can start now. Why shouldn't this work with Whitewater? Promise cooperation as long as you can, but drag out legal proceedings as long as you can.

Paul Sarbanes

Hillary admirer Judge Henry Woods will surely be overturned in ruling that Independent Counsel Kenneth Starr lacks jurisdiction in one case involving Arkansas Governor Jim Guy Tucker, but it does run the clock. Governor Tucker now wants his other case delayed while he litigates with the New York Times over access to a reporter's notes.

In response to a Congressional subpoena for notes on a suspicious-looking meeting on November 5, 1993, meanwhile, the White House first offers an attorney-client privilege claim that most lawyers rate in the tenuous-to-frivolous range. For starters, Mr. Clinton wasn't party to the meeting itself, normally a condition for such privilege claims, whether with a lawyer or in the confessional.

Then the White House dangles a claim of executive privilege, a more serious claim even though it lost for Richard Nixon. But it hasn't officially invoked executive privilege yet; two sets of litigation take longer than one. Finally, it faxed a deal to the D'Amato Whitewater Committee yesterday in which an offer to divulge the notes was freighted with dilatory restrictions. The committee rejected this ploy and voted to enforce the subpoena.

As the subpoena wends its way through the Congressional process, Senator Paul Sarbanes has to decide whether to join the Paula Jones ploy. On the Whitewater Committee, he's been the point man of the Democratic defense, and when the subpoena resolution reaches the Senate floor, probably sometime next week, he has the option of conducting a filibuster. It would guarantee more delay, and if he holds enough Democrats he could block the resolution permanently.

Senator Sarbanes and other Democrats, though, will have to consider whether the Paula Jones ploy might backfire. Newt-bashing didn't save the day in San Jose on Tuesday, where a concerted anti-Gingrich campaign left Republican Tom Campbell with 59% of the vote in a district where George Bush got 30%. Do Congressional Democrats really want to lash themselves to Bill Clinton's Whitewater mast, or is it time to look for the lifeboats?

Defending attorney-client or executive privilege won't be much fun. A filibuster would give us time to look up all the Sarbanes quotes on the subject from the Watergate era. Then there's the merit of the claim. The White House says the purpose of the November 5 meeting was to brief the new private counsel for the Clintons on a "torrent" of press coverage and other matters relating to Whitewater. But take a look at the chronology below — all the action leading up to the meeting took place before heavy press coverage of Whitewater. And further revelations keep coming; the November 5 meeting itself was disclosed only late last month through questioning of Mr. Lindsey by Senator Lauch Faircloth. If William Kennedy's notes on the meeting include something like "get Jean Lewis off the Madison case," we have a conspiracy to obstruct justice.

Just last week, too, the White House reported that the mystery phone number (202) 628-7087 was a trunk line bypassing the White

House switchboard in case it was overloaded "and may have been provided to certain individuals for that purpose." In other words, Hillary Clinton was bypassing the switchboard to call into the White House the night of Vincent Foster's death. And we learned that Whitewater documents were passed from Mr. Foster to Webster Hubbell during the Presidential campaign, and supposedly were stored in Mr. Hubbell's Washington basement. When they were delivered to Clinton attorney David Kendall, he returned them to the Rose Law Firm, where they later came to the attention of Senate investigators. Mr. Kendall's initiative in this matter suggests that Arkansas legal habits are a little much for a firm like Williams & Connolly.

This is also a point for Congressional Democrats to ponder in deciding whether to join the Paula Jones ploy. If they filibuster, it will be a wondrous spectacle; if they don't, their silence will have an eloquence of its own.

Whitewater, 1993

May 5: Small Business Administration Administrator Erskine Bowles informs White House Chief of Staff Thomas "Mack" McLarty of confidential criminal fraud investigation of Little Rock municipal judge David Hale, owner of SBA-chartered Capital Management Services.

July 21: In Little Rock, the FBI executes a search warrant on Mr. Hale's office.

July 22: White House Counsel Bernard Nussbaum and Maggie Williams, chief of staff to Hillary Clinton, search the office of the late White House Deputy Counsel Vincent Foster for a second time. Months later, it is revealed that Whitewater files were removed from the office.

Aug. 16: Paula Casey, a longtime associate of the Clintons, takes office as U.S. Attorney for the Eastern District of Arkansas.

Sept. 20: Ms. Casey turns aside plea bargain attempts from Mr. Hale's lawyer, Randy Coleman. Mr. Coleman had offered to share information on the "banking and borrowing practices of some individuals in the elite political circles of Arkansas."

Senior White House aide Bruce Lindsey discusses the Hale matter with Clinton commodities adviser James Blair.

Sept. 21: An assistant U.S. attorney in Ms. Casey's office notifies

SBA Administrator Bowles of the planned indictment of Mr. Hale.

Sept. 29: Treasury Department General Counsel Jean Hanson warns Mr. Nussbaum about confidential criminal referrals the Resolution Trust Corp. plans to issue in the case of Madison Guaranty Savings & Loan. The referrals mention the Clintons and Arkansas Gov. Jim Guy Tucker.

Oct. 4 or 5: Mr. Lindsey informs the president about the referrals. He later tells Congress he did not mention any specific targets of the referrals.

Oct. 6: President Clinton meets with Gov. Tucker at the White House.

Oct. 14: A meeting is held in Mr. Nussbaum's office with senior White House and Treasury personnel to discuss the RTC and Madison.

Oct. 27: Paula Casey rejects the RTC's first criminal referral in the Madison case.

Nov. 5: White House lawyers meet with the Clintons' personal attorneys at the offices of Williams & Connolly. Present for the White House: Mr. Nussbaum; Mr. Lindsey, a presidential aide not attached to the Office of White House Counsel; Associate White House Counsel William Kennedy III, a former partner in the Rose Law Firm; and Associate White House Counsel Neil Eggleston.

Present as personal lawyers: David Kendall of Williams & Connolly, lead attorney; Little Rock attorney Stephen Engstrom; and Denver attorney James Lyons, author of the 1992 "Lyons' Report" on the Clintons' finances.

Nov. 9: Jean Lewis, the lead RTC investigator on Madison, is abruptly removed from the case.

In Little Rock, Paula Casey recuses herself from the Madison probe.

Nov. 16: Mr. Eggleston reaches out to a political appointee at the SBA for confidential papers on the Hale investigation.

Hillary's Turn

In the first weeks of 1996, two documents long sought by Congressional investigators suddenly came to light. First was an undated 1993 memo by former Arkansas operative David Watkins, who at the time was serving as White House Director of Administration. In the memo, Mr. Watkins placed responsibility for the Travel Office firings squarely at the door of Hillary Clinton. "[Vincent] Foster regularly informed me that the First Lady was concerned and desired action—the desired action was the firing of the Travel Office staff," Mr. Watkins wrote in the memo.

Hard on the heels of that revelation came another bombshell. The White House suddenly announced that Mrs. Clinton's Rose Law Firm billing records, sought by Congress and under subpoena by the independent counsel for more than two years, had miraculously been discovered on a table in the "book room" of the White House residence.

The new documents posed serious problems for Mrs. Clinton. She had previously denied being involved in the Travel Office firings. Through a White House attorney, Mrs. Clinton had told Government Accounting Office investigators that she did "not know the origin of the decision to remove the White House Travel Office employees." The Rose billing records provided additional details about Mrs. Clinton's work on behalf of James McDougal and Madison Guaranty, including her involvement in the Castle Grande land deal. A Resolution Trust Corp. inquiry had determined that Mr. McDougal's Castle Grande dealings were a "sham transaction," and parts of the transaction figured in Independent Counsel Kenneth Starr's indict-ment of the McDougals and Governor Tucker for bank fraud.

In an unprecedented move, Mr. Starr subpoenaed the first lady to appear before a Whitewater grand jury. President Clinton also was served a subpoena: to appear as a defense witness in the Arkansas bank fraud case.

REVIEW & OUTLOOK

Who Is Hillary Clinton?

1. Mrs. Clinton does not know the origin of the decision to remove the White House Travel Office employees. She believes that the decision to terminate the employees would have been made by Mr. Watkins with the approval of Mr. McLarty.

2. Mrs. Clinton was aware that Mr. Watkins was undertaking a review of the situation in the Travel Office, but she had no role in the decision to terminate the employees.

Hillary Clinton

So begin answers to questions posed to Hillary Clinton by the General Accounting Office, submitted to the GAO by Associate White House Counsel W. Neil Eggleston on April 6, 1994. Now we get an internal White House memo telling an entirely opposite story; as excerpted nearby, David Watkins wrote that Mrs. Clinton made him do it. The White House's director of administration wanted to delay and give employees a chance to find new jobs, but she forced him to fire them out of hand. Apologies were eventually tendered to most, though former Travel Office head Billy Dale was charged with embezzlement; a jury acquitted him in two hours.

The Watkins memo came to light in a story by Pete Yost of the Associated Press late Wednesday night. It was also delivered about that time to Rep. William Clinger's House Committee on Government

Reform and Oversight — two and a half years after it was written and eight months after the committee's official request for all White House documents related to the Travel Office affair.

The stark conflict between Mrs. Clinton's categorical denials and other available evidence seems to fit a pattern that has rapidly developed in the last few weeks. In all, they raise the question, who, really, is Hillary Rodham Clinton?

* * *

There will be more to learn when Mr. Clinger's subpoenas catch up with Mr. Watkins. Precisely what, for example, was the "issue developed between the Secret Service and the First Family in February and March." Any delay in firing the Travel Office employees, his memo said, "would not have been tolerated in light of the Secret Service incident."

Then there's the note by a minor White House aide Mr. Clinger included in releasing the document, saying that "Susan Thomases went to David and Mac[k] but they wouldn't fire." It seems that on May 19, 1993, the day of the firings, Ms. Thomases was in the White House for six hours. This is the same Susan Thomases, of course, who suffered an amnesia epidemic (tellingly recorded by Ted Koppel on ABC's "Nightline" December 19) when questioned by Senator D'Amato's committee about events just after Vincent Foster's death. Significantly, Mr. Watkins's memo reports that Mr. Foster had been another messenger from the First Lady on the Travel Office, and many reports suggest this issue preoccupied the former deputy counsel shortly before his death. So with the memo Senator D'Amato has all the more reason to press his investigation of the handling of Foster documents.

* * *

Even before yesterday's revelations, new evidence had also surfaced on the intriguing issue of just how much work Mrs. Clinton did back at the Rose Law Firm for Madison Guaranty, the Whitewater S&L. "There was a very bright young associate in our law firm who had a relationship with one of the officers of Madison," she soothingly said at her pink press conference in April 1994. "The young attorney, the young bank officer, did all the work."

The young Rose attorney was Richard "Rick" Massey, and the young bank officer a Madison official named John Latham. In her notes of phone conversations with Webster Hubbell during the 1992

Presidential campaign, Ms. Thomases wrote that "Rick will say he had relationship with Latham and had a lot to do with getting the client in." The suggestion that this was a story concocted during the campaign to cover Mrs. Clinton's role is buttressed by other notes Ms. Thomases wrote at the time, including mentions that Hillary had "numerous conferences" on Madison and "she did all the billing."

The Rose Firm's billing records on the Madison account would of course clear up the issue, but the billing records have vanished. We know that some Rose documents on Whitewater passed from Mr. Foster to Mr. Hubbell during the Presidential campaign and were stored in the latter's basement. Ms. Thomases' notes on conferences and bills suggest the billing records may have been in existence at the time. The William Kennedy note on the November 5, 1993 meeting includes the lines:

"Vacuum Rose Law Files WWDC Docs — subpoena
"+documents — never know go out
"Quietly."

* * *

The Resolution Trust Corp. said at year end it would not sue Rose or Mrs. Clinton over the representation of Madison, but according to the Washington Post, it did send another set of interrogatories to Mrs. Clinton about her role at Rose in structuring parts of an especially suspicious Madison Guaranty land development called Castle Grande. The RTC, officially going out of business but being wrapped into the Federal Deposit Insurance Corp., wants to learn more about a $400,000 option agreement for a 22-acre parcel of Castle Grande land to be sold to Seth Ward by Madison. Mr. Ward is the father-in-law of Mr. Hubbell, the former associate attorney and Clinton crony now serving federal time for ripping off his former Rose colleagues. Federal bank examiners have characterized Mr. Ward as a "straw" purchaser for Madison. Mrs. Clinton apparently authored the option agreement, unless of course Rick would like to volunteer.

What Mr. Massey, now a partner in the Rose Law Firm, would presently say is another item of interest. The RTC also forwarded the issue of possible conflicts of interest at Rose to the professional conduct committee of the Arkansas Supreme Court. Ronald Clark, managing partner at Rose, said, "We don't think there is anybody currently with this firm that has engaged in any conflict."

* * *

In her pink press conference, of course, Mrs. Clinton didn't take an oath. During the Senate debate over subpoenas for the Kennedy notes, Senator Lauch Faircloth charged, "Mrs. Clinton may have made false statements — a federal crime — to the RTC about who was responsible for bringing Madison's business to the Rose Firm." Similarly, a current Newsweek story by Mark Hosenball and Michael Isikoff includes the intriguing line that Mrs. Clinton "has stated under oath that her involvement with Madison as a client was 'minimal.'" The Clintons have also been extensively deposed by Independent Counsel Kenneth Starr, who issued a statement yesterday that he was "distressed" not to have received the Watkins memo until after it had been given to the AP.

The Newsweek story also casts doubt on the official version of what happened to Whitewater itself. The Clintons' interest in the development was sold back to Madison owner James McDougal for $1,000 in December of 1992. It now develops, however, that Mr. McDougal didn't have the $1,000. Jim Blair, Clinton friend and Tyson Foods lawyer, loaned it to him. It was never repaid. Mr. Blair told Newsweek, "I didn't think the Clintons should go to Washington tied in to McDougal."

This was the same Jim Blair, of course, who figured in Mrs. Clinton's commodity killing — the pink press-conference topic. With Mr. Blair at her side, she ran $1,000 into $100,000 in a series of trades in cattle futures and other fliers. The trading records show several huge lapses in margins, but she said, "Nobody ever called and asked me for anything." She and Mr. Blair traded through the most heavily disciplined broker at the most controversial firm in the financial community's most speculative market. For our money, her most credible remark to date was quoted in the Washington Post: "The 1980s were about acquiring — acquiring wealth, power, privilege."

Whoever Hillary Clinton the First Lady ultimately may be, at this point there is very little reason to accept at face value her various professions on the Travel Office, her work at Rose, her commodity trades or her health care task force. In all of these things she was of course a surrogate for her husband, and was officially defended by the White House. So on Bosnia, Haiti, a balanced budget in seven years or professions of good-faith negotiation in the current government shutdown, there is less reason than ever to trust the credibility of Bill Clinton the President.

Editorial Feature

White House Stonewall Cracks

The memo excerpted below was released late Wednesday by the White House in response to an eight-month-old request by the House Government Reform and Oversight Committee for documents relating to the firing of seven White House Travel Office employees in May 1993. An internal White House review found the firings to have been "insensitive"; five of the employees were offered other federal jobs and another retired. Travel Office Director Billy Dale was indicted on embezzlement charges, but last November a jury took only two hours to acquit him. Mr. Dale believes his ordeal had its origins at the highest levels. An aide to President Clinton told him that "there was one person only that was responsible for what happened in your office this weekend, and that person occupies the Oval Office."

For over two years, the White House has denied that President Clinton or Hillary Clinton ordered or planned the Travel Office firings. The undated 1993 memo below is by David Watkins, then the White House director of administration, who handled the firings. It was written for then-Chief of Staff Mack McLarty, who said yesterday he had just seen it "for the first time" and that Mrs. Clinton had not ordered the firings. Mr. Watkins has not disputed the authenticity of the memo. It reveals that Mrs. Clinton personally ordered the firings and contradicts official statements that she made to the General Accounting Office (see accompanying editorial nearby). The White House claimed Mrs. Clinton "had no role in the decision to terminate the employees."

— John H. Fund

Privileged and Confidential

From: David Watkins

Subject: Response to Internal White House Travel Office Management Review

In an effort to respond to the Internal Travel Office Review, I have prepared this memorandum, which details my response to the various conclusions of that Report. This is a soul cleansing, carefully detailing the surrounding circumstances and the pressures that demanded that action be taken immediately. It is my first attempt to be sure the record is straight, something I have not done in previous conversations with investigators — where I have been as protective and vague as possible. . . .

With the recent release of GAO audits and the resultant press coverage and criticism of my office, setting the record straight on the Travel Office occurrences is important.

As you recall, an issue developed between the Secret Service and the First Family in February and March requiring resolution and action on your's and my parts. The First Family was anxious to have that situation immediately resolved, and the First Lady in particular was extremely upset with the delayed action in that case.

Likewise, in this case, the First Lady took interest in having the Travel Office situation resolved quickly, following Harry Thomason's bringing it to her attention. Thomason [a Clinton friend from Hollywood] briefed the First Lady on his suspicion that the Travel Office was improperly funneling business to a single charter company, and told her that the functions of that office could easily [be] replaced and reallocated.

Once this made it onto the First Lady's agenda, Vince Foster became involved, and he and Harry Thomason regularly informed me of her attention to the Travel Office situation — as well as her insistence that the situation be resolved immediately by replacing the Travel Office staff.

Foster regularly informed me that the First Lady was concerned and desired action — the action desired was the firing of the Travel Office staff. On Friday, while I was in Memphis, Foster told me that it was important that I speak directly with the First Lady that day. I called her that evening and she conveyed to me in clear terms that her desire [was] for swift and clear action to resolve the situation. She mentioned that Thomason had explained how the Travel Office could be run after removing the current staff — that plan included bringing in World Wide Travel to handle the basic travel functions, the actual actions taken post dismissal, and in light of that she thought immediate action was in order.

On Monday morning, you [Chief of Staff Mack McLarty] came to my office and met with me and Patsy Thomasson [a special assistant to the president]. At that meeting you explained that this was on the First Lady's "radar screen." The message you conveyed to me was clear: immediate action must be taken. I explained to you that I had decided to terminate the Travel Office employees, and you expressed relief that we were finally going to take action (to resolve the situation in conformity with the First Lady's wishes). We both knew that there would be hell to pay if, after our failure in the Secret Service situation earlier, we failed to take swift and decisive action in conformity with the First Lady's wishes. You then approved the decision to terminate the Travel Office staff. . . .

Mack McLarty

These employees work at the pleasure of the President and all in the White House Office should understand that there is extremely low tolerance for the severely negligent and unaccountable procedures followed in that office. In light of the First Lady's insistence for immediate action and your concurrence, the abrupt manner of dismissal, from my perspective, was the only option. . . .

As early as February, the intent of Management and Administration [Mr. Watkins' office] was to review and reorganize the Travel Office before October 1 into a leaner operation — just as with every other office. . . . That remained the plan until the intense pressures surrounding this incident arose in May. If given time to develop, the original plan to reorganize the Travel Office for a smooth transition in September would have allowed the Travel Office employees to seek other federal placement, along with other Executive Office of the President staff, in anticipation of the end of the fiscal year staff cuts; however, when pressure began to build for immediate action in the Travel Office, the long-term plans were short-circuited. . . .

Management and Administration had no part in bringing [Harry]

Thomason into the White House. In fact, the responsible office failed or intentionally neglected to inform Management and Administration of the nature of his work. Contact with this Office on the subject consisted only of the First Lady's Office calling to insist on immediate access for Thomason. . . .

I think all this makes clear that the Travel Office incident was driven by pressures outside my Office. If I thought I could have resisted those pressures, undertaken more considered action, and remained in the White House, I certainly would have done so. But after the Secret Service incident, it was made clear that I must move more forcefully and immediately follow the direction of the First Family. I was convinced that failure to take immediate action in this case would have been directly contrary to the wishes of the First Lady, something that would not have been tolerated in light of the Secret Service incident earlier in the year.

For this reason, I was forced to undertake the Travel Office reorganization without a business plan firmly in hand — something I had never before done in years as a management consultant, where such plans are my business.

All failings outlined in the Podesta Management Review [an internal White House critique of the Travel Office firings] were either mistaken and groundless criticism, or were based on actions dictated by the need for instant action. This reorganization required more careful review, but in this case that possibility was foreclosed. Delaying action was beyond my control.

REVIEW & OUTLOOK

Asides

More Travel Sleaze

Trying to fend off the weekend blizzard of Whitewater accusations, Clinton superlawyer Bob Bennett took to the airwaves to further trash Billy Dale, the unfortunate Travel Office director acquitted by a jury of his peers. Mr. Bennett, originally hired to defend President Clinton in the Paula Jones case, said people shouldn't "cry about" Mr. Dale's treatment because he had "offered to plead guilty to embezzlement and serve four months." This refers to a most unjudicial leak of abortive plea bargain negotiations – and a decidedly embellished one as well, since Mr. Dale in fact ran up legal fees of close to $500,000 by refusing to admit embezzlement. Mr. Bennett, even at his hourly fees still an officer of the court, should be ashamed of himself.

REVIEW & OUTLOOK

'And For Defamation'

On several occasions on and after February 11, 1994, Clinton, and his agents and employees acting pursuant to his direction, maliciously and willfully, defamed Jones by making statements which Clinton knew to be false.

So reads what to our minds is the most intriguing — though certainly not the most sensational — count in Paula Corbin Jones's lawsuit against Bill Clinton, which moved back into the public spotlight yesterday. Overturning a lower court, the Eighth Circuit Court of Appeals said the trial should go forward.

Mrs. Jones of course accuses the President of sexual harassment in a hotel-room incident while he was Governor of Arkansas and she was a minor state employee. The incident came to light as part of descriptions of Mr. Clinton's sexual habits by Arkansas state troopers, in particular Danny Ferguson, a co-defendant in the suit. She says she rebuffed the Governor's advances and that there were obvious "distinguishing characteristics in Clinton's genital area." Unless the Supreme Court takes the case, this will now all go to trial.

There isn't much precedent, needless to say, for such a lawsuit against a President. No cases cover unofficial acts by a President, though the case of *Nixon v. Fitzgerald* provided an immunity to civil suits over a President's official acts. The President's case, adopted by the lower court and an appellate defense, is that the bother of litigation would distract a sitting President and should be stayed until he left office.

The court held yesterday, though, that Mrs. Jones has a right to timely access to the judicial system. "We start with the truism that Article II of the Constitution, which vests the executive power of the federal government in the President, did not create a monarchy," Judge Pasco Bowman wrote for the court. "[T]he President, like all other government officials, is subject to the same laws that apply to other members of society."

In his concurring opinion, Judge C. Arlen Beam noted that Congress had created a special legal category of sexual harassment by state officials, so this was not a "run-of-the-mill tort claim." He added that "the actual impact of this litigation on the duties of the Presidency, if that is Mr. Clinton's real concern, is being vastly magnified."

Paula Jones

Even a cloistered judge, that is, understands that Mr. Clinton's real concern is suppressing the negative publicity, above all until after the next election. Which brings us to the defamation charges. After the troopers' accounts, in which her identity was clear to insiders, she told her side of the story and demanded an apology. She was met with a barrage of abuse on behalf of the President of the United States.

Speaking through White House officials and decidedly not under oath, Mr. Clinton said the hotel incident never happened and that he had never met Mrs. Jones. Dee Dee Myers, the White House spokesperson, said "it's just not true." Another White House aide characterized Mrs. Jones's account as "a cheap political trick." James Carville commented, "Drag a $100 bill through a trailer park and there's no telling what you'll find." Superlawyer Bob Bennett huffed that her suit was "really just another effort to rewrite the results of the election." He also referred to Mrs. Jones's story as "tabloid trash" — translation, Mrs. Jones was poor white trash.

The Eighth Circuit, interestingly, remanded to the lower court the question of Presidential immunity on the defamation charges, withholding judgment on whether White House bombast lies within the "outer perimeter" of the President's official responsibilities posited by *Nixon v. Fitzgerald*. But given such language, any sense of fairness surely entitles Paula Jones to a court ruling on who is telling the truth about the underlying incident. If her story is true, she has been damaged not only by the incident itself, but by the full power and authority of the Presidency itself.

In this particular White House, of course, personal assault is standard operating procedure. When Gennifer Flowers and Sally Perdue speak out about their relationships with the governor, they are cast as "bimbos" and threatened. When David Hale claims he was pressured into making illegal loans, he is branded a crook and a liar. When RTC investigator Jean Lewis testifies before Congress, Clinton surrogates trot out personal correspondence to attack her as an unstable right-winger. When a memo from Arkansas insider David Watkins shines a spotlight on Hillary Clinton's actions in sacking the Travel Office employees, suddenly Arkansas insider Mr. Watkins is not capable of telling the truth.

Against this, Paula Jones wants her day in court, and more power to her.

Letters to the Editor

The $100 Drag

Despite the arrogance Jim Carville reflects in his statement about Paula Jones ("Drag a $100 bill through a trailer park and there's no telling what you'll find"), he never addresses the core problem: What was Bill Clinton doing dragging C-notes through trailer parks? (" 'And for Defamation,' " Review & Outlook, Jan. 10).

For Mr. Carville's edification, what you generally find when you enter trailer parks are people who own their own homes. God forbid an insensitive Republican should make a statement like Mr. Carville's.

David HOGGE

Richmond, Va.

REVIEW & OUTLOOK

Smoke Without Fire

Except for the hired hands, no one any longer is much defending the Clintons on Whitewater issues. Instead, former defenders are scratching their heads over "a coverup without a crime" — why is the White House acting as if it has something to hide? Defenders have advanced to a state of cognitive dissonance, an awareness that beliefs conflict with evidence. The next step is immensely clarifying: OK, they're hiding something; the problem is figuring out precisely what.

Bill Clinton

This is not to neglect, of course, that a coverup is itself a crime. In the Watergate scandal, obstruction of justice was number one in the articles of impeachment approved by the House Judiciary Committee. The itemized list included making false and misleading statements to investigators, withholding evidence, coaching witnesses and "disseminating information received from officers of the Department of Justice of the United States to subjects of investigations." The "smoking gun" was a tape recording of President Nixon approving a plan to have the CIA ask the FBI to drop its investigation of the "two-bit burglary" at Democratic Party headquarters in the Watergate complex. Along the way, of course, there were 18 ½-minute gaps in recordings, packets of evidence being destroyed, assertions of executive privilege swept aside by the Supreme Court and other marks of efforts to hide the truth.

In Whitewater, the basic issue is quite similar. We are at a stage of Presidential cronies leaving high office for jail, battles over "attorney-client" privilege, suppressed White House memos suddenly emerging, billing records being discovered in implausible ways. To cover up "two-bit" transgressions back in Arkansas, we are entitled to suspect, the prerogatives of the Presidency are being abused. As a political and constitutional issue, of course, Whitewater doesn't approach the consuming pitch of Watergate, and probably never will unless President Clinton is somehow re-elected and starts a second term.

* * *

The nature of the Arkansas transgressions is suggested by the newly revealed billing records of Hillary Rodham Clinton's work for Madison Guaranty, James McDougal's S&L. She is currently claiming that the 60 hours of work fit under her previous characterization of "minimal," but the question is not so much how much she did as what she did. She used legal skills and political clout to keep the wayward thrift afloat.

In January 1984, the Federal Home Loan Bank Board questioned Madison's lending practices and instructed the Arkansas Securities Department to take steps to close it down. In March, Rose ("atten: Hillary Clinton") received

James McDougal

the first $2,000 monthly retainer from Madison. In January 1985, Governor Clinton appointed Beverly Bassett as Securities Commissioner. On April 4, Mr. McDougal hosted a fund-raiser for Governor Clinton in the Madison's lobby, contributions to which have drawn the attention of the independent counsel.

A cluster of Rose Law Firm billings to Madison shows up in late April, as Mrs. Clinton and others work on a recapitalization plan to save the foundering thrift. Among the records is an hour by Mrs. Clinton on April 29 for a telephone conference with Commissioner Bassett. The next day, the recapitalization plan is presented to the Arkansas Securities Department, and two weeks later Ms. Bassett informs Mrs. Clinton the plan had been approved. In the event it was never implemented, nor did Ms. Bassett close Madison.

A second cluster of Rose billings occurs in late 1985 and early 1986 under the heading "I.D.C." — the Industrial Development Co., which evolved into the development Mr. McDougal named Castle Grande. Mr. McDougal bought the former industrial park in October 1985 from three banks which held the mortgage. He paid $1.75 million, but regulations limited his investment to $600,000. So he arranged for Seth Ward, then another Madison insider, to hold $1.15 million as a non-recourse loan from Madison. Mr. Ward also got a 10% commission on each parcel sold.

The Rose "I.D.C." billings commenced in August and really picked up steam in November and December. Federal bank examiners were due back at Madison in February, and Mr. McDougal knew he had to deal with its poor financial condition and the insider loans. Another non-recourse loan for $525,000 had gone to Madison insider Davis Fitzhugh; Madison CEO John Latham switched it to a phony recourse note before bank examiners arrived; Mr. Latham later pleaded guilty to tampering with the Fitzhugh loan.

Federal investigators concluded that the Castle Grande land was "purchased and sold in a series of fictitious transactions." Mr. McDougal's complex series of loans and paybacks is now under investigation by the independent counsel. The counsel has the cooperation of Robert Palmer, who pleaded guilty to falsifying 25 appraisals for Madison. According to the Rose billing records, Mrs. Clinton had many conversations with Mr. Ward (as well as Webster Hubbell, his son-in-law) as well as conferences with Mr. Latham and Mr. Fitzhugh.

*   *   *

Mr. McDougal's relations with the Clintons are also instructive. He has claimed he put Mrs. Clinton on retainer after Governor Clinton jogged over one day and made the request, mentioning financial hardship. Mr. Clinton denies this ever happened. It is a matter of record, though, that in 1979 the Clintons formed a 50-50 partnership with Mr. McDougal and his wife Susan on the Whitewater Development Co. The idea was to sell land along the White River, but in the end Mr. McDougal heavily subsidized the operation, carrying some of the Clintons' losses. The appearance, in short, is that Mr. McDougal was providing the Clintons a one-way bet.

Another of the Clintons' close friends was Jim Blair, counsel to chicken king Don Tyson. (Beverly Bassett is now Beverly Bassett Schaffer, wife of Archie Schaffer, director of media and government affairs for Tyson Foods.) Mr. Blair, of course, was also adviser to Mrs. Clinton on her 1978 commodities trades, in which she parlayed $1,000 into $100,000. This took place as Bill Clinton's first gubernatorial campaign headed into its final lap.

Yet another friend was David Watkins, political adviser to the governor when he re-entered the governor's mansion in 1983. That year Mr. Watkins steered Mrs. Clinton into a cellular telephone franchise. Her $2,000 investment netted $48,000 five years later. Mr. Watkins, of course, wrote the White House memo fingering the First Lady in the Travel Office firings and mentioning an earlier incident with the Secret Service.

Hillary Clinton

David Hale, an Arkansas political figure appointed to a judgeship by Governor Clinton, was head of Capital Management Services, a federally backed small-business lender. He made a $300,000 loan to Susan McDougal in 1986 to keep Madison afloat. Some of this money apparently showed up in the Whitewater account. Mr. Hale, who pleaded guilty to defrauding the SBA, said he made the loan under pressure from Mr. McDougal and Governor Clinton. Both have denied the charge, and after his plea Mr. Hale has been cooperating with Independent Counsel Kenneth Starr.

And, of course, these are the instances and allegations we know about. The Clintons' circle of friends was even wider. There was David Edwards, the elusive currency trader at the center of a $23 million gift from the Saudis to the University of Arkansas and who had a long dinner with the President in Little Rock just before Vincent Foster's death. Also Dan Lasater, who ran a bond-trading house and was convicted of social distribution of cocaine, leaving his business to be run while he was in jail by Patsy Thomasson, later one of the White House aides who visited Mr. Foster's office the night of his death.

Meanwhile, the New York Post reported yesterday on correspondence in which the New York State Attorney General is inquiring about more than $100,000 in payments to Mrs. Clinton by the National Center on Education and the Economy, a charity based at the time in Rochester and since relocated to Washington. Mrs. Clinton sat on the organization's board, along with former New York Governor Mario

Cuomo and Ira Magaziner, later health czar. Board members were not paid, but Mrs. Clinton was hired apparently to direct some programs; Dennis Vacco, the new Republican Attorney General, is asking for contracts with her or the Rose Firm and a description of work performed.

Also yesterday, the Associated Press reported that President Clinton was informed in advance of the Travel Office firings, and met twice the week before with Harry Thomason. These findings were omitted from the White House internal review of the matter; the report's author told the AP the omission was "of no consequence," because Mr. Clinton took no action himself. Mr. Thomason, of course, owned the firm that stood to profit from the changes in handling of Travel Office business.

*　*　*

By this point, we should think, the smoke is getting pretty thick. Some little flames may be individually quenched, but there is a certain pattern to them. The Clintons had a lot of friends in the fast lanes in Arkansas, and the whole crowd trafficked in political influence and money. Nearly all of the people involved in these affairs, in Washington and back in Arkansas, are in various degrees of serious legal trouble or personal and political ruin. But Bill and Hillary are in the White House, the dissonance runs, unsmudged and unsullied.

REVIEW & OUTLOOK

Split Hairs

Mrs. Clinton: Castle Grande was a trailer park on a piece of property that was about 1,000 acres big. I never did work for Castle Grande. Never at all. And so when I was asked about it last year, I didn't recognize it, I didn't remember it. The billing records show I did not do work for Castle Grande. I did work for something called IDC, which was not related to Castle Grande.

Ms. Walters: Was that Seth . . .

Mrs. Clinton: And Seth Ward was involved in that . . .

Ms. Walters: Separate deal?

Mrs. Clinton: Separate deal completely.

We don't know whether audacity is congenital, but it was certainly on display in Hillary Clinton's appearance with Barbara Walters. In the wake of this misinformation, someone ought to put down the relation between IDC and Castle Grande. Briefly, everyone else knowledgeable about the deals thinks of them as one and the same; the problem of the day is trying to figure out what hairs Mrs. Clinton is splitting.

IDC stands for the Industrial Development Co., which held the mortgage on 1,000 acres of the partially developed Little Rock Industrial Park in southern Pulaski County. In October 1985, IDC sold this land to interests controlled by James McDougal for $1.75 million. Regulations prevented Madison Financial, the real estate subsidiary of Madison Guaranty S&L, from investing more than $600,000, and

Madison insider Seth Ward held the balance of $1.15 million, financed by a non-recourse loan from Madison. Federal investigators have characterized Mr. Ward's role as a "straw" purchaser, and the Resolution Trust Corp. wants to know more about a $400,000 option deal Mr. Ward cut with Madison.

A code on the option document indicates it was authored by Mrs. Clinton. The billing records show a number of conversations with Seth Ward while these deals were being consummated. By any definition, Castle Grande was located on the 1,000 acres purchased from the IDC; which name should be used is at most a semantic issue.

The best account of these transactions was a four-part series in the Arkansas Democrat-Gazette in August 1994, focusing on the part played in the Madison saga by Governor Jim Guy Tucker, since indicted with Mr. McDougal by Independent Counsel Kenneth Starr. The Democrat-Gazette describes the Little Rock Industrial Park transactions, and concludes, "The land was purchased in October 1985. McDougal named the project Castle Grande."

"McDougal dreamed of Castle Grande as an upscale working-class neighborhood featuring mobile homes, a shopping center, a convenience story and a truck stop. Castle Grande would be home to the businesses and industries that employed some of the residents," the newspaper continued.

Above art showing a sign for the Castle Grande shopping center, buildings owned by Castle Sewer and Water, a sign for Master Developers' undeveloped truck stop lot, and a photo of Etta's Place restaurant, the Little Rock paper wrote, "They called it Castle Grande. . . . Beginning in October 1985, Madison Financial Corp. purchased 1,000 acres of southern Pulaski County industrial property, kicking off a whirlwind of land deals and high-dollar loans. The selling spree, financed through parent company Madison Guaranty Savings and Loan, culminated on Feb. 28, 1986, the same day federal examiners arrived at Madison."

Mrs. Clinton seems to be contending the name Castle Grande applied only to the trailer park, and was unfamiliar to her. As it happens, her name also comes up in two other related matters Rose handled for Castle Grande.

In January 1986, Mrs. Clinton worked on research related to Mr. McDougal's plan to build a brewery. Some of the Rose vouchers carry the notion "CG" — Castle Grande. But in a memo to Rose attorney

Rick Donovan, Mrs. Clinton writes, "Charge Madison Guaranty/IDC." The vouchers also indicate she worked on Castle Sewer and Water, a complex deal for a sewer treatment facility, ultimately resolved by Governor Clinton, that has resulted in an indictment by Mr. Starr.

One of the main themes offered over the weekend by the Clintons and their attorneys is that they keep answering questions, but the questions just keep coming back. It's not hard to understand why.

REVIEW & OUTLOOK

Castle Whatever — Cont.

Yesterday we explored the semantics Hillary Clinton has woven around "Castle Grande" and "IDC," the point being that whichever name you use she was still doing legal work for Madison Guaranty and Seth Ward in the midst of transactions federal regulators described as "sham."

As it happens, the editors of the Washington Post yesterday took up the same subject in response to a letter from Mrs. Clinton's lawyer making the distinction between Castle Grande Estates, the trailer park, and Castle Grande, the name everyone else applies to the larger project. This hair needs to be split, the Post made clear, to defend Mrs. Clinton's answers to an earlier interrogatory from the RTC. While the exact exchange is not in the public domain, it seems she told the RTC she didn't believe she knew anything about Castle Grande — by which she now means the trailer park and not the larger project she called IDC. While we're on the subject, it would be instructive to continue the story.

The records clearly show that Mrs. Clinton billed Madison for work on the "utility" issue — whether Castle Sewer and Water, serving Castle Grande, qualified as a "public utility" under Arkansas law. The Rose analysis was done in preparation for Madison's February 1986 sale of Castle Sewer to Arkansas businessmen Jim Guy Tucker — the current governor — and R.D. Randolph. They financed the $1.2 million purchase with a non-recourse loan from Madison Guaranty for $1,050,000 and a $150,000 loan from David

Hale's Capital Management Services.

The sale was based on a $1.3 million valuation by Little Rock appraiser Robert Palmer, who pleaded guilty in December 1994 to falsifying 25 appraisals for Madison. Both Mr. Hale and Mr. Palmer are cooperating with Independent Counsel Kenneth Starr. The financing of the Castle Sewer deal constitutes one count of Mr. Starr's 21-count indictment against Governor Tucker, Mr. McDougal and his wife Susan.

By 1987, after Mr. McDougal had been removed from Madison by federal regulators, the Castle Sewer partners were looking to renegotiate their debt. They hoped to point to legislation to deregulate small utilities, which would allow Castle Sewer to raise its rates and service its debt. The bill passed both houses of the Arkansas legislature, but Governor Clinton vetoed it.

According to documents obtained by the House Banking Committee, Messrs. Tucker and Randolph proceeded to pressure Governor Clinton to reverse the veto. "Mr. Randolph dropped by to see you this morning to talk to you about the Water Bill you vetoed," reads an April 1987 memo from a staffer to the Governor. "He mentioned a meeting between you, Tucker and Jim McDougal a couple of years ago which involved $33,000." That happened to be the amount raised in an April 1985 fund-raiser in Madison Guaranty's lobby, including contributions from Tucker, Randolph and McDougal, and now under investigation by the independent counsel. The Post also reported earlier that Mr. Tucker's lawyers had threatened not to pay the loan on the grounds that the original purchase was invalid, a challenge that would have raised questions about the legal work done by Mrs. Clinton.

Mr. Tucker has denied the report, and in the event there was no need for him to carry out any threats. The water bill was passed again in a special session of the legislature, and Governor Clinton, in an abrupt reversal, signed the measure into law.

REVIEW & OUTLOOK

'We Need Our People In'

Today, David Watkins, the former White House administrator whose memo put Hillary Clinton and Travelgate on front pages and TV screens, will testify before a House committee. It is unclear to what extent Mr. Watkins, a former business partner and close friend of the First Lady, will seek to protect her. However, a growing body of supplementary evidence is eroding Mrs. Clinton's version of events. The question that keeps emerging is, why the urgency? Why did the Clinton inner circle feel it had to get its hands on the travel operation so fast?

David Watkins

The First Lady has spent recent days in the Clintons' familiar Didn't-Inhale Defense. No longer quite arguing that "she had no role" in the 1993 Travel Office purge, she now says her "mere expression of concern" could have been "taken to mean something more than it was meant." On Mr. Watkins, Mrs. Clinton now claims that "if you read his memo, he doesn't say I directly told him anything."

Rewind to the Watkins memo itself. Mr. Watkins writes: Mrs. Clinton "conveyed to me in clear terms her desire for swift and clear action." In May 14 notes recording his conversation with the First Lady before the firings, Mr. Watkins also wrote: "We need those people out — We need our people in — We need the slots." This version is backed up by contemporaneous notes by then White House chief of staff Mack McLarty, and aides Todd Stern and Lorraine Voles. Ms. Voles wrote that the First Lady's friend, Susan "Thomases went to Mack— Hillary wants these people fired — Mack wouldn't do it."

The Clintons' take on these events, now being pressed everywhere by their lawyers, is that the White House undertook to correct the Travel Office's "financial mismanagement." Our view is that this is a secondary story intended to divert attention from the main goal of simply seizing control of the travel business. There is reason to believe that the takeover was in train well before the Clintons actually entered the White House in January 1993.

In November 1992, two months before the inauguration, Steven Davison of World Wide Travel, the Little Rock agency that handled the Clinton campaign's travel, told Arkansas Business magazine that World Wide might open a Washington office to handle the travel needs of Presidential staff, a function long performed by the Travel Office. In December, Clinton aide Jeff Eller told several reporters that the new administration had plans to remove the Travel Office staff.

In January, Hollywood producer Harry Thomason's partner in the air charter business, Darnell Martens, drafted a memo in which he set out ways "to pursue Washington opportunities" for their firm. They included: "obtain some form of official status as advisors to the White House," a two-year evaluation of "all non-military government aircraft," "selection assistance and policy recommendations" for the FAA Administrator. Mr. Martens also suggested that the scheduling of White House press corps aircraft could be "done by TRM [Thomason's company] much as the campaign aircraft were handled." Finally, two days before the first request to Peat Marwick auditors for a hurried May 12 review of the Travel Office, World Wide Travel was contacted by Catherine Cornelius, a cousin of President Clinton, and told to get ready to take over the Travel Office.

Now, putting the gloss of innocence on this, one could say it was somehow the Clintons' prerogative to reorganize the Travel Office. But in the famous memo, even David Watkins notes that he'd never have crashed through such a reorganization without first devising some sort of business plan. Who would, really? That leaves us to explain the extraordinarily ramped-up sequence of events leading to the May firing of the seven career employees.

On May 12, Catherine Cornelius and Harry Thomason met with

Mr. Watkins to discuss their allegations against the Travel Office. Later that day, White House associate counsel William Kennedy contacted the FBI. When FBI agent Jim Bourke called back the next day, Mr. Kennedy demanded to know "within 15 minutes" what the FBI was going to do. Otherwise, he warned, the IRS would be called in instead, Later that day, Hillary Clinton separately asked both Mack McLarty and Vince Foster what was being done about "problems" in the Travel Office.

Hillary Clinton, Vince Foster, Mack McLarty, Bill Kennedy, David Watkins, the FBI, the IRS. This is an awful lot of heavy firepower being brought to bear all at once on transitioning a White House administrative function. And indeed David Watkins's May 14 notes make it clear that he himself wonders what's going on. Of the firings, his notes say:

"Can we close the operation on May 15 and continue to operate in the short term on the same or better level of service?"

"Do we hamper possible criminal investigation re disposal of evidence?"

"Why the rush?"

Five days later, under the constant prodding of whatever we're supposed to think the First Lady was conveying, the firings took place.

In recent days, Mrs. Clinton's advocates have been putting out that her failure has been in being too instinctively lawyerly. What's lawyerly about any of this? We don't see open bids being asked for a federal service. We see the Arkansas crowd targeting a White House function as their property, smashing some career small fry to get at it, and now in the person of the First Lady arguing, it was no big deal. They must figure the Beltway's willingness to be gulled is absolutely boundless.

REVIEW & OUTLOOK

Castle Grande—The Brewery

It's a busy time in Whitewater land. At the House Oversight Committee hearings into Travelgate yesterday, former White House administrator David Watkins enforced a television blackout on the proceedings, but stood by most of his story of Hillary Clinton's role in firing seven employees. Over at the Senate Whitewater hearings Tuesday, former White House associate counsel William Kennedy lectured on grammar, contending that in his note "Vacuum Rose Law Files," the word vacuum was a noun rather than a verb.

Amid these diversions, we're here to offer Part III of the Castle Grande saga. We've already talked about Mrs. Clinton's split hairs over Castle Grande Estates, the trailer park, and the IDC project, which everyone else is mistaken to call Castle Grande. And we talked about Mrs. Clinton's work on Castle Grande's sewer project, helped along by a timely reversal of a veto by the governor. So we really should complete the tour with Castle Grande, the Brewery.

According to documents released by the House Banking Committee and recently discovered Rose billing records, Mrs. Clinton represented Madison in issues relating to the construction of a brewery at Castle Grande (actually, Castle Grande Estates). Madison Guaranty owner Jim McDougal envisioned a brewery and "tasting room" as a tourist attraction. But there were two problems. Arkansas law did not permit both the manufacture and sale of alcoholic beverages at the same site. And Castle Grande was located in a "dry" township.

In December 1984, Mr. McDougal attacked the first problem by sending gubernatorial aide Betsey Wright a copy of a bill allowing the Arkansas Alcoholic Beverage Control Board (the "ABC") to license manufacturing facilities for on-premises sale of alcohol. "Governor Clinton has made a commitment concerning this bill which I need to discuss with you at your convenience," reads an attached McDougal note. Two months later, the regulation was changed.

In a memo attached to the Castle Grande documents, the House Banking Committee notes that Mr. McDougal's "request for favorable legislative treatment coincided with substantial payments of principal by McDougal-controlled entities on the Clintons' personal Whitewater debts." To wit, more than $22,000 on a co-signed McDougal-Clinton note at Citizens Bank.

After securing the regulatory change, Mr. McDougal attacked the "dry" problem by employing Mrs. Clinton to study this and related matters. In a January 1986 memo, Mrs. Clinton and Rose attorney Rick Donovan determined that the regulations originated in a township that no longer existed, and the law thus might be considered "dissolved" by the ABC, despite precedent running against such an interpretation.

Six weeks earlier, Mr. McDougal had written in a memo to Seth Ward, a Madison insider, about a proposal by Arkansas beer tycoon Bill Lyon, "Subject to approval by the ABC, Bill will place his brewery in the shell building, along with a tasting room. I have spoken with the Governor on this matter, and expect it will be approved." And in an undated follow-up memo to Rose attorney Rick Donovan, Mrs. Clinton wrote that she gave the legal memo to Mr. Ward, and suggested devising "a strategy to approach the ABC to argue the 'dissolved township' theory." It seems Jim Guy Tucker's law firm reached an opposite judgment, and suggested a township referendum.

By August 1986, federal regulators removed Mr. McDougal from Madison, and his plans to develop Castle Grande became moot.

REVIEW & OUTLOOK

The Clinton Tag Team

Back in one of its early incarnations, you may remember, Bill Clinton's Presidential campaign had a slogan, "buy one, get two." The subsequent cookie-baking phase submerged the notion of a dual, husband-and-wife Presidency. But it emerged again inauguration week, when Mrs. Bill Clinton quickly became Hillary Rodham Clinton, about to remake the nation's health care system.

Hillary Clinton

We recite this history because the First Lady has seemed to stand almost alone at the center of the revelations of the past two weeks, culminating in yesterday's astonishing testimony that the missing Rose Law Firm billing records suddenly appeared in the "book room" next to her study in the family quarters of the White House. Aide Carolyn Huber undoubtedly told the same story when she testified before Independent Counsel Kenneth Starr's grand jury in Little Rock on Wednesday, and the documents themselves are presumably being tested for fingerprints in line with usual forensic procedures. They are known to be annotated in the handwriting of the late Vincent Foster, and it's also known that documents from his office passed through the family quarters before being turned over to the Clintons' personal attorneys. Clinton defenders object to the Ockham's Razor connection of these facts.

It is a good time to reflect on who resides in the family quarters.

True, it's difficult enough to imagine Bill or Chelsea or Socks poring over Rose billing records. True too that the White House went out of its way to shovel a Bill Safire column out of the snow to keep Hillary on the point. But one presumes the two halves of the dual Presidency share pillow talk. And while Mrs. Clinton clearly has a mind of her own, it has to be a stretch to depict her as a loose cannon on the White House deck. Their whole history from Arkansas to the present suggests a political-managerial-financial tag team. Which is to say what ought to be obvious, that the controversy swirling around the First Lady inextricably involves the President.

Take the Travel Office affair, for example. For openers, Hillary Clinton obviously has no official power to fire White House employ-

Bill Clinton

ees. President Clinton bears the power and the real responsibility for whatever his Administration does. But even laying that aside, it now appears the President was told about the firings in advance, though afterward he explained, "All I knew was there was a plan to cut the size of the office, save tax dollars." Of course, Mrs. Clinton also denies she had any significant role in the firing of Billy Dale and his six colleagues.

In his testimony Wednesday before the House Oversight Committee, former White House administrator David Watkins sketched his view of the event: "I was in the chain of command — the President, the First Lady, [!] McLarty, me. It was me. I'm accountable." But he added, "Was there pressure? Did I feel pressure of the desires and wishes of others? Yes, I did." Mr. Foster, for example, "regularly informed me that the First Lady was concerned and desired action — the action desired was the firing of the Travel Office staff," Mr. Watkins wrote in his now-famous memo. And if Mr. Foster was speaking for the First Lady, the First Lady must be presumed to speak for the President.

Indeed, calendar notes finally turned over to House investigators by Hollywood producer and travel-company impresario Harry Thomason show that he had two meetings with the President the week before the firings, and shortly after each met with Catherine Cornelius, later designated to take over the office. The usual denials apply, but Mr. Dale tells us a high aide to President Clinton told him at the time that "there was one person only that was responsible for what happened in your office this weekend, and that person occupies the Oval Office."

Or take the Arkansas transactions surrounding the Castle Grande development, which we've detailed this week. Yes, Mrs. Clinton did legal work for parts of Jim McDougal's real estate development, and answered RTC interrogatories in a way that now has her wrapped in split hairs. But it was not Mrs. Clinton who reversed a veto of legislation helpful to keeping a Castle Sewer loan afloat. Nor was it Mrs. Clinton mentioned in a memo alluding to political contributions at a Madison fund-raiser. Nor was it Mrs. Clinton cited in a memo Mr. McDougal delivered to Betsey Wright on a bill to facilitate a brewery there: "Governor Clinton has made a commitment."

Or take, for that matter, Whitewater Development Co. itself. Bill was as much a partner as Hillary, and both profited when Mr. McDougal absorbed losses. And while Hillary took the legal plan to recapitalize the foundering thrift to Arkansas Securities Commissioner Beverly Bassett, it was the Governor who had appointed the Commissioner three months earlier.

And, of course, Mr. McDougal claims Governor Clinton jogged by to suggest he put Hillary on retainer. While Mr. McDougal is scarcely the most credible witness, the fact is that $2,000 checks started arriving at the Rose Law Firm to Hillary's attention. By the way, this was before Rick Massey even joined Rose, shattering the story that he brought in the Madison account. Also, of course, David Hale, now a Starr witness after his guilty plea, also claims Governor Clinton pressured him into making a $300,000 loan to Madison Guaranty, some of which ended up in the Whitewater account.

Or take, for that matter, Mrs. Clinton's $100,000 in commodity profits. Perhaps Tyson Foods Counsel Jim Blair "advised" her in these transactions because he liked the cadence of the name Rodham. Or his interest might have been piqued by her husband's growing political prospects. The Clinton tag team, after all, filed a joint tax return.

Now, we dwell on this because of a theme that, at least until the Huber testimony yesterday, seemed to be buzzing around the Beltway press hive. Namely, that you can't impeach a First Lady, that the President has been floating above the controversy, that no crime has been suggested and is in any event Mr. Starr's turf, that continued emphasis on scandal is (gasp!) political, that with an election approaching all this should be closed down so the electorate can ponder the future of Medicare. So let's deep-six Whitewater, as we deep-sixed it back in 1992.

What are your deepest suspicions, this line of logic asks. OK, our deepest suspicions are that back in Arkansas the Clinton tag team was engaged in a pattern of sleazy operations, and that when they arrived in Washington they abused the powers of the Presidency to thwart investigation of them. Whether the sleaze amounted to indictable crimes we will leave to Mr. Starr, but the coverup is the reason articles of impeachment were voted against Richard Nixon. These are perhaps only suspicions, but various people keep asking.

It is far better, we submit, to air fully such suspicions now, even if partisans like Alfonse D'Amato are the messengers. What are political campaigns for, after all, if not to air and prove or refute issues of both policy and character? For the Republic, clearly the worst outcome would be to bury suspicions until after the election, and to have them re-emerge and proven true at the start of a second Clinton term.

Counteroffensive—
Washington

As Republicans battled their way through the Presidential prima-ry season, the Whitewater counteroffensive took on a new life in Washington. Efforts increased to discredit Whitewater figures such as Kenneth Starr, Alfonse D'Amato, Billy Dale and others who might prove damaging. In one emblematic incident, superlawyer Robert Bennett, the President's personal attorney, attacked Mr. Dale— already driven from his job, bankrupted, charged with felonious con-duct and acquitted in a jury trial—in a televised interview.

The Senate Whitewater Committee, meanwhile, continued to stitch together the threads of the complicated story into a damning portrait of official misconduct and Arkansas sleaze. In another round of questioning before the Committee, former Associate Attorney General Webster Hubbell admitted while he was negotiating a plea bargain with Mr. Starr he was paid an undisclosed sum by a billion-aire pal of the President, Indonesian financier Mochtar Riady. Mr. Riady's Lippo Group was a former business partner in Arkansas with investment giant Stephens Inc. and later attempted to buy the Hong Kong branch of BCCI. In another surprise, Richard Ben-Veniste, the former Watergate prosecutor and now Democratic counsel to the Whitewater Committee, turned out to have been an attorney for DEA/CIA-connected Mena drug smuggler Barry Seal. Mr. Ben-Veniste told the Journal, "I did my part by launching Barry Seal into the arms of Vice President Bush, who embraced him as an under-cover operative." The Journal noted that "Mr. Ben-Veniste's remark is an implicit warning that if pushed far enough Whitewater will start to implicate Republicans as well as Democrats. Fine by us."

By March, Senate Democrats had closed ranks around the Clintons and mounted a lengthy filibuster against renewing the mandate of the Whitewater Committee. Though the Committee would convene later for a few weeks, the filibuster proved effective. The Senate probe was dead, killed by the minority.

REVIEW & OUTLOOK

Asides

Attack Lawyer Called Off

The White House retreated this week from recent attacks on the character of Billy Dale, the White House Travel Office director who was found innocent of embezzlement charges last year. Recall that Bob Bennett, President Clinton's private lawyer, had incorrectly told ABC that in plea negotiations with prosecutors Mr. Dale "was willing to plead guilty to embezzlement and serve four months in jail." Yesterday, White House spokesman Mike McCurry rebuked Mr. Bennett for his "objectionable" statements. "We didn't put Bennett out to say anything bad about Billy Dale," Mr. McCurry said. But the Associated Press reports that a senior White House official said President Clinton earlier had told Mr.

Robert Bennett

Bennett he did "a great job" in his ABC interview and subsequently expanded his role in defending the Administration. In addition, talking points sent out by the First Lady's office for Democratic defenders of the Administration recommended attacking Mr. Dale for office mismanagement. The Administration's handling of Whitewater has become so chaotic it can't even keep its political spin cycles in order.

Letters to the Editor

Robert Bennett on Billy Dale

Your Feb. 1 editorial "Attack Lawyer Called Off," was incorrect in several respects. I was not ordered to attack, nor was I called off or admonished. Had your editorial writers read Mike McCurry's statements of Jan. 31 or the Associated Press reports regarding Mr. McCurry's press conference, you would not have written such a misleading editorial.

Your comment that I incorrectly characterized Billy Dale's plea offer on ABC is also wrong. In the letter embodying that offer — which was a matter of public record and confirmed in public statements by Mr. Dale's lawyer prior to my remarks on ABC — it is stated: "Mr. Dale will enter a plea of guilty to a single count of 18 U.S.C. Section 654." That statute reads in relevant part, "Whoever, being an officer or employee of the United States . . . embezzles or wrongfully converts to his own use the money or property of another . . ." shall be fined or imprisoned or both. Also, as part of the proposed agreement the letter in relevant part states, "The United States agrees that it will not seek a sentence in excess of four (4) months imprisonment," and that "the United States agrees that it will not oppose Mr. Dale's request that at least one-half of that term be served under home confinement." A careful reading of the Dale plea letter, obviously released by Congress and not the Department of Justice, leaves little doubt that Mr. Dale and his attorney did not view Mr. Dale as a victim of a frame-up or other conspiracy.

Finally, let me make it clear that it is a terrible distortion of the record to suggest that I "attacked" Mr. Dale. In response to Congressman Clinger, who has repeatedly suggested on ABC and other shows that the acquittal of Billy Dale means that there was no misconduct at the Travel Office and that somehow his acquittal proves there was a political conspiracy to frame him, I suggested that this was nonsense. Mr. Dale was indicted by a grand jury of citizens of the District of Columbia after a thorough investigation and presentation of evidence by career professionals in the Public Integrity Section of the Department of Justice, and not by political appointees. Of course, Mr. Dale, like all citizens, was presumed innocent before trial, and with his acquittal no one should suggest that he was guilty of a crime. However, his acquittal does not mean that he was framed or that the "disastrously" run travel office was free of misconduct. Indeed, a reading of Mr. Dale's trial transcript and the undisputed public record clearly rebuts any such suggestions.

ROBERT S. BENNETT

Washington

* * *

FEBRUARY 7, 1996

The Conspiracy Against Billy Dale

Robert Bennett's Feb. 2 Letter to the Editor ("Robert Bennett on Billy Dale"), in which he tries to defend his unfounded attacks on my client, is incorrect in several respects. First, Mr. Bennett's purported "careful reading" of the letter I wrote to the Department of Justice on Nov. 30, 1994, and his quotation from that letter is highly selective and misleading. The argument he advances based upon the language of that letter — that there is "little doubt that Mr. Dale and his attorney did not view Mr. Dale as a victim of a frame-up or other conspiracy" — is, to use Mr. Bennett's words, "a terrible distortion of the record."

Let me make clear that Mr. Dale and his attorney believe that the removal of Mr. Dale and his colleagues from the Travel Office, and Mr. Dale's subsequent prosecution, were indeed the product of "efforts by a clique of Arkansas and other political supporters of the Clinton Administration to take over the Travel Office in order to reap substantial financial rewards from both the media charter service and the Travel Office's commercial component that was responsible for booking business and personal air travel . . . for White House staff." This quote — which I would hope leaves little doubt about our view of the matter — is from a lengthy pleading filed in federal court more than a year ago. It is part of the "public record" on which Mr. Bennett purports to rely. That pleading sets out in detail the basis for our belief: (1) that the investigation of Mr. Dale had its genesis in a desire to reward World Wide Travel Service for its critical assistance during the Clinton presidential campaign; and (2) that there was reason to believe that, to achieve their goal, White House officials "had removed from the Travel Office and kept from the prosecutors" logs maintained by Mr. Dale to account precisely for the money he was charged with embezzling.

I asserted in that document, and others filed with the court: (1) that these logs were removed in order to give the supposedly independent review team hired by the White House the incorrect impression that Mr. Dale could not account completely for press funds, thereby providing a plausible reason for the decision, reached long before the financial review, to fire Mr. Dale and his colleagues; and (2) that these logs would demonstrate completely Mr. Dale's innocence of the charges against him. These logs, which are still missing, were never part of the supposedly "thorough investigation and presentation of evidence [to "a grand jury of citizens of the District of Columbia"] by career professionals in the Public Integrity Section of the Department of Justice" that Mr. Bennett cites for his specious claim that there was "misconduct" in Mr. Dale's management of the Travel Office. It is hardly an accident that this is the case; the history of the White House's persistent refusal to cooperate with the Justice Department in this investigation and others is well-documented in the public record.

Back in January 1995 we sought court permission to serve subpoenas on the White House and others in order to gain access to the memoranda and other documents that have since been given to Rep. Clinger's committee. Had we been granted permission, the full nature of the conspiracy that victimized Mr. Dale would have been brought to public light at that time. Most important, the public would have learned then that Mr. Bennett's client, Harry Thomason, by advancing the outrageous and self-serving lie that Mr. Dale had demanded kickbacks in exchange for Travel Office business, set in motion the events that led to Mr. Dale's removal and prosecution. In the course of their lengthy investigation of Mr. Dale, the prosecutors could find no evidence to support Mr. Thomason's claim. They could find no one who disputed the view of numerous witnesses who had known Mr. Dale for decades that his honesty and integrity were above reproach.

Mr. Bennett is also incorrect in his suggestion that my Nov. 30, 1994, letter to the Justice Department constitutes a willingness by Mr. Dale to admit the charge of embezzlement, for which he was acquitted. Mr. Bennett accurately quotes the first sentence of that letter: that Mr. Dale was prepared to enter a "plea of guilty to a single count of 18 U.S.C. Section 654." For some reason, Mr. Bennett chose to omit the sentence that immediately follows: that Mr. Dale would not admit to any intent to defraud or to permanently deprive anyone of the money that was represented by the checks he deposited in his personal account. It was no accident that we included this condition. As a lawyer of Mr. Bennett's experience and exceptional ability must know, the crime of embezzlement requires either an admission by the defendant or proof by the prosecution of that which Mr. Dale always denied. Mr. Bennett's omission of this condition in describing my letter to the prosecutor is akin to describing the Washington, D.C. skyline but omitting the Washington Monument and the Capitol dome.

By offering to end the case without admitting all the elements necessary to prove the charge, Mr. Dale and I were engaging in a practice that has been an accepted part of criminal procedure since 1970, when the Supreme Court sanctioned it. It is employed in a variety of circumstances in which a person faced with an expensive and wrenching criminal trial seeks to avoid that trial while maintaining his innocence. Certainly the Justice Department understood Mr. Dale was not admitting embezzlement; that is why it refused to end the case on the terms we offered. As events turned out, Mr. Dale told the jury precisely that which he offered to admit a year earlier. Under proper instructions on the law from District Judge Gladys Kessler, a Clinton appointee, the jury promptly found Mr. Dale not guilty, precisely because there was no proof that Mr. Dale engaged in the conduct that we denied in the Nov. 30 letter.

This letter should never have become the subject of public debate. It was a confidential communication. One senior Justice official said its leak was "outrageous"; and it is being investigated by the department's Office of Professional Responsibility. Mr. Bennett's bald assertion that it was "obviously released by Congress and not by the Department of Justice" suggests he has highly relevant information on this score. I hope Congress provides him with an opportunity to share his evidence publicly.

Mr. Bennett also claims that "a reading of Mr. Dale's trial transcript and the undisputed public record" demonstrates that the Travel Office was "disastrously run." The record demonstrates no such thing. Mr. Dale acknowledged during trial that a single decision on his part — to use his personal funds to cash certain checks made out to the Travel Office — was a "disastrous" one. No one (other than Mr. Bennett and his clients) has ever suggested that Mr. Dale's management of the principal functions of the Travel Office was less than exemplary. Unlike the documented practices of the current Travel Office, Mr. Dale paid his vendors on time, billed the press on time, balanced the checkbook, and never had planes land at the wrong airport, as occurred several months ago.

Finally, we challenge Mr. Bennett to produce the evidence to support the irresponsible claim he made on ABC that the Travel Office was engaged in other unspecified misconduct; or his equally irresponsible suggestion on CBS that members of the Travel Office had been involved in conduct that violated "customs law and state tax laws." Absent his production of evidence in support of these claims, we call upon Mr. Bennett to promptly and publicly acknowledge his error.

STEVEN C. TABACKMAN
Attorney for Billy Ray Dale
Washington

* * *

Robert Bennett's defense of himself for his gratuitous comments and involvement concerning the Billy Dale case is both passing strange and not worthy of an able trial lawyer. If his recent public pronouncements concerning the case were not provoked or inspired by his representation of the Clintons, then he is nothing more than a noisy busybody; if he is not advancing his clients' interests, then he should stick to his own cases and not try to sully Mr. Dale, who obviously has suffered enough.

Perhaps the most incredible parts of Mr. Bennett's letter are the many sinister conclusions he draws from Mr. Dale's attempt to plea bargain. Mr. Bennett may be the bar's most prodigious plea bargainer, and he well knows that many times those indicted, especially federally, decide to plea bargain to avoid the horrible strain of trial and the huge cost required to defend against almost any U.S. indictment.

Mr. Bennett suggests that the acquittal of Billy Dale does not suggest a political conspiracy to frame him. But Mr. Bennett must know that such suspicions by many are based not only upon the acquittal alone. That suspicion is heavily fueled by information that has finally become public concerning the uninspiring activities of the Clintons and the Clintons' friends who wanted to take over and earn large profits from the operations of the White House Travel Office; Mr. Dale was manifestly an impediment to their uninspiring effort.

Mr. Bennett would be wise to heed the advice of the French philosopher who sagaciously said, "We all talk nonsense on occasion, the vice is to do so seriously."

DON H. REUBEN

Chicago

REVIEW & OUTLOOK

The Clinton Judges

In his State of the Union address, President Clinton declared a campaign of talking right, no doubt also intending to solidify his coalition by governing left. One of the quickest ways to cut to the real nature of an incumbent President, trying to divine what he would actually do in a second term, is to look at his judicial appointments.

We have already discussed the case of Judge Harold Baer Jr., a 1994 Clinton appointee who threw out a drug arrest in New York, though police had caught the drug-runners' driver red-handed and seized 80 pounds of cocaine and heroin. The police had no reason to search the car, Judge Baer declared, because running from the cops is ordinary behavior in the neighborhood in question.

Today we would like to take up one of the President's pending appointments, the nomination of attorney Bruce Greer as a federal district judge in the Southern District of Florida. The nomination excited our attention when we learned that Mr. Greer had been a partner in a defunct law firm with a name riveted in our memory: Arky, Freed, Stearns, Watson & Greer. The firm collapsed in 1985 when Stephen Arky committed suicide amid the financial wreckage of Ronnie Ewton's ESM Government Securities and Marvin Warner's Home State Savings Bank.

* * *

Mr. Greer's nomination is now before Senator Orrin Hatch's Judiciary Committee, which has yet to schedule hearings. On January 22, the Miami Herald complained that "some Republicans want to delay President Clinton's judicial nominees as long as possible and ultimately beyond an election that they hope to win." The editorial did not mention Arky Freed and all that, nor for that matter Mr. Greer's legal work on behalf of the Herald. We second the call for early hearings. We'd like to learn a lot more about Mr. Greer's former firm, and provide the prospective judge an opportunity to explain his role in it.

Mr. Greer was recommended for the post in July 1993 by Senator Bob Graham, Democrat of Florida. Senator Graham also supports another Floridian due to appear before the Judiciary Committee, Democratic Party fund-raiser Charles "Bud" Stack. Mr. Stack raised millions as candidate Clinton's 1992 Florida finance chairman and in 1994 helped organize a Miami gala that brought in $3.4 million for the Democratic Party. President Clinton nominated him for a seat on the 11th Circuit Court of Appeals last November.

Critics on the right, such as the Free Congress Foundation, complain that the selection is a patronage payoff; critics on the left, such as the Alliance for Justice, want Mr. Stack's 17-year membership in the Riviera Country Club explored. Membership in the Riviera, which for years reportedly had an unofficial policy of excluding blacks and Jews, sunk the 1991 nomination of U.S. District Judge Kenneth Ryskamp to the 11th Circuit. Mr. Stack, who quit the club in 1993, says he worked to expand minority membership; the same argument was made by Judge Ryskamp.

*　*　*

Mr. Greer's nomination languished in White House limbo for two years without formally going to the Judiciary Committee. Meanwhile, though American Bar Association judicial ratings are supposed to remain confidential until Senate hearings — except if your name is Robert Bork — reports began to circulate that Mr. Greer had been ABA rated as "not qualified." But last August, apparently as a reflection of what forces ultimately prevail in Mr. Clinton's Administration, the Greer nomination was sent to the Senate.

Mr. Greer was a partner in the Arky firm from 1976 to 1985. Also in 1976, Stephen Arky began a close working relationship with his friend Ronnie Ewton, a government securities trader and the founder of ESM Securities. Mr. Arky was the son-in-law of Democratic Party financier and former Carter Administration ambassador to Switzerland Marvin Warner, owner of Home State Savings Bank of

Ohio; Mr. Warner also was second cousin to state comptroller Gerald Lewis, Florida's top banking and securities regulator. Mr. Warner's bank became Mr. Arky's biggest client.

In 1985, ESM imploded in the midst of a gigantic securities' repurchase scam, causing $100 million in losses in Florida and touching off a bank crisis in Ohio, where Mr. Warner's Home State Bank lost $150 million and was shut down. Mr. Arky killed himself that July, leaving behind a note declaring his innocence in the ESM collapse. Mr. Ewton and Mr. Warner subsequently went to jail for securities and banking fraud.

The odd cast circulating through the halls of the Arky firm also included radical feminist lawyer Patricia Ireland, now President of the National Organization of Women, and Jack Ryan, until recently the acting head of the Resolution Trust Corp. Mr. Ryan also is riveted in our memory: He was director of banking supervision and regulation at the Federal Reserve when the corrupt Bank of Credit & Commerce International illegally gained control of First American Bank in Washington. He left the Fed in 1985 to join the Arky firm as a financial consultant, returning to government service 18 months later. By mid-1994 he was running the RTC.

Whitewater aficionados of course know Mr. Ryan as one of the Clinton Administration officials who wanted to be able to say that "Whitewater did not cause a loss to Madison" Guaranty S&L, according to RTC investigator Jean Lewis's account of her conversation with RTC attorney April Breslaw. Indeed, one of the unanswered questions of the Whitewater probe is what role Mr. Ryan played in gagging Ms. Lewis and other potential Whitewater whistleblowers.

* * *

What does this have to do with Mr. Greer? Part of Mr. Greer's duties at the Arky firm included dealing with state and federal regulatory agencies such as those headed by Mr. Ryan and Florida Comptroller Lewis. According to South Florida Business Journal, for example, Mr. Greer fought off a 1978 U.S. Securities and Exchange Commission probe of ESM that included an SEC request for documents relating to companies controlled by Mr. Warner. Mr. Greer battled the SEC to a standstill, after the agency had charged that ESM was engaged in a "scheme to defraud." The SEC dropped the case in 1981. Four years later, ESM went down with at least $250 million in losses.

At the time, the Miami Herald wrote that "the agency legally responsible for regulating government securities dealers like ESM — the office of Florida Comptroller Gerald Lewis — did nothing, despite warning signals." Mr. Lewis dismissed the public reports of his inaction as "hindsight" and defended his relationship with Mr. Warner, his cousin. "My decisions have never been affected by a relation," he told the newspaper.

After Arky Freed's collapse, Mr. Greer founded Greer, Homer & Bonner. One of Mr. Greer's clients was CenTrust Savings Bank Chairman David Paul. In 1994 Mr. Paul, at the center of one of the S&L crisis's biggest scandals, was sentenced to 11 years in prison and ordered to pay $65 million in fines and restitution for looting CenTrust. What makes Mr. Paul's bank especially worthy of notice is that it also was a BCCI satellite.

At one time its largest shareholder was BCCI front man Ghaith Pharaon. In 1985, BCCI parked $25 million with the bank to help Mr. Paul dress up his books. Mr. Paul also became famous for his efforts on behalf of many Florida Democrats, including Mr. Greer's current nomination patron, Senator Graham, and Comptroller Lewis, who was voted out of office in 1994 after a 20-year reign. Among Mr. Paul's favors: loans of the CenTrust jet and contributions to Democratic Party fund-raisers.

Mr. Greer's known connections to Mr. Paul date back to 1987, when his new firm was one of several companies signing generous deals to lease space in Mr. Paul's CenTrust Tower. Mr. Paul "used his connections with law firms and other companies that did business with the savings and loan to fill up the building," the Miami Review reported. Later, when federal and state regulators — including the RTC and Mr. Lewis — finally went after CenTrust, Mr. Paul hired Mr. Greer as his personal lawyer in a dispute over a $30 million art collection allegedly built with depositors' money.

The $12 million in assets Mr. Greer and his lawyer wife list on their financial disclosure form includes a $900,000 limited partnership in Cen Office Building Ltd. Public records in Florida indicate that the property was once owned by CenTrust. The details of this transaction should be explored, as should Mr. Greer's relations with another intriguing client, financier Victor Posner.

* * *

Now of course lawyers are entitled to have clients, and those clients are likely to be people in trouble with the law. There is no reason to accuse Mr. Greer of anything criminal, and no one has done so. But the issue is scarcely whether he should be sent to jail; it is whether his career should be rewarded with a lifetime appointment to the federal judiciary. In that context, his list of associations is far too rich for our blood.

If President Clinton is serious about the themes he enunciated in his State of the Union (for example, "I challenge all our schools to teach character education, to teach good values and good citizenship"), he could start to demonstrate it by withdrawing the Greer nomination. If not, let's proceed with full, complete and open hearings to learn what kind of judges we could expect in four more years of the current Administration.

REVIEW & OUTLOOK

Asides

A Hubbell Clarification

The White House's Whitewater spokesman Mark Fabiani charged Wednesday that Rep. William Clinger's subpoenas for 28 Travel Office documents were more about "headlines than facts." In fact, the Clinger headlines were pretty small, sitting below the big head-lines about Webster Hubbell's testimony. The former associate attor-ney general testified that those Madison Guaranty/Hillary Clinton billing records that sprouted on a table in the Clintons' book room were taken by him without permission from the Rose Law Firm and given to Vincent Foster in 1992. The committee said it will deploy a "process of elimination" to determine who next held, saw or moved the famous files.

Editorial Feature

Razorback Money Drops Clinton, Backs Bob Dole

By MICAH MORRISON

"It's a stunning measure of how disillusioned and disappointed people have become with Bill Clinton in the White House," a spokesman for Bob Dole's presidential campaign said with a chortle last year, when the Los Angeles Times dug up campaign-finance records showing that Arkansas investment giant Stephens Inc. and poultry powerhouse Tyson Foods had turned their back on Bill Clinton and were sending money to Mr. Dole.

In covering the Whitewater affair and Arkansas adventures, articles and editorials in this newspaper have often noted that both Tyson and Stephens were early supporters of the first Clinton presidential campaign. In the weeks following Mr. Clinton's 1991 announcement, each raised about $20,000 for the nascent effort. Warren Stephens, president of Stephens Inc., later said he had raised more than $100,000 for the Clintons by the middle of 1992. And when the Clinton campaign began to run out of funds in advance of the critical New York primary, Worthen Bank — in which the Stephens organization had a 25% stake at the time — extended a $3.5 million line of credit. So it is only fair to report now on where the big Arkansas money is putting its bets this year.

As with many big political contributors, the Arkansas heavyweights are spreading the money, with Federal Election Commission records showing dollops for the Gramm and Alexander campaigns, as well as Democratic Party causes. They do not show much in the way of direct Clinton campaign contributions, except for a few lower-level Stephens employees.

This time around, though, the favorite of big Arkansas business does appear to be Mr. Dole. In addition to Tyson and Stephens, Arkansas heavyweights Riceland Foods and Alltell Corp. have contributed to the Dole campaign. The dough, however, is not exactly rolling in. Charles Murphy, retired head of Murphy Oil Corp. and Mr. Dole's Arkansas finance chairman, says he has raised "about $90,000," but expects that figure to increase dramatically in the coming months. Mr. Murphy, a globe-trotting former Clinton supporter, says he switched to Mr. Dole because the president "has gone from being a disappointment to an embarrassment. It's just devastating to hear what is said about him around the world, his vacillations."

Jackson Stephens

Burned by Whitewater, Tyson Foods maintains a pointed silence on Bill Clinton these days and tries to keep a low profile. Last year, Tyson executives and their political action committee gave $5,000 to Mr. Dole's campaign and $23,500 in fluid "soft money" to national GOP committees, according to FEC records. "We are going to be less active" in presidential politics this year, says Tyson spokesman Archie Schaffer. "Sen. Dole is a friend of production agriculture and recognizes the importance of what we do, but there never have been any close ties. We haven't given Sen. Dole or any other presidential candidate money" since 1995.

Stephens Inc.'s relationship with Sen. Dole is much more complex and intriguing. The longtime head of the world-wide investment firm, Jackson Stephens, is an old friend and political ally. Mr. Stephens and the Doles have apartments at the exclusive Sea View Hotel in Bal Harbour, Fla. So does top Dole supporter Archer-Daniels-Midland chairman Dwayne Andreas.

In 1995, according to FEC records, Stephens family members and company executives donated $6,250 to the Dole presidential campaign. Mr. Stephens also donated $50,000 to Mr. Dole's Better America Foundation, which shut down in June following complaints about its tax-exempt status. Including donations from the Stephens Overseas Services PAC, the Stephens organization also gave about $90,000 to GOP national committees, $70,000 of it in soft money that can be used to support various candidates.

Stephens Inc. also employs a controversial figure in the world of the Doles, David Owen. Mr. Owen, a former banker and lieutenant governor of Kansas, was a top Dole aide and financial adviser until he was ousted from Mr. Dole's 1988 presidential campaign amid reports that he mismanaged a blind trust for Elizabeth Dole and violated campaign finance laws. Mr. Owen went to jail for seven months in 1994 on an unrelated tax-evasion charge and last year paid the FEC $13,000 in fines on the campaign-finance violations.

Mr. Owen has been a Stephens employee in Kansas for "a long time," Warren Stephens says. "My recollection is we first met him in some connection with Dole." Currently, however, Mr. Owen seems to be an enemy of Mr. Dole; he recently told the New Yorker that he'd been "made a scapegoat for Dole" − "He betrayed me."

What Mr. Dole's enemy is doing working for Jack Stephens, one of Mr. Dole's friends, is one of those happenstances that fascinate observers of the enigmatic chairman of Stephens Inc. As readers of this newspaper know, Mr. Stephens's range of acquaintances runs the gamut from the corrupt bankers of BCCI to virtually every modern American president. He was, for example, an Annapolis classmate of Jimmy Carter.

According to Mr. Murphy, the Dole finance chairman in Arkansas, Jack Stephens remains influential. He advises the Dole camp and "is a factor to be reckoned with in the national campaign," Mr. Murphy says. So is Vernon Weaver, a Washington lobbyist for Mr. Stephens and head of the Small Business Administration under Jimmy Carter. Mr. Weaver, says Mr. Murphy, "is pretty active in the Dole campaign. You can be sure that's a reflection of Jack Stephens's feelings."

Mr. Morrison is a Journal editorial page writer.

REVIEW & OUTLOOK

The Other Timetable

While his potential Republican challengers have been cudgeling one another in the snows of Iowa and New Hampshire, President Bill Clinton has been cozy in the White House conducting business as usual. His wife set a new First Ladyship record, for example, by being hauled before a grand jury. And the President himself has been subpoenaed for the Arkansas trial of his Whitewater business partners and his successor as governor.

The Republicans have the primary timetable — New Hampshire now followed by Delaware on Saturday and Arizona next Tuesday. But Mr. Clinton has the testimony timetable. The Arkansas case goes to trial March 4; a companion case awaits an Eighth Circuit reversal of Clinton-crony Judge Henry Woods. The Appellate Court has already said the Paula Jones case can also proceed. Senator Alfonse D'Amato's hearings come up for a renewal vote next week, and Congressman Bill Clinger has issued 28 new subpoenas in his Travelgate lying probe. Meanwhile the Starr and Smaltz investigations tick away.

White House stonewalling and document denial have succeeded in stalling all of this into the middle of the Presidential election — so Democrats can cry partisan politics if, say, in the Castle Grande land flips Mrs. Clinton winds up an "unindicted co-conspirator," as Richard Nixon did in Watergate. This is all the more reason to wrap up what the public has learned, or should have learned, about Whitewater while Republican battles have hogged the headlines.

* * *

- Mrs. Clinton's four-hour appearance before the grand jury January 26 was the direct result of the mysterious peregrinations of the Rose Law Firm billing records. As the world now knows, White House aide and former Rose employee Carolyn Huber discovered the records in the "book room" of the White House residence last August. The sudden emergence of the files, sought by investigators for more than two years, clearly angered the independent counsel, who had previously merely deposed the First Couple at the White House.

- The Rose billing records are yielding new clues about Mrs. Clinton's dealings with Madison insiders, as suggested by Senate investigators at the February 6 hearings with a panel of Federal Deposit Insurance Corp. officials. Mrs. Clinton billed Madison for conferences on: February 28, 1986, the day Mr. Ward received a $1.15 million Castle Grande loan; April 7, when Mr. Ward received a $300,000 note on Castle Grande; and on May 1, when Mr. Ward's option agreement with Madison was approved. It further turns out that Mr. Ward's attorney, Alston Jennings, visited Mrs. Clinton at the White House in August 1995, about the time that Mrs. Huber spotted the records in the book room.

- At the Senate Whitewater hearings, new details continue to emerge about Castle Grande, Madison, and the Clintons' relationship with Arkansas regulators. Beverly Bassett Schaffer, the former head of the Arkansas Securities Department, testified that she had in fact discussed a recapitalization plan for Madison in a phone call with Mrs. Clinton in 1985. Mrs. Clinton has dismissed the call as simply a perfunctory inquiry about an address. Ms. Schaffer also acknowledged that a year later she gave Governor Clinton's office a "heads-up" about a move by bank regulators to remove Mr. McDougal from Madison. In a July 2, 1986, note to a top Clinton aide, Ms. Schaffer wrote: "Madison Guaranty is in pretty serious trouble. Because of Bill's relationship w/McDougal, we probably ought to talk about it."

- The White House damage-control team was so worried about what Mrs. Schaffer might say, we learned from testimony by former communications director Mark Gearan last week, that adviser Harold Ickes suggested an emissary go to Little Rock to make sure she got her story straight. "Bev. Bassett is so f——— imp[ortant]," Mr. Gearan's notes on Mr. Ickes's remarks read. "If we f— this up, we're done." The Gearan notes, which miraculously appeared about two weeks ago, show near-panic on the eve of the appointment of the first independent counsel. Mr. Ickes declared that Mrs. Clinton was "adamantly opposed" to an independent counsel, as was the other veteran of the Watergate investigation, White House Counsel Bernard Nussbaum.

• Down in Little Rock, meanwhile, the case in which the President will testify concerns charges of bank fraud and conspiracy against Arkansas Governor Jim Guy Tucker and Madison owners James and Susan McDougal. The 21-count indictment includes an allegation that Mrs. McDougal was the recipient of an illegal $300,000 loan from for-

Susan McDougal

mer municipal judge David Hale's Capital Management Services, a Small Business Administration-backed company. Mr. Hale claims that then-Governor Clinton and Mr. McDougal pressured him into making the loan. Mrs. McDougal says it never happened, and needs Mr. Clinton to back her up. President Clinton will take the stand — probably via satellite or videotape — and be open to cross-examination by the independent counsel. Mr. Starr may even want to know whether President Clinton and Governor Tucker really discussed the Arkansas National Guard in their meetings in October and November of 1993, as news of the Madison criminal referrals first roiled the White House.

• In a response to supplemental interrogatories from the Resolution Trust Corp., Mrs. Clinton acknowledged she authorized the destruction of Rose files on Madison back in 1988. This was a time when the S&L was collapsing in a welter of fraud allegations and Bill Clinton was contemplating a run for the White House. At least two of the files related to work on Castle Grande.

• Clinton crony Webster Hubbell testified on February 7 that shortly before Mr. Clinton's inauguration he removed files from the Rose Law Firm relating to Mrs. Clinton's legal work on a number of issues, including Madison Guaranty, taking originals and not making copies. Mr. Hubbell, the former Associate Attorney General and son-in-law of Madison insider Seth Ward, is now doing time for ripping off the Rose firm, where he was a senior partner. He said that the last time he saw the Rose billing records, Vincent Foster had them, and acknowledged that the files "could have been" in Mr.

Foster's office the night he died. Secret Service guard Henry O'Neill has testified that he saw Margaret Williams, Mrs. Clinton's chief of staff, emerge from Mr. Foster's office that night with an armful of documents. Ms. Williams denies Mr. O'Neill's account, but with her incredible answers to a whole series of other questions, any sensible person will believe Mr. O'Neill and conclude that Mr. Foster's office was rifled the night of his death and a coverup has proceeded ever since.

*   *   *

Democratic campaign officials have been scouring the financial resumes of all the GOP contenders for "another Whitewater." Steve Forbes won't release tax records, for example. Lamar Alexander's Tennessee friends cut him in on some successful deals. Bob Dole hob-nobs with Dwayne Andreas (Ethanol Inc.) in Florida's Sea View Hotel. Pat Buchanan is pals with textile protectionist Roger Miliken. All this should be duly recorded and kept in mind.

For another Whitewater, though, you'd need, let's see: a mysterious suicide and vanishing records; a failed S&L and a failed SBIC with the taxpayers left to bail out the loss; a spate of Travelgate subpoenas, a sexual harassment suit, a friendly judge stalling hearings, an Associate Attorney General in jail, three independent counsels at bay, two business partners in the dock and a partridge in a pear tree.

Editorial Feature

The Investigation Must Continue

By Orrin G. Hatch

Today the Senate is scheduled to vote on whether to extend the lifetime of the special committee on Whitewater. I believe that the Senate must agree to allow the committee to complete its work, which has been hampered by repeated delays and obfuscation on the part of the White House. As the New York Times observed last week, to ask the senators on the special committee to stop their investigation now "would be a dereliction of their duties."

Whitewater involves the failure of a federally insured savings and loan, Madison Guaranty, at a cost to taxpayers of $60 million, and we have a duty to investigate whether President and Mrs. Clinton were involved. It is for this very reason that the special committee must be allowed to continue its efforts to conduct a fair, careful and thorough investigation.

In particular, the special committee needs to investigate and resolve the following issues:

• *How did Mrs. Clinton's Rose Law Firm billing records mysteriously appear in the White House reading room, and who put them there?*

The answer to this question is not just an insignificant whodunit. These records had been under subpoena by the independent counsel for almost two years. Apparently, these records are marked with handwriting identified as the late Vincent Foster's. Were these records in Mr. Foster's office when he died, and were they removed by the first lady's assistants to conceal them from federal investigators?

• *Who brought Madison Guaranty into the Rose Law Firm as a client, and who had primary responsibility for the account?*

Mrs. Clinton claims that a then-wet-behind-the-ears, first-year associate brought in the client; the associate denies this. The newly found billing records show that Mrs. Clinton performed some substantial work on Madison matters and that she billed about 60 hours of work to the account. They also show that on 53 different days Mrs. Clinton worked on Madison matters and that she had 33 conferences with Madison employees.

• *Did Mrs. Clinton attempt to benefit from her relationship with her husband, then-Gov. Clinton, in representing Madison Guaranty before Arkansas regulators?*

Mrs. Clinton's billing records show that she talked with Beverly Bassett Schaffer, who was appointed by Gov. Clinton as Arkansas securities commissioner, before Madison Guaranty applied for permission to issue preferred stock, and they agreed that the stock issue could go forward. The offering would have allowed the rapidly deteriorating Madison Guaranty to stay afloat financially longer than it did, which would have increased the losses to the American taxpayer.

Records also indicate that Mrs. Clinton terminated her representation of Madison Guaranty only days after Ms. Schaffer notified Gov. Clinton's office that Madison was in trouble.

• *What was Mrs. Clinton's role in the ill-fated Castle Grande deal, and did she know of and assist Madison in creating what the Resolution Trust Corp. has concluded was a "sham transaction" designed to conceal Madison's true ownership interest in the project?*

Castle Grande was a Madison Guaranty development that failed at a cost to taxpayers of about $4 million. Mrs. Clinton claimed to federal regulators that she never worked on Castle Grande but did work on Industrial Development Corp., which was just another name for the Castle Grande project. Madison used Seth Ward as a front man to nominally purchase an interest in Castle Grande. Mr. Ward is the father-in-law of Webster Hubbell, the former managing partner of the Rose Law Firm — and former associate attorney general — who is now serving a prison sentence for mail fraud. Mrs. Clinton's billing records show 16 separate conferences with Mr.

Ward and 14.7 hours billed to this seemingly fraudulent project.

- *Have President and Mrs. Clinton's lawyers and assistants attempted to impede the investigations into Whitewater by the independent counsel and by the Senate special committee?*

Then-associate White House counsel William Kennedy's notes from a November 1993 meeting apparently state "vacuum Rose Law Firm files" and then "Documents — never go out quietly." We have learned that these Rose Law Firm documents may have been kept by Mr. Hubbell in his basement, and that these documents may have been in Mr. Foster's office when he died. Did Mr. Kennedy's notes refer to a past or future attempt to destroy or hide documents under subpoena by the independent counsel and the special committee? It took several hearings and meetings of the special committee, a full vote of the Senate and the threat of a civil suit before the Clintons agreed to release the notes.

William Kennedy

- *Did the first lady or her aides order White House counsel Bernard Nussbaum to prevent Justice Department investigators from searching Mr. Foster's office after his death?*

On July 22, 1993, Mr. Nussbaum reneged on an agreement with the Justice Department to search Mr. Foster's office. Records indicate that earlier that morning a flurry of calls occurred between several parties: Margaret Williams, the first lady's chief of staff; Susan Thomases; the Rodham residence, where Mrs. Clinton was staying during Mr. Foster's funeral; and Mr. Nussbaum. A White House lawyer remembers being told by Mr. Nussbaum that morning that the first lady and Ms. Thomases were concerned about law enforcement having "unfettered access" to Mr. Foster's office. But Ms. Williams and Ms. Thomases have suffered convenient memory loss about the substance of those phone calls. We must have the truth about those calls.

- *Was there an effort to interfere with the investigation into Whitewater?*

We have notes taken by Mark Gearan, then White House communications director, of a Jan. 7, 1994, meeting, which took place just a few days after President Clinton had read a newspaper editorial about Ms. Schaffer. Mr. Clinton wrote on the copy, "will she hold up?" Mr. Clinton also spoke to her at a basketball game in Arkansas. At this meeting, Harold Ickes, deputy White House chief of staff, says that someone should be sent to make sure Ms. Schaffer had her story straight and that holes had to be poked in "their" story. Mr. Ickes also apparently declared that if this was not taken care of, "we're done." Was there an attempt either to influence Ms. Schaffer's story or to convince her to change her recollection of important events?

• *Who ordered the firing of Billy Dale, head of the White House travel office, and his staff, and why?*

In written answers to the General Accounting Office, a White House lawyer stated for Mrs. Clinton that she did not "know the origin of the decision" to fire the travel office staff and that she had "no role" in the decision. But David Watkins, former White House head of personnel, states that Mrs. Clinton conveyed to him "her desire for swift and clear action to resolve the [travel office] situation" that plainly included firing the staffers and replacing them with employees of television producer and Clinton friend Harry Thomason. Two other memos support the veracity of Mr. Watkins's account.

Some have questioned the importance of Travelgate. Certainly there is nothing wrong with addressing office mismanagement, but it is another thing entirely to accuse those managers of embezzlement and then to prosecute them with the full resources of the federal government. This is why I have introduced a bill to reimburse Mr. Dale for his legal expenses. Travelgate is also of central importance to the Whitewater investigation because it appears that the travel office firings may have been a factor that led Mr. Foster to kill himself.

To many informed people, the Whitewater affair appears to be the classic story of unscrupulous dealings intended to benefit the political elite and an effort to bury the truth when questions were raised. The White House's delay in cooperating with the investigation has produced the need to extend the special committee's life span for as long as necessary. Subpoenaed documents mysteriously turn up two years later. The White House continues to refuse to turn over other relevant documents, such as e-mail records.

Because of what many people believe to be the obvious delay and obfuscation by the White House, the Senate has not had these questions answered, so we must extend the special committee's mandate until it completes its investigation thoroughly and fairly. We are still at the point where the Clintons can change course and provide the American people with a full and open explanation. Let's hope they do.

Sen. Hatch (R., Utah) is chairman of the Senate Judiciary Committee.

REVIEW & OUTLOOK

Who Is Mochtar Riady?

Mr. Chertoff: I guess the question is really this, it is whether, in connection with this representation, you received a large amount of money and that may have had an impact on the degree of your cooperation with the Independent Counsel or with us?

Mr. Hubbell: That's pretty rotten.

Shortly after this exchange, Senator Alfonse D'Amato intervened to cut short questioning of Webster Hubbell by Whitewater Committee counsel Michael Chertoff. A New Republic writer described the exchange as "Chertoff's first major gaffe." Perhaps, but as the transcript printed nearby shows, the questioning did establish something: Between the time Mr. Hubbell resigned as associate attorney general and went to jail, he was paid to represent the Lippo Group.

Lippo, in case you're wondering, is a huge conglomerate based in Indonesia. Its assets are estimated at $6 billion, and it concentrates mainly on banking and real estate in Indonesia and Hong Kong. It also does infrastructure projects in China and owns Lippo Bank of California. It was founded by Mochtar Riady, who rose from poor circumstances in Jakarta to become a highly successful executive at the private Bank Central Asia before founding his own empire. The family interests are represented by his sons Stephen in Hong Kong and James in the United States.

The Riadys are members of predominantly Muslim Indonesia's tiny but fantastically successful ethnic Chinese minority. Last year

Forbes magazine wrote that Indonesia had 10 billionaires, six of them new. Most, including Mochtar Riady and Liem Sioe Liong of the Salim Group, owner of the bank where Mr. Riady got his start, have close ties to Indonesia's President Suharto. In case you're wondering whether Mr. Hubbell is an expert on Javanese legal customs or perhaps Irian Jaya property claims, the Riadys are also old Arkansas hands.

One of Mr. Riady's early U.S. investments was Worthen Bank of Arkansas. In 1984, in a partnership with Arkansas financier Jackson Stephens, Lippo bought $16 million of Worthen stock and installed James Riady in Little Rock as a director of the bank. "Mochtar Riady and Jack Stephens owe their friendship to the troubles of another noted financier, Bert Lance," a 1985 story in this newspaper reported. At one point Mr. Riady had offered to buy Mr. Lance's 16% stake in the National Bank of Georgia, but later withdrew, and the shares were eventually sold to Ghaith Pharaon, front man for the corrupt Bank of Credit & Commerce International.

Mochtar Riady

Curiously, Lippo brushed up against the BCCI scandal again in 1991, when its Hong Kong Chinese Bank offered to buy the Hong Kong Bank of Credit & Commerce after regulators seized it. The purchase fell through, but one BCC executive ended up as a senior vice president of Lippo Group Marketing; he was among four former BCC officials reprimanded by a Hong Kong judge in 1995 for laundering money for drug baron Law Kin-man. The money-laundering did not involve Lippo, and a spokesman tells us the executive has since emigrated.

The Worthen purchase started a period of intense collaboration between Stephens and Lippo, with a wide variety of deals, including the purchase of Hong Kong Chinese Bank. A 1994 report by Hong Kong's Securities and Futures Commission criticized a Lippo acquisition in which it was assisted by Stephens Finance. An official of Stephens Inc. told us this week, however, that all business affairs between the Arkansas investment giant and Lippo ended in the late 1980s.

But a relationship seems to remain between the Riadys and President Clinton. The Lippo boardroom in Hong Kong is decorated with a portrait of Mochtar Riady with Bill and Hillary (as well as a photo of Stephen Riady and President Bush). The family patriarch was invited to the Clinton inauguration. James Riady attended the pre-inaugural economic summit in Little Rock, the Asian Pacific Economic Conference in Seattle in November 1993, a June 1994 salute to Vice President Al Gore in Washington, and was on hand for President Clinton's November 1994 visit to Indonesia. In connection with the Jakarta visit, Commerce Secretary Ron Brown staged an orgy of contract signings for U.S. business ventures in Indonesia.

Also on hand for these meetings was Maria Haley, a director of the Export-Import Bank and previously an Arkansas official in charge of international business development. She says that Governor Clinton's romancing of the Riadys was what any governor would do to encourage local growth. Mrs. Haley's former husband, lawyer John Haley, is co-defendant with Arkansas Governor Jim Guy Tucker in the case now under appeal after Clinton pal Judge Henry Woods ruled it was beyond the jurisdiction of Independent Counsel Kenneth Starr.

Given this history, Mr. Chertoff's line of inquiry certainly seems appropriate, and well worth pursuing in further private depositions of Mr. Hubbell. The explanation of Mr. Hubbell's work may be entirely innocent, though our inquiries with Lippo in Los Angeles and Hong Kong produced no comment. Mr. Hubbell's phone logs as associate attorney general show calls from James Riady, and clearly he did have a prior relationship with Lippo, presumably through the Rose Law Firm.

The fact remains, though, that while Mr. Hubbell was negotiating his plea bargain with Mr. Starr, he was being paid by a billionaire pal of the President. In the plea bargain, he admitted to mail fraud and tax evasion and agreed to cooperate in exchange for a reduced-sentence recommendation. When the time for sentencing came, Mr. Starr showed what he thought of Mr. Hubbell's cooperation; there was no recommendation for leniency.

Editorial Feature

Mr. Hubbell and the Lippo Group

Following are excerpts from a Senate Whitewater Committee hearing on Feb. 7. A related editorial appears nearby.

Majority Counsel Michael Chertoff: Mr. Hubbell, I want to ask you in connection with, I guess, judging the quality of your testimony, whether you have had discussions with anybody in the last couple of years concerning any financial arrangements that might be made in terms of work or any other kind of financial arrangements when you get out of jail?

Webster Hubbell: Me?

Mr. Chertoff: I don't mean with your wife or family. I mean, with anybody who has a business or anything of the sort.

Mr. Hubbell: No, I have not.

Mr. Chertoff: Are you familiar with a group called the Lippo Group?

Mr. Hubbell: Yes.

Mr. Chertoff: What kind of entity is that?

Mr. Hubbell: They are a group in Indonesia that at one time had a major ownership of Worthen Bank.

Mr. Chertoff: Have you had discussions with anybody, either from the Lippo Group or representing the Lippo Group, concerning whether you might do any business with them or work for them when you get out of jail?

Mr. Hubbell: No, I have not.

Mr. Chertoff: Have you had discussions with representatives of the Lippo Group at all in the last three years?

Mr. Hubbell: Yes.

Mr. Chertoff: When?

Mr. Hubbell: When I left the Justice Department prior to my pleading guilty.

Mr. Chertoff: What were the nature of those discussions?

Mr. Hubbell: I'm sorry, I can't disclose those.

Mr. Chertoff: Did it involve a financial — something of a financial nature?

Mr. Hubbell: I was — can I consult with my lawyer?

(Witness conferred with counsel.)

Mr. Hubbell: Mr. Chertoff, I don't think I am violating the attorney-client privilege. The Lippo Group itself was not my client, but a representative of that group — one of their affiliates was a client of mine, and all of the nature of the conversations I had related to that representation. That representation occurred in the summer and fall of 1993 — '94, excuse me.

Mr. Chertoff: Over what period of time, how long did the representation last?

Mr. Hubbell: It lasted — it lasted until I pled guilty in 1994.

Mr. Chertoff: Which was when?

Mr. Hubbell: December of 1994.

Mr. Chertoff: So it lasted for over a year?

Mr. Hubbell: No. No, I left the Justice Department in April, and I believe I started representing them sometime in the summer of 1994.

Mr. Chertoff: So it lasted for about five months?

Mr. Hubbell: Yes.

Mr. Chertoff: You were in practice in Washington?

Mr. Hubbell: Yes.

Mr. Chertoff: Did you have other clients?

Mr. Hubbell: Yes.

Mr. Chertoff: Had you had a pre-existing relationship with this group?

Mr. Hubbell: Yes.

Sen. Paul Sarbanes (D., Md.): Mr. Chairman, how does this — I am not quite sure —

Mr. Hubbell: I want to make clear, I have had no discussions about getting paid by anybody when I leave jail. I have no employment opportunities at this moment.

Mr. Chertoff: I guess the question is really this, it is whether, in connection with this representation, you received a large amount of money and that may have had an impact on the degree of your cooperation with the Independent Counsel or with us?

Mr. Hubbell: That's pretty rotten.

Mr. Chertoff: I am just going to ask you the question about what the nature of the arrangement was.

Mr. Hubbell: I was doing work for the client and they paid me like the other clients —

Mr. Chertoff: On an hourly basis?

Mr. Hubbell: No. I will not represent anybody on a hourly basis anymore.

Chairman Al D'Amato (R., N.Y.): Let me suggest this. I am going to suggest any further questions along this line, that we take them in a private deposition. And I will ask counsel to not go forward as it relates to pursuing this line. I think that would be in the best interest, if there — you know, if there are facts that we should know, why then, that's — we can pursue it. If there's information that is not relevant, why, then, there is no need to bring it out in a public way. So it would seem to me that that would be the best, and I would ask Mr. Chertoff to suspend any further questioning of Mr. Hubbell as it relates to this particular area that has been opened up.

Webster Hubbell

Sen. Sarbanes: Could I suggest that that suggestion might have been advisable some time ago before all of these innuendoes were thrown out on the record. It may in fact be terribly unfair.

Mr. Hubbell: I think it is awful unfair. I would have to say that the chairman has done everything possible, I have answered questions now, for people, for a year and a half. Anybody who asks a question, I've answered. I have never invoked the privilege. I have never done anything but answer your questions for a year and a half. And now to imply that I am not entitled to work at all, Mike, between that time and wanting to know about my clients, I am entitled to say something. I have for a year and a half been hauled all over this country, answering questions, and I've answered every dadgum one of them.

And I am a little bit upset that, after it is over, somebody wants to know about my private business like there's something wrong with me trying to do some work and support my family. I have a wife and four children, and I needed the work and I did. But there wasn't anything improper with it and nobody promised me a damned thing.

Chairman D'Amato: Well, I think, Mr. Hubbell, you are certainly entitled to put that answer on the record, and I accept it. And I suggest that, if there be any further need to explore that avenue, that we do it in camera, by way of deposition, so that we can ascertain whether or not there is any relevance or not. It would seem to me that would be the manner in which we should proceed.

REVIEW & OUTLOOK

The Coverup Filibuster

While the Republicans have been grabbing headlines battling in primaries, Democrats have quietly unleashed a filibuster to close down the Whitewater hearings, asserting that the hearings are merely a partisan exercise uncovering nothing new.

Despite such surprises as the sudden appearance of Hillary Clinton's billing records, filibustering Senators manage to keep a straight face most of the time. Also despite the start of Independent Counsel Kenneth Starr's trial of Arkansas Governor Jim Guy Tucker and others, after which important new witnesses would become available to the committee. And as we pointed out recently, the hearings have already established that Webster Hubbell was at the same time negotiating a plea bargain with Mr. Starr and being paid by Indonesian billionaire Mochtar Riady, a Clinton buddy. Democrats object to asking such innocent questions as how big a fee the former associate attorney general received from Mr. Riady's Lippo Group and for what work, if any.

The Democrats got their chance to filibuster such questions because the D'Amato committee needs to have its authorization renewed. Democrats are blocking a vote, and a cloture motion comes up Tuesday. The Republicans will not have the 60 votes needed to break a filibuster, assuming all the Democratic Senators will enlist in the Whitewater coverup.

In addition to covering up for the Clintons, the Democratic Senators have a special reason to cut off the next round of hearings.

They're expected to deal with Arkansas, and particularly with Dan Lasater, the Little Rock bond magnate convicted of cocaine distribution. Richard Ben-Veniste, Watergate prosecutor and Democratic counsel in the Whitewater hearings, astonishingly turns out also to have been an attorney for the late Barry Seal, the cocaine smuggler who operated out of Mena airport in Arkansas. According to minutes obtained by Dow Jones News Service of a high-level Resolution Trust Corp. meeting, Mr. Lasater "may have been establishing depository

Richard Ben-Veniste

accounts at Madison and other financial institutions and laundering drug money through them via brokered deposits and bond issues." So one of the big questions in the impending round of hearings ought to be whether there were connections between committee witness Lasater and former Ben-Veniste client Seal.

We called Mr. Ben-Veniste to chat about this Friday, after learning of the link from the book "Kings of Cocaine," by Guy Gugliotta and Jeff Lean. He blamed Republicans for our inquiry, and called it "a pathetic indication of how little gas is left in the other side's tank." But yes, he did represent Mr. Seal when he was convicted in a drug case in Florida. But, he added, "I didn't know anything about Barry Seal's connections to Mena airport and this fellow Lasater."

Mr. Ben-Veniste says he did read reports of a possible Seal-Lasater link as he was preparing to sign up to defend Whitewater for the Democrats, though he "thought the reports were part of the lunatic fringe." But, he told us, "for the sake of appearances, and out of an abundance of caution, I told Senator Sarbanes that I simply would not have anything to do with the Lasater part of the inquiry." This is news to us, and we wonder how Senator Sarbanes expected to explain it if the hearings are authorized and Mr. Lasater testifies.

Mr. Seal's retention of Mr. Ben-Veniste is especially ironic in light of the recent attacks on the former associations of David Bossie, the most energetic and successful Whitewater investigator on the Republican side of the aisle. Mr. Bossie started poking into Whitewater in 1993 for Citizens United, run by Floyd Brown, author of the independent Willie Horton commercial in the 1988 presidential campaign. When Mr. Brown put out a fund-raising letter bragging about giving Mr. Bossie his start, Democrats went ballistic, especially Senator Carol Moseley-Braun. Heaven forbid a staffer should have worked for Floyd Brown, a political heavy. But no problem, what passes for logic runs, to have worked for Barry Seal, a notorious cocaine smuggler whose ghost lurks on the fringes of the commitee's inquiry.

Mr. Ben-Veniste told us one other intriguing thing. To wit, "I did my part by launching Barry Seal into the arms of Vice President Bush, who embraced him as an undercover operative." And indeed, after his conviction, Mr. Seal contacted the South Florida Drug Task Force then run by Vice President Bush, and went on to become a spectacular informant for the Drug Enforcement Administration and flew at least one mission to Central America for the CIA. He was murdered by Medellin cartel hitmen in 1986, leaving many questions about Mena, drugs, the CIA and law enforcement in Arkansas. Mr. Ben-Veniste's remark is an implicit warning that if pushed far enough Whitewater will start to implicate Republicans as well as Democrats.

Fine by us. Much of the American public already has a bipartisan distrust of all of Washington, as Ross Perot's voters made clear in the last Presidential election. In particular, presumptive GOP nominee Bob Dole carries the burden of an insider image. But as Senate majority leader he has the power to make Democrats pay dearly for a filibuster joining the Whitewater coverup. If he wants to be a "comeback adult," one of the best things he could do is to make sure dirty linen is appropriately washed.

Counteroffensive— Arkansas

In March, Kenneth Starr's first Whitewater trial—the bank fraud case against Arkansas Governor Jim Guy Tucker and James and Susan McDougal—got under way in Little Rock amid general prognostications of failure. Mr. Starr received some good news, however, when the Eighth Circuit Court of Appeals reversed Judge Henry Woods's dismissal of the separate tax fraud case the independent counsel had brought against Governor Tucker. The Eighth Circuit upheld Mr. Starr's jurisdiction in the matter and took the extraordinary step of bouncing Judge Woods from the case.

The long bank fraud trial was marked by the videotaped testimony of President Clinton as a defense witness, the lengthy examination of Arkansas insider David Hale, and a train of witnesses and documents supporting the 21-count indictment. As the trial moved toward conclusion, Mr. Starr came under increasing attack in the media by allies of the Clintons; The Wall Street Journal also was criticized, particularly in Arkansas, for its extensive exploration of Whitewater, including Mena, drugs and the mysterious deaths of teenagers Kevin Ives and Don Henry.

In another ominous sign for the White House, Mr. Starr assumed jurisdiction over the Travel Office affair.

Editorial Feature

The Arkansas Machine Strikes Back

By MICAH MORRISON

LITTLE ROCK, Ark. – The first trial resulting from Kenneth Starr's Whitewater probe has quickly turned into a split-level struggle. In the courtroom, Mr. Starr's prosecution team is carefully building a complex fraud and conspiracy case against Arkansas Gov. Jim Guy Tucker and James and Susan McDougal, the former owners of Madison Guaranty Savings & Loan. But on a second level well understood here in Arkansas, the trial is a blow aimed at the heart of a political machine that has dominated the state for more than 40 years and succeeded in sending one of its luminaries to the White House.

Jim Guy Tucker

The machine is fighting back, and among those savvy in the ways of Arkansas justice, the early betting is not on Mr. Starr. Up against an entrenched system with every interest in seeing him fail, the independent counsel faces a host of obstacles, including the sheer complexity of financial fraud cases, media that often show a home-team mentality, and intimidation of witnesses by means both cunning and audacious.

Mr. Starr did win one round last week, when several aspects of the Arkansas defense proved too much for the U.S. Court of Appeals for the Eighth Circuit in St. Louis. On Friday, the court issued a series of rulings striking down challenges to the independent counsel. In the most spectacular decision, the higher court not only reversed Clinton crony Judge Henry Woods, but took the extraordinary step of bouncing him from Mr. Starr's case.

Judge Woods had been presiding over a separate fraud charge against Gov. Tucker and two business associates concerning the acquisition of a cable TV franchise and related loans. The judge ruled that this matter was beyond Mr. Starr's jurisdiction, essentially adopting the reasoning of Justice Antonin Scalia's dissent when the Supreme Court ruled 8-1 to uphold the independent counsel law. In appealing, Mr. Starr also asked that the judge be removed because of his longstanding associations with the Clintons.

"Judge Woods's link with the Clintons and the Clintons' connection to Tucker have been widely reported in the press," the three-judge appellate panel noted. Softening the blow with an expression of "confidence" in Judge Woods's ability to handle the trial fairly, the panel wrote that reassignment nevertheless was necessary "in order to preserve the appearance as well as the reality of impartial justice." Judge Woods complained that he might be the first jurist in "Anglo-American history who has been removed from a case on the basis of newspaper accounts, magazine articles and television transcripts."

In another ruling, the Eighth Circuit panel rejected an attempt by Little Rock businessman Eugene Fitzhugh to back out of an early plea bargain struck with the independent counsel's office. The appellate court also upheld subpoenas issued by Mr. Starr in an investigation of possible federal banking crimes involving contributions to Bill Clinton's 1990 gubernatorial and 1992 presidential campaigns by bankers Herby Branscum and Robert Hill. Taken together, the rulings appear to be a strong vote of support for Mr. Starr and a signal that the appeals panel will not countenance any shenanigans in Arkansas.

The trial currently under way in U.S. District Judge George Howard Jr.'s courtroom in Little Rock does directly concern Madison Guaranty, the Whitewater-connected S&L, and David Hale's federally backed investment company, Capital Management Services. Gov. Tucker and the McDougals face serious prison time if convicted on all 21 counts in Mr. Starr's indictment. It charges that from 1985 to 1987 Mr. Tucker and the McDougals used Madison and Capital Management Services for a series of about $3 million in fraudulent loans and land deals.

Bill and Hillary Clinton — partners with the McDougals in the Whitewater land development project — are not named in the indictment. But several counts relate to Castle Grande, the Madison deal Mrs. Clinton worked on as a Rose Law Firm attorney. Other counts involve a $300,000 loan from Mr. Hale to Susan McDougal deposited in a Madison account. Mr. Hale claims that then-Gov. Clinton and Mr. McDougal pressured him into making the loan; President Clinton has dismissed the Hale allegation as "a bunch of bull."

One problem Mr. Starr faces is sheltering his witnesses from intimidation and retribution. In January, for example, it was revealed that Mr. Starr had given immunity to Municipal Judge Bill Watt, a business associate of Mr. Hale who could presumably corroborate some of his claims. After several Arkansas journalists pointed out that Mr. Watt was about to qualify for a generous retirement package, the Little Rock Board of Directors — a kind of city council — revoked a 1993 ordinance that had created the pension. Mr. Watt told the Arkansas Democrat-Gazette that he thought the sudden vote of the city board was due to "outside interference, like Whitewater." Board members deny the charge and hold out the possibility that the pension issue will be addressed next year — that is, after Mr. Watt testifies.

The Watt incident was illustrative of the excruciating position of the Arkansas media. As is the case in many small states, the Arkansas press is controlled by financial interests closely tied to the political establishment, but reporters and editors are also acutely aware of the state's seamy side. In editorial commentary and political cartoons, the state's largest newspaper, the Democrat-Gazette, generally portrays Mr. Starr as a GOP carpetbagger intent on an eventual Supreme Court seat. "It is about time to begin asking if Kenneth Starr is really interested in wrongdoing by public officials in Arkansas," writes Democrat-Gazette columnist John Brummett, "unless those public officials happen to be bigtime Democrats targeted by Republicans."

But at the same time, the Democrat-Gazette devotes enormous news-side resources to the Whitewater story. The paper's four-part August 1994 examination of the Castle Grande land deals, for example, has never been topped. It has blanketed the current trial, printing pages of full-text opening statements and court rulings. The newspaper also published the names, hometowns and occupations of the entire jury. "Publishing those names," complains one lawyer involved in the case, "opens up room for all sorts of prejudice to develop, all sorts of attempts to influence the panel." Executive Editor Griffin Smith Jr. defended the decision to publish; he told the weekly Arkansas Business, "The identities of the jurors are something the public has a right to know, just one more fact about the case."

In another media development, Little Rock's ABC affiliate, KATV, yanked a reporter off the Whitewater story last month after a complaining phone call from Gov. Tucker. The reporter, David Schuster, had been taken off on-air reporting of Whitewater once earlier, after what turned out to be an incorrect report that the governor's lawyers had visited with the Starr team to discuss a plea bargain (they had only discussed legal logistics). When Mr. Schuster ventured back in front of the camera on Feb. 5 at 5 p.m. with a Whitewater story, an angry Gov. Tucker was immediately on the phone from a Washington meeting. Mr. Schuster did not make the 6 p.m. report. KATV news director Bob Steel took the blame for the incident, telling the Democrat-Gazette that he was the one who initially suggested to the governor that Mr. Schuster be barred from the story. "I don't particularly like chief executives making my assignments," Mr. Steel said, "but I put myself in a box."

Attitudes toward Mr. Starr pale, however, in comparison to those toward Mr. Hale, former Arkansas insider turned lead prosecution witness. The former municipal judge pretty much set the Whitewater probe into high gear with his allegation against Mr. Clinton in September 1993. Since then, he has been pilloried as a lying, cheating scoundrel out to save his own skin by pointing the finger at enticing political targets. Mr. Hale clearly is anything but a choir boy — his sentencing on two felony counts of conspiracy and mail fraud, in fact, is slated for next Monday. But his defenders say he has been fully cooperative with Mr. Starr and is genuinely committed to rooting out corruption in Arkansas.

Mr. Hale's supporters say the media attacks — which they claim are orchestrated from the White House — and the felony sentencing in mid-trial are intended to undermine the star witness's credibility. But that appears to be the least of Mr. Hale's problems. After months of negotiations, an Arkansas state official, Pulaski County Prosecuting Attorney Mark Stodola, last month pitched a hand grenade into the Starr camp. He wrote that he planned to prosecute Mr. Hale for a felony insurance code violation, involving lying to regulators and the possible theft of $150,000 from National Savings Life Insurance Co., which Mr. Hale also owned.

"[I]t would be highly unusual, if not unprecedented, for a state prosecutor to initiate separate criminal charges against an individual cooperating in an important federal investigation, during the course of that person's cooperation," a statement released last month by Mr. Starr's office said. The statement also said that any state law violations by Mr. Hale could be presented and taken into account at his sentencing; Mr. Stodola rejected the offer.

Mr. Stodola is one of three Democrats running in the primary for the congressional seat being vacated by Rep. Ray Thornton. Arkansas Insurance Commissioner Lee Douglass recommended that Mr. Hale be charged; Mr. Douglass was appointed to his post by Gov. Bill Clinton and re-appointed by Gov. Tucker. Both Mr. Stodola and Mr. Douglass deny that any political influence was exerted on them in the Hale matter.

David Hale

Sam Dash, Mr. Starr's ethics adviser and the former chief counsel to the Senate Watergate committee, met with Mr. Stodola in January, and said the county prosecutor appeared to be under "heavy political pressure." Mr. Dash told the Democrat-Gazette that the pressure on Mr. Stodola to file charges against Mr. Hale "could have been a strategy to embarrass or discredit an important witness in an important prosecution." According to congressional sources, Senate Whitewater Committee members are preparing a letter to Attorney General Janet Reno asking for a probe of the Stodola affair.

Mr. Hale — who has received threats of physical harm and has been in hiding for two years — is terrified by the state prosecution, according to friends in Little Rock. Mr. Hale is keenly aware of the sort of threat he poses to the Arkansas machine; while crusading against corruption in the 1960s, newspaper publisher Gene Wirges was indicted seven times, once was sentenced to three years at hard labor until it was revealed that the chief witness against him had lied, and escaped several attempts on his life. Mr. Hale's friends say he fears that Mr. Stodola will arrest him when he appears at the Tucker trial, and that he would not survive the night in an Arkansas jail.

As the main event unfolds here in Little Rock, courthouse cynics say Kenneth Starr can't win because he doesn't understand how to deal with the political machine. What you need in Arkansas, this argument runs, is not a polite Virginian such as Mr. Starr but a mean junkyard dog to bite off a few heads. But the Tucker-McDougal prosecution appears to have settled into a steady procession of Madison officials, associates and documents. While Mr. Hale is vital in implicating Bill Clinton, the trial actually involves Mr. Tucker and the McDougals; here the prosecution has other witnesses, by all indications including the real estate appraiser in the alleged land flips.

And Mr. Starr does appear to enjoy not only the backing of the Eighth Circuit, but the quiet support of ordinary Arkansans tired of their political machine. Presumably these are the sort of folks who sat on the Arkansas grand jury that brought the indictments, and perhaps on the trial jury hearing them. Maybe in the end the cynics will be proved wrong.

Mr. Morrison is a Journal editorial page writer.

Editorial Feature

Whitewater Reconstructed

By ROBERT L. BARTLEY

Since James B. Stewart combines a lawyer's perseverance in research and a novelist's eye for detail, those of us who know him were always confident he'd turn Whitewater into a whopping good read. With "Blood Sport: The President and His Adversaries," he's crafted, if not a definitive account of the scandals surrounding the Clinton White House, certainly an evocative one.

We start the story with Susan McDougal setting out for her first visit to what became the Whitewater property "wearing bell-bottom pants and a tight white top" on a "mild, brilliantly sunny winter day in early 1978." We end it in November 1994, with a phone conversation between Bill Clinton and Bernard Nussbaum, with the president hinting he wished he'd taken *Susan McDougal* the advice proffered by the resigned White House counsel. In between, "Blood Sport" (Simon & Schuster, 479 pages, $25) piles nuggets of detail into mountains of impression.

The result is a devastating personality sketch of the Arkansas crowd in general and Hillary Clinton in particular. The overwhelming impression is the pervasiveness of lies — from the draft record to the Gennifer Flowers case, to the state troopers, to the health care task force, to the Travel Office firings, to responses to investigations by, say, the General Accounting Office. And all of this is backed by inside anecdote, courtesy of the inside if limited access won with the help of Mrs. Clinton's confidant Susan Thomases, who incited the former Wall Street Journal reporter and page-one editor to take up a book, presumably in her expectation it would somehow help calm the roiling Whitewaters.

While the narrative pace grips the reader, however, it also extracts its price. Skilled writers understand that they are captives of their literary format, whether a Shakespearean sonnet or a 30-second sound bite, or the contemporary fly-on-the-wall insider account invented by Theodore H. White, and embellished by Bob Woodward into the art of reconstructed conversations. In an epilogue on sources, Mr. Stewart is entirely honest about this, reminding the reader his quotes are accurate – not literally, only substantively. And I completely believe, indeed attest, that he talked to hundreds of people, did his best to get everyone's side and made detached judgments about who and what to believe – even if the demands of the form preclude him from sharing any of this with you as the narrative rolls along.

The reader is left with a choice: Suspend disbelief and accept the account as written. Or, engage in a constant guessing-game with the author: Whose word is he accepting now, and do I agree with his judgment about the accuracy and verisimilitude of the presumed source? Book sales attest there's a place for this kind of journalism, honestly admitted. Still, it's not quite what we think of journalism in writing a daily news account, a front-page piece in this newspaper, or even for that matter in our commentary or editorial opinion.

Mr. Stewart honed this style in his earlier best-seller "Den of Thieves," about Michael Milken and other "inside traders." The book, and the Pulitzer Prize Mr. Stewart shared with Daniel Hertzberg, now deputy managing editor, was based on reporting done for the Journal. Here on the editorial page, by contrast, Mr. Milken was defended by another lawyer-journalist, L. Gordon Crovitz, now an important Dow Jones executive as editor and publisher of The Far Eastern Economic Review.

At the time, I thought the Journal "insider" articles were a big service, because without them no one would have known what was going on. When they described police in flak jackets raiding Princeton-Newport Securities, you could take it as showing the seriousness of the charges, but you could also take it as showing the prosecutors as silly, thuggish or both. And the other half of the Stewart-Hertzberg Pulitzer entry, their account of credit problems nearly breaking the market just after the 1987 crash, was simply the most impressive piece of financial journalism I have ever read.

By the time the "insider trading" material was massaged into a fly-on-the-wall narrative, though, it had all of the shortcomings of the genre. But given the Zeitgeist of the era, no one cared. No one listened when the few Milken supporters who could be found complained about reconstructed conversations. The New York Times Book Review sent the volume to a previously (and since) obscure financial writer whose distinction was caustic criticism of Mr. Milken, Wall Street and the 1980s. And when Mr. Stewart honestly recorded in an epilogue that most of the vaunted convictions had been reversed by the Second Circuit Court of Appeals, no one noticed that this trashed the thrust of the preceding narrative.

Michael Milken

If the commercial success of the fly-on-the-wall account depends crucially on the Zeitgeist, the reportorial success depends on the author getting the big picture right. I do not think the big picture was a den of thieves, for example; it was arch con-man Ivan Boesky succeeding again, playing on the ambition and vanity of prosecutor Rudolph Giuliani to cut himself a good deal by promising a bigger fish, Mr. Milken. (See "Payback," the 1995 book by University of Chicago law professor Daniel Fischel.)

In "Blood Sport," Mr. Stewart's big picture is that because of deep character faults the Clintons badly handled a series of misfortunes, from the financial collapse of Whitewater to the suicide of Vincent Foster. This is surely better than having someone of Mr. Stewart's energy and rhetorical skill reviving the charge that our editorials drove Mr. Foster to suicide; in this respect the book treats us entirely fairly. And indeed, at least at first blush, this time he seems to agree with what we have so extensively written about Whitewater. He has turned on Ms. Thomases, the conventional wisdom runs, and joined the critics. Frankly, I wonder whether, net-net, this is the real effect.

First of all, reconstructed conversations are open to attack. John Brummett, the high muzzle-velocity Whitewater skeptic at the Arkansas Democrat-Gazette, scores in his review of "Blood Sport."

One of the book's telling tidbits about Mrs. Clinton is her imperious refusal to get out of a failing Whitewater because she'd been promised it would pay for Chelsea's college education. This has to come from Susan McDougal, the only other person in the room, and why should we believe her? In "an arguable outrage," Mr. Brummett continues, Ms. Thomases's account of a conversation with Mr. Foster "puts words in a dead man's mouth," including a worry that David Watkins would lie about Hillary's role in Travelgate. This is an

Susan Thomases

attempt to discredit a Watkins memo that later surfaced, and Mr. Brummett quotes a friend of the deceased, "if Foster indeed confided in Susan Thomases 'then killing himself was his second most irrational act.'"

The demands of narrative, though, also whiz the reader by inconvenient incriminating details. We never hear, for example, of Secret Service guard Henry O'Neill, who testified he personally saw Margaret Williams, Mrs. Clinton's chief of staff, leave Mr. Foster's office the night of his death with arms full of files. Instead, we get only what must be Mr. Nussbaum's account, that he and Mrs. Williams and Patsy Thomasson "turned out the lights" after briefly looking for a suicide note. Ms. Thomasson, too, is identified simply as "Watkins's deputy." She is in fact a long-time Arkansas political operative and a controversial figure in Washington; she ran Arkansas bond dealer Dan Lasater's business while he was in jail on cocaine charges. Mr. Lasater, employer of Roger Clinton, racetrack buddy of the president's mother and contributor to Clinton campaigns, has no index entry in "Blood Sport."

Mr. Stewart's lively but uneven melange is being spun in two vastly different ways. Among the media's personality mavens, it's devastating. Maureen Dowd of the New York Times is far more vitriolic about Hillary than these pages ever have been or would dare to be. But notice the first comment out of the White House from press secretary Michael McCurry: "One judgment is inescapable. A Pulitzer Prize-winning journalist has spent months investigating the so-called Whitewater matter and has found precious little news to impart to his readers."

The current fallback position of the Clinton campaign is precisely this: nothing new. Now a super-journalist has investigated and written a long book, so we know everything and can put it behind us. We always knew the Clintons were white trash, but where are the crimes?

In fact, Mr. Stewart's account and particularly his footnotes are littered with prima facie crimes. It is a federal crime to submit a false financial statement while seeking a mortgage from an insured institution. It is a crime to offer an Arkansas trooper a federal job as an inducement for silence. It is a crime to tell clever lies to government investigators such as the General Accounting Office. Mr. Stewart is too good a lawyer not to recognize large areas of criminal concern, but adds, "Factual issues of knowledge and intent loom large in whether any of these laws were broken." Worse could have been said, of course, of the legal contraptions to which Michael Milken was coerced to plead.

Then too, the narrative of "Blood Sport" essentially ends in March 1994, the same time as the book of Wall Street Journal articles we published 18 months ago. Events since then are merely noted, and much is omitted or glossed over in the interests of making the narrative move. For anyone who fails to understand these severe limitations, Mr. Stewart's in-depth look and a narrow slice of the story creates a misleading impression of exhaustiveness. If you ignore Dan Lasater and concentrate on what Susan McDougal wore to Whitewater in 1978, you may create a devastating sketch, but you're not going to break much news.

Susan Thomases was surely never so naive as to think she could keep Jim Stewart in her pocket, and she surely has an acute understanding of the vulnerabilities she has been trying to defend. What did she really want and expect? One of Mr. Stewart's tantalizing nuggets is her reaction to the original Whitewater story by Jeff Gerth of the New York Times back in 1992. Most others in the campaign were in panic, though Mr. Gerth's editors had packed the story with qualifications and caveats. By contrast, "Thomases was thrilled. She thought it was incomprehensible."

"Blood Sport" is of course anything but incomprehensible. But while Simon & Schuster's publicity hype has permeated the conventional wisdom, count one Whitewater maven who suspects that Ms. Thomases is far from distraught.

Mr. Bartley is editor of the Journal.

REVIEW & OUTLOOK

Asides

Who Is Micah Morrison?

So asked an editorial in Friday's Arkansas Democrat-Gazette, stung by Journal editorial page writer Micah Morrison's article last week on the trial of Governor Jim Guy Tucker. It included a few paragraphs on the tenor of coverage by the local press, and in Arkansas as everywhere, the press has the thinnest skin around.

So the Arkansas press is in an uproar, even including the Democrat-Gazette, whose editorial page editor is Paul Greenberg, who tried to tell the nation for years that Bill Clinton was "Slick Willie." While the offending article also had compliments for the paper, Mr. Morrison says he did have some lumps coming for attributing to it a cartoon in the weekly Arkansas Times. However, he denies that he hugged Debbie Gershman, spokesperson for Independent Counsel Kenneth Starr, as the Democrat-Gazette reported the day before. He also denies, as the editorial variously charged, that his prose was "turgid," or in a "half-Karl Marx, half-Jules Verne mode" or that he was a "space-age visitor" who had "only begun to degravitate" or that he indulged in "gonzo journalism."

Mr. Morrison had asserted that the local press has a "home-team mentality," and what the reaction says about this we leave readers to judge. But any Arkansan with information he or she would rather entrust to Mr. Morrison can leave a message at 212-416-2581.

Letters to the Editor

Gonzo Journalism Isn't Micah's Style

Portraying Micah Morrison as a gonzo journalist, as the press in Little Rock evidently did (Asides, March 25), is low burlesque, akin to claiming Joan Rivers is a topless dancer.

Mr. Morrison's March 19 investigative piece on Arkansas simply falls short. It's almost dull. We in Colorado, where Hunter Thompson and others have set the standard, could give Little Rock editors a few pointers on how to recognize the real gonzo. Mr. Morrison should have:

Raced down Main Street under suspicion of driving while impaired and, when apprehended, issued a press release saying police were trying to silence him on orders of the "Whitewater Gang."

Gotten himself in a sex-harassment hassle with a lady author seeking to interview him.

Showed public awareness by telling the "little people" of Arkansas they were being ripped off by overcharges on drugs — both prescription and the street kind.

Micah Morrison a gonzo? Happily, he's not even close.

LEE OLSON

Lakewood, Colo.

Editorial Feature

Too Many Outside Counsels

There currently are five independent counsels who have been in business a combined 4,189 days and have spent more than $50 million. One investigation goes back six years, involving alleged wrongdoing in the Reagan administration.

Although there have been only 17 independent counsels, often

Politics & People

By Albert R. Hunt

called special prosecutors, since this post-Watergate-era reform was enacted, there is a growing sense that the independent counsel statute needs to be curtailed. Rep. Jay Dickey (R., Ark.) is pushing a major overhaul in the House.

A catalyst may be a little-noticed hearing five weeks ago. An unusually diverse panel of experts — independent counsel Lawrence Walsh, a target of many Republicans for his Iran-Contra inquiry; Joseph diGenova, a prominent Republican prosecutor and once an independent counsel; Abner Mikva, a former federal judge and White House counsel in the Clinton administration, and Theodore Olson, a former Reagan administration official and himself once a target of an independent inquiry — agreed the independent counsel law is in dire need of reform.

Mr. Olson, understandably bitter about the lengthy and futile investigation of him for supposedly misleading Congress, wants to dump the law altogether. The others, however, agreed that in at least three contemporary cases an independent counsel would be justified: Watergate, the Iran-Contra scandal and the present Whitewater investigation. But most other investigations, they argued, could be undertaken by the Justice Department.

In recent years the debate over the statute unfortunately has been all-or-nothing: Keep it as is or kill it. That's a false choice. Instead it ought to be changed in several substantive ways.

• The threshold for appointing an independent counsel needs to be raised. Currently if there is a specific allegation and a credible source against the president or anyone in his cabinet or political family, the pressure is on the attorney general to request an outside investigation. This grew out of the Nixon administration's crimes. That White House and Justice Department couldn't be trusted; in reaction, Congress cast a wide net on who would be covered by the statute and when.

That scope ought to be narrowed and the criteria toughened. An independent counsel is desirable for public confidence when there

Current Investigations			
INDEPENDENT COUNSEL	SUBJECT	APPOINTED	COSTS* (In mil.)
Adams/ Thompson	HUD	3/1/90	$24.5
Fiske/Starr	Clinton	1/24/94	$19.5
Smaltz	Espy	9/9/94	$3.37
Barrett	Cisneros	5/24/95	$0.22
Pearson	Brown	7/6/95	$0.16
*Through Sept. 1995			
Source: General Accounting Office			

are serious allegations against the president, probably when they are against the attorney general, or in those unusual cases where the Justice Department would face a clear conflict. As Mr. diGenova says, it should be reserved "for those rare instances where there could be a constitutional crisis or where the president's interest is so obvious and acute that the attorney general faces a clear conflict of interest."

This probably would have eliminated almost two-thirds of the independent counsel investigations. Some, like the current inquiry into Housing Secretary Henry Cisneros, would have been dismissed quickly by any prosecutor not constrained by this law. Some more serious allegations, like the HUD scandal in the Reagan administration, could have been handled through normal investigative and prosecutorial channels.

Above all, don't make it any worse. The normally sensible House Judiciary Committee chairman, Henry Hyde, proposes to extend this law to members of Congress. But whether it's the indictment of a powerful member like Dan Rostenkowski or the conviction of two Democratic congressman over the past seven months, the evidence shows there is no need to broaden the coverage of this law.

• Ideological opposites Ted Olson and Abner Mikva, as well as Rep. Dickey, agree the independent counsel should be a full-time job, requiring a leave of absence from regular jobs.

"It is absolutely essential that the independent counsel should be free from any concerns that he or she has conflicting interests," says Mr. Mikva. "The investigation ought to be completed as quickly as possible."

These worries have been driven home by Whitewater counsel Kenneth Starr, a widely respected conservative who nonetheless is raising ethical eyebrows with his outside business and political activities while serving as an independent counsel. He has not suspended ties to his law firm, which was being sued by the Resolution Trust Corp. at the same time the Whitewater counsel was investigating the RTC's role. He has continued to take on politically charged cases, such as representing major tobacco companies against the government, and to make political contributions. (The Arkansas Times, using Freedom of Information requests, revealed that Mr. Starr's ethics adviser, Sam Dash, the former Watergate counsel, is being paid a princely $3,200 a week for his services.)

This is all in the context of the well-known desires of Mr. Starr, a distinguished solicitor general in the Bush administration, to be appointed to the Supreme Court someday. His decision to haul Hillary Clinton before a grand jury rather than simply take more testimony from her was viewed by even some non paranoiac Democrats as grandstanding, underscoring the desirability of tapping someone without political ambitions.

Ken Starr insists he's not dragging out the inquiry and is devoting his "full energies" to it, but the facts belie that. If he wants to maintain his good reputation and retain public confidence, he ought to cease all outside activities immediately; that ought to be a requirement for future appointments.

• The way independent counsels are named needs to be changed. Currently, Chief Justice William Rehnquist names a panel of three federal judges. The current panel is dominated by Judge David Sentelle, a politically motivated justice with close ties to the Jesse Helms right-wing organization in North Carolina.

Indeed, Judge Sentelle lunched with Sen. Helms and North Carolina Sen. Lauch Faircloth, who had been demanding a new Whitewater prosecutor, shortly before his panel decided to sack the previous counsel and appoint Mr. Starr. Messrs. Sentelle, Helms and Faircloth insist the subject never came up. Sure. A better method, suggested by Judge Mikva, would be to each year select a three-member panel, by lottery, from the 13 chief judges around the country.

An underlying assumption in these charges is there won't be another political cipher as attorney general. There's no guarantee of that. But there are checks and balances — chiefly Congress, the press, and career investigators and prosecutors. If a Justice Department took a dive in investigating a cabinet member or ally of the president in today's environment, the political costs likely would be high.

Letters to the Editor

What's Sauce for the Goose . . .

Al Hunt has now concluded that it is too easy to unleash independent counsels on executive branch officials. Where has he been the last nearly two decades since the birth of this law in 1978?

I don't remember Mr. Hunt having second thoughts about the independent counsel law when it was used first to delay the appointment of my former boss, Edwin Meese, to the attorney general post, and used again to try to force Mr. Meese from office. In fact, every aspect of Mr. Meese's and his family's life were investigated at various times by no less than three independent counsels at a cost of tens of millions of dollars. Yet despite all the negative leaks from investigators to reporters, who were all too willing to print them, Mr. Meese wasn't charged with so much as jaywalking. Where were the voices of "reform" then?

Another recent critic of this law is Abner Mikva. Mr. Mikva left his lifetime position as chief judge of the Court of Appeals for the District of Columbia, which he received from President Carter, to serve as President Clinton's White House counsel. Mr. Mikva then left the Clinton White House and the swirl of ethics charges there after about one year's time. But before serving on the bench or at the White House, Mr. Mikva was a Democratic congressman who voted to create the independent counsel law. Now he, like Mr. Hunt, has second thoughts. The law, he tells us, is in need of "reform."

One "reform" suggested by Mr. Mikva, and duly reported by Mr. Hunt, is not a reform at all, but a partisan criticism of Whitewater

Independent Counsel Kenneth Starr. Mr. Starr is the subject of a concerted attack by Clinton supporters in and out of the media who claim his private law practice creates a conflict of interest. Although the law has always allowed independent counsels to maintain their private practices, and most do, suddenly Mr. Starr is faulted for doing so.

According to Mr. Mikva, "It is absolutely essential that the independent counsel should be free from any concerns that he or she has conflicting interests. The investigation ought to be completed as quickly as possible." Compared with, say, former Iran-Contra Independent Counsel Lawrence Walsh's seven-year reign and unimpressive results, Mr. Starr's investigation is a paragon of efficiency. He has achieved numerous guilty pleas and indictments since his appointment.

Kenneth Starr

But Mr. Starr's private law practice has nothing to do with the speed of his investigation. That charge should be aimed at the Clinton administration and their supporters. For instance, Clinton officials have delayed providing information to investigators in response to subpoenas, with one miraculous document discovery after another; interference by a local Democratic prosecutor in Arkansas, who is also running for Congress, is another obstacle Mr. Starr is forced to overcome; and Mr. Starr was forced to appeal outrageous rulings by a federal judge in Arkansas, who also happens to be a close Clinton friend, which, although successful, drained resources and caused delays. Mr. Mikva's "reform" won't fix these problems.

And what are the supposed "conflicts" that cause Mr. Mikva concern about the Starr investigation? Well, for instance, Mr. Starr represents tobacco companies, which are at odds with Clinton administration policies; he represents the Republican National Committee, which, of course, is the party of Lincoln, not Clinton; and he represents Wisconsin Gov. Tommy Thompson in school choice litigation that is supported by conservatives. Hence we're to believe Mr. Starr has it "in" for Mr. Clinton. What nonsense.

Mr. Starr's ethics adviser is former chief Watergate counsel Sam Dash, a Democrat. Mr. Dash sees no conflict. Is he out to get Mr. Clinton, too? Is his judgment impaired by the tobacco companies, the

GOP and the rest? Moreover, if, as the argument goes, Mr. Starr's representation of these clients creates a partisan appearance, I suppose when President Carter appointed then-Congressman Mikva — a partisan liberal Democrat — to head the second most powerful court in America, Mr. Carter created a conflict as well. After all, the question can be asked: Did Mr. Mikva bring his well-known liberal ideology to the bench? Did his partisan political experience influence his judicial duties?

In truth, Mr. Hunt and Mr. Mikva confuse ethical conflicts, which do not exist in this case under any standard of review, with their partisan desire to assign partisan motives to Mr. Starr. Funny how tight the shoe fits when it's on the other guy's foot.

Mark R. Levin
Landmark Legal Foundation

Washington

(Landmark is co-counsel to former RTC Criminal Investigator Jean Lewis.)

REVIEW & OUTLOOK

The Travel Office Phase

The Whitewater coverup has been in high gear the past couple of weeks, with Senate Democrats filibustering against further investigation, the Pillsbury reports being disinterred to exonerate the Clintons, and various worrywarts suddenly discovering that Independent Counsel Kenneth Starr works for a big law firm. We take this as a sure sign that Mr. Starr's probe is hitting some sore spots, not only with his current prosecution in Little Rock, but, even more portentously, with his assuming jurisdiction over the White House Travel Office firings.

Nearby we reprint some excerpts from reports by the law firm Pillsbury, Madison & Sutro — for the benefit of readers whose curiosity may have been piqued by Anthony Lewis in his syndicated column or Garry Wills in the New York Review of Books. Reporters regularly covering Whitewater have downplayed these reports, understanding that their charter was merely cost-benefit analysis on whether the regulators can raise money through litigation. The last supplemental report, under charter from the FDIC rather than the RTC, did take a distinctly different tone, rather gratuitously adopting Mrs. Clinton's denials and memory lapses at face value. Perhaps the firm felt this necessary to defend earlier conclusions after release of the Rose billing records, but even this report had to state that it exonerated no one.

Whatever the specifics, we have fundamental doubts about using lawsuits to bolster the public fisc, but in the S&L crisis such cost-benefit analysis was ubiquitous and many prominent firms came out on the wrong side. Mr. Starr's firm, Kirkland & Ellis, settled a suit over its representation of an S&L, though Mr. Starr had nothing to do with it personally and his arrangements passed muster with his ethics counsel, Democrat Sam Dash of Watergate fame. We have repeatedly written that the very notion of an "independent counsel" is a walking conflict of interest, and Antonin Scalia eloquently expressed this view before the Supreme Court. But eight other Justices went the other way, and now come Mr. Lewis and others to complain that the institution is out of control. Meanwhile, a federal judge in Arkansas just ordered a new grand jury to continue Mr. Starr's probe.

The White House is energetically fanning the embers of defense because of the coming election and the allegations arising in the Little Rock trial of sometime associates of the Clintons. But most acutely, we suspect, because Mr. Starr's mandate has been broadened formally to include the Travel Office scandal. On March 22, the three-judge court supervising Mr. Starr broadened his jurisdiction at the request of Attorney General Janet Reno to include the David Watkins memo that seems to conflict with Mrs. Clinton's testimony about her role in the Travel Office firings. The court gave Mr. Starr the power to "seek indictments and to prosecute any person or entities involved."

In April 1994, the White House responded on Mrs. Clinton's behalf and at her direction to interrogatories from the General Accounting Office. Answers include the likes of, "Mrs. Clinton was aware that Mr. Watkins was undertaking a review of the situation in the Travel Office, but she had no role in the decision to terminate the employees." This year, she submitted a 25-page affidavit responding to inquiries from Rep. William Clinger's Committee on Government Reform and Oversight. The categorical denials have faded into a series of evasions recorded in the accompanying box score.

Now, the Travel Office firings did not take place a decade ago, but in 1993. Nor in Arkansas, but at 1600 Pennsylvania Avenue. What Mr. Starr is now investigating is not an old land transaction, that is, but how the Clinton Administration conducted the business of the Presidency.

It's clear on the face of matters that the Travel Office employees were fired to make way for Arkansas cronies — adjuncts of the "political family" David Hale depicts taking care of each other financially and otherwise. The firings were obviously precipitous, based on the first available accusations. The FBI was called to help, and the IRS invoked. Indeed, the IRS promptly began to investigate UltrAir, the previous contractor. The episode resulted in a criminal prosecution of former Travel Office head Billy Dale, on charges promptly chucked out by a jury. At least prima facie, the Travel Office episode was about an Administration using the law enforcement powers of the government to throw someone in jail because he was in their way. In polite circles, this is called an abuse of power.

Then, too, there is the coverup, with the possibility of obstruction of justice. Attorney General Reno's letter to the court said Mr. Starr may as well handle the Watkins memo because he already "has notified me that he is investigating possible false statements concerning the travel office firings made to his office in the course of its inquiry into the suicide of former deputy White House counsel Vince Foster." This might have to do, for example, with the adventures of the handwritten notebook in which the late deputy White House counsel recounted his deep Travel Office concerns. The White House did not notify investigators of this document until July 1994, nearly a year after Mr. Foster's death and the week following the Fiske report on it. The document was not actually delivered to Mr. Starr until April 1995.

The Arkansas phase of Whitewater is relevant because this is where the Clinton people learned to behave this way. But filibustering Democrats want no further character witnesses about the

Box Score: *Congressional Travel Office Probe*
Hillary Clinton March 21 affidavit:

QUOTES	NUMBER
"I do not recall"/"I cannot recall".	21
"I do not believe".	9
"I have no knowledge"/"I have no first-hand knowledge"/"I have no personal knowledge". . . .	7
"It is possible"/"It is quite possible that I had"/ "It is possible that I may have".	4
"I simply don't know"/"I don't know"/ "I do not know how"/"I do not know what".	4
"I believe".	3
"I may have spoken".	3
"I have no specific recollection".	2
"I may have expressed the view".	2
"I cannot identify".	2
"I do not know for certain"/"I do not know how".	2

Also: "It is hard to remember"/"I have tried to state . . . such recollections as I have"/"It is . . . difficult now to distinguish"/"I believe I became aware"/"I do not remember precisely"/"I have a vague recollection"/ "I am not aware"/"He may have mentioned"

Clintons and their coterie. No one in the Senate has any memory of a filibuster being used to block funding for oversight hearings; if Republicans had filibustered Iran-Contra, the air would have been filled with talk of impeachment.

In its broadest sense, from the Ozarks to the White House, Whitewater is an endless web of lies and deceptions, abuse of prerogatives and casual obliviousness to the law. Democrats have a particular reason to filibuster, of course, because the next phase of the Senate hearings will be about Dan Lasater, cocaine-convicted bond dealer and Clinton crony. That is, they would open the question of whether the same behavior pattern applied to the Arkansas drug scene, not only seamy but sinister.

Editorial Feature

The Pillsbury 'Exoneration'

Recently, reports from the law firm Pillsbury, Madison & Sutro have been cited by critics of Whitewater hearings as justification for closing down any further investigations into the matter. However, a fuller reading of the reports may lead to a different conclusion. Following are excerpts from the various reports, plus excerpts from a staff review of the reports by Rep. Jim Leach's House Banking Committee. The reports were addressed to the Resolution Trust Corp., as it wound up its mandate last year, and to the Federal Deposit Insurance Corp., which assumed jurisdiction as the RTC dissolved:

A Report on Certain Real Estate Loans and Investments Made by Madison Guaranty Savings & Loan and Related Entities (Dec. 19, 1995):

To establish a claim not barred by the statute of limitations, the RTC must prove fraud or intentional misconduct. . . . [A]ny potential defendants can be expected to argue that they acted in good faith and therefore lack the requisite intent.

It is anticipated from the statements made by several witnesses that Jim McDougal, Jim Guy Tucker, Chris Wade and Bill Henley will argue that the 1308 Main Street and Castle Grande transactions were arm's-length sales of the properties with profits accruing to the individuals involved and that they were an exercise of prudent business judgment. . . .

Similarly, the Castle Grande transactions will be cast as arm's-length for-profit investments, albeit by people close to McDougal. It was argued in the McDougal criminal trial that people known to the institution were better risks than strangers. This defense was successful in the criminal trial, but the prosecution was less than vigorous.

When all factors are taken into consideration, litigation with respect to these two projects may only be marginally cost-effective. If vigorously defended, they could be expensive to litigate, and, given the likelihood of a hometown jury, there is no certainty as to the outcome — despite a factual pattern which would amply support claims for fraud, conversion and abetting. Additionally, any claim of conspiracy is presently grounded only in circumstantial evidence. Finally, there are relatively few potential defendants against whom the RTC would be able to take a judgment and who would be financially able to satisfy that judgment.

A Report on the Representation of Madison Guaranty Savings & Loan by the Rose Law Firm (Dec. 28, 1995):

The evidence does not provide a basis consistent with the extender statute on which to assert claims against the Rose Law Firm that could be pursued in a cost-effective manner. Accordingly, it is recommended that no further resources be expended on this part of the investigation.

A Report on the Rose Law Firm's Conduct of Accounting Malpractice Litigation Pertaining to Madison Guaranty Savings & Loan (Dec. 28, 1995):

Litigation costs: A case against the Rose Law Firm based on the foregoing could not be litigated to judgment in a cost-effective manner. Preparing and trying such a case would involve many depositions (both of Rose Law Firm lawyers and others), heavy use by both sides of expensive experts and probably a fair amount of motion practice. There is no reasonable likelihood that such a case could be prepared and tried for $200,000. Thus in all probability, the expense of litigating the matter would exceed the maximum recovery. Regardless of whether it won or lost at trial, the RTC would lose money on the case. . . .

Recommendation: While a claim could be stated against the Rose Law Firm, litigation would be difficult, the outcome would be uncertain and the expected recovery would not cover the costs of the litigation, much less lead to a net recovery for Madison Guaranty's estate. Thus, it is recommended that such litigation not be pursued.

A Supplemental Report on the Representation of Madison Guaranty Savings & Loan by the Rose Law Firm (Feb. 25, 1996):

On or about January 4, 1996, billing records pertaining to the Rose Law Firm's representation of Madison Guaranty were discovered at the White House. The records are responsive to the RTC's subpoena on the Rose Law Firm in February 1994. The records also are responsive to the RTC's subpoenas served on President and Mrs. Clinton in June 1994.

On January 5, 1996, David E. Kendall, counsel to the President and Mrs. Clinton, sent PM&S a copy of these billing records. The records shed new light on work performed by the Rose Law Firm for Madison Guaranty in 1985 and 1986. Had they been available earlier, the records would have eased the task of determining what services the Rose Law Firm performed for Madison Guaranty. That task was made more difficult by the absence of billing records and other records of the work performed, notably the absence of any files documenting the Rose Law Firm's work on the acquisition of Castle Grande. . . .

The new evidence has very little effect on the analysis of what the Rose Law Firm knew and did before the acquisition of the IDC property closed. The new evidence shows that, after the acquisition closed, lawyers at the Rose Law Firm (and in particular Mrs. Clinton) had more contact with Seth Ward and performed more services for Madison Guaranty than previously was known, but there remains no substantial evidence that these lawyers knew or intended to aid and abet McDougal's apparent misconduct. . . .

For purposes of this report, the ultimate question is not whether McDougal or Ward could profitably be sued, but whether the Rose Law Firm aided and abetted them in what looks like fraudulent or intentional misconduct. . . . Despite the new billing records, the extent of the Rose Law Firm's involvement in the IDC acquisition is not well documented, and it has been further obscured by faulty memories. . . .

It simply would not be persuasive to argue that, for $21,000, McDougal corrupted the Rose Law Firm and convinced half a dozen lawyers, most of whom he did not know, to join him in a scheme to violate the law. Odd as he might seem, McDougal did not involve large groups of strangers in his schemes. Instead, McDougal typically involved a close group of long-time friends and trusted associates in his plans, and nobody else. And typically it was the same people, over and over, friends and vassals who dated back to McDougal's youth. . . .

The Clintons (like Senator Fulbright) were not old cronies . . . instead, they fall into a different group. They were not confidantes but people who McDougal wanted to claim as friends. . . .

Conclusion: The evidence taken as a whole does not amount to convincing proof that the Rose Law Firm knowingly aided and abetted a fraud, or a scheme to circumvent the Arkansas investment limitation regulation. This conclusion does not necessarily mean that the evidence exonerates anyone; it simply means, given the applicable legal standards and the statutory mandate under which the FDIC operates, that no reasonable basis has been found to recommend the filing of a claim relating to IDC/Castle Grande against the Rose Law Firm.

*   *   *

From an April 3 memorandum to Chairman James Leach from the staff of the House Banking Committee, commenting on the Pillsbury reports:

The Legal Threshold . . . .

The factual findings contained in Pillsbury's report suggest that if held to a gross negligence standard — or some other legal standard not requiring a showing of fraud or intentional misconduct — Rose might well have faced liability for its legal work on the Castle Grande project. . . .

Quid Pro Quos . . .

Pillsbury's puzzling assertion that there is no "suggestion" that improper quid pro quos passed between Governor Clinton and the owner of a state-chartered savings & loan that retained the Governor's wife to represent it before state regulators appointed by her husband is belied by a substantial body of documentary evidence released by the House Banking Committee at its hearing last summer. Those documents reflect a pattern of special treatment accorded McDougal and Madison Guaranty during Governor Clinton's tenure, including but not limited to the following examples:

• Governor Clinton intervened on McDougal's behalf with State Health Department officials who had protested sewage treatment deficiencies at one of Madison's real estate development projects, and helped to secure favorable state consideration of a proposal to construct a "brew pub" at another McDougal-controlled development;

• Governor Clinton directed major state agencies to lease sizable office space from Madison Guaranty when less costly and more suitable space was available elsewhere in Little Rock;

• Governor Clinton appointed Madison Guaranty's President to the state savings & loan commission;

• Governor Clinton appointed as the state's top S&L regulator an attorney who had represented Madison in private practice, and whose candidacy for the post was endorsed by McDougal; and

• Under Governor Clinton, Madison Guaranty was permitted to grow 25-fold during a brief four-year period, and to continue operating long after its insolvency was established.

The Heart of the Matter

. . . [W]ith respect to the facts, Pillsbury's various reports largely substantiate the circumstances that the House Banking Committee outlined at its hearings in August 1995, namely, that the Clintons used their positions of power and influence in Arkansas to avoid substantial personal liabilities that otherwise would have accrued from the failed Whitewater real estate investment. . . . Placed in this context, what Pillsbury views as Rose's relatively trivial billings for representing Madison takes on greater significance. . . .

Pillsbury's various reports have been repeatedly invoked in recent weeks as part of a public relations offensive designed to convince a skeptical public that the Clintons have been "exonerated" of any wrongdoing in the Whitewater circumstance. The reports are simply not consistent with such an interpretation.

Editorial Feature

Whitewater: Not a 'Trivial Matter'

In recent weeks, Joe Conason, executive editor of the New York Observer, has emerged as the White House's leading defender on Whitewater. He has appeared on PBS's "Charlie Rose Show" and CNN's "Crossfire" to accuse James Stewart, the author of the best-selling book "Blood Sport: The President and His Adversaries," of inaccurate reporting on Whitewater. He also co-authored a lengthy piece in the Nation magazine accusing Independent Counsel Kenneth Starr of conflicts of interest. This week, Mr. Conason wrote an Observer article reporting that Sam Dash, the Democratic counsel to the Watergate committee who now serves as an ethics adviser to Mr. Starr, didn't view Whitewater as important. Mr. Starr said Mr. Conason's column "recklessly misquotes and mischaracterizes" Mr. Dash's views. Mr. Dash himself issued a four-page statement rebutting Mr. Conason's interpretation of their conversation. Mr. Conason faxed us a five-page response saying he stands by his story. Excerpts from Mr. Dash's statement follow:

In my 40 years of public life, since serving as District Attorney of Philadelphia in 1956, this is the first time I have found it necessary to respond this way to a news story quoting me. I have been quoted thousands of times in the past, and although, like others in my position, I have not always liked the way a story came out, I had to agree it was fair reporting. Not so Joe Conason's story about me published today in the New York Observer.

This past Monday, I agreed to talk to Mr. Conason about my role as Ethics Counsel to Independent Counsel Kenneth Starr, as I have done with numerous reporters over the past months, with Mr. Starr's approval, in order to provide some accounting of the unusual process of oversight and review Mr. Starr has set up to ensure objectivity and fairness in the investigations and prosecutions under his responsibility. What I said to Mr. Conason was pretty much what I have said to other reporters, who have published stories about these interviews. As can readily be seen by reading these stories, I have reported on the conduct of the Independent Counsel and his staff clearly in a way that has been supportive of their integrity and fairness . . . and I have had no reason to change my views on these matters.

One would not think so, however, on reading Mr. Conason's account of my interview. He reports me as trivializing the charges under investigation by the Independent Counsel; second-guessing the validly of the prosecution in Little Rock; claiming that the lawyers working for Starr have to be "reined in" or they will abuse power; and threatening to quit my position. How Mr. Conason could have derived any of these views on my part from my interview bewilders me. I believe, from what he said to me, that these are Mr. Conason's positions. Unfortunately, he has permitted them to be expressed in his story through quotations he erroneously attributes to me.

Sam Dash

I want to respond specifically to some of Mr. Conason's misquotations:

• (Conason) "Samuel Dash . . . doesn't think there is much to the Whitewater affair . . . and that it may have not ever merited the appointment of an independent counsel."

I actually said that Whitewater cannot be compared to Watergate as a national scandal, but that what Whitewater has come to mean under Mr. Starr's investigation . . . is a very important and significant matter which had to be investigated by an independent counsel.

• (Conason) "Even there (the present charges being tried in Little Rock), however, he (Dash) has reservations. 'There may have been fraud in the Tucker-McDougal case,' he said, 'But if Bill Clinton was not President, would anybody have looked into it? No.'"

I actually expressed no reservations about the indictment returned by the grand jury, now the basis of the trial in Little

Rock. My reference to Mr. Clinton being President was in the context of telling Mr. Conason that if Mr. Clinton were not President, there would be no basis to appoint an independent counsel, and that, therefore, there may not have been an investigation of these important charges. My statement was in support of the Independent Counsel legislation. But Mr. Conason's report makes it look like I was attributing partisan political motives to the investigation.

• (Conason) Quotation attributed to Dash: "None of what was said by Hale about conversations he had with the President has any relevance to the charges against Tucker and McDougal."

I did not make such a blanket statement. I repeatedly emphasized to Mr. Conason that I was speaking only of those conversations which Hale has alleged he had with Mr. Clinton alone.

• (Conason) "He (Dash) acknowledges that the independent counsel engaged him in a 'Faustian Bargain' to defuse early doubts about Mr. Starr's partisanship."

The term "Faustian bargain" is foreign to me. I have never used it, and certainly did not use it in my interview with Mr. Conason. . . . It is a strong term indicating selling one's soul, which is entirely out of bounds in any effort to describe the relation that was established between Mr. Starr and me. . . .

• (Conason) "Given his continuing doubts about Whitewater. . ."

I expressed no such doubts about "Whitewater" as it is being investigated by Mr. Starr — but, on the contrary, expressed strong support of his investigations. . . .

• The last paragraph of Mr. Conason's story is pure fiction. In it he represents that I have threatened to quit, and that by so doing, I hold some power over Mr. Starr which "ensures that Whitewater ultimately concludes as the trivial matter it is." I have neither suggested nor threatened that I will quit as Ethics Counsel. As I told Mr. Conason, I have discussed with Mr. Starr that I may not be able to perform this role this summer, since I will be in Heidelberg, Germany, serving as an exchange professor at the University of Heidelberg Law School. . . . I stressed to Mr. Conason that I believed it [Whitewater] was not a "trivial matter," as he suggested, but an important and significant matter that needed the attention of the criminal justice system, and particularly that part of the system that called for an independent counsel.

Editorial Feature

The Lonely Crusade of Linda Ives

By MICAH MORRISON

ALEXANDER, Ark. — Linda Ives appears to be a simple house-
wife — born in 1949, graduated from Little Rock's McClellan High
School, and married to Larry Ives, an engineer on the Union Pacific
railroad. But her tale is one of the most Byzantine in all Arkansas,
involving the murder of her son and his friend, allegations of air-
dropped drugs connected to the Mena, Ark., airport, a series of
aborted investigations and, she believes, coverups by local, state
and federal investigators.

The case started nine years ago, when Bill Clinton was governor
of Arkansas. Today, with Mr. Clinton in the White House, it is still
rattling through the state, with one of the principal figures making
bizarre headlines in the local press as recently as the last few weeks.
Above all, the "train deaths" case opens a window into the seamy
world of Arkansas drugs.

The bare facts of the case are these: At 4:25 a.m. on Aug. 23, 1987,
a northbound Union Pacific train ran over two teenagers, Kevin Ives
and Don Henry, as they lay side by side, motionless on the tracks.
Arkansas State Medical Examiner Fahmy Malak quickly ruled the
deaths "accidental," saying the boys were "unconscious and in deep
sleep" due to smoking marijuana. "We didn't know anything about
marijuana at the time," Mrs. Ives says. But when medical experts
found the explanation implausible, "we really began asking questions." The families held a press conference challenging the ruling,

which received wide publicity in Arkansas.

This in turn provoked an investigation by a local grand jury in Saline County, a largely rural area between Little Rock and Hot Springs. Ultimately the bodies were exhumed and another autopsy was performed by outside pathologists. They found that Don Henry had been stabbed in the back, and that Kevin Ives had been beaten with a rifle butt. In grand jury testimony, lead pathologist Joseph Burton of Atlanta said that the boys "were either incapacitated, knocked unconscious, possibly even killed, their bodies placed on the tracks and the train overran their bodies." In September 1988, the grand jury issued a report stating, "Our conclusions are that the case is definitely a homicide."

The teenagers told their parents they were going out for a night of deer hunting by spotlight. From the beginning allegations of a drug connection haunted the case. One police report filed seven months after the deaths reads, "Confidential Informant states that she has been told that the area the two boys died in is a drop zone for dope." The case soon became a local cause celebre. A Republican candidate for sheriff in heavily Democratic Saline County held a press conference by the railroad tracks where the two teenagers died, promised to crack down on "drug lords" operating in the area, and won an upset victory.

On taking office, however, the new sheriff passed the investigation along to Chuck Banks, U.S. attorney for the Eastern District of Arkansas during the Bush administration. Mr. Banks's office was probing allegations of drug-related corruption among Saline County officials. At the same time, another investigation was opened by Jean Duffey, a deputy prosecutor heading a newly created drug task force for the state's Seventh Judicial District. Drawing on interviews with area residents and informants, the task force developed a theory that the area was used as a site for drug drops by plane. "We had witnesses telling us about low-flying aircraft and informants testifying about drug pick-ups," Ms. Duffey recalled recently.

Ms. Duffey also says that her supervisor, outgoing Prosecuting Attorney Gary Arnold, gave her a strange order upon her new appointment. "He told me, 'You are not to use the drug task force to investigate any public officials.' At the time, I assumed it was because of the U.S. attorney's investigation. But as soon as my undercover agents hit the streets, they began linking public officials to drug dealing. So I began funneling that information to the U.S. attorney's office."

Eight months after taking the post of drug task force coordinator, Ms. Duffey was fired amid allegations of financial mismanagement, child abuse and official improprieties. The Arkansas State Police subsequently found no basis on which to charge her with mismanagement of task force funds and state welfare authorities cleared her of the abuse allegation. Ms. Duffey next received a subpoena that apparently would have forced her to reveal the identity of her informants — to some of the very people being probed for drug corruption, she claims. She chose to ignore the subpoena, she says, "rather than showing up in court and refusing to testify and being jailed for contempt. I feared for my safety in an

Linda Ives

Arkansas jail. Then the judge issued a felony arrest warrant — 'failure to appear' usually is a low-level misdemeanor — and told the newspapers I was a fugitive. That's when I left the state."

Ms. Duffey attributes the "smear campaign" and subpoena that forced her from the state to Dan Harmon, who had won the Democratic nomination for prosecuting attorney for the Seventh Judicial District. While he did not take office until January 1991, he had considerable influence in 1990 because the Democratic nomination ensured he would eventually gain the post. Interviewed this week, Mr. Harmon says that Ms. Duffey is a "crackpot" and that he was "planning to replace her when all hell broke loose."

Ms. Duffey says that matters were a great deal more serious than a personal dispute between her and Mr. Harmon: "My agents were turning up information linking Mr. Harmon to drugs, that's what the real problem was." Mr. Harmon also was identified in leaked investigative documents as a "target" in the 1989-1991 U.S. attorney's drug-corruption probe, and Ms. Duffey says the reason she did not respond to Mr. Harmon's attacks was that the U.S. attorney's office was assuring her that his indictment was imminent. But in November 1990 the case supervisor, Assistant U.S. Attorney Robert Govar, was removed from the investigation and U.S. Attorney Banks took charge.

In June 1991, Mr. Banks announced that the investigation was over. "There's not going to be any pressing of indictment against Mr. Harmon or any other public official," he said. "We found no evidence of any drug-related misconduct by public officials." Mr. Banks added that there would be no arrests in connection with the deaths of Kevin Ives and Don Henry.

Bill Clinton's gubernatorial administration assumed a role in the Ives and Henry case shortly after Dr. Malak's marijuana-induced accidental death ruling. Dr. Malak, an Egyptian-born physician appointed medical examiner during Mr. Clinton's first term, already had been buffeted by a number of controversial cases. With public pressure growing over botched tests and faulty handling of evidence in the train deaths affair, Gov. Clinton called in two out-of-state pathologists to review the work of the medical examiner and the state crime lab, where the autopsies had been conducted.

But when the Saline County grand jury probing the case attempted to subpoena the outside pathologists, Gov. Clinton balked. Betsey Wright, his chief of staff, submitted an affidavit saying she did not "know when the two pathologists will return to Little Rock" and that their contract with the state was to "make a job performance evaluation, not to provide a second opinion on specific cases." The grand jury responded by issuing a subpoena to Ms. Wright herself on May 25, 1988, and the next day issued its initial ruling of "probable homicide" in need of further investigation.

Two months later, Gov. Clinton revived a long dormant state Medical Examiner Commission to handle the Malak controversy. The panel was headed up by the director of the Arkansas Department of Health, Joycelyn Elders. In January 1989, the Medical Examiner

Commission ruled on the Malak case. There was "insufficient evidence at this time for dismissal" of Dr. Malak, Dr. Elders announced. Nine months later, Gov. Clinton introduced a bill to make the state more competitive in hiring forensic pathologists — by giving Dr. Malak a $32,000 pay raise; the state Legislature later cut the raise by half. Ms. Wright says the salary was raised in anticipation of removing Dr. Malak and attracting a new medical examiner. Dr. Malak was eased out of his job and given a position as a Health Department consultant to Dr. Elders a month before Gov. Clinton announced his presidential run.

A Los Angeles Times report in May 1992 notes that Dr. Malak's other controversial cases included one involving Mr. Clinton's mother, nurse-anesthetist Virginia Kelley. It said Dr. Malak's 1981 ruling in the death of one patient Mrs. Kelley was attending helped her "avoid legal scrutiny" in that death when she was already a defendant in a negligence suit in another patient's death. The suit was eventually settled by the hospital; Mrs. Kelley's hospital privileges were revoked in 1981 and she withdrew from practice.

Linda Ives has developed more sinister explanations for the Clinton administration's solicitude for Dr. Malak, charging that "high state and federal officials" have joined in an attempt to cover up the deaths of the boys and drug-related activities in Saline County. Taking allies where she can find them, she recently teamed up with California-based Jeremiah Films to produce a just-released videotape of her story. The company previously produced the notorious "Clinton Chronicles" videotape, but Mrs. Ives promises that she has "exercised full editorial control" over the new tape, and says that portions of the proceeds will go to "a special Civil Justice Fund we've established to find a courageous lawyer and finance a wrongful death lawsuit."

Of course, Mrs. Ives's own perceptions are colored by a nine-year obsession with her son's death. "I firmly believe my son and Don Henry were killed because they witnessed a drug drop by airplane connected to the Mena drug smuggling routes," Mrs. Ives says. "It's the only thing that could explain everything that has happened." It's well established that self-confessed cocaine smuggler and Drug Enforcement Administration informant Barry Seal operated out of Mena, in western Arkansas. Although he was murdered 18 months before the death of the boys, reports of Mena-connected drug activities persisted for years.

Police records also show that one of the early investigators on the train deaths case was Arkansas State Police Officer L.D. Brown, a former security aide to Gov. Clinton who is now cooperating with Independent Counsel Kenneth Starr's Whitewater probe. He says that he was ordered off the train deaths case in 1988. "I was told it had something to do with Mena and I was to get off it," Mr. Brown said in a recent interview. The superior officer who gave him the order died of cancer in 1994.

Last July, in an interview with American Spectator editor R. Emmett Tyrrell, Mr. Brown claimed that he worked briefly for Barry Seal, and that when he informed Gov. Clinton of Mr. Seal's activities,

Dan Lasater

Gov. Clinton told him that it was "Lasater's deal" and that he was not to worry about it. Dan Lasater is the Little Rock bond dealer and Clinton supporter arrested for cocaine distribution in 1986, in the same probe that netted Roger Clinton, the president's brother. While Mr. Lasater has received far less publicity than Hillary Clinton's financial transactions, veteran Arkansas observers have long viewed him as one of Mr. Clinton's most troubling connections. The new round of Senate Whitewater hearings reauthorized yesterday will provide a glimpse of Mr. Lasater, since the next stage of investigation will delve into some of his deals.

As Mr. Lasater was being charged with cocaine distribution in 1986, the DEA confirmed that he was the target of a drug trafficking probe involving his private plane and a small airstrip at the New Mexico resort, Angel Fire, which he had purchased in 1984. In the transcript of his interview with the FBI, Mr. Lasater identifies a police officer named Jay Campbell as an old friend. He also says that Mr. Campbell was a member of a DEA task force and had flown on his plane. Mr. Campbell — working a narcotics beat at the time for a nearby town's police force — was subpoenaed by the original Saline County grand jury and appears in police reports on the train deaths case.

Mr. Lasater could not be reached for comment. Mr. Campbell, now a lieutenant in a Pulaski County (Little Rock) narcotics unit, says that Mr. Lasater was only an "acquaintance" and that he was not a member of a DEA task force at the time, though he later served on several federal probes. He vigorously denies any involvement in the train deaths case and says he was "dragged into" the probe by a publicity-seeking Dan Harmon, then serving as special prosecutor for the Saline County grand jury.

One of the most constant and puzzling counterpoints in Linda Ives's lonely crusade has been Mr. Harmon, today still prosecuting attorney for the Seventh Judicial District. Initially, he led the aggressive Saline County grand jury that had the bodies exhumed. He even worked on the case as a volunteer before requesting that the presiding judge appoint him special prosecutor to supervise investigation of the deaths. Mr. Harmon had previously served as an elected county prosecutor in 1978-1980, then declared bankruptcy and briefly decamped to California before returning to Arkansas and private practice. Mr. Harmon won his 1990 election as prosecuting attorney by capitalizing on publicity gained as special prosecutor in the train deaths, and has held the post ever since.

At the time of his election, Mr. Harmon was a suspect in the U.S. attorney's corruption probe. "Dan Harmon. . ." states a February 1990 U.S. Attorney's Office memorandum leaked to the Arkansas press, "has been identified as a target in this investigation." One of the cocaine dealers targeted in the probe allegedly was connected to Mr. Harmon. The dealer, the memo says, "may have been involved, indirectly, in the murders of Kevin Ives and Don Henry." Mr. Harmon was cleared in June 1991 when U.S. Attorney Banks announced that he had found no evidence of drug-related misconduct by officials.

It appeared that the crusade was over. But in 1993, Mrs. Ives persuaded yet another new Saline County sheriff to reopen the train deaths probe. Detective John Brown was assigned the case. He says he was soon approached by a high-ranking state official who told him "it would be best if I just left this thing alone." But Mr. Brown did not leave it alone. In fact, Mr. Brown says that he turned up a new witness in the case. According to Mr. Brown, the witness claims that he saw Mr. Harmon on the tracks the night the boys were killed. Mr. Harmon dismisses the charge as "totally ridiculous."

But the new witness appears to have triggered an FBI probe. Mr. Brown says he was in the process of checking out the allegation when he mentioned it to a local FBI official who, much to Mr. Brown's surprise, immediately took the witness into protective custody and polygraphed him. "The FBI then said they were taking over the case and wanted everything I had," Mr. Brown recalls.

Jean Duffey, the former drug task force head, says the FBI contacted her in March 1994 — three years after she fled the state — telling her that a new investigation of the train deaths and official corruption was under way, and asking for her assistance. Linda Ives also says that after about 18 months of extensive contacts, the FBI broke off communication with her last August, shortly after a summary of the case was forwarded to current U.S. Attorney Paula Casey.

In November, Mrs. Ives had a final meeting with FBI officials. Apparently, the FBI was backing away from the case, particularly the second autopsy. At the November meeting, Mrs. Ives says, "[FBI agent] Bill Temple told me, 'It's time for you to realize a crime has never been committed.'" Mrs. Ives and Ms. Duffey then went public with the charge that the FBI was participating in a "coverup" of the controversial case.

The FBI has not responded to numerous requests for comment on its agents' conversations with Mrs. Ives. In virtually the only FBI comment on the case, I.C. Smith, the Little Rock FBI chief, gave a brief interview to the local Benton Courier in which he denied that his office was covering anything up. He said that the main obstacle was "the very real problem of determining whether federal jurisdiction would apply." Mr. Smith also suggested that Agent Temple had been "misquoted" and would not have spoken in such a "cold-hearted manner" to Mrs. Ives.

Mrs. Ives sticks by her story, and ridicules Mr. Smith's suggestion that jurisdiction might be at issue. "It's a federal corruption probe they've been working for 18 months," she says. "It's ludicrous to believe the FBI would work a case that long without knowing if they have jurisdiction."

In a memo on the Benton Courier article sent to Mr. Smith (and also sent to six Arkansas media outlets), Ms. Duffey says Mrs. Ives's account of the conversation was confirmed by Phyllis Cournan, another FBI agent in the room at time. Ms. Duffey's memo also says that in 1994 Ms. Cournan told her that the FBI had recommended that Mr. Banks, then the U.S. attorney, be charged with obstructing justice. Mr. Banks, now in private practice in Little Rock, did not respond to requests for comment.

Meanwhile, Dan Harmon has again been making news in Arkansas. His ex-wife, Holly DuVall, was arrested Nov. 30 after making a call from Mr. Harmon's phone to an undercover agent to buy a small amount of methamphetamine. Eleven days earlier, she had made news when local police searched her rented condominium near Hot Springs at the manager's request, following an altercation. They found an empty cocaine evidence package that should have been locked in the safe at Mr. Harmon's drug task force; federal investigators were soon visiting the condo and Mr. Harmon's office.

On March 18, Ms. Duffey went public with charges against Mr. Harmon on a local TV broadcast, "The Pat Lynch Show." One newspaper, the Malvern Daily Record, ran with the story, under the headline "Duffey alleges Harmon at scene of teens' murder." Four days later, Mr. Harmon announced that he was a Democratic candidate in the primary for Saline County sheriff.

Paula Casey

The next day, he was arrested on felony kidnapping and aggravated assault charges after allegedly dragging Ms. DuVall from her car and taking her on a 100-mile-per-hour ride. After a few days in jail and a brief hunger strike, Mr. Harmon held a press conference to deny kidnapping Ms. DuVall and denounce his arrest as a "political" move to undermine him. In regard to the train deaths allegations, Mr. Harmon says he plans to sue Ms. Duffey, Mr. Lynch and the Malvern Daily Record.

In mid-January the state cut off funding for Mr. Harmon's drug task force, and on Jan. 28 the Arkansas Democrat-Gazette reported that "Federal investigators are said to be building a racketeering case against people associated with the now-defunct Seventh Judicial District Drug Task Force." Arkansas State Police officials confirm that a corruption probe is under way. Mr. Harmon is not worried. "Nobody has questioned me," he says. "Nobody has informed me I'm a target. It's all just innuendo in the local press."

The results of any continuing federal investigation touching on the Ives and Henry deaths will be presented to Mr. Banks's successor as

U.S. attorney for the Eastern District. So Linda Ives's crusade will end up in the hands of Ms. Casey, the longtime Clinton ally and campaign worker who recused herself from Whitewater cases only after making several crucial decisions. President Clinton appointed her U.S. attorney in Little Rock in August 1993, shortly after his unprecedented demand for the immediate resignation of all sitting U.S. attorneys. Mrs. Ives says she is not optimistic about Ms. Casey. "But then," she adds, "it's not like I'm going to go away, either."

Mr. Morrison is a Journal editorial page writer.

Editorial Feature

Why Starr
Is Suddenly
In the Cross Hairs

Two years ago this column frowned on President Clinton's legal defense fund, highlighting the role played by a Los Angeles lawyer and Democratic activist, Ron Olson. So imagine my surprise when I soon received a private letter, from a prominent Republican, ripping me for ripping Mr. Olson.

The letter writer was Kenneth Starr.

This happened before Mr. Starr was asked to be the independent counsel for Whitewater, and long before the current campaign to portray the former solicitor general as a ferocious, ethically chal-

Potomac Watch

By Paul A. Gigot

lenged GOP partisan. Those of us who know Ken Starr find this last idea amusing. What we've pondered is the opposite — that Mr. Starr's judicious, establishment instincts might cause him to shrink from pursuing the facts if they led into the White House.

Yet the campaign to morph Mr. Starr into Al D'Amato continues to spread with barely a dissent. What began as a crusade in the liberal tabloids broke out this week into a New Yorker magazine assault by Jane Mayer. Her work, in turn, has been invoked by the New York Times in urging Judge Starr to resign.

All of which meshes beautifully with a White House defense that has become breathtaking in its simplicity: Portray everyone looking into Whitewater as a vicious, eye-bulging partisan. Defense lawyers everywhere know this strategy well: Blame the cops and beat the rap. It worked for Johnnie Cochran.

It's also worked with fellow Democrats, who have circled the wagons better than the Montana Freemen. Whitewater is unique among modern scandals in its display of party loyalty. When Republican presidents have been caught up in ethics probes, a Bill Cohen or Warren Rudman has always intoned that the facts aren't proven but the accusations are too serious to ignore, etc. And the press applauds them for rising above partisanship, etc.

Democrats have shown little such independence on Whitewater. Especially now that Mr. Clinton has vetoed Newt Gingrich's agenda, Democrats in Congress have been stalwart even to the point of associating themselves with White House stonewalling.

Kenneth Starr

The White House was shrewd to answer every substantive question on Whitewater by changing the subject to an attack on Al D'Amato. This deflection has worked so well that Senate Democrats felt no backlash when they filibustered to delay, and finally this week to limit, the probe. The New York Times, which now wants to cashier Mr. Starr, has barely noticed this broad-daylight coverup. Even the miraculous, years-late appearance of Hillary Rodham Clinton's Rose Law Firm billing records in January has now faded into media uninterest.

This means the only remaining Whitewater threat is Mr. Starr, who is now getting the D'Amato treatment himself. His sins include doing what nearly every other special counsel has done, and what the counsel law itself anticipates, which is to work for a law firm (Kirkland & Ellis) and represent clients. The one Kirkland client with even a tangential association to Whitewater, International Paper, was dropped by the firm when Mr. Starr became special counsel. He also stands accused of representing causes (such as school choice for poor African-American kids in Milwaukee) that are also favored by conservatives — which is said to be a conflict because these same conservatives don't like Bill Clinton!

Moreover, Mr. Starr's critics are less conflicted about some conflicts than others. A year ago Mr. Starr's law firm pried out of the New Yorker's Jane Mayer a humiliating public apology regarding her 1994 book, "Strange Justice." Ms. Mayer and co-author Jill Abramson all but accused Bush White House assistant counsel Mark Paoletta of breaking the law: "Such stage directions from the White House appear to have been in direct violation of the federal anti-lobbying act."

Strange journalism, thought Mr. Paoletta, who retained Kirkland to fire a letter to Ms. Mayer's publisher requesting an apology and retraction for defamation. After some resistance, Houghton Mifflin's general counsel wrote Mr. Paoletta last July 28 "on behalf of the authors," stating that "this passage was never intended to state or suggest that you yourself had violated any law." The authors also agreed to pull the sentence from the paperback and later editions of the book. Even the best journalists sometimes make mistakes. But one would have thought that while alleging conflict of interest about Mr. Starr, Ms. Mayer would have disclosed her own.

In any event, Ms. Mayer breaks the political code when she admits that a battered Mr. Starr serves multiple White House purposes. If he fails to press charges, the Clintons will hail his conclusion for being all the more credible. But if he does indict someone in the White House, perhaps even the first lady, his case can then be attacked and dismissed as tainted. At a minimum, he might be intimidated into delaying things until after the election.

However it all turns out — and most people are waiting to see what evidence Mr. Starr actually turns up — you have to admire the brazenness of White House Whitewater strategists. They're just better than Republicans at the smashmouth politics of ethics, tougher and unhindered by scruple.

Review & Outlook

Asides

Mena Cynics

The Associated Press reported last week that investigators for the House Banking Committee have been taking depositions in Mena, Arkansas. As readers of this page know, Mena is at the center of a swirl of allegations involving covert U.S. activities, cocaine smuggling and money laundering. Among those deposed was Charles Black, a former area prosecutor who once attempted to investigate Mena. "My cynical belief is that there is a lack of motivation in either party to fully and properly investigate," Mr. Black told the AP, "because the results will damage as many Republicans as Democrats." Let's hope the House committee has the courage to prove the Mena cynics wrong.

REVIEW & OUTLOOK

Clinton Under Oath

Looking back through American history, no Presidency raises deeper philosophical issues than Bill Clinton's. The core questions of his Administration, indeed his life, are the core questions of epistemology: What is truth? Does it exist? How can we tell?

What's more, the best description we've heard of Mr. Clinton is that he's our first totally existential President, for whom there is no past, no future, only the present moment. It is not so much that he lies in any calculating sense, but that he has the capacity actually to believe whatever the moment requires. This allows him to project his patented sincerity, as deep-felt on one side of the issue one day as on the other side the next. He is consummately the man from whom you would buy a used car.

Bill Clinton

This remarkable trait has served him well, carrying him from a dysfunctional family to a youthful audience with President Kennedy to Oxford to the governorship and ultimately to the highest office in the land. Repeatedly, he has used it to charm his way out of contradictions that would have tripped up any ordinary liar.

As a candidate, his sincere demeanor allowed him to navigate our Washington bureau's revelations of his constantly changing stories about his draft status during Vietnam, a series of equivocations and contradictions that should have sunk nearly any other candidate. When Gennifer Flowers turned up with her tape recordings, he went on CBS to tell a national audience "that allegation is false," that she herself had said they hadn't been together for 10 minutes in 10 years. Pressed whether he was "categorically denying that you ever had an affair with Gennifer Flowers," he was able to reply, "I've said that before and so has she." It developed, of course, that three state troopers on Mr. Clinton's security detail said they'd handled hundred of phone calls between the two and often driven Governor Clinton to Ms. Flowers's apartment.

By now, this part of Mr. Clinton's personality has been elevated to mythic proportions. A whole book, "Primary Colors," has been written about it, and it can be read as an ultimately sympathetic one. Unless the Paula Jones case is settled, a jury will have to decide which of two people in the room is telling the truth. At times, and for some audiences, the President's personal peccadilloes are almost part of his charm.

As a President, though, Mr. Clinton's ability to tell two stories has certain shortcomings. It seems, for example, that Congress and the public were both convinced Mr. Clinton was opposed to supplying arms to the Bosnians, while he was relying on the Iranians to do that very thing. The Chinese leadership is no longer inclined to believe him after his Administration told them it would never give a visa to Taiwanese leader Lee Teng-hui. It used to be thought, back in the days of Presidents Johnson and Nixon, that a "credibility gap" was a fatal White House disease.

Which brings us to the intriguing spectacle about to take place Sunday, as Bill Clinton is examined under oath and pain of perjury. He's been called as a defense witness in the Arkansas land-flipping trial of his onetime buddies and business partners James and Susan McDougal, and his successor as governor Jim Guy Tucker. Indeed, since Governor Tucker must surely be too smart to take the stand and even Jim McDougal is not that crazy, President Clinton seems likely to be the main defense witness.

So it will fall to the President to discredit David Hale, who's confessed his own felonies and turned state's evidence. Mr. Clinton is of course not himself on trial, and indeed some of the counts do not depend on Mr. Hale's testimony. But the defense strategy has been to wrap itself around the President; in their courtroom-steps comments, indeed, the defense attorneys often seem more intent on protecting the President than protecting their clients. So while Mr. Clinton's testimony Sunday will be videotaped and temporarily sealed, presumably it ultimately will be introduced and released.

The defense will ask Mr. Clinton to rebut Mr. Hale's testimony about a meeting with the two of them and Mr. McDougal at a trailer in the Castle Grande real estate development. Mr. Hale said they talked about the urgent need for a $150,000 loan, later raised to $300,000, and that the Governor said his name should not come up. The President has publicly dismissed Mr. Hale's claims as "a bunch of bull," and Mr. Clinton stated in May 1995 written answers to a Resolution Trust Corp. inquiry, "I am certain I never pressured Hale or any company he owned to make any loan."

Read closely, neither of these "denials" measure up to the CBS Gennifer Flowers's standard. But then, CBS cannot indict for perjury. Ray Jahn, who will lead the examination for Independent Counsel Ken Starr, will want to know whether any such meeting took place or might have taken place. The President will not know what Mr. McDougal may ultimately say, especially if convicted on other counts. Nor can he know what the Independent Counsel's office may already have; it is an exceedingly thorough collection of lawyers. This week Roger M. Adelman was named head of the Travelgate part of Mr. Starr's investigation; he's a white-collar crime specialist who's tried some 250 criminal cases, including a conviction in the Abscam Congressional scandal. We presume the chills this must be sending down White House spines explains the President's televised swipe at Mr. Starr yesterday.

We've long thought that the worst possible outcome of the Whitewater scandal would be that Mr. Clinton would charm his way to re-election, then to have evidence emerge of offenses too serious to ignore. This is, after all, what happened with Richard Nixon's obstruction of justice. The shortest route to this outcome, it occurs to us, will be for the President to toy with perjury this Sunday.

Arkansas—A Verdict

Much to the shock of American punditry, the Whitewater jury returned convictions against all three defendants in the Arkansas corruption trial. Governor Tucker announced he would resign and pass the baton to his Republican Lieutenant Governor, Mike Huckabee. Mr. Starr's critics fell silent.

Editorial Feature

Whitewater: The Prosecution Rests

By MICAH MORRISON

LITTLE ROCK, Ark. – The prosecution has now rested in the only Whitewater trial to date; yesterday U.S. District Judge George Howard Jr. winnowed some of the 21 counts against Arkansas Gov. Jim Guy Tucker, James McDougal and Susan McDougal, and today the jury will return to hear the defense. Whatever the ultimate verdict, Mr. Starr's case deserves its moment of attention. It's never easy to follow a legal argument on the basis of day-by-day news accounts, and this case is further clouded by the drama of recorded but still undisclosed testimony by President Bill Clinton concerning allegations by David Hale, former judge and now confessed felon. That drama, at least, should soon be resolved, as Mr. McDougal's attorney has announced that the tape will be played in court today. At its heart, though, the case against Gov. Tucker and the McDougals is a rather pedestrian one, familiar enough in the wake of the great savings and loan collapse of the late 1980s.

Mr. McDougal's Madison Guaranty S&L was taken over by federal regulators, and liquidated at a cost to taxpayers usually estimated at $60 million. Mr. Hale's Capital Management Services, a federally sponsored Small Business Investment Company, also collapsed at a taxpayer cost of about $3 million. The prosecution alleges that along the way the defendants milked these institutions to line their own pockets, bilking the taxpayer, and it turns out, some of their business associates as well.

The defense's strategy — both inside the courtroom and in the public-relations air war to shape national perceptions of the trial — has been to attack the government and the witnesses, particularly Mr. Hale, who was sentenced to 28 months in prison and ordered to pay $2 million in restitution for his role in defrauding Capital Management. In his opening statement, Sam Heuer, Mr. McDougal's lawyer, set the tone by calling Mr. Hale "the most deceitful person you'll ever hear of in your life." Mr. Heuer argued that Mr. Hale had concocted his charges because he was in trouble with the FBI and "knew that Jim McDougal was a good personal friend of Bill Clinton." Mr. Heuer attacked the independent counsel as "a prosecution machine on a mission." Why, he asked the jury, "is this case so important to them? Because Bill Clinton is the sitting president of the United States." Clinton vs. Hale, in fact, appears likely to be the

James McDougal

cornerstone of the defense's case, and it has been an effective one, particularly in the spin war to protect Mr. Clinton, who is involved because he and Mrs. Clinton were partners with the McDougals in Whitewater Development Co.

Beyond doubt, Mr. Hale has been central to the prosecution effort. "He was an insider. He knew how the system worked. He knew about the deals. Some of them were merely patronage, some were merely unethical, but some are crimes," Hickman Ewing, leader of Mr. Starr's prosecution effort, explained at Mr. Hale's sentencing. "As time has gone along, because of Mr. Hale's coming forward," he elaborated, "now there are others who admitted their wrongdoing, and now who are cooperating with the government."

The confessions of others, the prosecution clearly believes, bolster Mr. Hale's own credibility. But by now the prosecution is not betting the farm on him; the evidence has taken on a life of its own. With the defense about to open, Mr. Starr's team has offered ample evidence — even absent Mr. Hale's direct testimony — of land flips, straw purchases, bogus loan applications and other white-collar rape and pillage.

Mr. Hale, for example, provided information leading to guilty pleas by real-estate agent Larry Kuca and Stephen Smith, a former aide to Gov. Bill Clinton. Both admitted to obtaining fraudulent loans from Capital Management, pleading guilty to single counts of conspiracy to misapply funds. Both testified at the trial. Mr. Kuca testified that Mr. McDougal had directed him to divert $143,000 to a McDougal-controlled enterprise, Campobello Properties. Mr. Smith, a shareholder with Mr. McDougal and Mr. Tucker in the Kings River Land Co., testified that he falsely obtained $65,000 from Mr. Hale's lending firm and used it to pay off a Kings River note; yesterday, Judge Howard dropped Mr. Tucker from the Kings River counts.

One of the most important guilty pleas obtained with Mr. Hale's help was that of Robert Palmer, an appraiser who cooked up the inflated land valuations that provided the paperwork for loans to be issued by Madison. Mr. Palmer has pleaded guilty to one felony count of conspiracy and admitted to doctoring and backdating dozens of appraisals. He provided testimony on a number of key counts in the indictment, including a $755,000 inflated appraisal for a loan to a Hale frontman and a $1.3 million appraisal for a Madison loan to a company controlled by Mr. Tucker.

David Hale

With such witnesses and access to documents, the government has been able to buttress the counts on which Mr. Hale testified with others that in no way turn on his personal credibility. Two of them are worth a closer look:

Count 12 of the indictment is emblematic of the cozy deals and colossal arrogance of the Tucker-McDougal enterprise. It alleges that the McDougals and Mr. Tucker engaged in a classic land flip of a sewer and water utility, located in Mr. McDougal's Castle Grande development, by purchasing the property and then reselling it at a falsely inflated value financed by a loan from Mr. McDougal's S&L.

In January 1986 Madison Financial, an arm of the S&L, bought the sewer property for $450,000. About five weeks later, it resold the property for $1.2 million to Castle Sewer, a company formed for the purchase of the utility by Mr. Tucker and a partner, R.D. Randolph, a former bulldozer operator. Madison issued a loan of $1.05 million toward the purchase price of the newly appraised property. Who benefits? Mr. McDougal recorded a paper profit of $600,000 to help him ward off bank examiners. Susan McDougal, registered as a broker for Madison's real-estate arm, pocketed three checks totaling $85,000 as a "commission" on a deal she apparently had nothing to do with, though the judge dismissed her on this count.

Mr. Tucker, meanwhile, had submitted a loan proposal to Mr. Hale's Capital Management for "operating capital and for maintenance and painting of the water tank" at the utility. He got $150,000. But instead of being used for painting and maintenance, the money went right to Mr. McDougal as a downpayment on the property, the

Susan McDougal

prosecution says. Mr. Tucker benefited by getting a utility with a real value of about $450,000, while putting up no money and not signing any loan guarantees.

Testifying against Mr. Tucker and the McDougals were several key players in the transactions. Mr. Palmer, the appraiser, testified that he was instructed by a top Madison official to come up with a figure "somewhere around" $1.2 million. Don Denton, Madison's former chief loan officer, detailed aspects of the transactions and identified appraisal memos, loan documents and checks entered into evidence.

Mr. Tucker's former partner, Mr. Randolph, was on the stand for five days with what the Arkansas Democrat Gazette called "some of the most damaging testimony" against Mr. Tucker. Mr. Randolph painted a devastating portrait of a business innocent manipulated in the Castle Sewer scheme and related transactions. Mr. Randolph testified that he wasn't aware that the property they had purchased for $1.2 million had only weeks earlier been purchased for one-third the price. And it wasn't until years later, Mr. Randolph testified, that he learned that Mr. Tucker had stuck him with sole responsibility for the $150,000 Capital Management note — his largest single debt when he was forced into bankruptcy.

Four other counts in the indictment — and the tale of another hapless innocent — center around a building on Main Street in Little Rock that Mr. McDougal allegedly swapped through a series of straw purchasers to generate profits for himself and his buddies. The first McDougal nominee, the indictment alleges, was Mr. Tucker. He bought the dilapidated building at 1308 Main in February 1984 with a $45,000 Madison loan.

In March 1985, Madison assigned the mortgage on the property, then held by Mr. Tucker and his wife Betty, to a Madison employee named Lisa Aunspaugh, who was 20 years old at the time. Her only previous employment had been a year at minimum wage in an interior design shop. With Madison rapidly expanding its holdings and Susan McDougal busy remodeling properties, Mr. McDougal had hired Ms. Aunspaugh and set up a business account for her in the name of Designers Construction. He also provided the financing for her to buy a house at his Maple Creek development and a new Mercedes.

After the assignment of the 1308 Main Street mortgage, Ms. Aunspaugh testified, Mr. McDougal instructed her to write a check for $12,000 to the Tuckers on the Designers Construction account and deliver it. In October 1985, at Mr. McDougal's direction and with a Madison loan, she purchased the Main Street property for $125,000. Ms. Aunspaugh and Mrs. McDougal moved their remodeling business into the building. Three months later, again at Mr. McDougal's direction, Ms. Aunspaugh sold the property to Mrs. McDougal's brother, Bill Henley, for $190,000. Mr. Henley subsequently produced a lease dated August 1985 and claimed that Madison — through the Susan McDougal-Lisa Aunspaugh enterprise — owed him $18,000 in back rent. Never mind that Mr. Henley didn't buy the building until January 1986. Madison paid him the $18,000.

Who benefits? The prosecution says that the Tuckers wound up with $12,000 after simply holding the building for a year for Mr. McDougal and paying taxes and interest. Mr. McDougal used Ms. Aunspaugh as a straw purchaser for a $125,000 loan from his S&L for a property he secretly controlled. Then he sold it for a $65,000 profit that went into the Designers Construction account under his control, and arranged a backdated bogus lease to funnel $18,000 to his brother-in-law. After the collapse of Madison, Ms. Aunspaugh was dunned by the IRS for $58,000 in back taxes and faced foreclosure action on her Maple Creek property. Ms. Aunspaugh's testimony was backed up by former Madison officials, who identified loan documents, deeds, and numerous checks written on the Designers Construction account. The defense vigorously attacked Ms. Aunspaugh, forcing her to concede she had lied to IRS investigators in the past about the status of the Maple Creek property and income from the Designers Construction account.

When the defense opens its case, today, it's expected to argue that these were merely business decisions gone bad. Defense attorneys may argue that the Tuckers realized only a modest profit from the Main Street transaction, for example, and that the deal was a good faith effort to improve a rundown area of the capital. In the Castle Sewer transactions, similarly, Gov. Tucker will probably argue that Mr. McDougal failed to honor important side agreements to bring in new sewer and water hook-ups. It is not clear, however, whether the defendants will testify in their own behalf, or how Mr. McDougal, for

example, would perform under cross examination. Now that the defense gets its turn, doubtless the jury will hear a lot more about the vileness of Mr. Hale, the evil political intentions of the independent counsel and the intrusions of outsiders wanting to tear down the great state of Arkansas.

Presumably President Clinton's testimony will impugn Mr. Hale, who claims that he met with Mr. Tucker and then-Gov. Clinton to dis-

Jim Guy Tucker

cuss money to clean up the "political family," which led to an illegal $300,000 loan to a front company, Master Marketing, set up in Mrs. McDougal's name. The prosecution presented its final witness on Friday, FBI agent Michael Patkus, who testified that he had traced nearly $50,000 from the McDougals' private account at Madison to two payments benefiting Whitewater Development. The prosecution contends that the payments — $24,455 for a loan payment, and $25,000 as a downpayment on a tract purchase from International Paper — flowed from the Master Marketing loan from Mr. Hale's Capital Management.

Courtroom pundits opine that the jury of ordinary Arkansans may be finding the complex fiscal maneuvers bewildering. Yet it isn't very difficult to figure out who did what to the likes of Lisa Aunspaugh and R.D. Randolph — folks much more similar to the jury than Gov. Tucker and the McDougals. Some Whitewater buffs criticize the prosecution for failing to seek a change of venue when the Arkansas Democrat Gazette took the legal but unusual step of publishing the names of the jury pool; they worry that the governor of any small state would have various ways of influencing individual jurors.

Yet at the moment, Gov. Tucker is not particularly popular; in an

April Democrat Gazette poll, only 19% of the voters believed his claim of innocence in the fraud trial. He also recently suffered blistering defeats in special elections for a constitutional convention and a $3.5 billion highway construction bond issue. There are signs, indeed, that the political machine is breaking up, with Arkansas on its way to becoming a two-party state.

In part this is a kind of radiating effect from the attention Whitewater brought to this state. Mr. Starr's indictments, after all, were voted up by an Arkansas grand jury; he has produced nine guilty pleas and a federal judge recently decided his charges required yet another grand jury. Whitewater prosecutors are slated to start a new trial on June 17 against two Arkansas bankers charged with illegally funneling campaign funds to Mr. Clinton's 1990 gubernatorial run. Separately, two state officials were recently indicted on mail fraud charges in a local prosecution.

In another corruption case, former Secretary of State Bill McCuen recently plead guilty to various counts of bribery, tax evasion and accepting kickbacks. When a Pulaski County judge slammed him with a 17-year prison term, the Democrat Gazette saluted the severity of the sentence, marveling, "What's happening here? Is political corruption going to be taken with a new degree of seriousness in this state?"

Good question.

Mr. Morrison is a Journal editorial page writer.

REVIEW & OUTLOOK

Executive Privilege?!

"We've told everybody we're in the cooperation business. . . . That's what we want to do. We want to get this over with."
— PRESIDENT CLINTON, *January 12, 1996, after the belated discovery of Travel Office memos and Whitewater billing records.*

Yesterday, the House Government Reform and Oversight Committee voted to hold the White House in contempt of Congress. Far from being "in the cooperation business," the Clinton Administration is claiming executive privilege in defying bipartisan Congressional subpoenas for documents relating to the Travel Office scandal. This is a stretch.

Not since Richard Nixon has an Administration sought to withhold material on so tenuous a legal claim. In 1974, the Supreme Court unanimously held in U.S. v. Nixon that without a claim protecting "military, diplomatic or sensitive national security secrets" the court could not uphold a generalized Presidential claim of confidentiality. That decision didn't directly address claims of executive privilege against demands by Congress for information.

While it is likely to lose in court, the White House has apparently decided its interests are better served by delaying the timely production of documents, no matter how severe a confrontation with Congress that provokes.

Next week will mark the third anniversary of the purge of seven career Travel Office employees and the unexplained involvement of the FBI and the IRS in the affair. Travel Office Director Billy Dale was indicted on embezzlement charges, and there is evidence his ordeal had its origins at the highest levels of the White House. A jury took two hours to acquit him.

For three years various government entities have tried to find out who did what in the bizarre Travel Office firings and why. The White House clearly doesn't want anyone to understand what lay behind this fiasco, seemingly content to ride out a record of evasion, obfuscation and stonewalling.

The General Accounting Office conducted the first investigation of Travelgate. Hillary Clinton told the GAO she had "no role in the decision" to fire the Travel Office employees. That "no-role" claim was contradicted this past January by the discovery of a 1993 memo from former White House Administrator David Watkins, in which Mr. Watkins admitted he had not been "straight" with GAO investigators and that the First Lady had ordered the firings. Thus, White House stonewalling had produced an incomplete GAO report. Using understatement, the GAO's Nancy Kingsbury told Congress last year, "I can't say that there was quite as generous an outpouring of cooperation in this case as might have been desirable."

William Clinger

Even the Administration's own Justice Department ran into a White House's stonewall. Lee Radek, the head of Justice's Public Integrity Section, noted in a 1994 report, "At this point we are not confident that the White House has produced to us all documents in its possession . . . the White House's incomplete production greatly concerns us."

Michael Shaheen of the Justice Department's Office of Professional Responsibility was more direct. When the late Vincent Foster's Travel Office notebook was turned over two years after his death, Mr. Shaheen wrote, "We were stunned to learn of the existence of this document since it so obviously bears directly upon the inquiry. . . . Even a minimum level of cooperation by the White House should have resulted in its disclosure to us at the outset of our investigation."

Rep. William Clinger, the Pennsylvania Republican who chairs the Government Oversight Committee, has sought documents relating to a possible Travel Office coverup for three years. After official document requests last year weren't complied with, the committee on a bipartisan vote issued subpoenas for them last January 11. Since then the White House has turned over some files, including a never-before-seen handwritten note from David Watkins to Hillary Clinton in which he stressed to her that information he had given the GAO that she had wanted to replace Travel Office employees with "our people" was "reported out of context." Mr. Watkins concluded by saying he regretted "innuendoes related to your involvement in this affair. I have always known who my 'client' is."

But the White House is now claiming for an unspecified number of remaining documents that all are covered by executive privilege. It won't provide a brief description of what documents it is refusing to turn over, so that the validity of its claim can be judged. Rep. Clinger says his committee had no choice yesterday but to vote to ask the full House to hold White House Counsel Jack Quinn, Mr. Watkins and another former White House aide in criminal contempt of Congress for failing to comply with the subpoenas.

The Clinton White House's claim of executive privilege is pushing way out on the frontier. Ronald Reagan, in a memorandum to department heads, ordered that congressional information requests "be complied with as promptly and as fully as possible." He cited as the basis for an executive-privilege claim national security, foreign relations or "the performance of the Executive branch's constitutional duties." How do the Travelgate firings fit into any of that?

Of course, the court battles over this could be dragged out so that any embarrassing revelations are delayed until after the election. Perhaps the assignment will go to Judge Royce Lamberth, who wrestled with the health-care task force's earlier document stonewall. Congressman Clinger put the issue squarely yesterday: Travelgate "at the bottom is a scandal about the character of this presidency."

Review & Outlook

Majesty of the Presidency

So President Bill Clinton, who is not on trial in Little Rock, testifies, naturally grabbing national headlines. But Governor Jim Guy Tucker, who is on trial, does not take the stand. With the President's endorsement, the defense rests.

No matter that the Presidential testimony is peripheral to most of the indictment, this may work. There is no predicting what a jury may do, especially in highly publicized cases such as the O.J. Simpson and first Menendez brothers trials. And jury sentiments, specific evidence aside, sometimes carry truths of their own. The 12 jurors in Little Rock, most of them high school graduates, are entitled to believe they owe some deference to the office of the Presidency. Mr. Clinton played this card skillfully, with all the surface sincerity we now know so well.

There does remain, however, the little matter of the evidence presented in the courtroom, detailed on this page by Micah Morrison on May 7. The various counts of the indictment against Governor Tucker and James and Susan McDougal charge fraud and conspiracy, in transactions that contributed to the collapse of Mr. McDougal's Madison Guaranty Savings & Loan. Aside from the President, the only other defense witness was Mr. McDougal, whose rambling testimony was mostly helpful to the prosecution — for example opening a way to introduce his earlier statement to the FBI that Governor Tucker was a "thief who would steal anything that wasn't nailed down."

Mr. Clinton's testimony served two purposes: He was a character witness for the defendants. And especially, he came to impugn the testimony of David Hale, the former Arkansas insider who gave the prosecution its leads in the case. The defense theory is to make the case not People v. Tucker and McDougal, but Hale v. Clinton.

Yet in fact the prosecution presented not only Mr. Hale but a whole series of other witnesses. Larry Kuca, a real estate agent involved with Madison projects, and Stephen Smith, a former aide to Governor Bill Clinton, testified after entering their own guilty pleas on fraudulent loans. Don Denton, former chief loan officer for Madison, testified for the prosecution and identified numerous loan documents and checks. Robert Palmer admitted doctoring and backdating a series of appraisals he had done in connection with Madison loans, and testified that a Madison official instructed him to come up with an appraisal "somewhere around" $1.2 million on a key loan from Mr. McDougal's Madison to Governor Tucker's Castle Sewer Co.

R.D. Randolph, a former bulldozer operator who was Governor Tucker's partner in Castle Sewer, testified at length, saying he did not know their company purchased the property for three times the price paid for it a few weeks earlier. And also that he did not understand that Governor Tucker stuck him with sole responsibility for a loan to the company from Mr. Hale's small-business loan company. Also testifying for the prosecution were Lisa Aunspaugh, who served as a front for Mr. McDougal in loans and transactions that benefited Governor Tucker and others. As well as Dean Paul, the principal in the original loan that prosecutors argued was the taproot of the conspiracy uniting Mr. Tucker, Mr. McDougal and Mr. Hale.

Nothing in the President's videotape touched on any of this. His dispute with Mr. Hale concerns other counts, covering a loan Mr. Hale made to Susan McDougal's Master Marketing. Some of this money ended up with Whitewater Development Co., jointly owned by the McDougals and the Clintons. Mr. Hale testified he and Mr. Clinton and Mr. McDougal met to plan the loan, while Mr. Clinton denied "any suggestion that I tried to get money from him." Clearly there's a dispute here, with, for what it's worth, Mr. McDougal taking the President's side. We presume Judge George Howard will instruct the jury that this testimony pertains only to the Master Marketing counts.

The defense will argue that Mr. Hale made up everything to involve the President as a distraction from his own crimes, so the jury should ignore all of his testimony. And by inference, we presume, it should also ignore Mr. Kuca, Mr. Smith, Mr. Denton, Mr. Palmer, Ms. Aunspaugh, Mr. Paul and Mr. Randolph. But if Mr. Hale simply made up everything, why have all these people corroborated parts of his testimony, and indeed why have some of them admitted their own guilt?

And why, pray tell, didn't the Governor of Arkansas want to take the stand to deny he's a thief? The jury is not supposed to consider a defendant's failure to testify, of course, but this obligation does not extend to voters choosing their state officials. The Governor would seem to have every political reason to testify, except that he probably figures his political goose is already cooked. A poll showed only 19% of Arkansans believe his denials, and he's suffered stinging defeats of referendum proposals.

Bill Clinton

As for Mr. Clinton, he's likely to have further opportunities to display his skill at testifying. Independent Counsel Kenneth Starr has another case ready to go June 17 that even more directly concerns the President, charging that two Arkansas bankers illegally diverted money into his 1990 gubernatorial campaign. The defense has announced it will require the President's services. The Eighth Circuit Court of Appeals ruled last week that the Paula Jones sexual harassment suit against Mr. Clinton should go to trial May 16 as scheduled; though the President's lawyers will seek further delay by appealing to the Supreme Court.

The Supreme Court may also eventually get the contempt citations Rep. William Clinger's oversight committee voted last week against Presidential counsel Jack Quinn and others. Though the President did not actually sign a letter claiming executive privilege, Mr. Quinn asserted it anyway on documents pertaining to the Travel Office firings. (In that case a jury believed defendant Billy Dale rather than prosecutors ultimately commanded by Mr. Clinton). *U.S. v. Nixon*, the key Supreme Court ruling in Watergate, was of course a definitive executive privilege case.

In all of these controversies, the Clinton strategy is delay. Push the matter into the campaign so you can yell partisan politics. Push disclosure beyond the election so you can claim the voters knew all and don't care. Push into a second term, so you can wave any charge aside with the majesty of the Presidency, as Mr. Clinton did so masterfully for the benefit of Jim Guy Tucker and Jim McDougal.

Editorial Feature

Despite Polls, History Favors Dole

By ROBERT L. BARTLEY

It is never safer to go out on a limb than when you're going against the current conventional nonsense. So you read it here first: This fall's election is Bob Dole's to lose.

The assumption that Mr. Dole has already lost, of course, is just now the starting point for all political thinking. Even his decision to leave the Senate is being billed by Democrats as an act of desperation, and by pundits as an effort to "revive" his "moribund" campaign — though in fact he's not even officially nominated. The traditional starting date for a campaign is Labor Day, indeed, and it's not yet Memorial Day. The Dole defeat has become an idee fixe the likes of which we've not seen since Hillary Clinton and 500 experts were going to think real hard for 100 days and remake 14% of GDP.

In my book, Mr. Dole rates as the favorite for one simple reason: In our last nation-wide elections, his party won a historic victory behind the biggest vote swing since 1932. (In the process, by the way, confounding all the polls and pundits that now write off Mr. Dole.) After the 1994 congressional elections, Walter Dean Burnham, our leading student of electoral cycles, wrote that it had "many characteristics of an old-style partisan critical realignment," suggesting that the Republicans might dominate for a generation or more. Nobel Prize-winning economic historian Robert W. Fogel wrote that the roots of the sweep were essentially religious, that it was a symptom of "The Fourth Great Awakening."

That is, the 1994 results were driven by very deep currents in American society. By changes in religious sentiments. By the internationalization of the economy, reducing the margin of the welfare state. By the end of the war culture, with its impetus to centralization, that has persisted since 1914. By the empowering technologies of the information age. All of these powerful trends point to a smaller, less ambitious, less intrusive and more responsive government. Mr. Dole and his party are the social vehicle for and political beneficiary of these changes, or at least ought to be. And, without some good reason to believe otherwise, we should assume these same trends will dominate November's election.

Bob Dole

The big reason to think otherwise, everyone keeps hearing, is that Mr. Dole is "20 points behind" in public opinion polls. First of all, it's a 20-point Clinton lead in some polls, with others at somewhat lesser margins. At this stage of a campaign, variability and volatility in poll numbers is quite unremarkable. In January 1980, a Gallup Poll had Jimmy Carter ahead of Ronald Reagan by 62% to 33%, but in November Mr. Reagan won the popular vote by nearly 10 points, almost 51% to only 41%, and the electoral vote by 489 to 49. Similarly, in May 1988, Michael Dukakis led George Bush by 54% to 38%, but in November Mr. Bush won, 53% to 46%.

Four years later, Mr. Bush was so invincible in the early polls that he scared most Democrats out of the race, leaving the nomination to Bill Clinton. With Ross Perot drawing 19% of the vote, President Bush sank to 37%. Bill Clinton won with 43.0%, the cheapest win since Woodrow Wilson, though only marginally less than the 43.4% victory recorded in 1968 by Richard M. Nixon. Standard polling language includes the phrase "if the election were held today," meaning the whole exercise is based on a false premise. When November dawns, experience teaches, having been ahead in the polls matters far less than having found the right side of history and the issues.

Bill Clinton is of course no fool and, under the tutelage of his latest spinmeister Richard Morris, is scrambling to change sides, or rather to get on both sides at once. "The era of big government is over," he professed in his State of the Union address — though he tells the Washington Post's E.J. Dionne Jr. he wants "a different kind of government activism." He wants school uniforms — though his party filibustered funding for the District of Columbia to kill a voucher program for the poorest schools. He endorses Wisconsin Gov. Tommy Thompson's tough welfare reforms — though the fine print disavows any similar national program. He seizes on photo ops like signing a law on reporting the location of sex abusers, any handy Olympic event and Adm. Jeremy Boorda's memorial service.

This rhetorical zag to the right probably does have a lot to do with the improvement in the president's poll numbers. The American people quite rightly give a sitting president the benefit of the doubt; they want to believe he embodies their ideals and values. But come election time these same people are quite capable — as Gerald Ford, Jimmy Carter and George Bush discovered — of cashiering an incumbent they find wanting. So the question is, come November will the people really believe in Bill Clinton as an apostle of smaller government and traditional values?

Reasons to doubt include Mr. Clinton's considerable baggage, starting with the Democratic Party. For the election will not be Bill Clinton vs. Bob Dole, but the Clinton team vs. the Dole team. Mr. Clinton said his cabinet "looks like America." I doubt that America agrees. A glance through the prospective committee chairmen if the Democrats retake Congress shows a hallelujah chorus for big government. The tort lawyers have been awarded with vetoes; missile defense has been stopped on ideological grounds; the Justice Department still pushes affirmative action. Can Mr. Morris succeed in keeping anyone from noticing?

Then too, the people have not lately been tolerant of political deception. They turned out President Bush largely over his breaking his "read my lips" pledge, and elected a Republican House largely on the specific promises in the "Contract With America." Are they really ready to believe that a president whose major initiative was national health insurance has now changed his spots? While Mr. Clinton is probably the best one-on-one salesman our politics has ever seen, over time he runs a risk of overselling, of being seen willing to say anything and adopt any position in the interests of re-election.

Especially so given Mr. Clinton's vulnerability on the character issue, manifest in his administration's manifold petty scandals. Independent Counsel Kenneth Starr has one jury deliberating and another trial ready to roll in June. Rep. William Clinger's House Oversight Committee has voted contempt citations against White House Counsel Jack Quinn, who now claims executive privilege over a pile of documents on the Travel Office firings. The fired Travel Office workers, meanwhile, have filed suit against presidential buddy Harry Thomason. The Supreme Court is now considering whether to accept the Paula Jones sexual harassment suit. The White House claims that all of this is a wide-ranging anti-Clinton conspiracy, of course, but it certainly creates the potential for shock waves to presidential credibility between now and November.

In a sense, predictions about November depend on your assessment of the American people. Predictions based on current polls and the considerable tactical skill of the Clinton/Morris operation implicitly assume the electorate is not bright enough to see through an obvious masquerade. Mr. Morris is the political incarnation of movie impresario Joseph E. Levine, who once declared, "You can fool all the people all the time if the advertising is right and the budget is big enough." But if the people are cannier than that, as Abe Lincoln held and I think history suggests, and if they really want a smaller government and traditional values, they're likely to pick the Republican ticket. They did precisely this, after all, not only in the 1994 congressional races but in five of the last seven presidential elections.

In the face of this electoral history, expectations of a Dole defeat are currently being fed by the Beltway press pack. To be sure, an important part of the bad-mouthing has come from conservatives such as William Kristol, Bill Bennett and Robert Novak. But these seeds landed in fertile ground, given the liberal Democratic instincts of the Washington press corps. The Freedom Forum, a press foundation, recently released a survey of 139 Washington reporters and bureau chiefs. It found that 89% voted for Bill Clinton and 7% for George Bush, and that only 4% were registered Republicans, while 2% identified themselves as conservatives.

Members of the press say that these lopsided numbers are offset by "objectivity," but everyone else recognizes this assertion as preposterous. In my observation, the measure of "objectivity" comes largely from peers within the group the Freedom Forum poll so tellingly describes. This peer pressure is reinforced by an elaborate system of rewards and punishments such as the Pulitzer Prizes, Gridiron Club memberships, invitations to the appropriate dinners, cocktail parties, breakfasts and so on. It is not that anyone sets out to slant the news, merely that liberal premises and assumptions emerge repeatedly and predictably from what Tom Bethell of The American Spectator has christened "the hive."

Between elections, the media "spin" is a considerable power in American politics, as Newt Gingrich has ruefully discovered. We now read that Mr. Gingrich is the most hated man in American politics, and that his "Contract" has been a failure. It's true that the House Republicans may have overpromised and overreached, but that is typically the way anything gets done in today's politics. Mr. Morris is walking proof that Mr. Gingrich and his Republicans have totally changed the terms of debate in Washington. And over the threat of a presidential veto, the Republican Congress has produced the first year-over-year cuts in discretionary spending in a generation, passed a phase-out of crop subsidies and surrendered congressional power to a presidential line-item veto. In any historical view, this is a remarkable record of change for any one Congress.

As the lightening rod for these changes, Speaker Gingrich has been hit with a storm of bad press, mostly based on the 69 ethics charges his Democratic opponents have officially filed. Of these, 68 have been officially dismissed. Most intriguing are those concerning writing books and teaching, intellectual pursuits beyond your average politician. Meanwhile, the speaker impresses audiences outside the Beltway, at the Council on Foreign Relations in New York for example, as one of the most original thinkers in American politics. Never has the discrepancy between the image and the man in person been so great.

Presidential and other political campaigns are important not least because they give politicians direct access to voters, unfiltered by press intermediation. The hive responds to this threat to its position by pumping for campaign finance limitations and complaining about "negative" ads. In a campaign the people are listening and focusing, much less inclined to take their impressions secondhand. Predictably, Republicans do better in elections than between them, especially if they campaign as Republicans.

The real danger to the Dole campaign is that if Beltway Republicans start to believe the polls and the press, predictions of defeat will become self-fulfilling. We are seeing some of this already. Witness Sen. Alfonse D'Amato trying to repackage himself as an anti-Gingrich liberal; he even has his own Dick Morris named Arthur Finkelstein. (In fact, the New York senator has political problems because he sought to disempower his fellow Republicans by freezing candidates out of the state's primary.) A similar course is being urged on Sen. Dole by longstanding fans and well-wishers like Mark Shields, Mary McGrory, Kevin Phillips and William Schneider. They urge him to use his departure from the Senate to distance himself from the House Republicans, instead of using it to liberate himself from constant compromises in the interests of "the legislative process."

Mr. Dole, however, is showing signs of finding his stride. He not only displayed decisiveness and discipline in the decision to resign, but has assembled a stable of good speechwriters and convened first-rate economists to devise a tax strategy. No doubt he will want to polish the rough edges of the "Contract," but surely he will not be foolish enough to cooperate in his opponent's frenetic efforts to blur the differences between them. Whatever the current conventional wisdom, the Dole team's path to victory follows the themes that won so handsomely the last time out.

Mr. Bartley is editor of the Journal.

REVIEW & OUTLOOK

The Smaltz Probe Reborn

The seemingly dormant investigation of Independent Counsel Donald Smaltz into the activities of former Agriculture Secretary Mike Espy came to life this week with the indictment of two Mississippi farmers for fraudulently obtaining $777,000 in crop subsidies. More interestingly, the indictments also shed light on what might prove to be a much more consequential story, the heretofore murky struggle between Mr. Smaltz and the Department of Justice.

Donald Smaltz

According to documents unsealed this week in Washington by the three-judge special division of the U.S. Court of Appeals responsible for oversight of independent counsel, Mr. Smaltz applied in January to expand his probe into a "related matter." In his application, Mr. Smaltz cited section 594(e) of the independent counsel statute, which states that a counsel "may ask the Attorney General or the division of the court to refer to the independent counsel matters related to the independent counsel's prosecutorial jurisdiction, and the Attorney General or the division of the court, as the case may be, may refer such matters."

While other such requests have gone first to the Attorney General, Mr. Smaltz instead went straight to the appeals court special division. The Justice Department opposed both Mr. Smaltz's referral and the means by which he sought it. Justice argued that 594(e) requires the concurrence of the Attorney General, and that the new matter was not sufficiently related to Mr. Smaltz's original grant of jurisdiction. The judges rejected these arguments in an April 1 opinion, observing, "The plain language of section 594(e) in no way suggests the concurrence of the Attorney General is required before the court can refer a related matter to an independent counsel at the counsel's request; rather, it plainly contemplates the opposite."

This opinion, however, was carefully worded to preserve confidentiality, making it hard to judge the merits of Mr. Smaltz's request. The special division said only, without specifying any names, that the new matter was "demonstrably related" to Mr. Smaltz's original mandate. While the decision was not widely covered, Bruce Brown of Legal Times observed that "the panel, for the first time since the 1978 independent counsel law went into effect, held that an independent counsel who wants to widen an investigation can go directly to the special panel without having to seek the approval of the Justice Department."

Without the particulars of the case, of course, it was impossible to tell whether Mr. Smaltz was being overly aggressive. Now, at least, we know what the flap was all about. With Wednesday's indictments, the special division unsealed its April 1 order allowing Mr. Smaltz to expand his probe into the activities of Ronald Blackley, Mr. Espy's former chief of staff at Agriculture, "related to any application, appeal or request for subsidy made to or considered by the United States Department of Agriculture," or any intervention in the subsidy process.

The indictment concerning the Mississippi crop payments alleges that "unindicted co-conspirator No. 2, who had been appointed to a senior position within the Office of the Secretary" by Mr. Espy, intervened in the subsidy application process to rig an inflated application for his Mississippi friends. Clearly this refers to Mr. Blackley. Which leaves us with the larger question of why the Department of Justice expended such prodigious efforts to block Mr. Smaltz from expanding his probe of Mr. Espy to include Mr. Espy's chief of staff. This hardly seems overreaching.

As aficionados of such matters, we recall that this is not the first time Mr. Smaltz has run into problems with Justice and other friends of Mr. Clinton. Mr. Smaltz's original September 1994 mandate, we recall, was to examine Mr. Espy's ties to agribusiness, including

Arkansas chicken giant Tyson Foods. One of Mr. Smaltz's finds in Arkansas was a former Tyson pilot who claimed he had flown cash-filled envelopes to Little Rock that he understood were intended for Bill Clinton. The Tyson folks reacted with outrage, sending their chief lobbyist to Capitol Hill to complain, marshaling their political allies, and denouncing Mr. Smaltz's nascent inquiry as a "political witch hunt."

Shortly after that, we recall, the Justice Department turned down a February 1995 Smaltz request to expand his probe. Chicken king Don Tyson faded from the news. In July of that year, Chief Judge John Garrett Penn of the U.S. District Court for the District of Columbia quashed several of Mr. Smaltz's subpoenas.

Now we learn that the Justice Department has continued its effort to curtail Mr. Smaltz. Seen in the light of recent Justice Department actions, the events of 1995 take on a more troubling aspect. Unless Justice can somehow explain its opposition to the modest request the judicial panel upheld, we have to ask whether Justice has simply been trying to kill the Smaltz probe. And if so, precisely why?

Review & Outlook

Immunize Hale

As the Whitewater trial in Arkansas ran its lengthy course, we kept reading that it came down to the word of David Hale, a confessed felon, against Bill Clinton, President of the United States. The jury's verdict is now in: It believed Mr. Hale.

Now, as we kept pointing out, the case was not really Clinton v. Hale. There were mountains of other testimony, including that of the  appraiser in land flips, against the defendants, James and Susan McDougal, Mr. Clinton's partners in the Whitewater venture, and Jim Guy Tucker, Mr. Clinton's hand-picked successor as Arkansas governor. The jury found the three had defrauded the government through Mr. McDougal's Madison Guaranty Savings & Loan and Mr. Hale's Capital Management Services. The jurors found that Mr. Hale's testimony was extensively corroborated by other evidence, but his inside account was the well from which Independent Counsel Kenneth Starr drew the other evidence; so his help does burnish his tarnished credibility.

David Hale

As for Mr. Clinton, obviously the jury was not blown away by Presidential testimony, despite efforts of the defense to wrap the defendants in their sometime buddy the President. Close observers of the trial recognized the jury could give the President a pass with an innocent verdict on the "Master Marketing" counts, which involved the illegal $300,000 loan Mr. Hale testified that the President helped solicit. These were the only counts to which Mr. Clinton's testimony was directly relevant, and were also the principal counts against Susan McDougal. But instead of deferring to the President and freeing Mrs. McDougal, the jury voted guilty on Master Marketing.

The big impact of the verdict is likely to be its effect on further investigations. Mr. Starr can only be encouraged to press even harder with his investigations; he has a trial starting in three weeks of two bankers on charges of illegally diverting money to Mr. Clinton's 1990 gubernatorial campaign. (He must be especially ebullient since he also won his much-criticized case to decertify the big tobacco class-action suit.) Governor Tucker now faces up to 10 years in prison, plus another trial on related counts. Mr. Starr may want to inquire about the content of the governor's meetings with Mr. Clinton immediately after the White House learned of the RTC criminal referrals on Madison.

We also think the verdict is a big message for Senator Alfonse D'Amato, who has seemed content to let his Whitewater probe fizzle out in the Senate. In recent weeks, for example, he let Senator Paul Sarbanes bully him into directing a subpoena for fingerprint tests on the notorious Rose-White House billing records to Mr. Starr, starting a fight with the independent counsel and guaranteeing the committee will not get the records. And he was quoted as saying the committee was concluding because potential hearings were "of no interest to the public."

Mr. D'Amato has been negotiating for a Hale appearance with Ted Olson, the big-time Washington lawyer now representing Mr. Hale. Mr. Olson has said Mr. Hale would claim the Fifth Amendment, unless the committee gives him use immunity for his testimony. Why not, since Mr. Hale has already been convicted of the federal offenses? The immunity would apply to a threatened prosecution by Pulaski County Prosecuting Attorney Mark Stodola, currently an Arkansas Congressional candidate. These threats against Hale are retribution and a warning to other potential cooperators, and are anything but a reason to deny a witness immunity for Congressional testimony. But Senator D'Amato has refused to press for the votes necessary for this step.

Then too, there is the matter of Dan Lasater, a sometime Clinton buddy, bond trader and cocaine convict. He came before the D'Amato committee and was asked whether he got favoritism from Governor Clinton's administration. But the real question about Mr. Lasater is whether he was laundering drug money through his bond trades, as an RTC investigative report explicitly speculates. In particular, there is the curious tale of Dennis Patrick, a Kentucky resident of little means who was talked into opening a trading account at Mr. Lasater's firm, and has records to show that about $60 million in bonds were moved through it.

No one on the D'Amato committee asked Mr. Lasater about Mr. Patrick because it was "out of scope," that is, not covered by the formal Senate resolution chartering the committee. But surely money laundering is within the scope of the Banking Committee, which Mr. D'Amato also runs. He owes it to a drug-worried public to haul Mr. Lasater back before the Banking Committee, get him to explain the Patrick matter, and follow where it takes him.

We would also hope, without much expectation, that the national media will be discouraged from burying the Whitewater story for the duration of this election, as it did for the duration of the 1992 one. And we would hope that spokesmen for the state of Arkansas stop complaining about the intervention of outsiders such as Ken Starr and ourselves. This verdict came from 12 ordinary citizens of Arkansas, clearly a wholesome force, and perhaps one that appreciates a little help from the outside.

REVIEW & OUTLOOK

The Whitewater Ado

"Much ado about nothing" is the spin now hurtling out of various Clinton precincts in the wake of Independent Counsel Kenneth Starr's victory Tuesday in the Tucker-McDougal fraud trial.

The line first out of the White House was that all this is happening to someone else. Mr. Clinton, who testified for the defense in the case involving his former Whitewater Development Co. partners and his handpicked successor as governor, was credible, the White House says, but irrelevant.

"We're letting the jurors' words speak for themselves," said designated White House spinmeister Mark Fabiani, who released seven pages of juror remarks culled from interviews and supportive of Mr. Clinton's testimonial appearance. Alas, missing from the Fabiani packet was juror Janice Greer's observation to the Associated Press about the Clintons: "I think he and his wife had just as much to do with it."

Spin, for all its shortcomings, normally has at least a toehold on reality. The political lexicon will have to search elsewhere for an apt description of Senator Christopher Dodd's performance Tuesday night on "Nightline." Senator Dodd castigated critics of the President for engaging in "guilt by association" and claimed that the Little Rock verdicts "had nothing to do with Whitewater."

This, among other things, is nonsense. For the benefit of people only now joining the ranks of Whitewater aficionados, we would suggest that two words in the entirety of the just-completed trial need be committed to memory: Master Marketing. Among the James and Susan McDougal convictions were four counts, the Master Marketing charges, which anyone paying attention knows were directly linked to Whitewater Development Co.

The purpose of President Clinton's videotaped testimony at the trial was to rebut the claims of former municipal judge David Hale that then-Governor Clinton and Jim Guy Tucker pressured Hale for a loan to help the "political family." Mr. Hale, who confessed to two felonies and cooperated with the prosecution, said he made the $300,000 loan to a McDougal front company called Master Marketing.

An FBI agent testified at the trial that he traced nearly $50,000 of those funds to two payments that benefited Whitewater Co. — $24,455 for a loan payment and a $25,000 down payment on a tract purchase from International Paper. Post-verdict juror deference to the Presidency aside, the jury's opinion was clear: David Hale had provided an accurate road map to Arkansas corruption, and one of those avenues led straight to Master Marketing, which funneled money to the Whitewater project.

Based on this FBI testimony, the Clintons as Whitewater partners were the beneficiaries of the Master Marketing fraud. We will quickly add, however, that so far only Mr. Hale's testimony directly links Mr. Clinton to the now-proved conspiracy to loot two federally backed institutions, the McDougals' Madison Guaranty S&L and Mr. Hale's Capital Management Service lending company. At this juncture, this is an essential distinction, and one might expect the President's defenders would make it. Instead, they're attempting to rewrite reality.

Tuesday "was the day Whitewater began," says Ted Van Dyk, a Democrat who has known both Clintons for years. "Democrats cannot pretend that Whitewater will go away. It probably will be a centerpiece of the campaign."

White House spinners had been so good for so long that they'd even persuaded Republicans it was all Whitewater under the bridge. Al D'Amato, pressed by his pollster, was ready to pack it in. That's why the convictions were such a shock here. Now the same apologists who would have buried Whitewater had this week's defendants been acquitted claim the conviction is old news from the president's pre-1992 past, like Gennifer Flowers and the draft.

But Whitewater won't go away this year precisely because it did go away in 1992. Imagine if Americans had known then what we know now: that the candidate's business partners had looted both a savings and loan and a fund to help the poor and minorities.

Or that $50,000 from that fund, according to FBI testimony at the Arkansas trial, made its way into the Clinton-McDougal Whitewater partnership itself. (So much for the spin that the convictions have nothing to do with Whitewater.) Or that lawyer Hillary Rodham Clinton had represented the McDougal S&L, at what Mr. McDougal says was her husband's request. Would it have mattered to voters?

Mr. Clinton had to worry it might have, which begins to explain why he and his wife have worked so hard to obscure their Arkansas past. Apologists keep saying that Whitewater is "smoke without fire," but now we know the fire was fraud and conspiracy. At a time when George Bush's son Neil was being pilloried merely for being an S&L director, the Clintons had good reason to avoid any association with S&L crooks. Other politicians have done more to avoid being embarrassed by less.

So starting in 1992 the Clintons ignored their late aide David Ifshin's advice to let it all hang out, turning instead to enforcer Susan Thomases to stonewall. We now know she did her job too well. A note recently turned up by the Senate Whitewater Committee has Ms. Thomases scribbling that "BC tells me to call Tucker" for Whitewater answers. That refers to soon-to-be-ex-Arkansas Gov. Jim Guy Tucker, now a 52-year-old felon who still refuses to cooperate with prosecutors despite facing 10 years in the big house. Ms. Thomases, as is her habit, said she didn't recall making such a call.

(Mr. Clinton called Mr. Tucker on Tuesday after his conviction; an intrepid White House reporter should ask the president if he'll rule out pardoning all of the Whitewater defendants.)

As the independent counsel's probe gains credibility, the Clintons may yet come to regret their attacks on Ken Starr's integrity. They insulted not only Mr. Starr but especially his staff of mostly career prosecutors. Those lawyers didn't appreciate being called Republican hacks. Now vindicated, these are the nonpartisans who will have the largest say in future decisions to indict.

The Clintons may also yet regret the "no crime, no foul" standard of accountability they've set for Whitewater. As Rep. Jim Leach (R., Iowa) has said all along, their role in Whitewater once might have been settled with disclosure and some civil sanctions. But instead of admitting mistakes, the Clintons dismissed their critics as partisans or liars.

Mesmerized by polls instead of reporting the facts, the Beltway press corps has reinforced the spin that only an indictment matters. But the irony is that this makes indictment the only option for a prosecutor who cares about official accountability. And the first lady is especially vulnerable given her flat-out denial, contradicted by former aide David Watkins, that she had anything to do with firing Billy Dale, among other discrepancies.

Bill Clinton's Whitewater strategy has been a four-year gamble that his political skills could overwhelm incriminating details. But thanks to a jury in Little Rock, voters are being reminded that the same president who has Ronald Reagan's charm also has Richard Nixon's scruples.

Washington: Curiouser and Curiouser

As the Presidential election season began in earnest, the Whitewater scandals appeared to be reaching critical mass. After a lengthy stonewall over document requests, the White House produced 1,000 of the 3,000 pages of documents sought by Rep. William Clinger in the Travel Office probe. Among the documents was a request to the FBI from White House personnel security chief Craig Livingstone for its file on Travel Office head Billy Dale—dated seven months after Mr. Dale had been fired—as well as a list requesting FBI files on several hundred former White House personnel, including prominent Republicans. The FBI had complied with the requests. "Filegate" quickly mushroomed into another crisis for the White House. New hearings were launched, Mr. Livingstone resigned and Independent Counsel Kenneth Starr's jurisdiction was expanded to cover the matter.

In the Senate, the bitterly divided Whitewater Committee issued its final report. The majority report cited a deliberate "pattern of obstruction" by the White House; the minority report condemned the inquiry as "partisan." The Journal noted that the majority report "lays fact upon fact, contradiction upon contradiction, which altogether becomes impossible to explain as anything but a conscious, consistent effort to reveal as little as possible about what once happened in Arkansas. If this isn't a coverup, it's the best imitation of one in the history of American government."

In Little Rock, Mr. Starr suffered his first setback on August 1, when a jury acquitted two Arkansas bankers on charges they illegally funneled money to the 1990 Clinton gubernatorial campaign. Two weeks earlier, Republican Mike Huckabee replaced Jim Guy Tucker, convicted in the first Whitewater trial on multiple fraud counts, as governor of Arkansas.

Mr. Clinton got a bit of good news when the Supreme Court decided it would hear his argument that as President he should be spared the distraction of the Paula Jones sexual harassment suit, a decision that effectively delayed the case from trial until after the election. But with Whitewater grand juries in Little Rock and Washington still hearing testimony, and Congressional hearings continuing to sputter along, issues of conduct and character were following the Clintons deep into Campaign '96.

Editorial Feature

Whitewater May Drown Democrats

By TED VAN DYK

We Democrats shouldn't fool ourselves. The conviction last week on 24 felony counts of Arkansas Gov. Jim Guy Tucker and Clinton associates James and Susan McDougal marked the beginning, not the end, of a looming political ordeal that could endanger not only the president and Hillary Rodham Clinton but hundreds of Democratic officeholders and candidates on the ballot this November. It also could set the stage for the ultimate triumph in 1997 of an unadulterated Contract With America, as interpreted by Speaker Newt Gingrich.

Of course the Clintons were found guilty of nothing last week. And they, as every American citizen, are entitled to be considered innocent of any and all charges until proven guilty. This is all the more true because the credibility of the presidency itself is at stake. No president, of either party, should be challenged lightly in lieu of compelling evidence that he had breached public trust.

Nonetheless we should have no illusions about what will follow. By convincing 12 Arkansas jurors that the charges against the Clinton allies had merit — and that he was not part of some partisan Republican cabal — Independent Counsel Kenneth Starr gained credibility and running room to pursue other cases that could come far closer to the Clintons.

In two weeks, Mr. Starr will bring to trial Arkansas bankers Herbert Branscum and Robert Hill for their alleged illegal diversion of bank funds to Bill Clinton's 1990 gubernatorial campaign. Both Mr. Branscum and Mr. Hill were appointed to state regulatory positions after approving loans totaling $180,000 to the Clintons. Yet another trial is pending in a separate fraud indictment brought against Gov. Tucker.

The "other" independent counsel, Donald Smaltz, who has been pursuing an investigation of, among others, former Agriculture Secretary Mike Espy and chicken magnate (and Clinton backer) Don Tyson, reportedly is close to bringing new indictments of his own. He also is reported to have turned over to Mr. Starr files and evidence that could be used in several other prospective cases. Among possible targets is Dan Lasater, a Clinton financial backer, big time bond trader, and convicted drug trafficker.

House Banking Committee Chairman Jim Leach (R., Iowa) and Sen. Alfonse D'Amato, chairman of the Senate Whitewater and Banking Committees, reportedly are ready to proceed with reports and hearings on matters as diverse as the Travelgate scandal (in which White House Travel Office employees were fired and then smeared); the Mena, Ark., airstrip associated with drug trafficking, payoffs and money laundering; and possible perjury and obstruction of justice by current and former White House staff and advisers.

Beyond this, Paula Jones remains out there with her sexual harassment charges against Mr. Clinton, whose attorney gave new visibility to the charges by claiming immunity for the president on the basis that as commander-in-chief he was akin to an active duty soldier. Then, way out there on the fringe, are investigations still under way into the death of Deputy White House Counsel Vincent Foster and of several scandal-associated Arkansans who expired under mysterious circumstances.

Presume for a moment that the investigations into unexplained deaths, narcotics trafficking and money laundering have nothing to do with the Clintons or flow from conspiracy-theorist imaginations. The rest of what generically has become known as Whitewater still could provide more than enough raw material to keep Republicans and media researchers busy until Election Day. In addition, we can expect Independent Counsel Starr to leverage his recent convictions to frighten into cooperation not only Mr. Tucker and the McDougals, but also literally dozens of big and bit players in Arkansas who now fear for their own futures as additional cases are pursued.

What can Democrats do? In previous presidential election years, incumbent Democratic presidents in trouble voluntarily have stepped down early in the election year rather than subject their party to divisive debate or probable general election defeat. In 1952 President Harry Truman stepped aside and, in 1968, Lyndon Johnson followed suit. Both did so because they were associated with unpopular wars (Korea and Vietnam) that had driven their popularity through the floor.

President Clinton's situation is different. There is no substantive issue creating a polarizing emotional divide in the party or country. And, unlike Truman and Johnson, he still maintains a respectable approval rating and leads his prospective opponent, Bob Dole, in opinion polls. At any rate, we are midway through the campaign year, and the nominating process is over.

In this circumstance our only option, of course, is to stick by the Clintons until and unless courts of law move against them. Yet congressional and other defenders of the president and first lady understandably will become wary as they fear they might be signing their own political death warrants by defending them against charges that subsequently might prove to be true. No matter, our first obligation as a party is to Stand By Your Man (and his Hillary).

Everything will change, however, if investigations and court proceedings result in one or more indictments against the first couple. Then the task will be to save the party and its candidates rather than let them be destroyed in a Clinton implosion. We as Democrats will have an obligation to forestall the Republican tidal wave that could take place in November, absent a Clinton withdrawal. A GOP landslide could provide hard-edged Contract Republicans with strong majorities in both houses of Congress and the ability to enact into law an agenda we have so far held in check.

Fortunately, there is time. Even though President Clinton has amassed the Democratic delegates necessary for his nomination, party rules provide that every delegate technically is unpledged in the event of an extraordinary circumstance. By our late August convention, it may well be that the charges and rumors will have been resolved and put to rest. However, if disastrous news hits the Clintons between now and late August, the responsibility of party delegates will be clear. It will be to call on the president voluntarily to step down and to make way for a substitute nominee — logically,

Vice President Al Gore, whose reputation for personal integrity is unsullied and who has kept full distance from Whitewater and related matters.

There is another possibility, of course. It is that the charges and investigations involving the Clintons will develop like those against President Richard Nixon in 1972. Before that election, a series of congressional and media inquiries began to establish that serious wrongdoing had taken place in the Nixon White House. Sen. George McGovern, the Democratic presidential nominee, strongly challenged President Nixon to answer these charges but was not taken seriously. Later, after President Nixon's second inaugural, a worst-case denouement took place and the country approached a constitutional crisis until Mr. Nixon was forced to resign. As Democrats there is little we can do about that eventuality but pray that it doesn't take place.

Al Gore

But if the outlook is clear and gloomy by August, we Democrats must think the unthinkable and be prepared to act on it. Otherwise, the growing Whitewater scandal could overtake and bury our party and its candidates. And all because we blindly walked to the guillotine chanting repetitively the Clinton mantra that "mistakes were made" but "we did nothing wrong."

Mr. Van Dyk, a 1992 adviser to presidential candidate Paul Tsongas, has been active in Democratic national politics since 1961.

Letters to the Editor

Whitewater Won't Drown Clinton

Ted Van Dyk's musings about the possibility of the president being driven from office by Whitewater are fanciful ("Whitewater May Drown Democrats," editorial page, June 3). During my career I have seen convicted defendants attempt to get leniency by making accusations against others. But the very document trail that convicted the Whitewater defendants makes it near impossible for them to manufacture accusations against the president. Career prosecutors of the type that Kenneth Starr has recruited do not bring cases against respectable citizens based solely on the word of plea-bargaining felons, particularly when the documents offer no support.

Moreover, there is not the slightest evidence in any of the Whitewater investigations that the president had any interest in making money. If James Stewart's book is to be believed, the president was almost negligent in his indifference to the financial condition of his family. The evidence bears this out. In a state in which three families — the Waltons, the Tysons and the Stephenses — generate many millions of dollars of legal fees, Hillary Clinton never got any referrals from them, despite her husband's political power. The few investments the Clintons appear to have made — a failed Whitewater land transaction and Mrs. Clinton's profits on cattle trades suggested by a close friend — are scarcely the stuff out of which cases are made; and the comparison either to Watergate or

Iran-Contra, where presidential power was abused, is totally misplaced.

New York

* * *

JULY 2, 1996

Whitewater Muddies 'Clean-Cut' Clinton

Arthur Liman's June 12 Letter to the Editor about Whitewater and related events in Arkansas was one of the best perspectives on the saga that I've read. As a New York Republican, I agree with Mr. Liman that the various Arkansas scandals (the Whitewater events, Madison Guaranty, the pork belly trades, and even the Foster suicide) are just not important enough to warrant being factors in the coming presidential election. Like Mr. Liman, I hope the election will be decided on issues of policy rather than personality.

However, Mr. Liman ignores two related points about Whitewater, and these could properly become issues that have some bearing on the election.

First, the Clinton campaign in '92 stressed a clean-cut candidate with a good-government background in Little Rock. Subsequent disclosures about Whitewater suggest this was not the case. Even if Whitewater events per se are weak tea, the disclosures are fair counterpoints to Mr. Clinton's rather vocal self-righteousness exhibited during the '92 campaign.

Second, the apparent coverup and endless stonewalling of Whitewater information by Mr. and Mrs. Clinton and their aides create troublesome questions of dissembling and incompetence. Malfeasance at the White House is a legitimate campaign issue.

Frankly, I wish Mr. Liman were right. I'd like to see the Arkansas events disappear as campaign issues. But every time I think this way, another unsavory tidbit comes out of the White House, such as the improper vetting of GOPers with secret FBI files. Like the more serious Watergate scandals, the legacy of Whitewater just won't go away.

JAMES RUDOLPH

New York

REVIEW & OUTLOOK

More Missing Documents

The Clinton White House has a problem with keeping records. Time and again it has suddenly uncovered items such as Rose Law Firm billing records, Vincent Foster's diary, the membership of the Magaziner health-care task force, or a memo contradicting the First Lady's account of the Travel Office firings months or even years after they were first sought by investigators. Now the notes that a White House lawyer took during investigative interviews with Hillary Clinton are missing. "We have looked everywhere we can look and we have not found any more notes," the White House spokesman Mark Fabiani announced Friday.

Clinton apologists will chalk this up as the umpteenth unfortunate example of White House "incompetence," but these aren't stupid people. The unavoidable issue is whether this should be seen more properly as attempts to thwart any discovery of the truth.

The latest missing notes were recorded by former White House associate counsel Neil Eggleston during meetings that White House aides had with General Accounting Office officials who were investigating the sudden firing of White House Travel Office employees. In addition, Mr. Eggleston told investigators he "presumably" took notes while he was interviewing Hillary Clinton to prepare her written answers to questions the GAO had posed to her about the firings.

In Mrs. Clinton's written response it was claimed "she had no role" in the Travel Office purge, a statement contradicted this past January by White House aide David Watkins's discovered memo in which he noted that Mrs. Clinton "conveyed to me in clear terms her desire for swift and clear action" to remove the Travel Office staff. The discrepancy between the account Mrs. Clinton gave the GAO and Mr. Watkins's memo was a main reason that Independent Counsel Kenneth Starr very recently hired two veteran prosecutors to conduct an expanded probe into Travelgate.

The now-missing Eggleston notes could be important in determining who did what in Travelgate. Staffers for Rep. William Clinger, the chairman of the Government Oversight Committee, discovered a 1994 memo from Mr. Eggleston to the Justice Department that indicated the notes' existence and that he didn't plan to turn them over to Justice as requested.

Rep. Clinger has become exasperated by what he calls "a culture of secrecy" at the White House. In January his committee issued a bipartisan subpoena for 3,000 pages of White House records on the Travel Office. It specifically requested the committee be informed "of any document which would be responsive and previously existed but you no longer have access to." Last week, after months of stonewalling and

William Clinger

hours away from a contempt of Congress vote, the White House produced 1,000 pages and provided an index of the other documents that together it said were a full accounting of "all documents relating to the firings." But the index includes no mention of the missing Eggleston notes. Then on Friday the White House said they'd looked everywhere but couldn't find them.

Of course, if this were the Nixon Watergate White House or the Reagan Administration, this incredible chain of events would have been screaming off the front pages over the weekend. But apparently the White House succeeded in its claims that the loss of the notes is no big deal because notes taken by other government officials at the same interviews are available. This means we're supposed to believe that Mr. Eggleston's notes were merely those of a recording secretary rather than the analysis of a senior White House lawyer. Further, apparently no one else was present during Mr. Eggleston's interview with Hillary Clinton at which he has testified that he "presumably" took notes. So we're also to believe that her final, terse written answers to the GAO were the sum total of what she told Mr. Eggleston.

This latest Lost and Found incident recalls to mind the recorded thoughts three years ago of White House aide Todd Stern, who conducted one of the early internal reviews of Travelgate:

"Problem is that if we do any kind of report and fail to address those questions, the press jumps on you wanting to know answers; while if you give answers that aren't fully honest (e.g., nothing re: HRC), you risk hugely compounding the problem by getting caught in half-truths. You run the risk of turning this into a coverup."

There is indeed a range of descriptions, across the political and legal spectrum, that may apply to these White House incidents. They are most certainly not mere incompetence.

REVIEW & OUTLOOK

Non-Denial Pardon

One of the legacies of Watergate was the art of evasion that became known as the non-denial denial. White House spokesman Mike McCurry managed a similarly stylish dodge Monday when he was asked what President Clinton thought about pardoning Whitewater felons Jim and Susan McDougal and Arkansas Governor Jim Guy Tucker.

Mr. McCurry: "I have heard absolutely nothing that would indicate that idea is being seriously entertained."

Q: "Well, I know, but can you rule it out? That's the question."

Mr. McCurry: "I haven't even heard anyone suggest that they would request such a pardon."

Q: "Well, you can't rule it out then?"

Mr. McCurry: "Mr. McDougal said he might consider doing that at some future date. I'm not even going to speculate on that. That would be as close to being a non-starter as I can imagine. But if something is officially — a pardon request is officially filed through the Justice Department through a very lengthy consideration, if something came through in that official channel, we would consider it at that time. But there is nothing that even remotely resembles that possibility pending."

Pending or not, we suspect a pardon is very much on the mind of the Whitewater felons, whose cooperation with the independent counsel might reflect on the President who could pardon them. We hope the press corps keeps at it and asks Mr. Clinton himself: Will you, sir, rule out a pardon for any or all of these Whitewater felons?

Editorial Feature

Arkansas Reform In Hands Of Huckabee, Starr

By Micah Morrison

In a stunning reversal for the political machine that has dominated Arkansas for decades, events in recent weeks have shoved the one-party state to the brink of historic reform. The May 28 resignation announcement of Gov. Jim Guy Tucker, convicted of bank fraud with James and Susan McDougal, is only the most visible sign of the shifting of the tectonic power plates. A week earlier, primary voters pointedly rejected or forced into runoffs candidates linked to the ruling elite, for the first time in Arkansas history fielding a strong statewide slate of Republicans. Speculating that the GOP could displace the Democrats in "one-party rule," the Arkansas Democrat-Gazette editorialized, "It may take some getting used to. Like an earthquake."

Mike Huckabee

Mike Huckabee is the young Republican lieutenant governor and Baptist preacher who will take the reins of state power when Mr. Tucker formally steps down. Mr. Huckabee said in an interview that he wants to be "a healer" for his state, but declined to discuss specific reforms before taking office. Yet in a sign perhaps of troubles ahead, Mr. Huckabee acknowledged he was "aware" of stories that state officials were shredding documents in anticipation of Gov. Tucker's departure. "Anyone in a state agency or any state officer that would do something probably illegal — and certainly unethical — would have to be looked into," Mr. Huckabee said.

Gov. Huckabee will have a lot to look into, but he'd better watch his back. A good early move would be to start cleaning up the cesspool that is Arkansas law enforcement. Above all, he needs to put his own people in control of the Arkansas State Police. In Arkansas, the state police function as a kind of gubernatorial Praetorian Guard. Pimping for then-Gov. Clinton, it appears, was the least of their sins.

Law enforcement officials say that the state police shut down cocaine probes into bond daddy Dan Lasater, chicken king Don Tyson and before the investigations ran their course. There is abundant evidence that some members of the state police spent years undermining inquiries into alleged drug smuggling at Mena airfield, finally driving its own investigator, Russell Welch, out of a job. And in the controversial "train deaths" case, law enforcement officials seem to have thwarted investigations into apparent links between the murder of two teenagers, drugs, and a local prosecutor, Dan Harmon.

Mr. Harmon is under investigation for a second time by the state police and FBI for corruption. He was jailed Friday for assaulting Arkansas Democrat-Gazette reporter Rodney Bowers, who tried to interview him about the probe. Mr. Bowers's injuries aren't serious, but the situation is painfully ironic. It's widely believed in Arkansas journalistic circles that Mr. Bowers has not been encouraged to write all he knows about the train deaths and Mena cases, while his newspaper's editorial page has expended much ink ridiculing stories on those subjects, particularly those by this writer.

On May 21 voters decided they'd had enough of Mr. Harmon, denying him a spot on the Democratic ticket in a run for sheriff of Saline County. The GOP slot was won by John Brown, a former detective who investigated the train deaths. Mr. Brown says if elected he will "fight public corruption in all forms" and pursue the case.

Voters also expressed their displeasure with Pulaski County Prosecuting Attorney Mark Stodola of Little Rock, forcing him into a runoff for the Democratic nomination for Rep. Ray Thornton's congressional seat. If elected, Mr. Stodola will become the de facto head of a diminished but still dangerous political machine. A longtime Clinton ally, Mr. Stodola last week signaled that he is still willing to play bully boy for the power elite when he restated his intention to use his prosecutorial powers to bring state insurance fraud charges against key Whitewater witness David Hale.

The message in any such Hale prosecution would be that new Whitewater witnesses are on notice that the state still has the power to punish them. This is not news to some of Independent Counsel Kenneth Starr's witnesses, such as Judge Bill Watt, whose pension was revoked, or former Madison S&L officer Don Denton, who friends say is in danger of losing his job at Little Rock airport.

Of course retribution is not news to Mena investigator Russell Welch. Nor is it news to Mr. Welch's colleague, former IRS investigator Bill Duncan, whose career was destroyed because he pursued the truth in the Mena affair. Nor is it news to former local drug task force head Jean Duffey, who was run out of the state after investigating the train deaths and Mena. Nor of course is it news to the state troopers who came forward with stories of Bill Clinton's sexual escapades, or to state police investigator J.N. "Doc" DeLaughter, whose career went down the drain after he started looking into Don Tyson and Dan Lasater.

Gov. Huckabee no doubt will be cautious about his dealings with Mr. Starr, but the two likely will establish some kind of quiet symbiotic relationship. Mr. Starr already is far down the road of liberating Arkansas from corruption. Mr. Huckabee's Baptist roots should allow him to do no less. The new governor can be of enormous help by signaling that state employees cooperating with Mr. Starr will not suffer retribution; let the truth set them free. And while he's at it, Mr. Huckabee should indicate that he's serious about getting to the bottom of Mena and the train deaths. He could start by consulting Bill Duncan, Russell Welch, Jean Duffey, Doc DeLaughter, and maybe even Rodney Bowers, about whom he should name to head the state police.

Mr. Morrison is a Journal editorial page writer.

REVIEW & OUTLOOK

Senators Join Coverup

After months of insisting that key Whitewater witness David Hale be called before the panel, Paul Sarbanes, Chris Dodd and other Democrats on the Senate Whitewater Committee reversed themselves, throwing up procedural roadblocks designed to make sure Mr. Hale never testifies on national television.

"It's obvious you're just trying to protect the President," Senator Richard Shelby angrily berated Democrats on the committee Wednesday. "Who else is afraid of David Hale's testimony?"

Indeed. Despite Mr. Hale's guilty plea to felonies, he proved an effective witness before an Arkansas jury, providing the road map and documents to convict Mr. Clinton's former business partners and his successor as governor of Arkansas. In the Arkansas trial, he testified about a meeting with then-Governor Clinton on loans to Susan McDougal's Master Marketing; the President denied this in his videotaped testimony. While the jury was not asked to judge the President's complicity, it did find the loans fraudulent. The White House knows that before the Committee, Mr. Hale would describe two further meetings with Mr. Clinton; voters would have to judge whether they could simply dismiss these accounts.

Mr. Hale has declared that unless he is given "use immunity," he will take the Fifth Amendment and refuse to testify. Use immunity simply means his Senate testimony could not be used in criminal proceedings against him. Having already sent Mr. Hale to prison, Independent Counsel Kenneth Starr says he has no objections to immunity. But Mr. Hale faces threats of an Arkansas state prosecution on a felony insurance code violation. The threat comes from a longtime Clinton crony in Little Rock — Pulaski County Prosecuting Attorney Mark Stodola. A two-thirds vote of the Whitewater Committee is needed to grant use immunity, giving the Democrats blocking power. They piously proclaim that heaven forbid the U.S. Senate should interfere with Mr. Stodola's plans.

In other words, the Senators and the President are hiding behind the skirts of an Arkansas political machine fighting for its own life. Mr. Stodola is using his position as prosecuting attorney to run for the U.S. Congress, and faces a June 11 runoff in the Democratic primary. If he wins the seat he will be the shining light of the Arkansas Democratic machine. His threats against Mr. Hale, who is after all already in jail, have little if anything to do with the state insurance code, and everything to do with retribution and intimidation of Arkansans cooperating with Mr. Starr.

David Hale

This is the way the Arkansas machine operates. In Little Rock, one witness at the Whitewater trial, Judge Bill Watt, had his pension revoked, while another, former Madison S&L official Don Denton, apparently is in danger of losing his job as a manager at the local airport. Ordinary federal corruption prosecutions in Little Rock have to proceed through U.S. Attorney Paula Casey, the longtime Clinton associate who refused a plea arrangement with Mr. Hale for the testimony that convicted Governor Jim Guy Tucker and the McDougals. Independent Counsel Kenneth Starr now provides an alternate path; his next Whitewater trial is slated to start June 17 and moves even closer to Mr. Clinton. The case against two Arkansas bankers involves contributions to Mr. Clinton's 1990 gubernatorial campaign and a 1991 Presidential exploratory committee.

Before Senators Sarbanes and Dodd joined the game, Arkansas tactics long since had infected the White House. When seven Travel Office employees stood in the way of appointing cronies, the Clinton Administration set out to destroy them, using the FBI and probably the IRS. This week, from a letter pried out of the White House by the strenuous efforts of Rep. William Clinger's oversight committee, we learned that the White House abused the FBI again seven months later. Someone using the name of then-White House Counsel Bernard Nussbaum lied to obtain confidential information from the FBI about Mr. Dale.

At the time, the White House was under intense pressure for the firings, and the Justice Department had brought embezzlement charges against Mr. Dale; a jury eventually acquitted him after two hours of deliberation. Mr. Starr is now looking into the Travel Office affair. On Capitol Hill, a bill to reimburse Mr. Dale for his legal expenses, which passed the House and would certainly pass the Senate if it reached a vote, has been put on hold by one of the major-domos of the Arkansas machine, Senator David Pryor.

We keep hearing that the Whitewater offenses are petty and a long time ago, and it is certainly true that other politicians such as Whitewater Committee Chairman Alfonse D'Amato have ethical problems of their own. But misuse of law-enforcement powers — threatening a prosecution to punish Mr. Hale as an adverse witness and using the excuse to avoid public scrutiny, or trying to destroy Billy Dale to justify your own clumsiness — this is corruption of an especially sinister cast. It seems to be a habit Mr. Clinton and his crowd carried from the Arkansas past to the Washington here and now.

REVIEW & OUTLOOK

Honest Mistake No. 99

White House spokespersons are by now so used to explaining their colleagues' actions as part of some incompetent Keystone Kops operation that they've probably programmed a computer user-key with the words "it was just a mistake" to save time on the spin cycle.

President Clinton now claims his aides kept the raw FBI files on 338 Republican appointees in the White House for two years because of "an honest bureaucratic snafu." This echo from the Watergate era is upon us, presumably, because the White House had days before admitted the "mistake" of obtaining the FBI files on Billy Dale, seven months after the director of the White House Travel Office was fired. Last Friday, the lawyer hired by the head of the White House personnel security office announced that the Dale incident was simply one part of the larger FBI file-collection effort. "A completely innocent explanation," concluded the White House's Mark Fabiani.

No doubt Mr. Fabiani's assurances will be enough to get most of the Beltway crowd to disperse and get back to work debunking the Dole campaign. Which leaves it to one congressman, William Clinger, to again expose the White House's theories to a reality check.

For three years the White House has done everything possible to avoid a full explanation of what happened at the Travel Office, from incomplete internal reviews to citing executive privilege to avoid turning over relevant documents to Rep. Clinger's House oversight committee.

After two years of seeing his requests for Travel Office documents stonewalled, Rep. Clinger and his committee sought a criminal contempt charge against the White House last month. White House Press Secretary Mike McCurry complained, "Chairman Clinger has 40,000 pages worth of paper and he all but wants the rolls of toilet paper in the men's room here. That's what he's after. He's gotten a little ridiculous." A day later, on the eve of a contempt vote by the House, the White House reluctantly released 1,000 of the 3,000 pages of documents sought by Rep. Clinger. The request for Billy Dale's FBI file was in that 1,000 pages.

Some toilet paper. Indeed, it was also confirmed from these 1,000 pages that the White House has "lost" the notes that Associate White House Counsel Neil Eggleston took during interviews on the Travel Office scandal conducted with White House aides. This mistake, the White House announced, was no problem because other people at the meetings took notes too.

By our count, the White House's explanation for the Billy Dale flap has changed five times since last Wednesday, culminating in the revelations about the mistaken 338 FBI files.

The White House's Mr. Fabiani now admits, "There's no question there are still unanswered issues." We agree, starting with the White House's continued insistence that executive privilege – a doctrine reserved for military or diplomatic secrets – can be cited to block release of the remaining 2,000 pages of Travel Office documents.

Aficionados of Clinton Administration "mistakes" know they've been around this particular track at least once before. In 1993 the Clinton State Department pulled and read the personnel files of 160 former Bush Administration employees. The State Department originally claimed that Clinton appointees Joseph Tarver and Mark Schulhof had gotten the files "by mistake" from storage. At the time, the Washington Post, noting that "this town went apoplectic" when Bush appointees in 1992 searched Mr. Clinton's passport files, called on the Clinton White House to "cut out the fancy dancing and come clean." After Secretary of State Warren Christopher read Inspector General Sherman Funk's devastating report, he fired the two Clinton aides.

Before the 338 FBI files surfaced, the work of Craig Livingstone, the 37-year-old Director of Personnel Security at the White House, had drawn rave reviews from such Clinton aides as George

Stephanopoulos. "Anything that has anything to do with security or logistics — Craig's going to take care of it," Mr. Stephanopoulos told the Pittsburgh Post-Gazette, Mr. Livingstone's hometown paper. "You don't have to tell him how to do it, when to do it. Just that it needs to be done, and he does it. And he knows how to cut through the bureaucracy and get things done."

But Mr. Livingstone's vaunted efficiency seems to have failed him at almost the same time that the White House was rummaging through the files of departed Republicans. In late 1993, then White House Press Secretary Dee Dee Myers and more than 100 White House staffers had not yet been given White House security clearances. Mr. Livingstone admitted to the Post-Gazette that "we had been remiss in the quickness of getting people cleared" for White House jobs.

We have arrived at a familiar place — the credibility gap. The trip required three years of evasions, half-truths, refusals to cooperate and sudden document discoveries. If the White House continues to withhold documents now, Congress should immediately move to cite the White House for contempt, launch inquiries about the missing Eggleston notes and call Mr. Livingstone to find out who programmed his tour through the Republicans' FBI files.

Editorial Feature

Inside the White House File Scandal

By GARY W. ALDRICH

I loved my career with the FBI and treasure my years as a special agent. Of the many assignments I was privileged to have over the course of a 26-year career, the highlight was the five years, just prior to my 1995 retirement, I spent assigned to the White House.

For more than three decades the FBI, the Secret Service and the White House Counsel's Office had worked as a team to clear the hundreds of new staff members who come with each new administration. This clearance process entailed a lengthy FBI background investigation to document the good character of every White House employee. It was a comprehensive and effective security system, perfected by six presidents to protect national security, the taxpayer and the White House itself.

But the things I saw in the last 2½ years of my tenure deeply disturbed me. And the recent disclosures that the Clinton White House requested, and the FBI provided, more than 340 background investigations on previous administrations' employees raise questions that pierce the very heart of national security, and call into question the relationship between the White House and the FBI.

Some presidents have made good use of the FBI background investigations, and some, to their regret, have not. But never before has any administration used background investigations of another president's political staff. FBI employees knew it would be wrong to give raw FBI files on political opponents to the other party. In fact, they knew it would be illegal, each disclosure a violation of the federal Privacy Act.

Why, then, did the Clinton administration request such files, and why did the FBI provide them? The White House's "explanation" — that it was "an honest bureaucratic snafu" — is really too much for this FBI veteran to believe. How does a unit at FBI headquarters copy and box for shipment to the White House Counsel's Office more than 340 highly confidential files, when the two FBI supervisors are both lawyers? Do the White House and the FBI really expect us to believe that the wholesale copying of hundreds of FBI files wouldn't raise an eyebrow? That the two FBI supervisors didn't know who James Baker was? If the FBI supervisors didn't know that hundreds of confidential files were going out the door, they were so grossly negligent as to imperil not only the civil rights of more than 340 individuals, but also national security.

In truth, I know that FBI management had plenty of warning that elements of security and background investigations were drastically wrong at the Clinton White House. As early as May 1993, Special Agent James Bourke, supervisor of the FBI office responsible for background investigations, had come under fire when, at the behest of the White House, he started a criminal investigation of seven innocent men in the Travel Office.

Not publicly known until now were the constant warnings that Mr. Bourke and other FBI management received from me and from my partner, Dennis Sculimbrene (who would go on to testify against his own agency and the White House as a defense witness in the Billy Dale trial). Why are Mr. Bourke and the good folks at the FBI just now finding serious reasons to check on the legitimacy of the requests of this White House? Documents exist that prove they have known about these problems for years. Mr. Bourke declined to be interviewed for this article, so one can only speculate as to why he ignored the repeated warnings. It may be that, like any bureaucrat, Mr. Bourke was simply trying to win favor from those he thought could advance his career — in this case, officials at the White House.

These allegations are more serious than anything we have seen in decades. So how can the White House, through Attorney General Janet Reno, be allowed to order the FBI to investigate itself? No federal bureaucracy is good at conducting an internal probe that has this kind of potential for explosive political revelation.

Right up to the time I retired in June 1995, Mr. Bourke and other FBI supervisors responsible for background investigations continued to honor each and every outrageous request the Clinton White House Counsel's Office made. Mr. Bourke cannot claim he did not know these requests were improper. He was well aware the Clinton administration had relaxed the security system at the White House so that those loyal to the administration could evade background checks. Other agents and I had told him so, and scores of documents going across his desk provided more evidence, just in case he did not believe his own agents. In fact, at the time the White House requested the files on previous administrations' appointees — one full year into the Clinton administration — more than 100 Clinton staffers, including then Press Secretary Dee Dee Myers, still had not been investigated by the FBI for passes or clearances.

Hillary Clinton

Yet the Clinton White House Counsel's Office apparently was wasting no time looking deeply into the background of anyone who was not lucky enough to have been hired by President Clinton. As Mr. Bourke also knew, permanent White House employees whose loyalty to the Clintons was in question were in for some "special" attention, Hillary Clinton style. For example, permanent employees in the White House residence who were suspected of being disloyal to the first lady were reinvestigated out of sequence, that is, early — in some cases four years before their periodic review was due.

Some of these staff members, appointed by Presidents Carter, Reagan or Bush, had just been cleared by the FBI. When I attempted to head off what appeared to be unnecessary and premature investigations by offering to obtain copies of the background investigations, my superiors at the FBI and Craig Livingstone, director of security for the White House Counsel's Office, effectively told me to mind my own business. What prompted the White House to investigate these staffers was a story, leaked to the press, that Mrs. Clinton had thrown a lamp at the president during a domestic argument. The Clintons had to know who the leaker was. Result: Decent, loyal, law-abiding citizens with spotless records were investigated by the FBI again, just to make sure. I believe that these permanent employees were being harassed and that if anything, anything at all, had turned up in a new FBI probe, they would have been summarily tossed out the door to "make slots" for the Clintons' people. And indeed, other employees besides Billy Dale were fired on the basis of these investigations.

At the same time, the White House was requesting copies of FBI investigations of hundreds of long-gone Reagan and Bush staffers. Why? Knowing that the Clintons casually used the FBI to weed out politically suspect employees, would it be so unreasonable to suspect them of also misusing the FBI to investigate political "enemies"?

Craig Livingstone

Statements by Clinton spokesmen that nobody looked at these FBI files are as plausible as saying that if 340 Playboy magazines were sent to a boys' high school, they would remain in their boxes, unmolested.

The safe where these secret records were allegedly kept was the size of a small bedroom. Maybe the files were taken out of the safe, and maybe they weren't. There was no need to take them out to examine them. Anyone — including Mr. Livingstone, whose desk was just outside the entrance to the safe — could have walked in, sat down at the table and perused the files to his heart's content. And the security office was equipped with a photocopy machine. I knew Mr. Livingstone as a fierce defender of the Clintons, especially Mrs. Clinton, who handpicked him for this sensitive position.

Which of these files were copied, and where were the copies sent? The time has come for real explanations, real investigations of the Clinton White House Counsel's Office and, sadly, maybe even of the FBI. In particular, Mr. Bourke and Mr. Livingstone should explain their roles. These FBI files could not have been requested, received and maintained without Mr. Livingstone's full knowledge, consent and direction. Mr. Bourke is responsible for protecting the FBI files and for ensuring the FBI's arm's-length relationship with this or any administration.

These two men should be brought before both a federal grand jury and Congress to account for this highly irregular conduct — conduct that has embarrassed the presidency and the FBI, undermined the public's trust in both institutions and potentially violated federal law. The Clinton administration has earned its reputation. But the FBI — my FBI — deserves better. Enough is enough.

———————————

Mr. Aldrich, an investigative writer, retired from the FBI in June 1995.

Letters to the Editor

What Are You Looking For, Mr. President?

Do you know what it is like to receive a telephone call late at night informing you that your name is on a list of people whose FBI files have been reviewed by officials in the Clinton White House?

Had it not been for the mystery surrounding the death of former White House Counsel Vincent Foster, or the myriad of unanswered questions surrounding the Whitewater investigation, I probably would have found President Clinton's excuse that this was "an honest mistake" a little more plausible. However, enough questions have been raised, particularly by Gary W. Aldrich, a 26-year career FBI agent who retired in 1995 after having spent five years working in the White House, that I do think an in-depth investigation is warranted. Who besides President Clinton believes this is an honest mistake? Certainly not the people whose FBI files were reviewed.

I am happily married, raising three children and living a pleasant life in Sacramento, Calif., 3,000 miles from Washington, D.C. My life has changed dramatically since my days at the White House 10 years ago when I was the director of Presidential Boards and Commissions. Today my exposure to the White House is limited to the stories I over-hear on CNN Headline News. So you can imagine the outrage I felt when I heard that Anthony Marceca, a White House official, had read my FBI file and passed on information to Craig Livingstone, director of White House Personnel Security.

Who do these people think they are? How can they be so cavalier? What were they looking for and what were they hoping to find? The oft-asked question "What did they know and when did they know it?" could not be more appropriate in this case.

When Rep. William Clinger, chairman of the House Government Reform and Oversight Committee, holds hearings I hope he will be successful in getting answers to these questions.

The irony of this cabal is that I have never seen my FBI file and have been told by the FBI that in order to receive a copy I would need to file a Freedom of Information Act request and wait "possibly years" because of a "backlog." It is rather amazing that an official in the Clinton White House simply placed a telephone call to the FBI and immediately had a "field day" reading through my file and several hundred others.

This is a perfect example of why many Americans have developed a distrust of government and politicians. For faith to be restored, honesty and integrity must replace impropriety.

Mr. President, what are you really looking for?

PAMELA KOEHLER ELMETS

Sacramento, Calif.

Editorial Feature

Whitewater Trial II

By MICAH MORRISON

LITTLE ROCK, Ark. — The curtain comes up today on the second trial stemming from Independent Counsel Kenneth Starr's Whitewater investigation. Mr. Starr's 11-count indictment charges Herby Branscum Jr. and Robert Hill, the owners of Perry County Bank in Perryville, Ark., with bank fraud and conspiracy. The indictment says Mr. Branscum and Mr. Hill hoodwinked regulators and funneled bank funds to "various state and federal campaigns, candidates and office holders," including Bill Clinton's 1990 gubernatorial campaign.

Mr. Clinton is not charged with any wrongdoing, though he figures prominently in the indictment and has been subpoenaed by Mr. Branscum to testify in his defense in a videotaped White House deposition slated for July 7. The prosecution team will be headed by Deputy Independent Counsel Hickman Ewing Jr., the soft-spoken former U.S. attorney from Memphis who was the behind-the-scenes manager of the successful prosecution of Arkansas Gov. Jim Guy Tucker and James and Susan McDougal. Attorneys for Mr. Branscum and Mr. Hill gave a glimpse of their game plan earlier this year when they released a joint statement denouncing Mr. Starr and saying their clients were being charged "only because they have past ties to the Democratic president of the United States." Mr. Branscum is a "pawn in a high-stakes chess game, the result of which may very likely determine the next president," said his attorney, Dan Guthrie.

Precisely which candidates other than then-Gov. Clinton benefited from the Perry County bankers' largesse is a mystery likely to be resolved later this week, following jury selection, when the prosecution presents its opening statement. But Mr. Starr's convictions in the Tucker-McDougal trial — as well as the separate investigation of the Senate Whitewater Committee, scheduled today to release its final report and close up shop — already have established a fundamental pattern beneath the complexities of the sprawling Whitewater affair: the use and abuse of Arkansas financial institutions as piggy banks for the political elite.

The current trial seems likely to turn on the same underlying issue. Mr. Hill was appointed by Gov. Clinton to the state Banking Board in 1986. Mr. Branscum, described by the Arkansas Democrat-Gazette as "the ultimate political insider," is one of Mr. Clinton's oldest political allies; their ties date back to 1976, when Mr. Clinton ran for attorney general. That year, then-Gov. David Pryor named Mr. Branscum head of the Arkansas Democratic Party, succeeding Mr. Clinton's boyhood friend Thomas "Mack" McLarty. Mr. Branscum was twice reappointed to the post by Gov. Clinton and later headed the state Claims Commission. The 1990

Kenneth Starr

Clinton gubernatorial campaign kept an account at Mr. Branscum's Perry County Bank, which also gave Mr. Clinton $180,000 in unsecured personal loans for the race. The loans, repaid on the eve of the 1992 presidential election, do not figure in Mr. Starr's indictment.

After the 1990 election, Gov. Clinton reappointed Mr. Hill to the Banking Board. Mr. Branscum was named to the influential Highway Commission, an independent agency that manages highway construction and maintenance contracts and is perhaps the most lucrative patronage post in the state.

Mr. Starr's indictment covers two main areas, both related to the 1990 campaign. It charges that Mr. Branscum, Mr. Hill and Neal Ainley, then president of the Perry County Bank, conspired to rip off the federally insured institution by misapplying bank funds to reimburse themselves and family members for donations to the Clinton campaign, among others, and then tried to cover up the scheme. The defendants and Mr. Ainley allegedly drew expense checks totaling about $12,000 from a Perry County Bank operating account as payments for various "legal and professional services" supposedly rendered to the bank. But the payments actually "were to reimburse the defendants, members of the defendants' families and others for political contributions they made at the direction of the defendants," the indictment says.

Among the potentially most damaging documents recorded in the indictment are three consecutively numbered checks totaling $7,000, drawn from the Perry County Bank operating account by Messrs. Branscum, Hill and Ainley on Dec. 11, 1990, and then deposited in their respective personal accounts. Three days later, the indictment says, Mr. Hill "hand-delivered at least $7,000 in political contributions" to Gov. Clinton. A few weeks later, the governor named Mr. Branscum to the Highway Commission.

Mr. Clinton committed no crime in accepting the money. The charges are against the defendants and hinge on their alleged misapplication of bank funds and use of false bank records in an attempt to cover it up. But the question of quid pro quo payments in exchange for political office hangs in the air.

The defense likely will claim that the expense checks were legitimate expenses and unrelated to the campaign donations. The problem with that line of argument will be Mr. Ainley, who in May 1995 pleaded guilty to two misdemeanor counts of concealing large cash withdrawals from the Internal Revenue Service and began cooperating with the independent counsel.

Mr. Ainley is Mr. Starr's insider — the David Hale of the second Whitewater trial — providing a guide to the alleged felonious practices. Presumably Mr. Ainley will testify about the details of a conspiracy to divert bank funds to various political campaigns. It also will be interesting to hear what he has to say about why Herby Branscum and Robert Hill were delivering money to Bill Clinton in December 1990.

According to the Washington Post, Mr. Starr has at least one other witness in addition to Mr. Ainley: former Perryville Mayor Richard Lee Tiago, who said Mr. Hill approached him about a Clinton donation "to help Herby get on the Highway Commission." The Associated Press also reports that Mr. Starr has a memo written by one of Gov. Clinton's secretaries, saying that Mr. Hill wanted to discuss Mr. Branscum's Highway Commission appointment when he dropped by on Dec. 14, 1990, to deliver the $7,000.

Mr. Ainley likely also will provide key testimony in the second area of Mr. Starr's indictment — a conspiracy to conceal from the IRS about $52,000 in two cash withdrawals turned over to Mr. Clinton's campaign treasurer, Bruce Lindsey, during the 1990 race, supposedly for a get-out-the-vote effort. The alleged crime, of course, lies not in giving the Clinton campaign its own money. Rather, the indictment charges that Mr. Branscum and Mr. Hill conspired with Mr. Ainley to hide the cash withdrawals from federal regulators by failing to file Currency Transaction Reports with the IRS, legally required for cash transactions over $10,000, and by falsely certifying to the Federal Deposit Insurance Corp. that CTRs had been filed. In one instance, the indictment alleges, Mr. Ainley went to the bank's mailroom at Mr. Hill's suggestion and intercepted an outgoing CTR, which he later turned over to Mr. Hill and Mr. Branscum.

Bruce Lindsey

Mr. Lindsey is a longtime Clinton confidant and now a senior White House aide. He was briefly named as a "target" in the probe of the cash withdrawals but later was notified by Mr. Starr that he would not be charged. But Mr. Lindsey is likely to emerge as a central figure in the trial. He signed four $7,500 checks that were bunched together for a $30,000 cash withdrawal. In March 1995, the New York Times reported that Mr. Lindsey also was the recipient of a second cash payment of $22,500; in May 1995, the Times reported that Mr. Ainley told prosecutors that Mr. Lindsey "directed him to illegally conceal cash payments to Mr. Clinton's 1990 campaign."

Doubtless the trial starting today will hold some surprises. But Perry County Bank is only one station on the sleazy trail of financial improprieties — and, as attested by the convictions and guilty pleas Mr. Starr has already obtained, outright crimes — associated with the Clintons' progress through the 1980s. The dollars do add up. Mr. Clinton received hundreds of thousands of dollars in loans in the early 1980s from the Bank of Cherry Valley, run by a political associate. One of those loans, in 1984, was for $50,000. The next year, another political associate, James McDougal, hosted a fund-raiser to pay off the Cherry Valley loan, a suspicious soiree apparently still under investigation by the independent counsel. By the time Madison imploded, the Clintons had already embarked on a new relationship with other political associates at the Perry County Bank. That relationship, as so often seems the case these days in Arkansas, proved profitable for the Clintons, but not for the people they left behind.

Mr. Morrison is a Journal editorial page writer.

REVIEW & OUTLOOK

'Pattern of Obstruction'

To anyone who still believes Whitewater is about some long-ago events in faraway Arkansas, we recommend yesterday's 1,200-page report by the Senate Whitewater Committee. Whether you agree or not with the majority's conclusions, it's impossible to read their report and not find that Whitewater has everything to do with the character of the Clinton Presidency. The Presidency's character surely is going to become one of the central voting issues of the November election.

The main virtue of the report is as a chronology of defensive, inexplicable behavior, which the majority concludes is a "pattern of obstruction." The report lays fact upon fact, contradiction upon contradiction, which altogether become impossible to explain as anything but a conscious, consistent effort to reveal as little as possible about what once happened in Arkansas. If this isn't a coverup, it's the best imitation of one in the history of American government.

The coverup pattern, we know from other sources, began with the Clinton campaign of 1992. The late David Ifshin, a friend-of-Bill who was then counsel to the Clinton campaign, advised the Clintons to respond to Jeff Gerth's New York Times queries about Whitewater by letting it all hang out. Instead Mr. Ifshin, who died recently of cancer, was dumped from the campaign, and Susan Thomases was put in charge of what we now know from numerous accounts was an attempt to push everything beyond that November's election.

The report shows how that pattern continued, in fact intensified, even after Mr. Clinton took office. We are reminded again how Paula Casey, Mr. Clinton's hand-picked U.S. attorney, recused herself from handling Whitewater only after she dismissed a criminal referral from investigators at the Resolution Trust Corp. That referral in turn became the basis for Independent Counsel Kenneth Starr's recent convictions, on 24 felony counts, of Mr. Clinton's former business partners.

Especially valuable is the report's account of the aftermath of Vincent Foster's suicide. In detail, the report describes how Mr. Foster was not a traditional White House counsel but effectively the

Vincent Foster

Clintons' personal attorney for Whitewater and other matters. He was the last person known to have personal possession of Hillary Clinton's famous billing records, which vanished during a two-year subpoena, only to appear, like some miraculous backyard apparition, at the White House in January.

The Foster suicide set off frantic White House activity, especially by Mrs. Clinton's aides, centering around his office. After meeting with Ms. Thomases, White House counsel Bernard Nussbaum then breaks his agreement with Justice Department lawyers and Park Police on how the suicide and office will be investigated. "Bernie," asks then-Deputy Attorney General Philip Heymann at one point, "are you trying to hide something?" A Secret Service agent saw Mrs. Clinton's top aide lifting documents out of the Foster suite. Mr. Heymann shortly decamped back to Harvard.

Relying on the word of small-fry and officials independent of the Clintons' circle, Republicans conclude that "these numerous instances of White House interference with several ongoing law enforcement investigations amounted to far more than just aggressive lawyering or political naivete." They are instead, "a highly improper pattern of deliberate misconduct." Democrats, in their side of the report, which also ought to be read, take the word of the Clinton friends who explain their odd behavior as chaos born of grief. The committee plans to put the complete report on a Web site later in the week.

We could list facts forever, but to our mind what matters is this "pattern" of conduct that has come to define the Clinton Presidency.

As the Whitewater report puts it, this White House has sought to "hinder, impede and control investigations" of all types, from Travelgate, to most recently citing executive privilege to avoid revealing that it had sought access to FBI files on political opponents. Whitewater isn't an exception; it's typical.

Back in November 1993, another official seeking information from this White House wrote that the Clinton Administration "submitted meritless relevancy objections in almost all instances." Its responses were "incomplete and inadequate." One was "preposterous." These were the words used by Federal District Judge Royce Lamberth to describe the Clinton administration's refusal to supply relevant documents about Mrs. Clinton's health care task force.

Democrats reply with their ritual defense that the majority is "partisan," and that Al D'Amato is a sleazeball himself. But Al D'Amato didn't cause the billing records apparition embedded with Mrs. Clinton's fingerprints. Republicans didn't coax Ms. Thomases into amazing memory loss, or numerous witnesses into contradicting the first lady on Castle Grande, on her representation of Madison Guaranty, and other matters.

One of the central issues here is whether the senior officials of this Administration have behaved mostly like the retinue in some 17th Century monarchy or as employees of a republic. Once the Clintons came to Washington, whatever Whitewater back in Arkansas was about turned into an attempt to use the powers of the presidency to conceal what they obviously considered to be at the least a large political embarrassment. Whether this "pattern of obstruction" became criminal behavior is up to Mr. Starr to decide. Whether this is the kind of Presidency America needs is up to the voters.

Editorial Feature

Dems Lash Selves To Clinton Mast; Bon Voyage!

President Clinton has apologized, in his fashion, for searching the FBI files of Republicans. What I want to know is when he's going to apologize to Democrats.

He might start with Jim Moran, the combative Virginia congressman who has been one of Mr. Clinton's most stalwart, not to say slavish, defenders. This has left him much more exposed than any Republican.

Potomac Watch

By Paul A. Gigot

"It's much ado about nothing," Mr. Moran declared on June 6, on PBS's "NewsHour With Jim Lehrer," mimicking White House talking points on the FBI file sweep.

"It was a clerk that did it," he added, climbing further onto a limb, and, "as Director Freeh of the FBI says, this was a routine matter handled in a routine way." We now know this "clerk" was a Democratic operative specializing in investigations, while Mr. Freeh admits "egregious violations of privacy."

Undaunted, Mr. Moran was back posing as Johnnie Cochran last Friday, spinning that "the problem all boils down to the fact that the Secret Service had an outdated computer list of people who had access to the White House." But yesterday the Secret Service told Congress it had no idea what list the White House is talking about. Perhaps the gentleman would like to revise and extend his remarks?

Give Mr. Moran credit for guts, if nothing else. Only a bold and loyal politician risks his own reputation by repeating whatever this White House tells him. But that's the way all congressional Democrats have behaved throughout the Clinton ethics travails, from Whitewater to Travelgate. They've dismissed it all as silly and partisan.

Democrats have lashed themselves to the Clinton mast, and either they'll ride out the storm or go down with him. Lately they must be consuming large doses of Dramamine.

This unanimous Democratic phalanx is unique in presidential scandals. When GOP presidents have hit heavy weather, a Bill Cohen or Jim Leach has always stepped forward, brow furrowed, to say that the facts must be learned, hearings must be held. When Ed Meese was under siege in 1988, then-Assistant Attorney General (and now Massachusetts Gov.) William Weld went so far as to resign in a moral huff. Though Mr. Meese was later exonerated, Mr. Weld had at least shown his independence.

John Kerry

Contrast that with Massachusetts Sen. John Kerry's down-the-line defense of the Clintons. As a member of the special Whitewater committee, the rare independence he could muster was to express incredulity toward Bernie Nussbaum, who had long since left the White House. Toward anyone currently on the payroll he was solicitous, to say the least.

This week Mr. Kerry joined his fellow Democrats in their searching judgment that because Al D'Amato is partisan, everything the White House says must be true. Mr. Kerry is running for re-election against Mr. Weld, so he'd better hope there aren't any more exploding Arkansas cigars.

Especially because the Democrats' own Whitewater report betrays that they really have no idea what the truth is. Regarding Hillary Rodham Clinton's billing records, which miraculously appeared two years late in the White House Book Room, Democrats wait until the last of their 400-some pages. Then they conclude Mrs. Clinton couldn't have played any role because her lawyer says she didn't.

Who did then? Democrats write that "it is possible that the

billing records were moved into or within the Book Room inadvertently" because "there was construction in and around the Book Room in the summer of 1995." Of course: The guys in hardhats did it!

Democrats redoubled their mast-lashing, "partisan" strategy last year when they concluded Mr. Clinton might be popular enough to save them from their Great Satan, Newt Gingrich. The president has helped with enough vetoes to keep honest liberals quiet. Democrats also counted on a media bored by Whitewater and a public cynical about politics. If voters think all politicians cut shady deals, then Mr. Clinton would satisfy community standards.

But the shock of the Whitewater convictions has upset this scenario. Rep. Marty Meehan (D., Mass.) yelped for weeks about independent counsel Kenneth Starr's ethics, but he's lost his voice since the convictions. Note, too, the silence this week of Democrats who weren't on the committee and thus weren't obliged to talk about Whitewater. Dick Gephardt wasn't looking for microphones. Even Virginia's Mr. Moran finally distanced himself from the White House this week, publicly apologizing to Billy Dale, the former Travel Office aide whose FBI file was also in the White House cache.

At least through November, Democrats will live in private fear that some new shoe will drop — on Whitewater, FBI files, or perhaps even a settlement of the Paula Jones sexual harassment suit, if the Supreme Court declines to hear a White House appeal that would delay the case past November.

Every Democrat's nightmare is to become the Charles Sandman of the 1990s. Watergate aficionados will recall that Mr. Sandman was the leader of the 10 House Judiciary Committee Republicans who bravely voted against impeaching Richard Nixon. In the next election, four of them lost, including Mr. Sandman.

REVIEW & OUTLOOK

Arkansas Burning?

In a column last week, "Latest Clinton Lie Hurts Arkansas," former Arkansas Democrat-Gazette managing editor John Starr berated President Clinton for casting a new blight on his already troubled state. "Carried away while expressing concern about a rash of arsons at black churches across the South," Mr. Starr wrote, "Clinton told his weekly radio audience that it was 'hard to think of a more depraved act of violence' and added, 'I have vivid and painful memories of black churches being burned in my own state when I was a child.'"

Trouble is, it never happened. "After Clinton floated the canard about black churches being burned in Arkansas," Mr. Starr wrote, "the Democrat-Gazette conducted an exhaustive check of civil rights leaders and found not one — I repeat, not one — who shared Clinton's painful memories of church burnings."

The director of the Arkansas History Commission says he's never known of a black church being burned in Arkansas. The White House released a list of three Arkansas churches that burned, but none of the fires were believed to be arson. "Clinton told a lie designed to make him look good with black supporters at the expense of the reputation of his state," Mr. Starr wrote. "What he did was inexcusable, and Clinton owes all of Arkansas an apology for having done it."

REVIEW & OUTLOOK

Paula's Day in Court

The law of course proceeds at its own majestic pace, and the Supreme Court is entitled to time to ponder the issues presented by the sexual harassment case against President Clinton by Paula Corbin Jones. Still, the delay in bringing the case to trial leaves voters rather at sea. The case against the President will still be pending when they are asked to decide yea or nay on his re-election in November.

Paula Jones

This is all the more perplexing because there is no guarantee the Court will ultimately rule in the President's favor. It has agreed to decide whether a civil suit against a sitting President should be delayed until he leaves office, thus postponing Mrs. Jones's day in court until after Mr. Clinton's re-election campaign. But the Circuit Court decided that the case should proceed; that the Constitution "did not create a monarchy." If the Supreme Court ultimately agrees, and if in the meantime Mr. Clinton wins re-election, *Jones v. Clinton* could become a spectacle dominating his second term.

To give readers and voters some appreciation of the stakes involved, we reprint nearby substantial excerpts from Mrs. Jones's original complaint, filed in Federal District Court in Arkansas. These are of course unproven allegations; the President says he has no recollection of meeting her. Yet at the same time these extracts come from official court documents on the public record, as opposed to rumor or hearsay. Different people will make different judgments on their credibility and relevance, but given the importance of an informed electorate and the public venue of the charges, we think the public has a right to know.

All the more so since the phrase "sexual harassment" has been expanded to embrace an almost endless array of workaday insensitivities. What Mrs. Jones alleges is instead an explicit sexual advance of the grossest order, by the chief executive of her employer, and with references to her departmental supervisor. Followed, when her story started to emerge, by a widely reported assault on her character from the White House itself. With or without current sensibilities, these are certainly serious charges.

The press, ourselves included, has suffered considerable confusion on the issue of reporting the sexual activities of politicians. We suspect that a suit like Mrs. Jones's would be front-page news immediately if brought against, say, the CEO of a Fortune 500 company — or for that matter a television evangelist or Hollywood actor. Yet with politicians in particular, we're torn between an imperative to inform the public and the sensible notion that even public figures are entitled to some final sphere of privacy.

This tension has resulted in a series of bizarre standards. John F. Kennedy charmed his way to a free pass, no doubt aided by the different mores of the age. His brother survived as a Senator after the death at Chappaquiddick, but the issue did hamstring his Presidential bid. Gary Hart was run out of a Presidential campaign over Donna Rice. Anita Hill was used to put Clarence Thomas through a wringer on far less serious and less recent accusations than those underlying the case just accepted by the court on which Justice Thomas now sits.

Bill Clinton by and large has been the beneficiary of yet another standard. His nationally televised admission of "problems" in his marriage, it runs, immunized him by establishing his philandering. So in the last campaign most of the press dismissed the Gennifer Flowers charges because a tabloid paid for her story. Even our editorials, often charged with malice against Mr. Clinton, did not make much of them. In retrospect, we think this was a mistake. The accounts of Arkansas state troopers later made clear that Ms. Flowers was essentially telling the truth, and Mr. Clinton's denials were essentially lies.

This was an important insight into the character that the Clinton Administration has displayed, not least in the current round of implausible explanations of misappropriated FBI files. By now, in one petty scandal after another, Mr. Clinton has spent any right to credibility. What reason on earth is there to believe his Presidential announcements, whether on tax cuts or Bosnia or the Middle East, let alone invocations of moral values?

There is a trendy notion that the public no longer cares, that indeed it finds Mr. Clinton's various transgressions amusing and charming. Perhaps, but we have a higher view of the public. We think it understands that campaign promises are only promises, and that sinners sin. But we think it can distinguish sin from depravity, and broken promises from credibility meltdown.

In any event, the public is entitled to make its own judgment, which means it is entitled to know what has been charged, without a filtering or bowdlerizing of documents already before the courts and long in the hands of reporters. And far better it should know now than halfway into the next Presidential term.

Editorial Feature

The Complaint Against the President

Following are excerpts from Paula Corbin Jones's complaint against President Clinton and Arkansas State Trooper Danny Ferguson, alleging that the president sexually harassed her. The complaint is dated May 6, 1994, and was filed in U.S. District Court in Little Rock.

On or about March 11, 1991, Jones began work as an Arkansas State employee for the Arkansas Industrial Development Commission (hereafter "AIDC"), an agency within the executive branch of the State of Arkansas. The Governor of Arkansas is the chief executive officer of the executive branch of the State of Arkansas.

Bill Clinton

On May 8, 1991, the AIDC sponsored the Third Annual Governor's Quality Management Conference (hereafter "Conference"), which was held at the Excelsior Hotel in Little Rock, Arkansas. Clinton, then Governor of Arkansas, delivered a speech at the Conference on that day.

Also on that day, Jones worked at the registration desk at the Conference along with Pamela Blackard (hereafter "Blackard") another AIDC employee.

A man approached the registration desk and informed Jones and Blackard that he was Trooper Danny Ferguson, Bill Clinton's bodyguard. Defendant Ferguson was at that time a law enforcement officer within the ranks of the Arkansas State Police and assigned to the Governor's Security Detail. He was in street clothes and displayed a firearm on his person. He made small talk with Jones and Blackard and then left.

At approximately 2:30 p.m. on that day, Ferguson reappeared at the registration desk, delivered a piece of paper to Jones with a four digit number written on it and said: "The Governor would like to meet with you" in this suite number. Plaintiff had never met Defendant Clinton and saw him in person for the first time at the Conference.

A three-way conversation followed between Ferguson, Blackard and Jones about what the Governor could want. Jones, who was then a rank-and-file Arkansas state employee being paid approximately $6.35 an hour, thought it was an honor to be asked to meet the Governor. Ferguson stated during the conversation: "It's okay, we do this all the time for the Governor." . . .

Trooper Ferguson then escorted Jones to the floor of the hotel suite whose number had been written on the slip of paper Trooper Ferguson had given to Jones. The door was slightly ajar when she arrived at the suite.

Jones knocked on the door frame and Clinton answered. Plaintiff entered. Ferguson remained outside.

The room was furnished as a business suite, not for an overnight hotel guest. It contained a couch and chairs, but no bed.

Clinton shook Jones' hand, invited her in, and closed the door.

A few minutes of small talk ensued, which included asking Jones about her job. Clinton told Jones that Dave Harrington is "my good friend." On May 8, 1991, David Harrington was Director of the AIDC, having been appointed to that post by Governor Clinton. Harrington was Jones' ultimate superior within the AIDC.

Clinton then took Jones' hand and pulled her toward him, so that their bodies were in close proximity.

Jones removed her hand from his and retreated several feet.

However, Clinton approached Jones again. He said: "I love the way your hair flows down your back" and "I love your curves." While saying these things, Clinton put his hand on Plaintiff's leg and started sliding it toward the hem of Plaintiff's culottes. Clinton also bent down to attempt to kiss Jones on the neck.

Jones exclaimed, "What are you doing?" and escaped from

Clinton's physical proximity by walking away from him. Jones tried to distract Clinton by chatting with him about his wife. Jones later took a seat at the end of the sofa nearest the door. Clinton asked Jones: "Are you married?" She responded that she had a regular boyfriend. Clinton then approached the sofa and as he sat down he lowered his trousers and underwear exposing his erect penis and asked Jones to "kiss it."

There were distinguishing characteristics in Clinton's genital area that were obvious to Jones.

Jones became horrified, jumped up from the couch, stated that she was "not that kind of girl" and said: "Look, I've got to go." She attempted to explain that she would get in trouble for being away from the registration desk.

Clinton, while fondling his penis said: "Well, I don't want to make you do anything you don't want to do." Clinton then stood up and pulled up his pants and said: "If you get in trouble for leaving work, have Dave call me immediately and I'll take care of it." As Jones left the room Clinton looked sternly at Jones and said: "You are smart. Let's keep this between ourselves."

Jones believed "Dave" to be the same David Harrington, of whom Clinton previously referred. Clinton, by his comments about Harrington to Jones, affirmed that he had control over Jones' employment, and that he was willing to use that power. Jones became fearful that her refusal to succumb to Clinton's advances could damage her in her job and even jeopardize her employment. . . .

Jones was visibly shaken and upset when she returned to the registration desk. Pamela Blackard immediately asked her what was wrong. After a moment, during which Jones attempted to collect herself, she told Blackard much of what had happened. Blackard attempted to comfort Plaintiff.

Jones thereafter left the Conference and went to the work place of her friend, Debra Ballentine.

When Ballentine met Plaintiff at the reception area, she immediately asked Jones what was wrong because Jones was visibly upset and nervous. . . . Jones then told Ballentine what had happened with Clinton in the hotel suite. . . .

Ballentine urged Jones to report the incident. Plaintiff refused, fearing that, if she did so, no one would believe her account, that she would lose her job, and that the incident would endanger her relationship with her then-fiance (now husband), Stephen Jones.

Later, on the same day, Plaintiff also described the substance of her encounter with Clinton to her sister, Charlotte Corbin Brown. . . .

Plaintiff continued to work at AIDC. One of her duties was to deliver documents to and from the Office of the Governor, as well as other offices within the Arkansas State Capitol complex. In or about June, 1991, while Jones was performing this duty, Ferguson saw her at the Governor's office and said: "Bill wants your phone number. Hillary's out of town often and Bill would like to see you." Plaintiff refused to provide her telephone number. . . .

On one occasion, Plaintiff was accosted by Clinton in the Rotunda of the Arkansas State Capitol. Clinton draped his arm over Plaintiff, pulled her close and tightly to his body and said: "Don't we make a beautiful couple — beauty and the beast?" . . .

Jones continued to work at AIDC even though she was in constant fear that Governor Clinton might take retaliatory action against her because of her rejection of his abhorrent sexual advances. Her enjoyment of her work was severely diminished. In fact, she was treated in a hostile and rude manner by certain superiors in AIDC. This rude conduct had not happened prior to her encounter with Clinton. Further, after her maternity leave she was transferred to a position which had no responsible duties for which she could be adequately evaluated to earn advancement. The reason given to her by her superiors for the transfer was that her previous position had been eliminated. This reason was untrue since her former position was not abolished. It was a pretext for the real reason which was that she was being punished for her rejection of the various advances made by Clinton described above. . . .

Jones terminated her employment and separated from AIDC service on February 20, 1993. On May 4, 1993, Plaintiff, her husband and child moved to California.

In January, 1994, Plaintiff visited her family and friends in Arkansas. While Jones was in Arkansas, Ms. Ballentine telephoned Jones to arrange a meeting for lunch. During the telephone conversation, Ballentine read to Plaintiff a paragraph from an article published in the January, 1994 issue of The American Spectator Magazine regarding Plaintiff's hotel suite encounter with Clinton.

The American Spectator account asserts that a woman by the name of "Paula" told an unnamed trooper (obviously Defendant

Ferguson), who had escorted "Paula" to Clinton's hotel room, that "she was available to be Clinton's regular girlfriend if he so desired," thus implying a consummated and satisfying sexual encounter with Clinton, as well as a willingness to continue a sexual relationship with him. . . .

Because the false statements appearing in The American Spectator article that Jones was willing to have sex with Clinton (and the innuendo that she had already done so when she left the hotel suite) threatened her marriage, her friendships, and her family relationships, Plaintiff spoke publicly on February 11, 1994, that she was the "Paula" mentioned in The American Spectator article, that she had rebuffed Clinton's sexual advances, and that she had not expressed a willingness to be his girlfriend. Jones and her lawyer asked that Clinton acknowledge the incident, state that Jones had rejected Clinton's advances, and apologize to Jones.

Clinton, who is now President of the United States of America responded to Jones' request for an apology by having his press spokespersons deliver a statement on his behalf that the incident never happened, and that he never met Plaintiff. Thus, by innuendo and effect, Clinton publicly branded Plaintiff a liar. Moreover, as recently as the week this Complaint was filed, Clinton, through his White House aides, stated that Plaintiff's account of the hotel room incident was untrue and a "cheap political trick."

Clinton hired an attorney, who, as Clinton's agent, said that Jones' account "is really just another effort to rewrite the results of the election [i.e. for President of the United States] and . . . distract the President from his agenda." The attorney further asked the question: "Why are these claims being brought now, three years after the fact?" The attorney also asked how Jones' allegations could be taken "seriously." These comments by Clinton's counsel, on behalf of Clinton, imply that Jones is a liar.

Dee Dee Meyers, White House Spokeswoman, said of Jones' allegations: "It's just not true." Thus, the pattern of defaming Jones continues to this date. . . .

Clinton's actions and omissions above stated caused Jones embarrassment, humiliation, fear, emotional distress, horror, grief, shame, marital discord and loss of reputation.

REVIEW & OUTLOOK

The Livingstone Standard

So control over the Clinton White House's office of personnel security was given to Craig Livingstone, a punk, and Tony Marceca, a political lowlife. And we're treated to hogwash that this is somehow just another emanation of Bill Clinton's affably chaotic personality.

A former Georgetown bouncer who once threatened to smash in a woman neighbor's face if she didn't quiet her dog, Craig Livingstone confessed in his deposition to the House Oversight Committee that he had used illegal drugs widely until 1985, had been fired from a job at Sears for irregularities involving merchandise and had been fired from another job because his employer no longer believed his claimed academic credentials. New York's Democratic Congressman Floyd Flake reported this week that he once got into an auto altercation at National Airport with Mr. Livingstone, who called Rep. Flake a "dumb-ass nigger."

Craig Livingstone

And of course Mr. Livingstone was assisted by Tony Marceca, who is somehow floating through life as an "Army investigator," since 1988 a permanent federal employee subject to Hatch Act prohibitions on political campaigning. Yet he previously happened to work on political campaigns for Ed Muskie, George McGovern, John Glenn, Gary Hart, Paul Simon, Walter Mondale and, most recently, Al Gore. In his deposition to the committee, Tony Marceca admitted to "some negative information in my background" relating to work he did for the Texas attorney general's office. On Tuesday, Mr. Marceca denied the accusation by former Hart campaign worker Dennis Casey that the man who until recently was "reviewing" White House FBI files once lifted $200 from the Hart campaign's petty cash box.

Testifying Wednesday, former White House associate counsel William Kennedy described the background matters in the Livingstone deposition as "items of concern," but "not killers as it were." Also, no one at the White House has a clue how Craig Livingstone got this job. Indeed, Mr. Kennedy suggested that the blame might lie with the late Vincent Foster.

Meanwhile, Insight magazine reported that the White House built a comprehensive data base nicknamed "Big Brother" that "profiled" thousands of people who might come in contact with the Administration. The data base included information on "favors" done for "contributors" to the Clinton campaign. Carlton Turner, an independent contractor hired for the job, says he was told the project was being done for the President and First Lady. Did Mr. Livingstone and Mr. Marceca, we have to wonder, also feed Big Brother?

Let's try to get something straight here: If all any of us does is scream about the obvious outrageousness of all this, the White House is going to go scot-free. Outrage alone means no one has penetrated to a serious understanding of the essential nature of this White House by way of Arkansas. It is simply not possible to match who and what Craig Livingstone is with the enormously sensitive office he controlled without being profoundly disturbed. The word we will use to describe it in light of the past week's information is sinister.

That is a serious charge, but we mean to clearly separate ourselves from the dominant view, notable among much of the journalistic community, that the Clinton crowd is just bumbling, baby-boomer innocents rolled in from Woodstock or M Street. They are not innocents. They are not bumblers. They know what they are doing, or trying to do.

The revelations this week of Dennis Sculimbrene further force one to such a conclusion. Detailed to the FBI's White House office since 1979, Mr. Sculimbrene has told a Senate committee that White House officials asked him to get FBI background information about Travel Office employees before they were fired. That was no innocent "mistake." The subsequent release of a memo by former White House aide David Watkins described Hillary Clinton demanding that he get "our people" into the Travel Office.

Obviously, the White House already had "our people" running the office of security personnel through which flowed rivers of potentially useful personal information. Retired FBI Agent Gary Aldrich reports, as John Fund notes in the article nearby, that the White House Counsel's office cut the Secret Service out of the traditional loop for handling matters pertaining to personnel security. That is not "bumbling." These columns reported two years ago that the Office of Administration, then run by Patsy Thomasson, had failed to complete security checks on hundreds of new White House aides, some of whom Ms. Thomasson said in a formal memo to Rep. Frank Wolf were participating in a mandatory White House drug-testing program.

The mantra that the Clintons have been the victim of incompetence and inexperience won't hold. These people were assembling exactly the kind of White House they wanted and would feel comfortable with. Despite William Kennedy's protestations, Craig Livingstone isn't just some loopy guy who wandered out of a Georgetown saloon into the White House. Craig Livingstone was in that highly sensitive job because, on the evidence that has emerged in the past week, his work was well up to the standard expected.

Editorial Feature

White House Insecurity

By JOHN H. FUND

Gary Aldrich never imagined he would become a government whistleblower. His 26-year career as an FBI special agent included a dozen major political corruption cases, all of which ended in convictions. In 1990, he became one of two FBI agents assigned to the White House to clear the background of presidential appointees. But as the Clinton administration took office in 1993, he watched in horror as a security system in place for 30 years almost completely collapsed. Efforts he and his partner made to warn their superiors were ignored, and Mr. Aldrich retired in 1995. He now repeats his alarm in an explosive new book, "Unlimited Access: An FBI Agent Inside the Clinton White House" (Regnery Publishing).

Mr. Aldrich has already made headlines with a June 13 article on this page in which he revealed that permanent White House employees who were suspected of being disloyal were reinvestigated up to three years before they were due, and asked to fill out forms that requested their tax records and political affiliations.

In his book, Mr. Aldrich reports that the White House Counsel's Office ended the longstanding practice of having the Secret Service comment on the "suitability" of presidential appointees and blocked Secret Service agents from even seeing background files for more than a year. Hundreds of White House employees, including Craig Livingstone, then White House security director, went months without permanent passes, even though some were handling classified material. The counsel's office showed little interest in the trouble-some background of many of its own appointees, but Democratic operative Anthony Marceca took the time to get FBI files on more than 700 other individuals, including one of the FBI agents assigned to the White House.

Mr. Aldrich reports that a White House computer expert told him that FBI agents working for then-Independent Counsel Robert Fiske had failed to examine the late Vincent Foster's computer. When it was finally located, the hard drive had been so badly damaged that none of its files could be read, and it was thrown away. He reports on conversations with Secret Service agents who claim President Clinton has left the White House late at night, for hours at a time, and without his Secret Service detail.

He details the unfair way in which Travel Office Director Billy Dale was railroaded out of his job and ultimately put on trial for embezzlement. FBI Agent Dennis Sculimbrene, Mr. Aldrich's partner at the White House, testified at Mr. Dale's trial that he had seen Clinton staffers going through the Travel Office, throwing documents away. Later Mr. Sculimbrene was upbraided by Mr. Livingstone: "I'm surprised you'd show your face in here. I don't appreciate what you did for Billy Dale, Dennis. It wasn't helpful." He replied that he had been subpoenaed and had simply told the truth, to which Mr. Livingstone replied, "Truth is whatever you want it to be."

Mr. Aldrich's book shows a clear disdain for the clothes, manners and language of the crowd the Clintons brought to Washington. He is clearly straight-laced, and some of his observations will strike read-ers as trivial. However, on matters of ethics and judgment the anec-dotes he has compiled are disturbing and not easily dismissed. No doubt the White House will attempt to discredit Mr. Aldrich and his book, but it won't find the mild-mannered career FBI agent an easy target.

Former FBI agents such as Mr. Aldrich are allowed to write books so long as they meet the bureau's concerns about privacy and nation-al security. When Mr. Aldrich submitted his book late last year, the FBI responded with several objections. Mr. Aldrich complied with most of them but declined to alter his scathing criticism on the lack of White House security. He is publishing his book without the bureau's written permission because he feels serious White House security problems are ongoing and won't end unless they're exposed.

He writes, "It wasn't long before I found evidence not only of real criminal activity, but of the willful endangerment of the president, the White House staff and national security."

Mr. Fund is a member of the Journal editorial board.

*   *   *

'A Whopper of a Mistake'

From "Unlimited Access" (Regnery Publishing) by Gary Aldrich:

One of the finest White House managers was Phil Larsen, head of personnel for the Office of Administration. But at the end of the first full week of the new Clinton administration, Phil called to say good-bye. He had submitted his resignation to David Watkins, and he was being careful about what he was saying over the phone. Why?

Larsen would tell me only that he didn't like what was going on and "I'm out of here." . . .

What had happened? Months later, when Congress's investigators, the General Accounting Office, stormed the White House to examine the files of the Office of Personnel, I found out. It seems that on 20 January 1993, when hundreds of Clinton people came to work at the White House, many didn't have a job. Hundreds were instructed to come or told, "Okay, come on in, maybe we'll have something for you to do."

They hadn't filled out forms, they hadn't submitted resumes, there wasn't even any proof that they were U.S. citizens! They weren't official U.S. government employees. So they couldn't get paid.

It eventually dawned on the Clinton administration that these people had to be given appointments. David Watkins called Larsen and told him to draw up the appropriate documents. Larsen told him, "Too late. It's illegal to grant appointments retroactively to pay people. We'd have to create phony documents to do that."

Watkins didn't care whether it was legal or illegal. He ordered Larsen to backdate forms and create whatever documents were necessary, phony or not, so Clinton's staff members could get paid. Larsen refused, and Larsen walked.

*   *   *

The new White House director of security was Craig Livingstone.

Craig had no experience in security issues. His only qualifications were that he was a 30-something friend of the Clintons and was built like an overweight bouncer. And his Washington career had opened with a bang. Federal employees were trying to find more than $150,000 worth of equipment lost or stolen from the inauguration—equipment that had been in the charge of Craig Livingstone. Further warning bells had gone off when Associate Counsel William Kennedy had asked me what the FBI thought of Craig's replacing Jane Dannenhauer and asked me in particular what the FBI would think if there were "character issues in his background." I responded gingerly, saying it was a post that should be filled with someone squeaky clean, before Kennedy cut me off: "I guess I see your point, but it doesn't matter. It's a done deal. Hillary wants him."

*　*　*

Melba was our office's GSA cleaning lady. She was almost always cheerful, but for the past several weeks she'd seemed sad or depressed.

"Melba, I don't mean to pry, but is there something wrong, something I can help you with?"

Melba thought for a moment, and a worried look crossed her face before she blurted, "Mr. Aldrich, sir, no harm intended, but these new people are terrible! Every day we go into their offices and clean up after them, and the very next day it's as if we had never been there before. They're messy people, Mr. Aldrich. These people are sloppy. Some are real slobs, sir! They throw garbage on the floor, or they throw cups of coffee and miss the waste can and it splashes all over the wall. And *they* don't clean it up!

"It's as if they don't care, Mr. Aldrich, and I hate to say this, and you must never repeat this as long as I'm here, but sir, President Bush's people were much neater *and* much nicer to us. And that's the God's honest truth, sir." . . .

It wasn't long before Melba told me she was taking early retirement. She didn't want to go, but she couldn't bear to stay; watching the White House deteriorate was just too hard.

*　*　*

The health care debate looked very different inside the White House than it did to the public. While the public was inundated by hard-luck stories of suffering poor people who had lost their insurance, the Clintons themselves were behaving like the most cutthroat corporate downsizers.

In an effort to make good on candidate Clinton's promise to cut the White House staff by 25%—a target the administration never reached—many longtime federal employees were fired. To staff the White House, the administration brought in a flood of interns and volunteers who worked not only without insurance, but also without pay (and frequently without professional standards of behavior).

Kept very quiet by the Clintons was the fact that many White House employees were hired as officially "part-time" staff to be paid at only 39 hours a week or less, even though there was plenty of work for them to do and they wanted to work full time. But denying them that extra hour of work a week allowed the White House to deny them a variety of benefits, the chief of which was *health insurance!*

*   *   *

At the end of my assignment at the White House I concluded that the Clintons might as well hitch a trailer to the White House and tow it to Little Rock; they had soiled the place. The U.S. Park Service hedge clipper in the Rose Garden had a finer character than the president of the United States. The sad thing was, the clipper knew it.

On my last day, I took one last stroll around the White House. I walked past the Rose Garden. As the Park Service employee clipped a hedge in front of the Oval Office, glancing occasionally at "the man" who was sitting behind the big desk, I wondered what might be going through the hedge clipper's mind. I think I know because so many of the permanent employees were thinking the same thing: "There's been a big mistake, a whopper of a mistake. How the heck did it happen, and what the heck are we going to do about it now?"

Editorial Feature

Filegate: A Family Affair

By CHARLES DONOVAN AND TERESA DONOVAN

For us, the capital theater called "Filegate" is a family affair. Brother and sister, one or the other of us worked in the White House from 1981 to 1993. Neither of us, thank goodness, was what the press is politely calling "luminaries." We labored in the obscurity befitting White House ghost-writers: Chuck wrote for Ronald Reagan's White House correspondence unit; Teresa performed similar duties for Vice President Bush, beginning in 1988 and continuing when he moved into the Oval Office the following January.

We welcome President Clinton's apology for his administration's acquisition of our FBI summary background files. But before describing why that apology isn't enough, we would like to do a little apologizing of our own. The first apology goes to Craig Livingstone and Anthony Marceca, the crack security team that laid hands on our files along with over 700 others. Gentlemen, we're sorry, our files must have been awfully dull — compared to what you're used to.

We extend a similar apology to the FBI agents who conducted the full field investigations necessary for us to be cleared for our White House passes. Most people imagine the lives of FBI agents to be full of intrigue, especially those agents who are assigned to protect national security.

But what could be intriguing about sleuthing in Cincinnati? Especially on the city's west side, which is notorious only for its lack of notoriety. True, that area was the original stomping ground of

Jerry Springer, who was the region's Great Democratic Hope before he became one of television's grand demagogic hypes. But that's as racy as it gets.

The lives of the Donovans were hardly the stuff of a Bob Woodward expose. Yes, it's true that some of our relatives speak to the ghosts of long-dead political figures — like Teddy Roosevelt — but only when those figures speak first. We were always taught to be polite to our elders.

We apologize as well for the numerous threads the FBI must have been forced to follow to get the full truth about us. From each of our eight brothers and sisters they must have gotten a different story. Surely the FBI must have been puzzled, for instance, to learn so much about the peccadilloes of the siblings christened Superman and Rat Baby at an early age.

Then there are the possible testimonies from our hundreds of neighbors in the west side's close-knit German-Irish community. Did anyone question the sanity of Jim Donovan and his late wife, Mary, for lavishing their love on such an unruly brood? Did Marge Parson tell the FBI

Craig Livingstone

about the many times the Donovan Christmas lights stayed up until July? Did whispers reach the agents' ears about the family's lax supervision of the chain-breaking Bruno, who locked wits with the fenders of three passing cars and lived to bark about it? Did the Kellers or Altmayers mention the paths Donovan feet wore as we cut through their backyards on the way to play wiffle ball? What about the ill-fated Pontiac LeMans that remained in the Donovan driveway for years, gradually transforming itself into a GM Terrarium because no one had the money to fix it?

We do not know the answers to these questions, but it is possible that Messrs. Livingstone and Marceca — and who knows how many others — now do. As for ourselves, we have no wish to know. And that's our point. Much has been made of the gross violation of privacy these files represent. Certainly, we are exercised by that violation of our own reasonable expectation of confidentiality. But the same concern applies to the privacy of those who spoke with the FBI about us, who also had reasonable expectations regarding their frank assessments of two people seeking to occupy sensitive posts in their national government.

No doubt, it would be intriguing to find out what all of these friends, neighbors, teachers and peers had to say about us. Like Huck Finn attending his own funeral, we might take morbid pleasure in having our self-images punctured or further inflated. Even so, neither of us has any plans to make a Freedom of Information Act request for copies of our files. After all, whatever our friends and  neighbors said in our behalf, we finished 12 years of White House service uneventfully.

The content of our files doesn't interest us, but knowing who has read them does. Chances are, we'll never get the full answer to that question. Obviously, no FBI field agents were present when these files circulated over to the Clinton White House — and who knows where else besides. The sting of that knowledge applies not only to those of us who worked in the White House, but also to the dozens of citizens, our neighbors and friends, whose private opinions have been splayed open by a nest of political hacks.

Anthony Marceca

Perhaps most galling of all, Filegate comes from an administration that racked up political points by trashing the ethics of its predecessors. But hypocrisy is like an ill-fitting suit. No matter how much you adjust your tie, you'll never look any better.

Mr. Donovan is senior policy adviser at the Family Research Council in Washington. Ms. Donovan worked at the White House through January 1993.

REVIEW & OUTLOOK

Mr. Foster & Mr. Livingstone

It is nearly three years since Vincent Foster's body was discovered at Fort Marcy Park, but mystery still cloaks events surrounding the suicide of the former deputy White House counsel. The mystery deepened in recent weeks with news that the White House operative most directly involved with the abuse of FBI background files was personnel security chief Craig Livingstone, a heretofore minor Whitewater player.

Vincent Foster

Mr. Livingstone resigned over Filegate, and White House aides moved quickly to put the issue behind them, eventually laying off responsibility for hiring him on Vincent Foster. "Vince decided to put him in the security office on a temporary basis," Presidential adviser George Stephanopoulos told ABC News. But former White House FBI agent Gary Aldrich says he was told by then-White House Associate Counsel William Kennedy that Mr. Livingstone was hired on orders of Hillary Clinton. Mr. Aldrich's claim was backed up by a former White House colleague, FBI agent Dennis Sculimbrene, who said in a June 19 interview with the Senate Judiciary Committee that Mr. Kennedy also told him that Mr. Livingstone was a Hillary Clinton hire. In Helsinki on Wednesday, Mrs. Clinton said of Mr. Livingstone: "I did not know him. I did not have anything to do with his being hired, and I do not remember even meeting him until sometime in the last year."

Notwithstanding Mrs. Clinton's recollections about her own association, there is indeed a Livingstone-Foster connection on the public record, but it may not be what Mr. Stephanopoulos had in mind.

* * *

Secret Service memos provided to the Senate Whitewater Committee show that Mr. Livingstone was one of the first to be notified of Mr. Foster's death. Mr. Foster's body was discovered at Fort Marcy Park around 6 p.m. Mr. Livingstone told Senate Whitewater investigators in a sworn deposition on July 10 last year that he was notified by the Secret Service at home around 9 p.m. Page 36 of the report on Mr. Foster's death by Robert Fiske, the first Whitewater special counsel, notes that the body "was taken to the morgue, where it was later identified by William Kennedy and Craig Livingstone, a Special Assistant to the White House Counsel." In his Senate deposition, Mr. Livingstone says that after identifying the body he went with Mr. Kennedy to Mr. Foster's home, where he stayed until 2 a.m.

After a few hours of sleep, Mr. Livingstone told Senate investigators, he drove back to Mr. Foster's home at 6:30 a.m., but stayed outside in his car, without notifying Foster family members, until 8 a.m. This strange behavior supposedly was to see if anyone from the press visited the family. Then he drove to the White House and was logged in by the Secret Service at 8:14 a.m.

Mr. Livingstone also says he visited the White House Counsel's suite several times that morning, but did not enter Mr. Foster's office or remove any documents. But according to a deposition given to the Senate Whitewater Committee by Bruce Abbott, a Secret Service officer on duty at the time, Mr. Livingstone that morning exited the West Wing carrying a brown "leather or vinyl-type briefcase, opening from the top, much in the fashion of a litigator's bag or lawyer's briefcase." A little later, Mr. Livingstone, accompanied by an individual not known to Officer Abbott, left the building again. "I observed that [unknown] individual carrying one or perhaps two boxes with what appeared to be, looked to me to be loose-leaf binders," Officer Abbott told Senate investigators.

Officer Abbott was sufficiently impressed by these events to notify his immediate superior at the White House, Dennis Martin. When Mr. Livingstone found out there was a Secret Service report on his actions, he contacted Mr. Martin in an unsuccessful attempt to learn

Officer Abbott's identity. "I think I called, made a friendly call and asked if we knew who was making the allegation," Mr. Livingstone said in his Senate deposition.

Now, we have heard much about the relevance of files and briefcases before. Secret Service Officer Henry O'Neill told the Senate Whitewater Committee that he saw Maggie Williams, Mrs. Clinton's chief of staff, leaving Mr. Foster's office the night of the death with an armful of files, which she denies. White House aide Patsy Thomasson told the committee she peeked into Mr. Foster's briefcase that night but did not see the torn-up yellow note "discovered" four days later. Park Police Sergeant Peter Markland said that then-White House Counsel Bernard Nussbaum did not let him look into the briefcase two days after the death. Foster family lawyer Michael Spafford testified he heard White House lawyer Clifford Sloan tell Mr. Nussbaum there were scraps of paper in the briefcase and that Mr. Nussbaum said they would get to it later; Messrs. Nussbaum and Sloan testified they did not recall the incident. Foster secretary Deborah Gorham testified that she had seen "something yellow" in Mr. Foster's briefcase and that Mr. Nussbaum later grilled her about it; Mr. Nussbaum suffered memory loss when questioned by Whitewater investigators about the incident.

Craig Livingstone

Meanwhile, there also are credible reports of a briefcase spotted in Mr. Foster's car in Fort Marcy Park, though the Fiske report does not list a briefcase among the articles found there. Journalist Christopher Ruddy has identified four witnesses who say they saw a briefcase. Two of the witnesses are motorists who stopped at the park; the other two are paramedics who were among the first at the death scene. All four have testified before the Whitewater grand jury in Washington, Mr. Ruddy reports.

*   *   *

It is not possible to know what all this ultimately adds up to, but it strikes us that the public record about security chief Livingstone's travels and actions through this period is incomplete. Perhaps, for instance, a personnel security chief more loyal to his patrons than to his sensitive office was the perfect candidate to retrieve the Foster briefcase and see that it was sanitized. Given Mr. Livingstone's intriguing comments to Senate investigators, his hard-to-miss appearance in the Fiske report and now his unusual handling of FBI files, certainly it was appropriate for Attorney General Janet Reno to recommend to the judicial panel that Independent Counsel Kenneth Starr be given authority over the Livingstone-Marceca operation.

As we have often noted, "Whitewater" is not merely about a land deal long ago. It is about behavior inside this White House. Craig Livingstone, a Clinton hire present at the identification of Vincent Foster's body and now seen as responsible for the misuse of sensitive FBI files, is a case in point.

Letters to the Editor

A Death and a Coverup

Your July 12 editorial "Mr. Foster & Mr. Livingstone" notes that Craig Livingstone was one of the first people to be notified of Vincent Foster's death, saying that he told Senate Whitewater investigators that he was notified by the Secret Service at around 9 p.m.

If this were true, it would mean it took nearly three hours for the U.S. Park Police to discover Foster was with the White House and inform the Secret Service, even though his White House photo ID was lying under his suit jacket on the front seat of his unlocked car. This suggests a degree of incompetence and sloth on the part of the Park Police that defies belief. It flies in the face of strong evidence that the Secret Service and senior White House officials learned of Foster's death an hour and a half to two hours earlier.

Foster's body was found by the police at 6:14 p.m. Park Police Sgt. Cheryl Braun told the FBI that she found Foster's White House ID around 7 p.m. and that 20 or 30 minutes later she informed her shift commander, Lt. Patrick Gavin, that the victim was a White House employee. Lt. Gavin told the FBI he called the Secret Service within 10 minutes of getting Sgt. Braun's message and that within 5 or 10 minutes he got a call from Bill Burton, assistant to White House Chief of Staff "Mack" McLarty.

If Craig Livingstone were the first to have been informed by the Secret Service, this chronology indicates he was called around 7:30, not at 9 p.m.

But the Braun/Gavin chronology is called into question by evidence that the Park Police did not delay opening Foster's car door for 45 minutes and were not slow to call the White House. There is evidence that some of the emergency rescue workers knew Foster was with the White House when they left the scene at 6:37 p.m. Park Police Sgt. John Rolla's notes indicate that he obtained Foster's Washington address from Lt. Danny Walter of the Secret Service soon after he arrived on the scene at around 6:35 p.m.

David Watkins, then assistant to the president for management and administration, testified before the Senate Whitewater Committee that when he asked his top aide, Patsy Thomasson, to search Foster's office for a note at around 10:30 p.m., "I also knew that the Park Police had been in touch with the Secret Service for some five hours before making that request." Five hours would be before Foster's body was found, but four hours would be close. The senators and their counsel didn't see the significance of that statement and failed to pin him down on the time. They did elicit the fact that he had been beeped by the Secret Service and informed that Foster had been found dead. He told them that the first person he called was Bill Burton, to tell him to inform Chief of Staff McLarty. He has said privately that he was beeped soon after he settled down in a theater to watch an early movie.

It appears the Park Police knew of Foster's White House connection within 15 or 20 minutes of finding the body and that they notified the White House promptly. It appears they have tried to conceal this fact in order to narrow the gap between the time they notified the White House and the time the White House claims it was notified. Sgt. Braun and Lt. Gavin stretched out the time about an hour, but that fell short of the time claimed by Mr. Livingstone and other White House officials. William Kennedy told the FBI that Mr. Livingstone notified him of the death between 8:15 and 8:30, telling him the body was en route to Fairfax Hospital. It arrived at the hospital at 8:30 p.m.

The question that cries out for an answer is why the White House wanted the extra time. What did they do with it?

The answer may lie in what a young woman named Rose Precupio told the FBI she observed while applying the president's makeup in the White House map room for his appearance on "Larry King Live" at 9 p.m. that night. She said that a man entered the room and informed the president that something had been found in Foster's office. Her story was a closely guarded secret until it was reported by Christopher Ruddy, the reporter who first revealed the disappearance of a briefcase that witnesses saw in Foster's car. (His report has been confirmed by questions — based on the young woman's story — that we know the FBI asked of the president's close adviser Bruce Lindsey.)

All those involved in this scandalous coverup should be called upon to testify under oath concerning what they know, when they knew it, to whom they communicated it, beginning with Park Police Sgt. John Rolla and ending with President Clinton. The president, according to the official version, was the last to know, having been kept in the dark until he finished the Larry King show at 10 p.m.

REED IRVINE
Accuracy in Media Inc.

Washington

Editorial Feature

Release the Clinton Whitewater Tapes

The videotape of President Clinton's testimony in the Whitewater criminal trial of Herby Branscum Jr. and Robert Hill is expected to be played this week to a federal jury in Little Rock, but if the president has his way, most Americans will never get a chance to see or hear him testify. The president and his lawyers argue that "respect for the Office of the President" prohibits public release of his videotaped Whitewater testimony.

Rule of Law

By Theodore J. Boutrous Jr.

The real reason for the president's resistance, however, is far less lofty: fear that his political opponents, not to mention David Letterman, Jay Leno and "Saturday Night Live," will have a field day if they ever get their hands on the videotapes. While the president may well be right, such purely political concerns are not nearly good enough to trump the public's First Amendment right to see these judicial records.

Mr. Clinton's testimony in the Whitewater cases is unprecedented. In addition to the current Branscum-Hill trial, which involves alleged campaign finance improprieties during Mr. Clinton's successful 1990 bid for re-election as governor of Arkansas, the president also testified earlier this year as a defense witness in the first Whitewater trial, which ended in felony convictions of his former business partners, Jim and Susan McDougal, and Arkansas Gov. Jim Guy Tucker.

Never before has a sitting president testified in two criminal trials.

Mr. Clinton's lawyers persuaded the judges in both cases that the president was entitled to special treatment out of deference to his official position and duties. Unlike every other witness, the president was excused from appearing live in Little Rock to testify in open court. Instead, he was permitted to give his testimony in secret from the White House in front of a video camera.

In the McDougal-Tucker case, the videotape of the president's testimony was later played to the jury and the handful of courtroom spectators and reporters who were present. A transcript of his testimony was thereafter released publicly. But Mr. Clinton filed a motion for a "protective order" seeking to ban public release of the videotape itself on the ground that "if copies of the videotape . . . were made available to the public, the tape would be subject to selective editing, out-of-context replays and similar misuse, as well as commercial and political exploitation." According to the president, the public should be barred from seeing his taped testimony in high-profile criminal trials because his "political opponents have already declared their intention to use portions of this videotape . . . in political 'attack ads.'"

Last month, Federal District Judge George Howard Jr. accepted this argument, and ordered that the videotape be kept under judicial lock and key. The major broadcast networks are appealing, and the case is set to be argued before the U.S. Court of Appeals for the Eighth Circuit on Aug. 12. Meanwhile, Federal District Judge Susan Webber Wright, who is presiding over the Branscum-Hill case, has ordered that the videotape of the president's testimony be kept under seal. The networks have filed a motion seeking public release of the videotape in that trial, and the president no doubt will oppose it.

The videotapes are judicial records that must, under the Constitution, be released to the public. As the Supreme Court has observed, "the courts of this country recognize a general right to inspect and copy . . . judicial records and documents." There is a strong presumption of openness that ordinarily precludes the sealing of judicial records, especially where there is a strong public interest at stake. The courts have held that only an overriding, compelling reason can defeat that fundamental constitutional right.

Mr. Clinton cannot possibly meet this test. There is a powerful public interest in the president's Whitewater testimony. Although the president argues that it is enough for constitutional purposes merely to release a written transcript of his testimony, the best way to determine whether a witness is telling the truth is to observe his demeanor while testifying — to watch his mannerisms, look into his eyes, see the expression on his face and hear the inflections and pauses in his voice. The American people are entitled to watch the tapes and judge for themselves the president's credibility under oath regarding Whitewater.

In support of his position against release of the tapes, Mr. Clinton's lawyers rely on easily distinguishable cases from the 1970s involving Presidents Nixon, Ford and Carter. The closest parallel is of a far more recent vintage. In 1990, a federal judge in Washington ordered that the videotape of President Reagan's testimony in the Iran-Contra Independent Counsel's prosecution of John Poindexter be released once the videotape was played for the jury.

Mr. Clinton asserts that the Poindexter case is inapplicable because Mr. Reagan had already left office and thus was "no longer charged with executing the constitutional responsibilities of the Chief Executive" when he testified. But the public interest in a sitting president's testimony is all the more intense — and the case for public release even stronger — precisely because be remains in office and is seeking re-election.

The president's concern that political foes, comedians and satirical commentators might "exploit" the videotapes to harshly criticize, or even to mock, him hardly qualifies as the sort of compelling reason needed to justify keeping the tapes out of the public eye. The Supreme Court said in its 1988 decision in Falwell v. Hustler Magazine that "the sort of robust political debate encouraged by the First Amendment is bound to produce speech that is critical of those who hold public office. . . . [P]ublic officials will be subject to vehement, caustic, and sometimes unpleasantly sharp attacks." Political attacks and humor are "often based on exploitation of . . . politically embarrassing events," and graphic depictions concerning politicians and other public figures historically "have played a prominent role in public and political debate." Thus, in Falwell, the court held that a parody about the Rev. Jerry Falwell published by Hustler was protected by the First Amendment even though it was "offensive to him, and doubtless gross and repugnant in the eyes of most."

The fact that the videotapes of Mr. Clinton's Whitewater testimony might be used in political speech and debate during an election year — the very essence of what the First Amendment is intended to foster and protect — is a potent ground for releasing the tapes, not a reason for keeping them secret. The American people, who put Mr. Clinton in the White House and will decide whether to do so again in less than four months, have a constitutional right to view the videotapes, regardless of the political consequences.

Mr. Boutrous is an attorney in Washington.

Editorial Feature

Huck Fini? Governor Meets Arkansas Machine

By MICAH MORRISON

Even the Arkansas Democrat-Gazette was appalled, talking of "checking the skies for aliens" and "some half-baked coup in a banana republic." In the end the good citizens of Arkansas got convicted Gov. Jim Guy Tucker to carry through with his resignation, but perhaps Monday will prove to be a learning experience for his replacement, Republican Mike Huckabee.

The Baptist preacher got an unsentimental education in the arrogance of power at his inauguration, when Gov. Tucker suddenly announced he was not resigning; Lt. Gov. Huckabee would only be "acting governor" while Mr. Tucker appealed his Whitewater convictions. By the end of the day, with the inauguration crowd growing uglier and Mr. Huckabee threatening impeachment proceedings, Gov. Tucker stepped down.

Mr. Tucker's 11th-hour attempt to overthrow the constitutional order was another manifestation of a corrupt political establishment that now reaches to Washington. Gov. Huckabee now faces a crucial decision, whether to fall in with the same political establishment that has long moved the levers of power behind the scenes, to act as a courageous reformer, or to become the Ostrich of the Ozarks, burying his head in the sand.

Mr. Huckabee may have learned something from Monday's episode, not to mention Gov. Tucker's last minute office-packing — 147 appointments last Friday alone. But the signs of a Huckabee turn-around are not encouraging. After this writer suggested in June that the new governor will need his own man running the state police, Mr. Huckabee told the Clintonoid weekly Arkansas Times that he was "outraged." He said "unequivocally" that State Police Commander John Bailey was "the one guy who has the safest spot in Arkansas."

While we hold no specific brief against Col. Bailey, that's too bad, because the state police holds the keys to unlocking some of the larger mysteries of Arkansas past and presumably present. Under Col. Bailey's watch, police brass smeared their own Mena, Ark., investigator, Russell Welch, with innuendo about what might be in his personnel file, and forced him from his job. Under his predecessor, Col. Tommy Goodwin, the mysteries of Mena unfolded, and cocaine and dirty money flooded the state. In this same era, Dan Lasater and Roger Clinton got wrist-slaps on drug raps.

Beyond the specific issue of law enforcement, Mr. Huckabee is forging alliances with the same business establishment that once backed Bill Clinton. According to recent campaign finance disclosure reports, top executives of investment banking giant Stephens Inc. and poultry packer Tyson Foods, among others, made significant contributions to Mr. Huckabee's Senate bid, abandoned after the Tucker conviction. The weekly Arkansas Business suggests that Stephens Inc. chairman Jackson Stephens or his son, company president Warren Stephens, are likely to wind up as members of Mr. Huckabee's kitchen cabinet.

It's perhaps inevitable that a governor would team with a state's biggest businesses, and join the chorus of civic boosting. Stephens and Tyson officials protest that they have been unfairly singled out by The Wall Street Journal and that they have an obligation to participate in the political and economic debate in Arkansas. Tyson officials also were active campaign contributors to Mr. Huckabee, and three top Tyson executives were named to his gubernatorial transition team. The former police commander, Mr. Goodwin, is a Tyson man from northwest Arkansas.

The extent of political and business intrigue in Arkansas is suggested by testimony Tuesday from presidential aide Bruce Lindsey, named as an unindicted co-conspirator in the trial of bankers Herby Branscum Jr. and Robert Hill. Mr. Lindsey asked the jury to believe that his writing of four separate $7,500 checks to cover a $30,000 withdrawal was motivated by "paranoia" that the big amount might be noticed by someone at Systematics, a bank-data processing firm controlled by Stephens family interests. He said he worried that someone there might pass on the information to Mr. Clinton's opponents for use in his successful 1990 gubernatorial campaign.

The Democrat-Gazette and other Arkansas civic boosters complain that in calling for reform of "Arkansas mores," we at the Journal smear the whole state. But in fact, we want to liberate the state from its longtime one-party dominance. If they don't want to listen to us, they could listen to Arkansas native Wesley Pruden, now editor of the Washington Times. We could not hope to do better than his May 31 column on reaction to convictions of Gov. Tucker and James and Susan MacDougal by Clinton apologists:

"Okay, so maybe there were some crimes down there. Maybe some people did rob banks. Maybe somebody did lie about how people did business with the state of Arkansas during the various Clinton administrations. Maybe, even, someone did lie about how she put her connections with the governor's office at the service of the clients of her law firm. Maybe the Democratic political establishment down there is a reeking stinkpile, but just because Bill Clinton was extruded from that reeking stinkpile doesn't mean that he was in any way a part of it or had anything to do with it. Now, could anyone imagine that?"

Mr. Morrison is a Journal editorial page writer.

JULY 22, 1996

REVIEW & OUTLOOK

Insecure White House

In May 1995, the Clinton Administration pre-emptorily closed Pennsylvania Avenue in front of the White House, without warning to local authorities, let alone motorists. The avenue was the city's main east-west artery, and to this day traffic patterns in downtown Washington remain disrupted, at huge inconvenience to local residents and visitors from around the nation. In the wake of the Oklahoma City bombing, this abrupt action was justified in the name of White House security.

No one can deny that the closing responded to a bona fide danger, especially with the spread of terrorism most likely on display yet again in last week's air crash. Yet we ought to be able to expect that an Administration willing to inflict such trouble on the public outside the White House would take security inside the White House with the same seriousness. Instead, as Congressional testimony from Secret Service agents showed again last week, the internal attitude can only be described as cavalier.

What kind of an Administration, after all, would name a political lowlife such as Craig Livingstone as its security chief? What does it mean when an Administration lets Mr. Livingstone and his sidekick Tony Marceca troll through hundreds of confidential FBI files on appointees of previous administrations? Mr. Marceca has now taken the Fifth Amendment, refusing not only to testify, but also to turn over a briefcase full of documents on his role in the file scandal. At least the Nixon Administration did not elevate its plumbers to the security office.

On a lesser level, senior aides did not think security important. When press secretary Dee Dee Myers was asked why she was wearing a temporary pass, for example, she said she hadn't had time to fill out the paperwork for a permanent one. Similarly, records released last week show that as late as December 1993, after nearly a year in office, the Security Office was requesting an extension of 90-day temporary passes for Ira Magaziner, the highly publicized health czar, and George Stephanopoulos, more recently point man in the campaign to discredit "Unlimited Access," the book by FBI agent Gary Aldrich.

Two years ago, former Senator Dennis DeConcini, then Democratic chairman of the Intelligence Committee, received reports from his staff that in March 1994 one-third of White House employees lacked permanent passes. He wrote to the White House raising concerns about security, and suggesting that Mr. Livingstone be replaced as head of security with a professional director from the Secret Service. He was rebuffed, despite the fact that months earlier Secret Service Supervisor Arnold Cole had raised concerns with White House Associate Counsel William Kennedy about "derogatory" security information in Mr. Livingstone's own background file, presumably concerning since-admitted drug use during the 1980s and disputes with two employers.

A principal root of the cavalier attitude toward security, to judge by the testimony to Rep. Bill Clinger's Oversight Committee, was a cavalier attitude toward records of drug use. Secret Service agents testified that they found 30 to 40 early appointees who had recently used cocaine, crack and hallucinogenic drugs. Concerned about the potential for blackmail, the Secret Service denied some of them passes, the Administration protested, and a program of individual random drug testing was set up as a compromise. The program applied to 21 employees, and the White House says those currently involved do not include any senior staff members.

As Senator DeConcini found, though, the White House has repeatedly rebuffed inquiries into security in general and drugs in particular. In 1994, Patsy Thomasson, then White House Director of Administration, told Rep. Frank Wolf's committee that "there have been no cases where the Secret Service recommended someone not have a pass and we have not responded as they asked us to." In light of the Secret Service's testimony, Mr. Thomasson's statement can now be said to be "inoperative."

When Newt Gingrich raised concerns about White House passes and drug use in 1994, White House Chief of Staff Leon Panetta reacted angrily: "These are reckless charges made. Reckless accusations that impugn people's integrity. No evidence. No facts. No foundation. Just basically smear and innuendo. The kind of thing that we rejected in this country a long time ago." On Friday a group of Republican Congressmen wrote Mr. Panetta asking whether he'd like to revise these remarks.

Which brings us to Mr. Aldrich, whose book "Unlimited Access" is well-entrenched on the best-seller lists despite the negative media reaction described alongside by Brent Bozell. It's true that a better editor might have helped Mr. Aldrich avoid some errors; none have been cited in his article on these pages. If the question is whether Mr. Aldrich has cited good sources for his anecdote about President Clinton sneaking out to the Marriott Hotel, the answer clearly is no.

Yet House Democrats raised procedural objections to delay depositions to Rep. Clinger's committee from Mr. Aldrich and his former partner Dennis Sculimbrene. Little wonder, for if the question is whether the Administration was irresponsibly lax on security, the answer just as clearly is yes.

Editorial Feature

Scandals and the Press

By L. BRENT BOZELL III

On June 13, this page dropped a bombshell — the firsthand account of a 26-year FBI veteran, Gary Aldrich, charging that top officials within the Clinton administration were raiding the personnel files of former Bush staff members. Two weeks later Regnery Publishing released "Unlimited Access," Mr. Aldrich's book blowing the whistle not just on Filegate, but also on the allegedly scandalous personal behavior of the Clintons and the White House staff. This was too much for the 89% pro-Clinton media. It took only days for Mr. Aldrich's credibility to be reduced to ashes, for him to become, in the words of New York Times columnist Maureen Dowd, a "crud peddler."

Gary Aldrich

It's worth taking a look at how the press has trashed Mr. Aldrich, if only to compare his treatment with the respectful attention granted to a far less credible peddler of left-wing conspiracy theories.

Initially there was intense media interest in the Aldrich story, but the administration had other plans. Fred Barnes reports in the July 22 issue of The Weekly Standard that, after "This Week With David Brinkley" booked Mr. Aldrich for its June 30 telecast, a phalanx of White House operatives lobbied ABC in an unprecedented demand that the segment be canceled. Though the Brinkley show kept Mr.

Aldrich on the program, the entire interview was adversarial. Ignoring the charges Mr. Aldrich was raising, all three panelists pounced on him for refusing to reveal his sources.

Within an hour after the show aired, producers from "Dateline NBC" and CNN's "Larry King Live" canceled their planned interviews. A bevy of other network shows also bailed out.

Simultaneously, the Washington press corps opened fire on the talking-head circuit. "The book is ludicrous. . . . It should've never been given credibility," snarled Time's Margaret Carlson on CNN's "Capital Gang." Her colleague, The Wall Street Journal's Al Hunt, said: "That book is so sleazy it makes you want to take a shower when you read it."

And then there's Eleanor Clift. On CNN's "Crossfire," the woman who denies any pro-Clinton bias, roundly denounced Mr. Aldrich. "Listen, he talks about things that are totally ridiculous. . . . He has no basis in fact. . . . This is right-wing fantasy!"

But the press corps has a different reaction to left-wing fantasies that impugn a Republican president. Back in the summer of 1980, the Reagan campaign warned of an "October Surprise," a back-room deal by the Carter administration to win the release of American hostages held in Iran in time for the elections. After the elections, President Reagan's enemies reversed the charges and accused the GOP of an "October Surprise" to keep the hostages in captivity until after the voting.

There was nothing offered to substantiate this conspiracy theory, yet for the next 10 years the story refused to die. On April 15, 1991, it was back in the news.

The New York Times Op-Ed Page published a lengthy manifesto from Gary Sick, a member of Jimmy Carter's National Security Council, formally accusing the Reagan campaign of carrying out the "October Surprise." Mr. Sick, like Gary Aldrich, used anonymous sources, including, he wrote, "a number of [whom] have been arrested or have served prison time for gun running, fraud, counterfeiting or drugs [and some] may be seeking publicity or revenge." The only sources Mr. Sick cited by name were Cyrus and Jamshid Hashemi, two brothers he described only as connected to Iranian revolutionaries and involved in international arms sales.

The Times headline screamed "The Election Story of the Decade" and the same TV networks that dismissed Mr. Aldrich after one appearance aired 27 stories on the "October Surprise" between April 15 and Dec. 31, 1991. Mr. Sick's op-ed was followed the next night by a PBS "Frontline" expose, "The Election Held Hostage," starring none other than Mr. Sick himself. This pseudo-documentary cited another source, Richard Brenneke, who claimed to have been in Paris in 1980 when Reagan campaign manager (and later CIA Director) William Casey made the alleged deal with the Iranians.

Bush spokesman Marlin Fitzwater, like Clinton mouthpiece Michael McCurry, tried to discredit the charges, labeling Mr. Sick "the Kitty Kelley of foreign policy," but the press would have none of it.

Columnist Mark Shields: "In his attack on Gary Sick, Fitzwater reveals more temper than judgment . . . . Gary Sick is an admirable and thoughtful former U.S. Navy captain." (May 11, 1991)

Carter State Department spokesman Hodding Carter, "Nightline": "Gary Sick has a reputation which he deserves for caution, for looking before he leaps, for thinking things through." (April 15, 1991)

Robert Koehler, Los Angeles Times: "Gary Sick, a highly respected former U.S. official . . ." (April 16, 1991)

Columnist Mike Royko: "He's an expert in foreign relations . . . and has a reputation for being an extremely intelligent, skeptical, systematic, probing thinker." (April 18, 1991)

Brian Duffy, U.S. News & World Report: "Gary Sick, a respected Middle East analyst . . ." (April 29, 1991)

Larry Martz, Newsweek: "Sick, a respected Columbia University professor . . ." (April 29, 1991)

So believable was this story that ABC's "Nightline" ran its own hourlong expose. The show's atmospherics included a dark set with no chairs, large pictures of Messrs. Bush, Reagan, Casey, Ayatollah Khomeini and others, and Mr. Koppel dramatically walking us through "the fog of rumor" in search of truth.

There was only one problem. There was no truth to the story. The evidence was there for anyone to see, provided by the handful of journalists who actually bothered to investigate it.

In The New Republic on Nov. 18, 1991, Steven Emerson and Jesse Furman blew the whistle on the Hashemi brothers. Mr. Sick had not disclosed that they were illegal arms dealers, indicted for shipping tens of millions of dollars of military equipment to Iran. They claimed to have met with Casey in Madrid during October 1980, yet after their indictments they never brought this information to the attention of their attorneys or the government — a surefire way to reduce their sentences. And the FBI had wiretaps of Cyrus Hashemi in his Manhattan offices on Oct. 21, 1980 — the day after he was supposed to have been with Casey in Paris.

What of Mr. Brenneke? He was uncovered in The Village Voice by former ABC producer Frank Snepp, who found credit card receipts placing Mr. Brenneke in Portland, Ore., at the time he claimed to be in Paris. So where did this whole conspiracy nonsense begin anyway? The answer was provided by Newsweek's John Barry, who traced its origin to an article in the Dec. 2, 1980, Executive Intelligence Review, published by Lyndon LaRouche.

Gary Sick

Even so, the Sick allegations triggered a congressional investigation. On Jan. 13, 1993, a bipartisan House task force released its report. The Reagan campaign was exonerated, but the report uncovered another "October Surprise" — an offer to Iran of $150 million in spare parts and $80 million in cash by the Carter White House in return for the hostages. The proposal was made by Warren Christopher, then deputy secretary of state, now secretary of state. When we asked if "Nightline" was going to cover the Christopher revelation, a producer replied, "That's a headline, not a 'Nightline.'" What of the paper that sponsored Gary Sick? The New York Times ran nothing about Mr. Christopher's role. How many stories on the network news? Not a one.

Mr. Emerson, a former correspondent for U.S. News & World Report and now an occasional contributor to this page, said it best. The "October Surprise" theory is "probably one of the largest hoaxes and fabrications in modern American journalism. . . . None of [the sources] had any documentation whatsoever. So I still question why major American journalistic institutions accepted on face value the statements of these fabricated sources."

This same journalistic community is telling us today that it is Gary Aldrich who lacks a threshold of credibility.

Mr. Bozell is chairman of the Media Research Center.

REVIEW & OUTLOOK

Who Is Arthur Coia?

Arthur A. Coia is president of LIUNA, the Laborers International Union of North America, which represents 700,000 construction workers, brick haulers and asbestos removers. He is also one of President Bill Clinton's most important political allies. His union lent President Clinton's inaugural committee $100,000, and contributed $1.1 million to Democrats in the 1994 elections. Mr. Coia has also served as vice chairman of numerous multimillion-dollar Democratic fund-raisers, including one in May of this year. He sits on the board of the "Back to Business" committee that takes out ads defending the Clintons on Whitewater, and in 1994 attended a White House dinner and an Oval Office meeting at which the President

Arthur Coia

gave him a personal golf club that now adorns his wall. And Hillary Clinton addressed his union's conference in Florida.

Mr. Coia's union is also the subject of a three-year Justice Department investigation; Justice delivered a draft civil racketeering complaint to the union on November 4, 1994. Its 212 pages minced no words, accusing LIUNA of being controlled by organized crime and calling for the removal of Mr. Coia and a federal takeover of his union. The complaint said Mr. Coia has "associated with, and been controlled and influenced by, organized crime figures." It detailed how Mr. Coia and his associates "employed actual and threatened force, violence and fear of physical and economic injury to create a climate of intimidation and fear." It charged that union leaders had conspired with such memorably named mobsters as Carmine (The Snake) Persico, Michael (Trigger Mike) Coppola and Anthony (Fat Tony) Salerno to loot the union of its health and welfare funds. Ron Fino, a former LIUNA official who became an FBI informant, made a 1993 declaration that "during my nearly 24 years in the Laborers' Union, I learned that the union was run by and for the benefit of the mob, its members, and its associates."

Mr. Coia, however, was somehow able to persuade Justice not to file the lawsuit. He strenuously denies having mob ties, and entered negotiations for a settlement. At first, the Justice Department didn't budge. "Coia has to go. Everything else is on the table," Paul Coffey, the head of Justice's organized crime section, told Mr. Coia's attorneys on November 16. But over time, Justice dropped the demand for his removal. A few days after Mrs. Clinton's Florida speech, Justice and LIUNA reached a consent decree. A few officials left, but Mr. Coia remains as president. The union pledged to allow members to vote directly for union leaders, appoint a former FBI official as inspector general and allow Justice to take over if the self-cleaning job failed.

After the consent decree was signed, Justice's demands that the union's top officers be directly elected were rejected. Justice had to deliver an ultimatum that they were prepared to take over before Mr. Coia agreed to a watered-down compromise. Despite Justice's allegations that union education and training funds had been siphoned off to benefit mob-controlled contractors, two federal cabinet agencies last year awarded multimillion grants to LIUNA to train workers.

Mr. Coia says the government did itself a favor by avoiding lengthy litigation and allowing him to clean up the union under Justice's supervision and that his personal ties to the Clintons played no role in Justice's consent decree. These ties, though, continue to be interesting. For one thing, his negotiation with Justice was conducted by Williams & Connolly, the Washington law firm that represents Bill and Hillary Clinton on Whitewater matters. (Though not by the Clintons' lawyer David Kendall but by Brendan Sullivan, who once represented Oliver North.)

Then, too, LIUNA was previously represented by Harold Ickes, now deputy White House chief of staff. In private practice, Mr. Ickes did a thriving labor union business, representing the LIUNA, a Hotel and Restaurant Employees local accused by the government of being mob controlled in 1992, and in 1986 a Teamsters local accused of using violence to silence dissidents. The Washington Times has reported that Mr. Coia has identified Mr. Ickes as his intermediary to President Clinton.

Then there is the curious role of Neil Eggleston, associate counsel at the White House until September 1994, and author of a 35-page memo to Mr. Ickes on the potential liabilities of the Clintons in Whitewater. LIUNA's internal prosecutor is Bob Lufkin, a former Justice Department official who was once a defense attorney for sometime LIUNA attorney Anthony Traini. Mr. Coia's Rhode Island law firm still takes messages for Mr. Traini. Mr. Lufkin brought in Mr. Eggleston as appellate officer, meaning that he will adjudicate disputes between union members and Peter Vaira, the union's internal hearing officer.

This consent decree has attracted some skeptics. For one, U.S. District Judge Emmet G. Sullivan. During a hearing on the consent decree, he asked, "Here's a man who's accused of being associated with organized crime. Why wasn't Coia removed?"

The House Judiciary subcommittee on crime will try to provide some answers to that and related questions in hearings starting today. Since the election looms, the White House response and probably the media spin will be that any trepidation about Mr. Coia's treatment is merely partisan politics, another "Republican attack."

REVIEW & OUTLOOK

No Questions Here?

Documents coming out of Rep. Bill McCollum's hearings on the Clinton Administration's relations with union president Arthur Coia establish that in 1994 the FBI wrote the White House Counsel's Office

that Mr. Coia "is a criminal associate of the New England Patriarca organized crime family" and that he had been the subject of an FBI criminal probe.

Abner Mikva, whose turn it was to be White House Counsel at the time, testified yesterday he never saw the letter. During a break in the hearings, he told reporters that the report was read by "probably a clerk in the office, maybe an intern." He also said such information

Arthur Coia

shouldn't be loosely bandied around the White House because of privacy considerations. We wonder if Security Chief Craig Livingstone got the word?

In another memo released yesterday, Paul Coffey, chief of the organized crime and racketeering section at Justice, wrote another prosecutor that Justice planned to file a civil suit against Mr. Coia's union, the Laborers International Union of North America, and noted that Hillary Clinton was scheduled to address the union's conference in Florida. "It is our understanding that Mrs. Clinton's staff has already been alerted by the Labor Department," he continued, that the suit would allege that the union has been dominated by organized crime "for at least two decades." In dealing with Mr. Coia the First Lady should understand, Mr. Coffey continued, "we plan to portray him as a mob puppet."

Mrs. Clinton did speak to the conference a year later, and Rep. McCollum counts 127 different contacts between Mr. Coia and President Clinton. We have already described on Wednesday, the settlement Justice finally reached with LIUNA. Mr. Coia stayed, on the promise that he'd clean up the union himself. He had previously described White House Deputy Chief of Staff Harold Ickes as his intermediary at the White House. And the appeal officer in the Justice Department's supervision of the cleanup just happens to be Neil Eggleston, the former associate counsel who did the big memo on the Clinton couple's criminal exposures in the Whitewater deal.

Was this a "sweetheart" deal, Rep. Charles Schumer asked. "No," replied Jim Moody, a former Justice Department official, though it was "different." John Keeney, acting head of the criminal division, said the agreement was unusual because no other allegedly corrupt union had ever asked for "such an opportunity" or agreed to cleanup conditions.

Meanwhile, LIUNA itself took out ads in the Washington Post denouncing Rep. McCollum's inquiries as "tabloid theatrics" (the most prominent mention of the hearings in the Post through Thursday, by the way). The AFL-CIO's Secretary-Treasurer Richard Trumka wrapped himself around LIUNA: "They're trying to silence us and they will not succeed." Back at the Department of Justice itself, assistant press spokesman Jim Sweeney ruled the inquiry "clearly a political charade."

What, the House of Representatives has the temerity to ask questions about the Justice Department? The very same Clinton Justice Department where a U.S. attorney resigned over Webster Hubbell's intervention in a corruption trial (our first "Who Is Webster Hubbell?" March 2, 1993). The same Justice Department that was overruled by the judicial panel when it opposed an expansion of the inquiry by Independent Counsel Donald Smaltz. The same Justice Department that lost its prosecution of Billy Dale after Travelgate. Why, how could anyone suspect political interference in a department like that?

REVIEW & OUTLOOK

Mr. Livingstone, We Presume

It's been nearly two months since Craig Livingstone became a household word for improperly obtaining FBI background files, but the more we learn about his rise from bar bouncer to White House security chief, the more interesting a character he seems.

Mr. Livingstone hit the news again last week when it turned out that notes taken during his routine background investigation back in 1993 show that White House Counsel Bernard Nussbaum told FBI agent Dennis Sculimbrene that Hillary Clinton had "highly recommended" Mr. Livingstone for his White House post. Mr. Nussbaum's lawyers added this to his list of denials, but no one has offered any plausible reason why Mr. Sculimbrene would have written this in notes from three years ago, before even the Travel Office firings and when Mr. Livingstone was an unknown.

Craig Livingstone

Gary Aldrich, another FBI veteran, had also reported that Mrs. Clinton was linked to Mr. Livingstone by William Kennedy, associate counsel and her former law partner. Mr. Aldrich's book "Unlimited Access" is about to become No. 1 on the best-seller lists of The Wall Street Journal, Publishers Weekly, the New York Times and others (despite the White House campaign to discredit him, or perhaps because of it). The Secret Service has noted that problems surfaced in Mr.

Livingstone's own background check; in a subsequent deposition, he's admitted using various drugs "up until about 1985" and being let go from two jobs over ethical problems. Mr. Aldrich says that to concerns that no one with this background should hold so sensitive a post, Mr. Kennedy said that Mrs. Clinton wanted it. She has denied even knowing him at the time, and it's possible that Mr. Kennedy, in charge of hiring heavies, invoked Mrs. Clinton's name as a drop-dead answer to any questions.

It does seem, though, that Mr. Livingstone somehow had picked up some clout around the White House. Consider documents obtained by Rep. William Clinger's House Oversight Committee. They include a memo to Abner Mikva, who was White House Counsel after Mr. Nussbaum and Lloyd Cutler but before Jack Quinn. Mr. Livingstone wanted a raise, which he said he'd already been promised. "I have seen this office through a few storms," he wrote, and "it would be wrong not to approve my request." He added, "I apologize for my tone but this is my last try to remain part of the team."

Now, personnel records show that between storms Mr. Livingstone worked banker's hours. His main job was to process White House passes, and seven months into the Administration a total of two permanent passes had been issued; as late as 14 months into the Administration one-third of White House employees lacked permanent passes. A month after his memo to Mr. Mikva his salary was boosted to $63,750, his third raise for a total of a 42% increase in two and a half years.

Among the "storms" Mr. Livingstone helped the Counsel's office to weather was the death of Deputy Counsel Vincent Foster. As we observed in "Mr. Foster and Mr. Livingstone" on July 12, the security chief was perhaps the first White House official notified of the death. Mr. Livingstone said he was notified at home around 9 p.m., roundly three hours after the body was found. Attempts to explain this three-hour delay are replete with contradictions.

Mr. Livingstone has testified that he and Mr. Kennedy went to the morgue to identify the body and that they returned to the Foster home and stayed until about 2 a.m. In further perusal of his depositions, it turns out that Mr. Kennedy left his car at the morgue, and that after they took Mrs. Kennedy home from the Foster residence, Mr. Livingstone drove Mr. Kennedy back to the morgue to retrieve his car. Then the security chief returned to the Foster home and sat outside in his car between 6:30 and 8:00 a.m., checking in at the White House at 8:14. Mr. Kennedy left his car at the morgue because he was distressed, Mr. Livingstone explained, and the purpose of the Foster home stake-out was to ward off the press.

Mr. Livingstone was also seen carrying files in the vicinity of the White House Counsel's office the following day, according to the deposition of Bruce Abbott, a Secret Service officer on duty at the time. Henry O'Neill, another Secret Service officer, also testified he saw Maggie Williams carrying armfuls of files out of Mr. Foster's office the night of his death. Both deny these accounts.

In his handling of FBI files, Mr. Livingstone faces potential criminal exposure for violations of the Privacy Act, misuse of government property and possible perjury and obstruction of justice. His assistant, Anthony Marceca, has already taken the Fifth Amendment in Senate testimony. Independent Counsel Kenneth Starr is in charge of the case, and we would hope that when he's in a position to explain the law to Mr. Livingstone, he asks about Mr. Foster, about "storms" and about remaining "part of the team."

REVIEW & OUTLOOK

Just a Minute

In the wake of the TWA crash and Olympic bomb, there's an understandable rush to dust off everything ever proposed as an anti-terrorism weapon. But let us suggest that before we accede to the Clinton Administration's request for new wiretapping powers for the

Craig Livingstone

FBI, we need some reassurance about the FBI, not to mention the Clinton Administration. Are the results of these wiretaps, for starters, likely to end up in the hands of a Craig Livingstone?

There was a reason, after all, why the Republican Congress hesitated on this request the first time around. To wit, the performance of our federal law enforcement apparatus at Waco and Ruby Ridge scarcely suggested they had earned our confidence and that they would prove discreet and wise with new powers to pry. Since, the FBI has turned cautious in confronting separatist groups, and while some complained it was too patient with the Montana Freemen, its tactics were confirmed by results.

Since then, however, we've learned that the FBI raised no questions in shipping more than 900 investigative files to the political hacks Mr. Clinton's people installed as security gatekeepers. Anthony Marceca, number-two heavy in the security office, even used his own background file as the basis for a libel suit against two women who had raised questions about him when questioned by agents. Despite the clarity of this lesson, the FBI now seems to have done it again.

Rep. William Clinger took to the House floor last week to describe the FBI actions surrounding his staff's discovery that the FBI had files quoting then-White House counsel Bernard Nussbaum as saying Mr. Livingstone had come "highly recommended" by Hillary Clinton. Rep. Clinger's staff had to dig deeply at the FBI to gain access to these notes; and when they did, the first thing the FBI did was give the White House a "heads up" that the committee was on to the inflammatory documents.

FBI General Counsel Howard Shapiro explained that once the notes were discovered he felt the bureau had a duty to tell "affected parties." In other words, the FBI apparently believes it should tell the White House whenever a Congressional oversight committee suspects wrongdoing. The White House proceeded to inform Mr. Nussbaum's lawyers about the notes. It seems that everyone was quickly informed about the existence of the notes except for Independent Counsel Ken Starr, who happens to be the legal official in charge of investigating Mr.

Anthony Marceca

Livingstone and Mr. Marceca. Mr. Starr took over the Filegate investigation last month because Attorney General Janet Reno said it would be "a conflict of interest" for the Justice Department to look into a matter involving the White House and FBI.

In addition to not including Mr. Starr as an "affected party" to be informed, the FBI also decided it was suddenly time to interview Dennis Sculimbrene, the FBI agent who took the notes in 1993. The day after the FBI contacted the White House, it dispatched two agents to his home to ask him if he had notes of the interview. According to Mr. Sculimbrene the agents told him "the White House was unhappy and concerned about this particular interview"; FBI spokesmen deny this.

Mr. Starr has complained about these actions, for example asking Mr. Shapiro to explain why the FBI agents were sent to interrogate Mr. Sculimbrene. Mr. Shapiro has replied that the FBI was concerned whether routine background interviews by agents were reliable. He will have a further opportunity to explain the bureau's actions this Thursday before Mr. Clinger's oversight committee. The answers will reach far beyond the Livingstone-Marceca episode.

In the dawning world we will need an FBI with strong powers. But that implies an FBI that will impose some checks on, rather than quickly adopt, the mores that a group of current occupants happen to bring to the White House.

JULY 31, 1996

Letters to the Editor

'Huck' Stood Tall And Didn't Blink

Micah Morrison's July 18 editorial-page commentary about Arkansas Gov. Mike Huckabee ("Huck Fini? Governor Meets Arkansas Machine") links unconnected events and gives no credit to Gov. Huckabee for the outstanding work he has already done.

The reason Jim Guy Tucker finally stepped down was because Huckabee stood tall and skillfully organized his ouster. In the first

Mike Huckabee

true test of his administration, Gov. Huckabee didn't blink, and the result was a truly ignominious ending to Mr. Tucker's political career. That initial act of political courage will probably do more to cement Gov. Huckabee's stature than anything else he does, yet Mr. Morrison barely mentions it.

Mr. Morrison cites the fact that the Arkansas business establishment gave money to Mr. Huckabee's U.S. Senate campaign as a worrisome sign of potential sell-out. That analysis misses the point. They gave money to his campaign because they wanted him out of Arkansas. A senator in Washington could do no harm to the home-state machine, but a governor could. The machine element wanted Mr. Huckabee out of the way so the party elite could select an "acceptable" replacement as lieutenant governor. Obviously that scenario hasn't worked. (And by the way, when the heads of the largest businesses in Arkansas send campaign contri-

butions, it hardly suggests the sort of intimidation that would

butions, it hardly suggests the sort of intimidation that would

-471-

butions, what's Mr. Huckabee supposed to do? Return them? If Micah Morrison truly believes that, then he isn't in touch with reality.)

Mr. Morrison seemingly wants to raze the state's entire political structure, consequences be damned. That's easy for an outsider to say; he doesn't have to live there. But there are solid reasons for a slower, more reasonable approach that makes significant reforms but doesn't destroy the entire political landscape. For one thing, that approach is much more likely to be successful. Healing language and steady, sensible reforms are more likely to yield results than the witch hunt Mr. Morrison clearly prefers.

Anyone who knows Mike Huckabee acknowledges that he is a man of unquestioned integrity who sticks to his principles. He took on Dale Bumpers in 1992; he took on the political establishment during the special election in 1993; he led the fight for lower taxes in the successful 1994 initiative campaign (also against the will of the entire political establishment). What more credentials does he need before Mr. Morrison gives him a break? He was only in office for three days before Mr. Morrison began raising the specter of capitulation and sellout.

Gov. Huckabee has already done more to break up the existing order in Arkansas than anyone, and instead of praising him, Mr. Morrison raises doubts about him. Fortunately, Mr. Morrison, with his appalling lack of judgment and shoot-your-friends mentality, is a mere journalist, while Gov. Huckabee is the person with the actual authority to build a consensus and get Arkansas moving in the right direction.

DOUGLAS GOODYEAR

Clemons, N.C.

REVIEW & OUTLOOK

Bad News

Yesterday was a bad day for lots of people — Independent Counsel Kenneth Starr, another set of political corruption prosecutors in Philadelphia, and also the President of the United States.

Mr. Starr suffered his first setback in Little Rock, when the jury in the Whitewater case acquitted two Arkansas bankers on four counts of the charges concerning donations to Mr. Clinton's 1990 gubernatorial campaign. It declared itself "hopelessly deadlocked" on the other seven counts against defendants Herby Branscum Jr. and Robert Hill. The acquittals included a conspiracy count on which Judge Susan Webber Wright had issued a ruling, required to admit certain testimony, that prosecutors had made a prima facie case that Presidential aide Bruce Lindsey qualified as an unindicted co-conspirator. The verdict shed little light on why Mr. Lindsey wrote four $7,500 checks for a $30,000 cash deposit. Mr. Starr earlier won a conviction against Governor Jim Guy Tucker and James and Susan McDougal, of course, and the Washington phase of his investigation rolls on.

Across the nation in Philadelphia, federal prosecutors also lost their case against 17-term Republican Congressman Joseph M. McDade, also acquitted after a jury initially pronounced itself deadlocked. Rep. McDade was accused of failing to report $100,000 in gifts, including campaign contributions, trips to Florida and Jamaica, Learjet flights, golf equipment, a week at a Delaware beach house, a Masters tournament jacket and $7,500 in scholarships for his son. He said failure to report was an honest mistake, and some of his staff took the stand to say it was their fault.

Speaker Newt Gingrich announced that Appropriations Committee Chairman Bob Livingstone will remain in that job. Rep. McDade would have been in line for the chairmanship, having already plastered his district with federal pork. He stepped aside because of his indictment, and has requested that Mr. Livingstone remain through the year. Mr. McDade has been diagnosed with Parkinson's disease, and had been hospitalized twice since the trial began June 10. Perhaps not guilty beyond a reasonable doubt, but at the very least a walking argument for term limits.

The setback for Mr. Starr should have made a good day for the Whitewater defense, but Mr. Clinton stepped all over his own spin by losing his cool in the Rose Garden. Responding to questions initiated by CBS correspondent Bill Plante, Mr. Clinton repudiated earlier statements by the White House spokesman and angrily refused to support Congressional legislation to reimburse fired Travel Office head Billy Dale for legal expenses. Mr. Dale was driven out of office to make way for Arkansas cronies of the Clintons and threatened with investigations by the FBI and IRS. Indicted by the Clinton Justice Department, Mr. Dale was acquitted by a jury in less than two hours.

Mr. Clinton testily made the point that his own people have also had to pay big legal bills, and it's OK with us if Congress also wants to pay legal bills for Maggie Williams or Josh Steiner. Indeed, we've suggested it pick up some of the President's own tab. But the real issue is whether the Justice Department indicted Mr. Dale to bail out White House bungling.

The department, of course, also declined to prosecute a major Clinton supporter, Laborers International Union head Arthur Coia, following a three-year investigation that linked the union boss to organized crime figures. And the FBI shipped 900 investigative files to White House heavies Craig Livingstone and Anthony Marceca, and gave the White House a "heads-up" that House investigators were closing in on notes saying that White House Counsel Bernard Nussbaum said Mr. Livingstone had been hired at the recommendation of Hillary Clinton.

In all, no big victories for anyone. Tomorrow is another day.

Letters to the Editor

Clift Notes on Klein, And Gary Aldrich

In response to "Scandals and the Press" by L. Brent Bozell III on your July 22 editorial page:

Newsweek journalist and TV pundit Eleanor Clift and former FBI Special Agent Gary Aldrich seem to possess remarkably similar professional traits. Each:

- Has devoted a respectable number of years to information gathering
- Protects his/her sources
- Enjoys a reputation for probity
- Doesn't hesitate to place personal opinions on record
- Considers himself/herself a defender of the White House

Interestingly, Ms. Clift, during a CNN "Crossfire" appearance in which she discussed her Newsweek colleague Joe Klein's novel "Primary Colors," and why his repeated denials of authorship should not diminish his journalistic credibility, argued that we should measure Mr. Klein against his entire body of work. On the other hand, she denounced Mr. Aldrich, saying, "Listen, he talks about things that are totally ridiculous. . . . He has no basis in fact. . . . This is right-wing fantasy!"

To be equally fair, Ms. Clift should consider Mr. Aldrich's "Unlimited Access" in the context of his 26-year FBI career. Is it possible that he knows, and can accurately report, more about present White House occupants than can Ms. Clift? Or does she fantasize?

In sticking up for colleague Klein's credibility (could his journalistic truth actually be stranger than his fiction?) while condemning Mr. Aldrich's reportorial veracity, Ms. Clift overlooks one obvious point: Both books, whether fiction or nonfiction, paint virtually the same unflattering picture of today's White House.

CHARLOTTE HALE

Savannah, Ga.

REVIEW & OUTLOOK

Claiming Political Privilege

President Clinton offered a rare public display of his usually private temper last week in the Rose Garden when reporters asked him about the Travel Office firings and drug use by his aides. These appear to remain sensitive subjects around the White House. We are now discovering why.

For almost a year the White House has been telling Rep. William Clinger's House Oversight Committee that executive privilege protected some 2,000 pages of documents on the Travel Office. But the picture now emerging from the papers and depositions given to the Clinger committee suggests that the White House's claims have mainly to do with political privilege, specifically the political vulnerability of the First Lady.

Recall that the White House's version of events leading up to the staff firings at the Travel Office began to unravel in January when a memo by former White House aide David Watkins clearly showed Mrs. Clinton behind the firings, suggesting there would be "hell to pay" if the dismissals weren't carried out. The White House and Mrs. Clinton disputed Mr. Watkins's account, but depositions released yesterday by Rep. Clinger's committee now offer solid support for the Watkins version.

Former Chief of Staff Mack McLarty says of the Travel Office in his deposition: "I believe the First Lady had a serious concern about this matter, and I felt a pressure from her to take it seriously and to act upon it, if necessary." In his deposition, Harry Thomason, the

First Lady's Hollywood pal, says: "I think that when the First Lady — the second conversation where it was more detailed — she said they ought to be gotten out." Before his death, Vincent Foster declined to reveal his contacts with Mrs. Clinton on the matter. When he was asked directly during an internal White House investigation if "anyone else" was "involved" in the firings he replied: "I think that's all I should say about that."

Surely we have reached a turn in this affair which justifies Rep. Clinger's skepticism about any White House concerns of privilege relating to the duties of the presidency. "Is this merely information which the President does not wish the public to know?" he properly asks.

The other issue that set off Mr. Clinton's anger at reporters last week was drug use by White House staff. Again recall the Administration's full-press campaign to discredit former FBI agent Gary Aldrich's book on White House security and drug problems. It emerged in testimony before the Clinger committee last week that the White House was handed an advance copy of the Aldrich manuscript four months before publication by the FBI's General Counsel Howard Shapiro. In fact, Mr. Shapiro hand-delivered it personally. Dennis Sculimbrene, the White House FBI agent who corroborated some of the Aldrich details on drug use, resigned last week after two high-level FBI agents interrogated him at home about notes he took suggesting that Mrs. Clinton had urged the hiring of Craig Livingstone as personnel security chief.

Indeed, the Clinger depositions shed light on the laxity with which White House officials let Craig Livingstone operate. Mr. Livingstone, who has admitted to illegal drug use in the 1980s, received a "higher than top secret" security clearance from the CIA on orders from former associate counsel William Kennedy. Charles Easley, a White House security official, says in his deposition that "on that basis" he renewed Mr. Livingstone's White House security clearance without looking at his background file. Mr. Easley now admits he made a mistake. He, incidentally, now serves as Mr. Livingstone's successor.

Based on his review, Rep. Clinger has asked the White House to turn over additional documents relating to Vincent Foster's office and other matters over which it still claims "executive privilege." If it fails to meet his August 16 deadline, he will move to have Congress hold the White House in contempt when it returns in September.

Editorial Feature

The Stonewall Excuses

The following is an excerpt from a statement issued Monday by Rep. William F. Clinger Jr. (R., Pa.), chairman of the House Government Reform and Oversight Committee. Rep. Clinger has announced that if his requests for more documents from the White House are not met by Aug. 16, he will renew his call for White House officials to be held in contempt of Congress.

Seeking White House Documents:

A Long Road From Foot-Dragging to Executive Privilege

In the course of [Congress's] trying to learn the facts, the White House has delayed, denied, and finally, when the Committee tried to call an end to its stonewalling—claimed executive privilege over relevant documents and refused to allow witnesses to testify to certain events when they appeared for Committee depositions. After reviewing many of the 2,000 pages of documents for which the White House claimed executive privilege, it is clear that most of these documents are not subject to any reasonable reading of executive privilege doctrine.

The President claims to be following the executive privilege doctrine as established in President Reagan's 1982 Executive Order. Quoting from this order:

"Executive privilege will be asserted only in the most compelling circumstances, and only after careful review demonstrates that assertion of this privilege is necessary. Congressional requests for information shall be complied with as promptly and as fully as possible, unless it is determined that compliance raises a substantial question of executive privilege."

"A 'substantial question of executive privilege' exists if disclosure of the information requested might significantly impair the national security (including the conduct of foreign relations), the deliberative process of the executive branch, or other aspects of the performance of the executive branch's constitutional duties."

Claims of privilege under this doctrine were waived purposefully by the President if there were any credible allegations of wrongdoing. For example, President Reagan waived all claims of executive privilege during the Iran-Contra investigation.

In light of the expansion of the independent counsel's jurisdiction into the Travel Office matter and, more recently, the FBI files matter, the President's actions are particularly troubling. Why, with ongoing criminal investigations, does the President still insist on keeping thousands of pages of documents from public scrutiny?

Numerous Claims of Executive Privilege in Committee Depositions

What is no less disturbing is the White House's insistence on claiming executive privilege over discussions of those documents in depositions. In their depositions, White House Counsel staff Jane Sherburne, Jon Yarowsky and Natalie Williams, as well as the First Lady's Chief of Staff Maggie Williams and former Press Secretary Lisa Caputo and numerous others, asserted executive privilege on dozens of occasions. The assertion of executive privilege over conversations with the First Lady has been made with troubling frequency. What constitutional basis exists for the President to assert executive privilege claims over conversations the First Lady had with staff?

Executive Privilege Claims Asserted for Political—Not National—Security Purposes

Why does the President persist in his efforts to shield documents under a seriously flawed assertion of executive privilege absent any national security interest or cited domestic policy matter? For example, how can the President justify a claim of executive privilege over notes that a White House Counsel took of discussions with attorneys for Harry Thomason or Mack McLarty regarding conversations each had with the First Lady about the Travel Office?

These notes are among those the White House insists on with-holding from public scrutiny under the umbrella of executive privilege. Although the White House and its apologists attempted to discredit Mr. Watkins's account, it appears the Counsel's office had confirming information at the time.

Conversations With the First Lady: Executive Privilege?

Are we to believe that conversations various individuals had with the First Lady about the Travel Office matter are of a national security concern or otherwise vital matters central to the constitutional duties of the Presidency? Or is this merely information which the President does not wish the public to know?

Furthermore, why was the White House Counsel's office used to sift through the various stories of key witnesses—including Harry Thomason, who was being investigated by the Justice Department for possible conflicts of

William Clinger

interest, as well as many others who may be appearing before a Grand Jury in conjunction with the Independent Counsel's investigation?

Debriefings With Outside Attorneys: Executive Privilege?

Another category of documents which the President has withheld from the public under a claim of executive privilege includes dozens of interviews with the attorneys representing Clinton White House staff and friends deposed in this investigation and the Whitewater matter. Even the much-proclaimed "independent" Peat Marwick employee, Larry Herman, appears to have allowed a debriefing concerning his interview with this Committee.

How can the President claim executive privilege over notes that are clearly debriefings of individuals or attorneys whose clients were questioned in the course of this or other related investigations? And again, why was the Counsel's office used in such a fashion? Did this waive the attorney-client privilege of the individuals involved when their attorneys transmitted this information to the White House? Is this material really subject to any serious claim of executive privilege or does it reflect a modus operandi in the Counsel's office that the President is not prepared to publicly defend?

White House Briefing Papers Created for Congress: Executive Privilege?

Extensively detailed briefing papers and a series of questions that were prepared by White House Counsel to script the Democrat members of the Committee on Government Reform and Oversight for hearings on the Travel Office also are included in the 2,000 pages of documents denied the Committee to this day. These documents outlined attacks on the Travel Office employees, attacks on the idea of conducting this investigation and even attacks on the Committee's staff. These scripts had detailed responses, for example, to any claims that the First Lady was involved with the firings, providing the explicit White House instructions to use such scripts only if the issue was raised during the hearing.

During a Committee deposition, the attorney for one of the individuals who created these documents, Associate Counsel Jon Yarowsky, offered that it would be entirely appropriate for the White House to do this and cited "the White House submitting the proposed questions for John Dean" during the Watergate hearings in his defense!

Can you imagine the uproar if President Reagan's Counsel had assisted Ollie North in his defense by crafting questions for the Republican Members of Congress and scripting attacks on Democratic members of the Committee? This White House continues to claim executive privilege over the scripts it fashioned for the Democrat Members of Congress to derail this investigation!

Information Concerning Vincent Foster: Executive Privilege?

Documents relating to Vincent Foster are another key area where the White House has taken extraordinary efforts to keep the information from the public. The White House redacted hundreds of pages relating to Mr. Foster's documents and the debriefings of witnesses that the Counsel's office obtained regarding Mr. Foster's documents.

These documents were clearly responsive to our subpoena but were almost entirely redacted. Why, after all of the mystery and diversions regarding Mr. Foster's documents, would the White House not want to put everything out on the table? Why the continued shell game? Three years after Mr. Foster's death it is sad that the White House continues to keep the public from the facts surrounding the handling of his documents and putting this matter to rest once and for all.

And again, what do these documents have to do with executive privilege? Is some national security concern at issue? What "substantial question of executive privilege" as defined in the Reagan privilege doctrine is served by keeping this information from public review?

REVIEW & OUTLOOK

Does Character Matter?

"Who Is Bill Clinton?" these columns asked back in 1992, observing that, "Every four years the Democrats send us another Governor we have to get to know." We had already learned of the Gennifer

Flowers episode, of course, and the changing equivocations on his draft record. Now, as our acquaintance with Mr. Clinton has deepened and ripened, the questions of character have steadily multiplied.

Yet as we move toward the election the series of scandals encapsulated as "Whitewater" does not seem to matter, at least if you choose to believe the polls. The Harris poll found that respondents who thought that the President or

Bill Clinton

Mrs. Clinton probably did something illegal in relation to the Whitewater case rose to 56% in early July from 52% a month earlier, while those who thought the President had probably tried to cover up wrongs rose to 59% from 56%. The same poll found that over the same month, the President increased his lead over Bob Dole to 22 percentage points, up from 18 points a month before. Other polls may not find such a large gap—the highly regarded Pew Research Center reported it at 11 points last week—but they all show that increasing doubts over character have had little effect on voting preference.

Which of course raises the question, does character matter, and if so why? While we've never had much time for the notion that politicians should be saints, it's also true that democracy is a compact of trust between the people and their leaders, especially their President. President Nixon was forced to resign not because of some two-bit burglary or even its coverup, but because the gradual revelation of a massive breach of trust with the people left him without the credibility to govern. In Whitewater and related Clinton scandals there has been no "smoking gun," but the character issue has eroded Mr. Clinton's credibility on several crucial particulars.

*   *   *

The most immediate of these concerns is the integrity of law enforcement, central to most of the swirling charges and suspicions. Whitewater is not simply an issue about a land deal in the Ozarks a decade ago; it is also an issue of how and why Jean Lewis, the RTC investigator probing Madison Savings and Loan, was yanked off the case while Bill Clinton was in the White House getting a "heads-up" from since-resigned Treasury and RTC officials. It is an issue of why the President met with since-convicted Governor Jim Guy Tucker shortly after learning of the RTC criminal referrals; was it really to discuss the Arkansas National Guard? It is about the President firing all incumbent U.S. Attorneys and filling the Little Rock post with his crony Paula Casey, who quickly proceeded to refuse the plea-bargain testimony that ultimately became the basis for Independent Counsel Kenneth Starr's successful prosecution.

Similarly, the recently revealed ravaging of FBI files has also damaged public confidence in that agency. With Craig Livingstone, appointed despite his own record of drug use, the Clinton crowd turned the White House Security Office on its head, ignoring security concerns within the White House and pawing through background files of political adversaries. We now learn that when former FBI agent Gary Aldrich submitted his book for clearance, the agency's General Counsel, Howard Shapiro, hand-delivered a copy to the White House so it could prepare its publicity counter-offensive.

The Billy Dale prosecution after the firings, meanwhile, raises the specter of law enforcement being used not only to cover up wrongs and gain political advantage, but as an offensive weapon against foes. Mr. Dale said records that would prove he handled funds properly vanished after he was evicted from his office, but even in their absence a jury immediately acquitted. Similarly, UltrAir, a Travel Office supplier used by Mr. Dale, found itself subject to a sudden IRS audit.

In the wake of the TWA bombing, Mr. Clinton now comes to Congress asking new wiretapping powers for the FBI. Perhaps it needs the powers, but how can Congress wisely grant them under current circumstances, with, to put a point on it, Mr. Shapiro still in the General Counsel's office? The character issue has already eroded the confidence in fairness so crucial to effective law enforcement.

* * *

Military leadership is traditionally an ultimate test of character, and even in the absence of big threats, the problems are already manifest in Mr. Clinton's excursion into Bosnia. The mission there seems to be postponing the outcome until after our November election, while preparing to reward "ethnic cleansing." Mr. Clinton's commanders have let it be known they are not prepared to receive an order to arrest war criminals, providing Mr. Clinton and equally cynical Europeans with the excuse they want. Yet the situation remains volatile, and Mr. Clinton is scarcely an inspiring figure to follow in war. On terrorism, similarly, his first response is to invite Gerry Adams of the IRA to the White House, and his second is to threaten allies over their adherence to cosmetic economic sanctions against Iran and Libya. This is anything but leadership.

Closer to home, leadership is also particularly lacking in what is above all a matter of character and symbolism, national drug policy. Revelations by Mr. Aldrich and others make clear that the Clinton crowd has trouble taking the drug issue seriously. Indeed, among the President's first acts was to gut the anti-drug office within the White House, and appoint an Arkansas spokesman for legalization as surgeon general, meanwhile bringing into the White House Patsy Thomasson, an associate of Arkansas drug convict Dan Lasater. Joycelyn Elders has now been replaced, though Ms. Thomasson remains, and Barry McCaffrey is revitalizing the drug office. But under Mr. Clinton's watch, drug use among teenagers has stopped declining and started to rise.

Finally, the issue of character and credibility permeates the

President's campaign strategy of trying to seize Republican issues. His guru Dick Morris presents the most right-wing Democrat candidate since Grover Cleveland, but what reason is there to believe? In a second term, will General McCaffrey stay, or will another Joycelyn Elders appear? What will happen in Bosnia with the promised December withdrawal? Will new Billy Dales be prosecuted? Is national health insurance really dead, or welfare reform finally accomplished? Will Mr. Clinton stay the course with his economic program, or suddenly appear with, say, new taxes or even a road-to-Damascus conversion to growth through inflation? Who is to say—given the President's existential, this-moment-only character?

* * *

The first business of a second term, indeed, would almost have to be settlement of the Paula Corbin Jones sexual harassment lawsuit, unless the Supreme Court reverses the appellate ruling that the trial should proceed. While Mr. Starr is now unlikely to bring new indictments before the election, his investigators are still in the field. We now learn that in addition to the David Watkins memo, "Mack" McLarty and Harry Thomason gave depositions casting further doubt on Mrs. Clinton's sworn statement that she had next-to-nothing to do with it. How would the Republic react to an indictment of the First Lady, let alone her conviction?

Would the President use his powers to pardon her, or for that matter others under suspicion or convicted? What about Governor Tucker, for example, who might have something to say about what he and the President discussed? And what if further investigation does uncover some "smoking gun," perhaps with Republicans still in control of one or both houses of Congress and ultimately the power of impeachment? Voters did give Richard Nixon a landslide in 1972, despite the Washington Post reporting on some campaign dirty tricks. But to reelect Mr. Clinton despite the rich menu before Mr. Starr would be like reelecting Mr. Nixon with Archibald Cox already in full bay.

* * *

With the current anomaly in the polls, the faddish interpretation is that the public is itself corrupt. That Americans want others to adopt traditional morality, but do not want to follow the rules themselves. That they want lower taxes and bigger entitlements too. That in Mr. Clinton they have the President they deserve. None of this corresponds to the American people as we know them.

We'd offer another reading. To wit, the electorate is currently in what psychologists call a state of "cognitive dissonance." The concept holds that people strive for internal consistency between beliefs and actions, and that evidence inconsistent with actions creates a dissonance that must somehow be resolved. Sometimes the resolution takes place by defense mechanisms, such as denial of the evidence. But often, a state of cognitive dissonance is an essential step in changing your mind.

A Whitewater Chronology

Editor's note: This special updated Whitewater chronology includes matters related to Bank of Credit & Commerce International, as well as Mena airfield and other Arkansas mysteries. It supersedes the chronology in Volume I of "A Journal Briefing: WHITEWATER."

1976

Bill Clinton is elected Arkansas Attorney General.

1977

Hillary Rodham Clinton joins the Rose Law Firm.

Arkansas financier Jackson Stephens of Stephens Inc. joins with a group of Arab investors to make an unsuccessful run at acquiring Financial General Bankshares in Washington, D.C.; the Arab investors would later be identified as principals and clients of Bank of Credit & Commerce International. BCCI founder Agha Hasan Abedi hires Bert Lance—recently resigned as President Jimmy Carter's budget director—as an adviser to the group. Amid the legal maneuvers surrounding the Lance group takeover attempt, a brief is submitted by the Stephens-controlled bank data processing firm Systematics; two of the lawyers signing the brief are Hillary Rodham and Webster Hubbell.

1978

August: The Clintons purchase a 230-acre land tract along Arkansas's White River, in partnership with James and Susan McDougal.

October: Mrs. Clinton, now a partner at the Rose Firm, begins a series of commodities trades under the guidance of Tyson Foods executive Jim Blair, earning nearly $100,000. The trades are not revealed until March 1994.

November: Bill Clinton is elected governor of Arkansas. He makes James McDougal a top economic adviser.

1979

Feb. 16:   The Federal Reserve rejects the bid by BCCI frontmen to take over Financial General Bankshares.

June: The Clintons and McDougals form Whitewater Development Co. to engage in the business of owning, selling, developing, managing and improving real property.

1980

November: Gov. Clinton is defeated by Republican Frank White. He joins the Little Rock law firm of Wright, Lindsey and Jennings.

1981

James McDougal purchases Madison Bank and Trust.

Aug. 25:   The Federal Reserve approves a new bid by largely the same Arab group of BCCI frontmen to acquire Financial General.

1982

Financial General changes its name to First American. Democratic Party icon Clark Clifford is appointed chairman. BCCI fronts begin acquiring controlling interest in banks and other American financial institutions.

In Arkansas, James McDougal purchases Madison

Guaranty Savings & Loan. It begins a period of rapid expansion.

November: Bill Clinton defeats Frank White, winning back the governor's seat.

1983

Capital Management Services, a federally insured small business investment company owned by Judge David Hale, begins making loans to the Arkansas political elite.

1984

Jan. 20: The Federal Home Loan Bank Board issues a report on Madison Guaranty questioning its lending practices and financial stability. The Arkansas Securities Department begins to take steps to close down Madison.

August: According to Mr. McDougal, Gov. Clinton drops by his office during a morning jog and asks that Madison steer some business to Mrs. Clinton at the Rose Law Firm.

November: Gov. Clinton wins re-election with 64% of the vote.

1985

January: Roger Clinton pleads guilty to cocaine distribution charges and is given immunity from further prosecution in exchange for his cooperation. He testifies before a federal grand jury and serves a brief prison sentence.

Jan. 16: Gov. Clinton appoints Beverly Bassett Schaffer, a longtime associate, to serve as Arkansas State Securities Commissioner.

March: Mrs. Clinton receives from Madison Guaranty the first payment of a $2,000-per-month retainer. Madison's accounting firm, Frost & Co., issues a report declaring the savings and loan solvent.

March 4: ESM Securities of Fort Lauderdale collapses after fraudulent trading, causing $250 million in losses and triggering a bank crisis in Ohio.

April 4: Mr. McDougal hosts a fund-raiser to help Gov. Clinton repay campaign debts. Contributions at the fund-raiser later draw the scrutiny of Whitewater investigators.

April 7: Securities firm Bevill, Bresler & Schulman files for bankruptcy amid fraud charges and an estimated $240 million in losses; one of the biggest apparent losers is Stephens-dominated Worthen Bank, which holds with Bevill $52 million of Arkansas state funds in uncollateralized repurchase agreements.

April 30: Hillary Clinton sends a recapitalization offer for the foundering Madison Guaranty to the Arkansas Securities Commission. Two weeks later, Ms. Schaffer informs Mrs. Clinton the plan is approved, but it is never implemented.

October: Mr. McDougal launches the Castle Grande land deal.

1986

Jan. 17: Michael Fitzhugh, United States Attorney for the Western District of Arkansas, advises the FBI that he is dropping the money laundering and narcotics-conspiracy case against Arkansas associates of drug smuggler Barry Seal. Arkansas State Police Investigator Russell Welch and Internal Revenue Service Investigator Bill Duncan, the lead agents on the case, protest; later, both are driven from their jobs.

Feb. 19: Barry Seal is gunned down by Colombian hitmen in Baton Rouge, La. Seal becomes the touchstone in murky allegations of cocaine trafficking, gun running, and intelligence-community activities swirling around his smuggling base at Mena in western Arkansas.

March 4: The Federal Home Loan Bank Board issues a second, sharply critical report of Madison, accusing Mr. McDougal of diverting funds to insiders.

April: Roger Clinton is paroled from prison.

April 3: David Hale's Capital Management Services makes a $300,000 loan to Susan McDougal in the name of a front, Master Marketing. Some of the funds wind up in a

Whitewater Development Co. account. Indicted for fraud on an unrelated transaction in 1993, Mr. Hale claims that then-Gov. Clinton and Mr. McDougal pressured him into making the loan.

August: Federal regulators remove Mr. McDougal from Madison's board of directors.

Oct. 5: Deceased Mena drug smuggler Barry Seal's C-123K is shot down over Nicaragua with an Arkansas pilot at the controls and a load of weapons and Contra-supporter Eugene Hasenfus in the cargo bay.

Oct. 24: Clinton friend and "bond daddy" Dan Lasater, and nine others, most of them from the Little Rock bond trading community, are indicted on cocaine charges. Roger Clinton, who has cooperated with the prosecution, is named an unindicted co-conspirator.

November: Gov. Clinton wins re-election. Gubernatorial terms are extended from two years to four.

1987

According to Susan McDougal, Whitewater records are taken to the Governor's Mansion and turned over to Mrs. Clinton sometime during the year.

Officials at investment giant Stephens Inc., including longtime Clinton friend David Edwards, take steps to rescue Harken Energy, a struggling Texas oil company with George W. Bush on its board. Over the next three years, Mr. Edwards brings BCCI-linked investors and advisers into Harken deals. One of them, Abdullah Bakhsh, purchases $10 million in shares of Stephens-dominated Worthen Bank.

Jan. 15: Dan Lasater begins serving a 30-month sentence for cocaine distribution. In July, he is paroled to a Little Rock halfway house.

Aug. 23: In a mysterious case later ruled a murder and linked to drug corruption, teenagers Kevin Ives and Don Henry are run over by a train in a remote locale a few miles southwest of Little Rock.

1988	
October:	A Florida grand jury indicts BCCI figures on charges of laundering drug money. It is the first sign of serious trouble at the international bank.

1989	
	Manhattan District Attorney Robert Morgenthau begins a wide-ranging probe of BCCI.
March:	Federal regulators shut down Madison Guaranty Savings & Loan, at a taxpayer loss of about $60 million. Mr. McDougal is indicted for bank fraud.
June 16:	Mena investigator Bill Duncan resigns from the Internal Revenue Service following clashes with Washington supervisors over the probe.

1990	
May:	Mr. McDougal goes to trial on bank fraud and is acquitted.
November:	Gov. Clinton is elected to a second four-year term, promising to serve it out and not seek the presidency in 1992.

1991	
January:	The Federal Reserve orders an investigation of BCCI's alleged control of First American Bank.
July 5:	Regulators world-wide shut down BCCI amid widespread charges of bank fraud and allegations of links to laundered drug money, terrorists and intelligence agencies.
Aug. 13:	Chairman Clark Clifford and top aide Robert Altman resign from First American Bank.
Oct. 3:	Bill Clinton announces his candidacy for president and attacks, among others, "S&L crooks and self-serving CEOs."

1992	
March 8:	New York Times reporter Jeff Gerth discloses the

Clintons' dealings with Madison and Whitewater.

March 20: Washington Times reporter Jerry Seper discloses Hillary Clinton's $2,000-per-month retainer from Madison.

March 23: In a hasty report arranged by the Clinton campaign, Denver lawyer James Lyons states the Clintons lost $68,000 on the Whitewater investment and clears them of improprieties. The issue fades from the campaign.

July 16: Bill Clinton accepts the Democratic Party's presidential nomination in New York.

July 22: A Manhattan grand jury hands up sealed indictments against BCCI principals, including Clark Clifford and Robert Altman. A week later, a grand jury in Washington and the Federal Reserve issue separate actions against Messrs. Clifford and Altman.

August: Clinton friend David Edwards arranges a $3.5 million lead gift from Saudi Arabian benefactors to the University of Arkansas for a Middle East studies center.

Aug. 31: Resolution Trust Corporation field officers complete criminal referral #C0004 on Madison Guaranty and forward it to Charles Banks, U.S. Attorney for the Eastern District of Arkansas. The referral alleges an elaborate check kiting scheme by Madison owners James and Susan McDougal and names the Clintons and Jim Guy Tucker as possible beneficiaries. Later, Mr. Banks forwards the referral to Washington. In the heat of the campaign, the issue is sidelined.

Nov. 3: Bill Clinton is elected president.

December: Vincent Foster, representing the Clintons, meets with James McDougal and arranges for him to buy the Clintons' remaining shares in Whitewater Development Co. for $1,000. Mr. McDougal is loaned the money for the purchase by Tyson Foods counsel Jim Blair, a longtime Clinton friend and commodities adviser. The loan is never repaid.

1993

Jan. 20:   Bill Clinton is sworn in as 42nd president of the United States.

February: Arkansas Gov. Jim Guy Tucker announces a $20 million Saudi gift to the University of Arkansas for a Middle East studies center.

March 24:   Year-old press clips about Whitewater are faxed from the office of Deputy Treasury Secretary Roger Altman to the office of White House Counsel Bernard Nussbaum. Mr. Altman also is serving as acting head of the Resolution Trust Corporation, an independent federal agency.

May 19:   The White House fires seven employees of its Travel Office, following a review by Associate Counsel William Kennedy III, a former member of the Rose Law Firm. Mr. Kennedy's actions, which included attempts to involve the FBI and the Internal Revenue Service in a criminal investigation of the Travel Office, are sharply criticized. Vincent Foster also is rebuked.

June 21:   Whitewater corporate tax returns for 1989 through 1991, prepared by Mr. Foster, are delivered to Jim McDougal's attorney.

July 17:   According to a White House chronology, Mr. Foster completes work on a blind trust for the Clintons. In Little Rock for a weekend visit, President Clinton has a four-hour dinner alone with old friend David Edwards, now in business for himself as an investment adviser and currency trader.

July 20:   The Little Rock FBI obtains a warrant to search the office of David Hale as part of its investigation into Capital Management Services. In Washington, Deputy White House Counsel Vincent Foster drives to Fort Marcy Park and commits suicide. That evening, Mr. Nussbaum, White House aide Patsy Thomasson, and Mrs. Clinton's chief of staff Maggie Williams visit Mr. Foster's office. According to testimony by a uniformed Secret Service officer, Ms. Williams exits the counsel's suite with an armful of folders; Ms. Williams denies the claim.

July 21: Early-morning calls are exchanged between Mrs. Clinton in Little Rock and White House operatives, including Maggie Williams and Susan Thomases. According to later congressional testimony, Mrs. Clinton's concerns about investigators having "unfettered access" to the Foster office are conveyed to White House Counsel Bernard Nussbaum. Mr. Nussbaum meets with Park Police and Justice Department investigators and agrees to a search of the office the following day. A figure of later controversy, White House personnel security chief Craig Livingstone, also is spotted in the Foster office area with files.

July 22: Mr. Nussbaum again searches Mr. Foster's office, but denies access to Park Police and Justice Department investigators. In an angry phone call, Deputy Attorney General Philip Heymann asks, "Bernie, are you hiding something?" Documents, including Whitewater files, are removed. Details on the removal of Whitewater files do not emerge for months.

July 26: A torn-up note is found in Mr. Foster's briefcase.

Aug. 14: In New York, Robert Altman is acquitted of bank fraud in the BCCI case; Clark Clifford's trial is indefinitely postponed due to ill health.

Aug. 16: Paula Casey, a longtime associate of the Clintons, takes office in Little Rock as U.S. attorney.

September: Ms. Casey turns down plea bargain attempts from David Hale's lawyer, who had offered to share information on the "banking and borrowing practices of some individuals in the elite political circles of the State of Arkansas."

Sept. 23: Mr. Hale is indicted for fraud.

Sept. 29: Treasury Department General Counsel Jean Hanson warns Mr. Nussbaum that the RTC plans to issue criminal referrals asking the Justice Department to investigate Madison. The referrals are said to name the Clintons as witnesses to, and possible beneficiaries of, illegal actions. The current governor of Arkansas, Jim

Guy Tucker, also is said to be a target of the investigation. Mr. Nussbaum passes the information to Bruce Lindsey, a top White House aide and Arkansas damage-control specialist.

Oct. 4 or 5: Mr. Lindsey informs President Clinton about the confidential referrals. Mr. Lindsey later tells Congress he did not mention any specific target of the referrals.

Oct. 6: President Clinton meets with Arkansas Gov. Jim Guy Tucker at the White House.

Oct. 8: Nine new criminal referrals on Madison Guaranty are forwarded to U.S. Attorney Paula Casey in Little Rock.

Oct. 14: A meeting is held in Mr. Nussbaum's office with senior White House and Treasury personnel to discuss the RTC and Madison. Participants at the meeting later tell Congress that they discussed only how to handle press inquiries.

Oct. 27: The RTC's first criminal referral is rejected in Little Rock by U.S. Attorney Casey.

Nov. 3: Associate Attorney General Webster Hubbell recuses himself from the Whitewater case.

Nov. 9: In Little Rock, U.S. Attorney Casey recuses herself from the Madison case; in Kansas City, RTC investigator Jean Lewis is taken off the probe.

Nov. 18: President Clinton meets with Gov. Tucker in Seattle.

Dec. 19: Allegations by Arkansas state troopers of the president's sexual infidelities while governor surface in the American Spectator and the Los Angeles Times.

Dec. 20: Washington Times correspondent Jerry Seper reports that Whitewater files were removed from Mr. Foster's office.

Dec. 30: At a New Year's retreat, President Clinton asks Comptroller of the Currency Eugene Ludwig, an old friend, for "advice" about how to handle the growing Whitewater storm.

1994

Jan. 20: Amid mounting political pressure, Attorney General Janet Reno appoints Robert Fiske as special counsel to investigate Whitewater.

Jan. 27: Deputy Attorney General Philip Heymann resigns.

Feb. 2: Mr. Altman meets with Mr. Nussbaum and other senior White House staff to give them a "heads-up" about Madison. Washington RTC attorney April Breslaw flies to Kansas City and meets with investigator Jean Lewis; in a secretly taped conversation, Ms. Breslaw states that top RTC officials "would like to be able to say that Whitewater did not cause a loss to Madison."

Feb. 24: Mr. Altman gives incomplete testimony to the Senate Banking Committee about discussions between the White House and Treasury on the Madison referrals.

Feb. 25: Mr. Altman recuses himself from the Madison investigation and announces he will step down as acting head of the RTC.

March 5: White House Counsel Bernard Nussbaum resigns.

March 8: Lloyd Cutler is named White House Counsel.

March 14: Associate Attorney General Webster Hubbell resigns.

March 18: The New York Times reveals Mrs. Clinton's 1970s commodities trades.

March 23: The Association of American Physicians and Surgeons files suit against Mrs. Clinton's health reform task force for violating the Federal Advisory Committee Act by holding secret meetings.

May 6: Former Little Rock resident Paula Corbin Jones files suit against President Clinton, charging he sexually harassed her while governor.

June 30: Special Counsel Robert Fiske concludes that Mr. Foster's death was a suicide and clears the White House and Treasury Department of obstruction of justice on the RTC contacts, opening the way for congressional hearings limited to the two subjects.

July 26:	Congressional hearings open.
Aug. 1:	The White House reveals that the Whitewater files removed from Mr. Foster's office were kept for five days in the Clintons' residence before being turned over to their personal lawyer.
Aug. 5:	A three-judge panel removes Mr. Fiske and appoints Kenneth Starr as independent counsel. Mr. Starr continues to investigate all aspects of Whitewater, including Mr. Foster's death.
Aug. 12:	The RTC informs Madison investigator Jean Lewis and two colleagues that they will be placed on "administrative leave" for two weeks.
Aug. 17:	Deputy Treasury Secretary Roger Altman resigns.
Aug. 18:	Treasury Department General Counsel Jean Hanson resigns.
Aug. 29:	The RTC files suit in federal court to compel the Rose Law Firm to turn over its client list in a conflict-of-interest probe.
Sept. 12:	Donald Smaltz is named independent counsel to investigate activities of Agriculture Secretary Mike Espy.
Oct. 1:	Abner Mikva replaces Lloyd Cutler as White House Counsel.
Oct. 3:	Agriculture Secretary Mike Espy resigns.
Nov. 8:	In a political earthquake, Republicans gain control of the House and the Senate.
Dec. 5:	In Little Rock, Madison Guaranty real-estate appraiser Robert Palmer pleads guilty to one felony count of conspiracy and agrees to cooperate with the Starr probe.
Dec. 6:	Former Associate Attorney General Webster Hubbell pleads guilty to two felonies in a scheme to defraud his former Rose Law Firm partners and says he will cooperate with the independent counsel.
Dec. 7:	Former Travel Office director Billy Dale is indicted on charges of embezzling office funds.

1995

Jan. 3:   Republicans on the Senate Banking Committee–poised to move into the majority and renew the Whitewater hearings–issue a sharply critical report based on the summer hearings. It accuses Clinton administration officials of "serious misconduct and malfeasance" in the matters of the RTC criminal referrals and later congressional testimony.

Feb. 28:   Arkansas banker Neal Ainley is indicted on five felony counts relating to Bill Clinton's 1990 gubernatorial campaign. He later pleads guilty to reduced charges and agrees to cooperate with the independent counsel.

March 21:   Whitewater real-estate broker Chris Wade pleads guilty to two felonies.

March 27:   Legal Times reports that Independent Counsel Donald Smaltz's probe has been "significantly curtailed by the Justice Department." In recent months, Mr. Smaltz had been exploring Arkansas poultry giant Tyson Foods.

May 5:   Mena investigator Russell Welch fights off an attempt by the Arkansas State Police to discredit him, but is forced into early retirement.

May 24:   David Barrett is appointed independent counsel to probe charges that Housing Secretary Henry Cisneros made false statements to the FBI.

June 7:   An Arkansas grand jury hands up indictments against Gov. Jim Guy Tucker and two business associates in a complex scheme to buy and sell cable television systems.

June 8:   Stephen Smith, a former aide to Gov. Bill Clinton, pleads guilty to misusing a Capital Management loan and agrees to cooperate with the independent counsel.

June 23:   A report for the RTC by the law firm Pillsbury, Madison & Sutro says that funds flowed to the Whitewater account from other Madison accounts, but adds that the Clintons "had little direct involvement" in the investment before 1988.

July 6:   Daniel Pearson is named independent counsel to probe business dealings of Commerce Secretary Ron Brown.

July 18: The special Senate Whitewater Committee opens a new round of hearings in Washington that quickly become mired in partisan disputes.

Aug. 8: In testimony before the House Banking Committee, RTC investigator Jean Lewis says there was a "concerted effort to obstruct, hamper and manipulate" the Madison investigation.

Aug. 17: Independent Counsel Kenneth Starr indicts Arkansas Gov. Jim Guy Tucker and former Madison Guaranty owners James and Susan McDougal for bank fraud and conspiracy.

Sept. 5: Federal District Judge Henry Woods dismisses the cable TV fraud case against Gov. Tucker and two associates, saying Mr. Starr has exceeded his jurisdiction; the independent counsel appeals Judge Woods's Court decision to the Eighth Circuit Court in St. Louis. The separate indictment against Gov. Tucker and the McDougals stands.

Sept. 20: White House Counsel Abner Mikva announces his resignation. The president names Jack Quinn, Vice President Al Gore's chief of staff, as his fourth White House counsel.

November: House Banking Committee Chairman Jim Leach informs colleagues that he will investigate allegations of drug smuggling and money laundering at Mena airport.

Nov. 16: After deliberating less than two hours, a Washington jury acquits former White House Travel Office head Billy Dale of embezzlement charges.

Dec. 29: A memo from former White House aide David Watkins placing responsibility for the Travel Office firings on Mrs. Clinton is discovered at the White House.

1996

Jan. 5: The White House announces that Mrs. Clinton's Rose Law Firm billing records, sought by the independent counsel and Congress for two years, have been discovered on a table in the "book room" of the personal residence.

Jan. 11: At a news conference, President Clinton says he is nearly broke and owes about $1.6 million in legal fees stemming from Whitewater and the Paula Jones sexual harassment suit.

Jan. 22: The White House announces that Mrs. Clinton has been subpoenaed to testify before a Whitewater grand jury about the missing billing records.

Feb. 5: Federal District Judge George Howard Jr. rules that President Clinton must appear as a defense witness in the bank fraud case against Jim Guy Tucker and the McDougals.

Feb. 8: The Wall Street Journal discloses that two of President Clinton's insurance policies have paid $900,000 into his legal defense fund.

Feb. 20: Arkansas bankers Herby Branscum Jr. and Robert Hill are indicted on bank fraud and conspiracy charges relating to Bill Clinton's 1990 gubernatorial campaign.

Feb. 29: The Whitewater Committee's mandate expires and Senate Democrats launch a filibuster to block an extension of the probe.

March 4: Gov. Tucker and the McDougals go on trial for bank fraud and conspiracy in Little Rock.

March 15: A three-judge panel of the Eighth Circuit Court of Appeals reinstates Independent Counsel Starr's indictment of Gov. Tucker and two associates in the cable television fraud scheme, and directs that Federal District Judge Henry Woods be removed from the case "to preserve the appearance of impartiality."

March 22: Independent Counsel Starr's jurisdiction is expanded to cover the Travel Office affair.

March 25: Arkansas insider David Hale is sentenced to 28 months in prison for defrauding the federal government.

April 3: Commerce Secretary Ron Brown and 32 others are

killed in a plane crash in Croatia.

April 28: President Clinton gives four hours of videotaped testimony in the White House as a defense witness in the Arkansas trial of Gov. Tucker and the McDougals.

May 28: An Arkansas jury convicts Gov. Tucker and the McDougals on 24 counts of bank fraud and conspiracy.

June 5: Documents obtained after a long struggle by the House Government Reform and Oversight Committee reveal that the White House has improperly obtained confidential FBI background files. "Filegate" mushrooms into another ethical crisis for the Clinton administration.

June 17: The trial of Arkansas bankers Branscum and Hill on charges of bank fraud relating to the 1990 Clinton gubernatorial campaign begins in Little Rock.

June 18: The Senate Whitewater Committee releases a 650-page final report detailing a "pattern of obstruction" by Clinton administration officials.

June 21: Independent Counsel Starr's jurisdiction is broadened to cover "Filegate."

June 25: The Supreme Court agrees to hear President Clinton's procedural appeal in the Paula Jones harassment suit, effectively delaying the trial until after the November election.

June 26 In an appearance before a House oversight committee investigating the Filegate affair, White House personnel security chief Craig Livingstone announces his resignation.

July 7: President Clinton gives videotaped testimony in the White House as a defense witness in the trial of Arkansas bankers Branscum and Hill.

July 15: Republican Mike Huckabee takes over as governor of Arkansas.

Aug. 1: A federal jury in Little Rock acquits Arkansas bankers Branscum and Hill on four bank fraud charges relating to the 1990 Clinton gubernatorial campaign: a mistrial is declared on seven other counts on which the jury deadlocks.

Acknowledgments

Many people at The Wall Street Journal played a part in producing "A Journal Briefing: WHITEWATER—Volume II." On the Editorial Page staff in New York, an array of editors, writers, production people and secretaries devoted care and extra time to the project, all while putting out a daily newspaper. Kenneth DeWitt, Rachel Laffer, Maria-Caroline Perignon and Virginia Bubek spent many hours on research, design and layout. On the technical side, a team of Journal computer whizzes and marketing staffers also lent a welcome hand. And Circulation Department workers in Chicopee, Mass., are making sure calls are taken and orders filled. Thanks go to all of them.

Index

A

Abbell, Michael, 90

Abbott, Bruce, 440-441, 467

Abrams, Elliott, 27-28, 84

Abramson, Jill, 339

Adams, Gerry, 486

Adams, James Ring, 25

Adelman, Roger M., 343

Adham, Kamal, 53, 144

Ainley, Neal T., 55-57, 68-69, 409-412

Albright, Harry Jr., 24, 144

Aldrich, Gary W., 401-407, 430-435, 439, 454-459, 465-466, 475-476, 478, 485-86

Alexander, Bill, 20

Alexander, Lamar, 276

Alltell Corp., 271

Altman, Robert

  BCCI and, 66, 81, 137, 142-144, 186-188, 190

  Currency Transaction Reports and, 69

  Espy probe and, 56

  Foster suicide and, 40-42

  Naqvi and, 23-26

D

E

F

G

America's Presidential Family," 139

Gubernatorial campaign funding trial, 381-384, 396-397, 408-412

Gugliotta, Guy, 290

Guinier, Lani, 195

Gurwin, Larry, 29, 50

H

Hale, Charlotte, 475-476

Hale, David

appearance at Senate Whitewater hearings proposed, 371, 395-397

Arkansas fraud charges against, 394, 396-397

Castle Grande project, 208, 245, 297

Clintons' links to, 116-117, 194, 218, 234, 239, 253

Clinton's videotaped testimony and, 342-343, 347-353, 358-360

McDougal-Tucker indictments and, 370-374

media attacks on, 298-299

plea bargain rejected, 96, 136, 146, 162

Senate investigation of, 199-200

Tucker's links to, 8-9, 83-86, 94, 121, 158, 174-176

"use immunity" plea of, 395-397

Haley, John, 83, 284

Haley, Maria, 284

Hammer, Armand, 25

Hankins, Jeff, 8

Hanson, Jean, 40, 42, 69, 162, 195, 219

Hardin & Grace, 114

Harken Energy Corp., 28-29, 50, 52-54

Harmon, Dan, 329-336, 393

Harriman, Averell, 5

Harriman, Pamela, 5-7

Harrington, David, 424-425

Hart, Gary, 195, 421, 426-427

Hasenfus, Eugene, 19, 28, 74

Hashemi, Cyrus, 457-459

Hashemi, Jamshid, 457-458

K

L

M

S

U

V

W

Wright, Susan Webber (Judge), 447, 473-474

Y
Yost, Pete, 223
Young, Buddy, 91

Z
Zayed al-Nahyan (Sheik), 144, 187-189, 191-192
Zeliff, Bill (Representative), 108